The Imperative of Modernity

The Imperative of Modernity

An Intellectual Biography of José Ortega y Gasset

ROCKWELL GRAY

UNIVERSITY OF CALIFORNIA PRESS
Berkeley   Los Angeles   London

Permission has been granted to reprint thirteen lines of poetry from "Spain 1937," by W. H. Auden, from *The English Auden: Poems, Essays and Dramatic Writings, 1927–1939*, by W. H. Auden, edited by Edward Mendelson, © 1978 Random House, Inc.

University of California Press
Berkeley and Los Angeles, California

University of California Press, Ltd.
London, England

LIBRARY OF CONGRESS
Library of Congress Cataloging-in-Publication Data

Gray, Rockwell.
    The imperative of modernity: an intellectual biography of José
Ortega y Gasset/Rockwell Gray.
      p.   cm.
    Bibliography: p.
    Includes index.
    ISBN 0-520-06201-9 (alk. paper)
    1. Ortega y Gasset, José, 1883–1955. 2. Authors, Spanish—20th
century—Biography. 3. Philosopher—Spain—Biography.
    4. Intellectuals—Spain—Biography. I. Title.
PQ6627.R8Z68 1989
868'.6209—dc19
                                   88-23311
                                     CIP

Printed in the United States of America

1 2 3 4 5 6 7 8 9

For my father, Rockwell Gray, who stands at the beginning; for George and Barbara Morgan, who helped me to open the doors of perception; for Madelyn, whose love and companionship have sweetened the years during which this book was built; and for Lowell, Zachary, and Elizabeth, whose voices ring just beyond my study door.

... to persuade the people of Madrid to concern themselves a bit with philosophy has been and still is the dream of my life.

—José Ortega y Gasset

Ortega y Gasset, after Nietzsche, is perhaps the greatest "European" writer.

—Albert Camus

CONTENTS

PREFACE

Since this study of José Ortega y Gasset has matured slowly, over a number of years, an autobiographical note on its inception and development may not be out of place. As Ortega was fond of observing, the themes we cultivate seem almost to have a life of their own as they spring up, ripen, and wither in our intellectual fields. But it is well for us occasionally to reckon their import for our own lives and those of our readers. The periodic apologia helps a writer to hone and direct his continuing efforts. At the same time, it directs the reader's attention to the "subtext" or larger purport of the author's work.

When I first encountered Ortega over three decades ago in an undergraduate introduction to Spanish literature taught by Professor A. David Kossoff, of Brown University, I found the philosopher's romantic vision of the Spanish landscape—probably in excerpts from "Tierras de Castilla"—exotic and enticing. It whetted my provincial New England appetite for experience of a culture that promised to complement the emotionally thin one of my childhood. Three years later, my initial interest was quickened by Professor Juan López-Morillas, a distinguished intellectual historian and a passionate student of Ortega's work. His advice and support sent me off to Madrid on a Fulbright Fellowship after my graduation from Brown. At that point, I was more interested in the poet and philosopher Miguel de Unamuno than in Ortega, but I recall purchasing the six gray volumes of what then constituted Ortega's *Obras completas* in the Espasa-Calpe bookstore on the Gran Vía. Still largely unread, these followed me in trunks until, about fifteen years later, I began doctoral work with the Committee on Social Thought at the University of Chicago. There Saul Bellow suggested I look into the man whose *Meditations on Quixote* I had summarized in Bellow's seminar on Cervantes's great novel. Having just tried, rather unsuccessfully, to teach Ortega's *What Is Philosophy?* in an introductory philosophy course at a small college in the city, I realized that the question of a philosopher's ability to reach a broad public arose naturally from the frustrations of that year of teaching. Although I had certainly lost my classroom public in the circuitous rhetoric of Ortega's pages, his own belief—stated in that book—that "clarity is the philosopher's courtesy" had been central, I realized, to his remarkable pedagogical mission in Spain.

While drafting a dissertation proposal in the summer of 1972, I could hardly imagine the many turns in the road ahead. I was to trace the entire course of a prolific and diverse career rich in institutional commitments and publishing ventures. No full-scale biography of Ortega existed in either Spanish or English, though a plethora of studies of his work and assessments of his person had accumulated since his death in 1955. My first approach would be to recreate, as far as possible, the ambience in which Ortega had cultivated the various audiences from which he hoped to build a native public receptive to his program for cultural modernization.

My project entailed a period of residence in Madrid and a series of interviews with many of those who had known Ortega and whose lives had been directly affected by his work. During the winter and spring of 1972–1973, living in the old Residencia de Estudiantes (which had come under the jurisdiction of the postwar Consejo Superior de Investigaciones Científicas) on the "hill of poplars" at number 21 Calle Pinar, I slowly made my way into Ortega's world. The very gardens where I walked before the midday meal at the Residencia had been frequented by the young Ortega, who often joined the preprandial *tertulia* (social-intellectual circle) that took place there in the years after World War I. And it was to the shelter of those historic buildings which he came in the summer of 1936, seriously ill, having fled his apartment with his family to escape the threat of random violence in the streets, before they were driven altogether from wartime Madrid. During my months in that relatively tranquil corner of the raucous and congested modern capital, I had the encouragement and wise counsel of Joan Connelly Ullman, who was in Madrid to work on her biography of the Spanish Socialist leader Pablo Iglesias. Her sound grasp of the nation's modern history became central to my halting efforts to recover a cultural milieu that the Franco regime had done its best to bury forever. My interviewees talked readily and generously of their memories of those earlier years, and both Soledad Ortega, Ortega's daughter, and Julián Marías, a former student of Ortega's, generously offered their counsel.

Back in Chicago for the next academic year, I submitted the first draft of my essay to Professor Edward Shils. He suggested that I view Ortega as a Spanish intellectual who wished to move from the "periphery" of his own culture toward the European "center" that defined the high culture of his day. This perspective added a new dimension to my earlier concern with the philosopher's relation to his native public: now I must see him in the wider context of European intellectual history in the early twentieth century. During the next few years, the book gradually matured, but the overall shape—the vital trajectory—of Ortega's life still eluded me. My concern with his various publics, both within Spain and abroad, was still a key motif, complemented increasingly by the issue of his generational membership. Ortega himself had made a seminal contribution to the small body of European theory on cultural and intellectual generations. One had to read only *The Modern Theme* and *Man and Crisis* to see that this theme had occupied him during the central period of his career.

My initial interest in the dilemma of a man who aimed to convey high theory to a heterogeneous and philosophically unsophisticated public emerged again as the book approached final shape. Ortega's role as a modernizing intellectual had to be set, I saw, in full biographical context. Yet the materials for this project remained limited. In Madrid his family held—as they still do—many of his letters and papers closed to all but a select few, who were thus able to study one facet or another of the life behind and within the work. For some time, I supposed that this policy rested on discretion regarding intimate details that might damage the posthumous reputation of the man whose memory they guarded and revered. I may, however, have been mistaken. For on the whole, Spanish culture has maintained a separation between the private and the public record, which has discouraged the development of a tradition of biography and autobiography comparable to that in the English-speaking world. In this sense, one might understand why no thorough life of one of the central figures in the nation's modern history had been published. In sum, my original assumption concerning the inaccessibility of certain primary materials for such a study no longer seems as likely as it did at first. Whatever the case, the portrait of Ortega presented in this volume, I now believe, comes as close as possible to being the missing life. This is, of course, an intellectual biography, in which the course of the man's days is subordinate to the development of his career.

In my later revisions of *The Imperative of Modernity*—a title that signalizes the governing passion of Ortega's pedagogical and philosophical work—I have seen how thorny is the task of portraying a man whose work is known everywhere in the Spanish-speaking world and currently fills twelve thick volumes of a much more complete *Obras completas*. Since the trajectory of Ortega's career is so intricate and diverse, it has been exceptionally difficult to order the story and get the priorities right. A just portrait must refer to the history of Spanish liberalism and reformism between the Revolution of 1868 and the outbreak of the Spanish Civil War in 1936. The story as told here includes the development of Spanish Krausism, that curious movement of intellectual and moral reform that began in Madrid around 1860, and a brief account of Francisco Giner de los Ríos's Institución Libre de Enseñanza (Institute of Free Education). Relevant too is the work of the prolix Generation of 1898, the cluster of Spanish writers who reached their intellectual maturity around the year of Spain's loss of the war with the United States.

But Ortega must just as certainly be seen in relation to the history of European philosophy at the turn and in the early decades of this century. As recent scholarship has shown, his central ideas were deeply indebted to the work of his neo-Kantian teachers in Marburg and to such thinkers as Friedrich Nietzsche, Wilhelm Dilthey, Max Scheler, Nicolai Hartmann, Edmund Husserl, and Martin Heidegger. Ortega brought his own thought to maturity in constant dialogue with these sources and in his determination to "overcome" the faults he perceived in the idealist and neo-idealist traditions of European thought. In addition, he was a signal member of the trans-European Generation of 1914, which provided Spain with its clearest example of a self-aware intellectual movement dedicated to the modernization of the culturally backward nation. If the writers of the preceding Generation of 1898 were the first in that country to identify themselves as "intellectuals," the young authors and reformist politicians who were ascendant at the outbreak of World War I would brilliantly exemplify that late nineteenth-century neologism.

Finally, this study seeks to remedy two forms of neglect in English-language publications relevant to understanding Ortega's career. First, most contemporary histories of European philosophy published in English omit even the briefest mention of philosophical thought in Spain, an oversight probably reflecting the common assumption that nothing worthy of mention existed south of the Pyrenees. In matters of poetry, music, and art, we readily grant that Spain has made interesting contributions during the present century; but we are not disposed to look there for important philosophical work. Even our broad surveys of modern intellectual history tend to give scant attention, if any, to the Iberian Peninsula. What we do have in this field are highly specialized studies, often written by Hispanists. Second, the existing studies of Ortega in English do little to establish the social and historical framework without which his work cannot be fairly assessed. Lacking this perspective, one is likely to vacillate between seeing him as a gifted man of letters who sprang up like a rare flower in a cultural desert and seeing him as a philosopher of sorts who wrote beautifully but hardly bears comparison with the seminal thinkers of our era. In this study, he is presented both as a philosopher *sensu stricto* and as a modern *philosophe* whose prodigious talents allowed him to do more than any other twentieth-century Spaniard to bring his country toward full membership in the spiritual and intellectual community of modern European nations.

ACKNOWLEDGMENTS

I extend my thanks to three persons at the University of California Press who have shepherded this book along its way. From the first, Scott Mahler's support of my work has been fervent and unwavering. His good taste and sound judgment are all one could hope from an editor. My copyeditor, Nancy Atkinson, brought to the manuscript a discriminating and passionate critical sense that made her a kind of ideal reader. Finally, the good cheer and good sense of Shirley Warren, managers editor, lightened my load in the final stages of work.

A word of particular thanks is also due Soledad Ortega of the Fundación José Ortega y Gasset in Madrid. Besides graciously extending permission for me to examine her father's restricted papers at the Library of Congress, she supplied several photos of her father and responded to my inquiries with lively interest.

BIOGRAPHICAL NOTE

The notable absence of a standard biography of Ortega is a major hindrance to any student of his work. Thus rendered vulnerable to ideological polemic and irresponsible speculation, his life has been variously represented, but always rather schematically. Indeed, Spanish history and letters generally have suffered, perhaps until recently, from the lack of fully developed genres of biography and autobiography, which have not found as rich soil in that socially conservative Catholic culture as they have elsewhere in Europe and in America. Similar to the bias that inhibited the acceptance and growth of psychoanalysis in Spain, this Spanish neglect of life writing as practiced, say, in Anglo-American letters stems from a sense that one's intimate life is not open territory for the incursions of scholars, journalists, and popular biographers. The well-worn topic of Spanish "dignity" points toward a characteristic reticence in the people, a feeling—particularly strong in Castile and the more northerly provinces—that one's domestic and erotic doings are one's own business. That stance in turn indicates a traditionally clearer division between public and private life than obtains elsewhere in the West. Consequently, Spaniards have preferred to keep their great men alive in ceremony and in informal memory rather than in intimate literary portraits.

But that bias is shifting, of course, as Spain ever more rapidly assimilates attitudes and modes characteristic of social and cultural modernization in the West. These include an increasing commitment to modern scholarly life writing, a more sophisticated historiography, and the cultivation of the social sciences as they have been practiced in much of Europe and the United States for several decades. This intellectual sea change has already begun to provide us with better resources for the study of the social and intellectual history of the Peninsula.

We may briefly summarize what is generally known about Ortega's life. He was born in Madrid on May 9, 1883, to José Ortega Munilla and Dolores Gasset Chinchilla. His mother was the daughter of the founder and owner of the distinguished liberal daily *El Imparcial*; his father, a well-known novelist and journalist, edited the paper's literary section and served from 1900 to 1906 as its director. In one sense, then, Ortega was born into letters, as his oft-cited quip —"I was born on a rotary press"—indicates. His early education took place in Madrid and El Escorial, where his family maintained summer quarters. At the age of eight, he entered a Jesuit school in the province of Malaga in the south.

Ortega had several informal teachers in childhood, not the least of whom was his gifted father. The young lad read eagerly in French and Spanish and already had a rich belletristic preparation when he entered the Jesuit university at Deusto in 1897 to follow a combined program of law and philosophy and letters. In 1898 he transferred to the Central University of Madrid, from which he received his *licenciatura* in 1902, the same year he began his journalistic career. In 1904 he took his doctorate at Madrid with a thesis on "The Terrors of the Year 1000: A Critique of a Legend," turning immediately afterward to Germany as the proper destination for a young man of philosophical vocation. Between 1905 and 1907, Ortega resided and intermittently studied in Leipzig, Nuremberg, Munich, Cologne, Berlin, and Marburg. But it was Marburg, where he studied under the university's two leading neo-Kantians, Hermann Cohen and Paul Natorp, which claimed his most serious attention, and he spent the better part of 1907 there.

Upon returning to Madrid in the fall of that year, Ortega began to write more frequently for *El Imparcial*, in which he had already published several critical essays. In June 1908 he was appointed professor of psychology, logic, and ethics at La Escuela Superior del Magisterio in Madrid, an institution he had helped to found. Established to train teachers for Spain's normal schools, La Escuela played a prominent part (until it was dissolved in 1932) in the numerous reforms of Spanish education carried out in the years just before World War I. The moment he gave his first class there in October 1909, the young Ortega began to play a decisive role in the cultural formation of the nation's youth. A year later he won the chair of metaphysics at the Central University of Madrid, left vacant by the death of the distinguished educator and statesman Nicolás Salmerón (1838–1908). In a heightened atmosphere of educational reform promoted by the Liberal prime minister José Canalejas,

Ortega's prestigious university position signaled the arrival of a new generation dedicated to the liberalization and modernization of the national culture. As the emerging leader of the Spanish Generation of 1914, Ortega, whose correspondence with prominent peers and older intellectual leaders in Spain was already voluminous, wielded an influence disproportionate to his small body of published work. More important, he had found for himself two key avenues to the public: the press and the university.

In the same year that he won his Madrid chair, Ortega married Rosa Spottorno Topete and, as if in accord with Freud's dictum that the capacities to love and work are the marks of the mature man, began to write prodigiously. Though named to the chair of metaphysics in November 1910, he did not immediately occupy it. He returned with his bride to Germany in January 1911, aided by a grant from Spain's Ministry of Public Instruction, and renewed his contacts in Marburg. There his first son, Miguel Germán, named in part for his father's second homeland, was born in May. By the end of 1911, Ortega had returned to Madrid to assume his chair and to proceed with his work as a philosopher and a social critic. From that time, he returned to Germany only once (briefly, in 1934) until 1949, after which he made several trips there. With the additional exception of two extended trips to Argentina (in 1916 and 1928), he was to remain on native ground until the outbreak of civil war in July 1936. It was the diverse work of those twenty-five years after 1911 that would make him the leading man of letters in prewar Spain.

As I will discuss later, Ortega's least public, most obviously specialized writing was done during this period at the Central University of Madrid, where he worked at the center of a quiet but extensive reconstruction of humanistic studies in Spanish higher education. Throughout the same years, he pursued a much more broadly public phase of his career with his journalistic labors for several small magazines (to which he contributed before and during the First World War) and for Madrid's two leading liberal dailies of the period, *El Imparcial* and *El Sol*. For the first, owned and run by relatives on his mother's side (the Gassets), he wrote between 1904 and 1917; for the second, which he helped to found, between 1917 and 1931. His affiliation with *El Sol* also involved him in the formation (in 1919) and later development of the Calpe (later Espasa-Calpe) publishing house, which soon made available first-rate literature from Spain and the rest of Europe in a modestly priced pocketbook series. Midway between the intimacy of his role as a university professor and the obvious prominence of his journalism stood his work as the founder (in 1923) and director of the monthly *Revista de Occidente* and the associated Revista press, which published in 1924 the first in a long line of translations of major works in European science, philosophy, history, and related fields. The *Revista*, which quickly became one of Europe's most distinguished intellectual journals, was directed toward the general educated public Ortega sought to form and augment in his native land. As such, it was at once a somewhat specialized yet widely influential publication.

In late June 1931, after the fall of Miguel Primo de Rivera's dictatorship (1923–1930) and the departure of King Alfonso XIII, Ortega was elected deputy to the Constituent Cortes (Congress) of the Second Spanish Republic. He came to that post as the voice of middle-class liberal intellectuals and professional men, whose support for the Republic he had rallied in the Agrupación al Servicio de la Republica, founded by him, Gregorio Marañon, and Ramón Pérez de Ayala on February 8, 1931. Ortega remained active as a deputy until 1932. In this role, the most overtly political one in his long and varied career, he had, perhaps, the least effect of all on Spanish culture.

In 1932 Ortega, feeling himself inefficacious in the rough-and-tumble of parliamentary debate and uninterested in the prosaic detail of politics, announced his withdrawal from active participation in the future of the Republic, which he nevertheless continued to support in principle. He wrote prodigiously during the politically turbulent years from 1933 to 1936, when the Spanish Civil War began with the uprising of July 18, 1936. Ill with a serious gastric disorder and fearful for his life, Ortega fled Madrid with his family on August 30, bound for Paris by way of Alicante, Marseilles, and Grenoble. The Ortegas arrived in the French capital in November of that year and remained there, with the exception of a trip to Holland in 1938, until early 1939, when Ortega was obliged to winter in Portugal to recuperate from a major operation. In the spring, he returned to Paris, but left again with his wife and only daughter for Argentina in August of that year. In Buenos Aires, he spent over two and a half financially difficult years of bitter exile.

By the spring of 1942, the Ortegas had moved to Estoril, a suburb of Lisbon, Portugal—a large step toward native soil. The next relatively tranquil three years seem to have been a period of withdrawn productivity for the philosopher. In Lisbon he wrote a number of short pieces and began to work on his study of Leibniz and the history of reason (published posthumously).

In August 1945, Ortega traveled to Madrid—the first visit in nine years—to feel out the ground for his possible return. He went back again in 1946 and, that May, gave the first of his postwar Spanish lectures in the Madrid Ateneo, which, from its founding as a private club in 1835 until the civil war in 1936, had been a major intellectual center for the promotion of parliamentary liberalism in Spain. Returning to Madrid yet again in 1948, Ortega founded the Instituto de Humanidades with the help of his disciple Julián Marías. For two years it offered a series of winter lectures and colloquia open to the general public, but an atmosphere of hostile criticism in the newspapers and in official circles eventually prompted Ortega to discontinue the experiment, his last formal work on Spanish soil. The remaining six years of his life, though filled with accolades from abroad and a busy lecture schedule in several countries, were dogged by failing health and his inability to reestablish a genuine forum in Madrid. His prewar public had of course been dissipated by the civil war, and his dominant role in the cultural life of the 1920s and 1930s now seemed a matter of the distant past.

In July 1949, Ortega, who by then enjoyed international renown, made his first trip to the United States to participate in the Goethe centennial in Aspen, Colorado, after which he traveled to Germany to speak at a German Goethe festival in Hamburg in August 1949. Both his growing reputation as a major European thinker and the grave decline of Spanish intellectual life under Franco led him in the following years to deliver a series of lectures and university courses in Germany. By the summer of 1955, which, as was his custom, he spent in Asturias, in the north of Spain, his health was clearly failing. On September 17 he returned to Madrid for diagnosis and treatment; his doctors discovered advanced, inoperable cancer of the stomach and liver. On October 18, 1955, Ortega died at his last Madrid residence, number 28 Monte Esquinza.

This brief biographical outline and the following study of his career are necessarily limited, for much remains obscure in Ortega's life. Only a handful of his letters has been published, and the most important of his private papers are still in the hands of his family. An adequate intimate biography of the man is yet to be written. Nevertheless, this study of his commitment to the modernization of Spanish culture provides a fresh context for understanding the life of a man who shaped the thoughts of millions of readers in Spain and abroad and established a new level of excellence for Spanish critical prose. I hope to show in the following pages why his example has provided intellectual and ethical inspiration for a distinguished minority of more recent Spanish writers and thinkers, whose work obviously carries his mark. Some of these men may justly be called his epigones; others are, more loosely speaking, simply admiring students of his literary style and his major ideas. For this select public he provided, as no other Spanish writer of this century, the model of serious critical thought and high aesthetic refinement, qualities all too rare in non-fiction Spanish prose before him.

Particularly after translations of *La rebelión de las masas* (*The Revolt of the Masses*) were published in the 1930s, Ortega progressively became an important writer outside of Spain, one of those world figures, those interpretive voices of Western culture, who represent the high development of European thought in this century: Freud, Nietzsche, Henri Bergson, Unamuno, Benedetto Croce, Paul Valéry, Jean-Paul Sartre, Albert Camus, Thomas Mann, Heidegger, Bertrand Russell and others. But such an image does little to illuminate the meaning of particular works by Ortega or to set them in the dual context of his Spanish citizenship and of the vast and disorderly corpus of his complete works. Neither does it help us to understand the complexity of his position regarding the "Europeanization" of Spanish culture, nor to grasp the rich ambivalences of his encounter with the idea of modernity. To such questions, set in biographical context, we now turn.

INTRODUCTION

Like many of his distinguished European peers, José Ortega y Gasset reached maturity at a time in recent history when the *Zeitgeist* appeared to undergo a radically new formulation. Born in 1883, he lived his youth and early adulthood in an atmosphere of heightened awareness of the end of one era and the beginning of another.

The approximately four decades between 1880 and the end of the Great War seemed to those who lived them—as indeed they seem to us in retrospect—a time of momentous cultural and historical change. In his *Education*, published toward the end of this period, Henry Adams characterized the late nineteenth century—filled as it was with disturbing speculations on the *fin de siècle*—as a time of crisis in Western man's sense of himself and the world. Concepts as fundamental as those of space and time were undergoing transformation in every sphere of cultural activity from the novel and visual arts to theoretical physics. Proust, Picasso, and Einstein, together with thinkers like Bergson and William James, all challenged older notions of location, duration, memory, and perception. The new culture of space and time, as it has been called, was accompanied by a sharpened sense of man's historicity and his ineluctable entanglement in a world troubled by the absence of enduring or immutable truths. Traditional religious beliefs, upon which relatively fixed definitions of human nature had been based, were undergoing attrition, a process only accelerated by the later ravages of a world war that redrew the map of Europe known to the nineteenth century. In physics, Einstein's general theory of relativity introduced a paradigm shift, while in art the rise of cubism altered an entire tradition of naturalistic perception. In philosophy, post-Kantian thought took a phenomenological turn that redefined the relationship between consciousness and the world of its "intended" objects. In psychology, Freud probed the strange logic of dreams and subconscious thought, while writers as diverse as Nietzsche, Dostoyevsky, Ibsen, and Joyce paralleled his investigations in works that sounded a new note in European letters. The two generations of artists and thinkers who came to maturity, respectively, in the 1890s and around 1914 felt that they worked in a kind of watershed period that divided the older world of bourgeois European civilization from a new era.

Extraordinarily sensitive to the *Zeitgeist* of this period, Ortega appeared early in the twentieth century as a major witness to the end of a historical and cultural order marked by almost ecstatic expectations of renewal. When one tries to define the conditions shaping Ortega's perspective, it is erroneous to assume—as Spanish intellectuals of the time often did—that the Spain of his youth was altogether a culturally stagnant backwater of Europe, a traditionalist and decadent society entirely peripheral to the transformations taking place in countries north of the Pyrenees. Despite the backwardness characteristic of much Spanish life as measured against advances in material welfare and innovations in thought and mores elsewhere in Europe, Spain too was undergoing the breadown of an old monarchical order and experiencing, though only in Madrid and Barcelona, the growth of a modernist movement in art and thought. A Spanish liberal political tradition had developed in the nineteenth century, which also witnessed the emergence of secular thought as an alternative to what was still a predominantly Catholic culture.

Influenced by political and cultural unrest in Spain and by his study of philosophy in Germany between 1905 and 1911, Ortega came to share with other European intellectuals of his generation a dazzling vision of modernity as it was being defined all over Europe— in Vienna, Paris, London, Berlin, Zurich, Prague, Stockholm, St. Petersburg, Moscow, Rome, Milan, Barcelona, and Madrid. In a great diversity of forms, they expressed their perception that the end of the nineteenth century and the early years of our own constituted a crisis in Western culture. Just before the Great War, anxiety over the end of the old order mixed with great expectations of the future. In fact, many intellectuals of the time welcomed the prospect of a European war precisely because they thought it would purge the continent of the vestiges of a moribund past. The frisson of impending apocalypse fused with the yearning for a cultural rebirth—a yearning characterized by a heightened sense of discovery in the sciences, philosophy, literature, theater, art, architecture, and other fields. Men and women of many circles and persuasions—artistic and theoretical as well as political—marked the coming "New Age" with feelings ranging from fear and rue to bravado and awe. Ortega, as we shall see, defined his particular place in this broad movement by declaring that the modern era in European philosophy—which, presumably, began with Descartes—was to be succeeded by a new philosophy of human life as understood through what he came to call *la razón vital* (vital reason) and, later, *la razón histórica* (historical reason).

Altogether, a peculiar intensity marked the thought and expression of the period. Both in Spain and elsewhere in Europe many writers sought a vision of life that would compensate for the apparent decline of the Christian faith. In an increasingly agnostic or simply secularized cultural climate, some embraced the "religion" of life itself, as Richard Ellman has noted of several English and Irish authors of the Edwardian period. In Edmund Gosse, Samuel Butler, W. B. Yeats, James Joyce, E. M. Forster, and D. H. Lawrence, one finds the transfer of religious terminology to everyday existence, which is then celebrated as "epiphanic" or sacred:

> A kind of inner belief pervades their writings, that the transcendent is immanent in the earthly.... As Conrad said it in his preface to *The Shadow-Line*, "the world of the living contains enough marvels and mysteries ... acting upon our emotions and intelligence in ways so inexplicable that it would almost justify the conception of life as an enchanted state." The central miracle for the Edwardians is the sudden alteration of the self.[1]

In post-Christian terms, self-transformation stood in for the workings of divine grace or the blessing of Christ upon one's life. Far from simply waning, the central belief-system of Western history left in its wake a multitude of cultural and psychological responses that must be understood as direct reflections of the shock men experienced at the "death" of God.[2] The tense, self-conscious assertion of life's inherent meaning was one of these. For many, the earlier, spontaneous wellsprings of faith were increasingly replaced by William James's "will to believe" and by the hallowing of the "precious moment" caught and held in all its magic. Throughout Western culture one could recognize the need to invest significance in a world apparently divested of its authorizing Creator, who, if not dead, was eclipsed or withdrawn.

In some thinkers, this need issued in new philosophies of culture and history, for if God could no longer be held responsible for a grand pattern of human existence over the ages, accounts alternative to the Christian teleological one had to be found. One of these, deeply influenced by the Darwinian revolution, was the organic metaphor, which likened the growth, maturation, and decay of cultures to the ontogenetic and phylogenetic rhythms of animal existence. One variant of this figure of thought was the seasonal metaphor. Although much older as an analogy for man's life than the biological model, the seasonal one took on new meanings in an age persuaded to assign to cultures their "springtimes," "autumns," and so on. Another, related variant was the diurnal metaphor, also venerable but newly fashionable, which likened the rise and fall of cultures and eras to that of the sun through the heavens. Some philosophers combined threads of all these interrelated models, most notably Oswald Spengler in the widely influential *Decline of the West*.

In the early stages of his career, Ortega, though unconvinced by Spengler, found the biological metaphor compelling. Although he later rejected its simplistic aspects in favor of a more sophisticated vision of cultural and historical change, traces of the analogy with animal life remained in his mature writings, concerned as they were with rooting culture in life, very much including the human body. In addition, he embraced the metaphor of the day's passage, perhaps borrowed from Nietzsche's *Zarathustra*, in order to confirm his conviction that his generation was called to define the "high noon" of Spanish culture in the postmodern period, the beginning of which coincided with his youth. His concept of the "height" or "level" of the times (*la altura de los tiempos*) was essentially an extension of the idea that human culture moves in a rhythm of ascendancy and decline. Following the diurnal figure of thought, Ortega saw his early work as the dawn of a new Spain; and in the 1920s and early 1930s, he indicated that both in his own philosophical work and in the political future of the nation high noon was imminent. Much as Lewis Mumford in the same years reenvisioned the development of nineteenth-century American culture in terms of the "Golden Day" and the "Brown Decades," Ortega employed cosmic or natural imagery to invest the course of his own times with significance.

The new "Golden Day" of Spain as conceived by Ortega and his generation was, in fact, only one version of the pervasive sense throughout Europe that the old order was spent and must be overturned. Yet as fundamental ideas of space, time, culture, history, political and social order, and human existence itself were being boldly revised in turn-of-the-century Europe, the forces of tradition and reaction, moved to "cultural despair" by the threat of too rapid change, pitted themselves against defenders of the new. In this dialectic, "antimodernism" became a prominent feature of the cultural and intellectual scene. In France, anti-Dreyfusards, seeing "the Jew" as a harbinger of moral decay and the break down of social order, organized against Dreyfusards, much as defenders of property, church, and state stood up throughout the Continent against exponents of communism, secularism, and socialist internationalism. In Bismarckian and Wilhelmine Germany, powerful banking and industrial interests gave an imperialist thrust to the nation's rapid economic growth around 1900, foreshadowing Germany's future role in twentieth-century Europe. But the expanding German middle class and the great entrepreneurs, arising in a newly unified nation without a seasoned tradition of political liberalism, welcomed neither modernism in art and thought nor calls for social justice and greater democratization of the political process. At the turn of the century, Spain, stung by the loss of her last colonies in the war with the United States in 1898, was rapidly approaching a series of crises that would fracture the old parliamentary order of the Restoration years (1875–1902) and end the Bourbon monarchy in 1931. During the Restoration period the frequent cries of Spanish intellectuals for "regeneration" of the nation's cultural and political life peaked in the voices of the brilliant Spanish literary movement known as the Generation of 1898, which flourished around the year of Spain's defeat in the Spanish-American War. Their lament—for the nation's military humiliation as well as for its longer history of decline—was taken up in turn by the cluster of young Spanish writers and politicians whose tasks were specified by Ortega's early writings. This cluster formed part of the trans-European movement that was later dubbed the Generation of 1914. In the larger context of Europe this generation's coming of age was defined by the outbreak of the Great War, while in neutralist Spain the flourishing of the movement was linked perhaps less to international than to domestic events—events in which Ortega played a key part. Among them were the establishing in 1913 of the reformist Liga de Educación Política Española (the Spanish League for Political Education), which Ortega helped to found out of concern for the moribund parliamentary system bequeathed to the nation by the Restoration; his epoch-making speech of 1914, "Vieja y nueva política" (Old and New Politics); and the publication of his first book, *Meditations on Quixote* (*Meditaciones del Quijote*), also in 1914. By that time he had developed a voice that distinguished his work from that of the men of 1898 and marked him as the obvious leader of the younger generation.

In the pan-European atmosphere of impending death of old forms, ideology flowered on all sides and manifestos proliferated. Art itself became freighted with theory, while physics, abandoning its old empiricist moorings, seemed more and more to resemble a sublime intuition, a kind of "poetry" of the universe. Psychology, philosophy, and literature all reflected an introspective turn, a new awareness of perception and consciousness. A more sophisticated sense of human time as subjectively experienced was fostered by Bergson's philosophy and William James's psychology and by numerous novelists of the time; yet even as people began to grasp more fully the "flow" of lived experience, an ecstatic awareness of the present moment in knife-edged separation from past and future appeared in much *fin de siècle* expression, conveying both elation and distress. In short, the cultural ferment that preceded 1914 explains how Virginia Woolf could say, in a much-quoted remark, that "on or about December, 1910, human character changed."[3] Arbitrary and literally incredible as the observation seems, it catches something that many participants in the drama of those years felt.

Historians are divided on the applicability of the metaphor of "watershed" to the decades on both sides of 1900. While the anguished voices of writers of the period from many countries portrayed the time as one of unprecedented changes on all fronts, more sober, subsequent assessments suggest that major lines of continuity can be divined throughout the *fin de siècle* and prewar period. Most students of the time agree, however, that Europe was intellectually shaken by innovations in art, philosophy, and science, and that the sociopolitical shock of four years of continent-wide war was no less profound. The voices that gave definitive expression to this idea were those of the Generation of 1914.

In neutralist Spain, the crisis of European civilization represented by the Great War was felt at a distance—a fact that confirmed the widespread perception among Spanish intellectuals that their culture had existed for centuries on the periphery of European cultural development. Indeed, Spain's decline as a major world power had been progressively evident since early in the seventeenth century; and well before 1914, the Spanish crisis of 1898, a cry of distress by numerous prominent writers over the political and moral decline of the nation, had been at once part of the pervasive cultural pessimism of the European *fin de siècle* and a more immediate reaction to Spain's loss of her last overseas colonies in the war with the United States. In this context, during the years just before 1914, the young Ortega y Gasset, inheritor of a rhetoric of death and regeneration, emerged as the outstanding Spanish voice of the new generation, combining in his work the themes of Spain's backwardness and Europe's cultural sea change.

The former issue involved him deeply in a political critique of the old parliamentary-monarchical order, while the latter cast him in the role of a harbinger of cultural modernism. In fact, these two strands of his thought were not separate, for he perceived native political reform as but one face of his nation's pressing need to enter the mainstream of European history, while his self-appointed mission of philosophical renewal, nourished by study with the neo-Kantians of Marburg and by the phenomenology of Max Scheler and Edmund Husserl, was ultimately rooted in his assessment of Spain as a culture vitiated by anarchic "subjectivism" and a vulgar sensualism. In other words, his political and his philosophical programs came at a historical juncture (both at home and abroad) that forced him to define the imperative to live " at the level of the times," an elusive concept most fully articulated only later in *The Revolt of the Masses* (1930).

In the years after his return from Marburg in 1911, Ortega defined his role in Spain as that of a herald of the dawning age, a prophet calling a wayward and indifferent people to heed the cultural development he discerned in other parts of Europe. He saw as no other Spaniard before him, including Miguel de Unamuno (1864–1936), that Spain must define itself by standards established beyond its frontiers. This perception implicated him in a dialectic of tradition and modernization, a framework that lent to his projects of political and cultural reform an urgency that greatly amplified the sense of crisis proclaimed by his intellectual forebears in the Generation of 1898 (Unamuno, Pío Baroja, Antonio Machado, Azorín, and others). In order to mount his program, Ortega became the outstanding Spanish spokesman of the *Zeitgeist* enunciated by the many European creators of the new culture. His vision of a Spain historically removed from the development of the rest of Europe sharpened his spatial perception of his nation as geographically beyond the pale, a lonely peninsula bounded by Gibraltar and the august Pyrenees range. In this view, Spain was both literally and figuratively on the edge of modern times. Its sense of time was controlled by old forms—Kant had called it derogatorily "the land of ancestors"—just as its sense of place was symbolically defined by the Pyrenean wall. Madrid was literally a long journey from Paris, Berlin, and London, and it seemed ages away from the concerns animating the life of those capitals.

Ortega's plan to overcome the cultural distance between Spain and the rest of Europe prompted him to project his own modernist sensibility upon his languishing native land. In this regard he was like many other modern intellectuals who wished to see the drama of their own thoughts writ large in the records of their people. Thus his reformist projects—the central topic of this essay—were never simply disinterested or altruistic but were instead rooted in the fusion of his own calling to civic pedagogy with the developing history of Spain. As he phrased it in 1910, all significant teaching was "social pedagogy," for the reform of thought and character must result in the renewal of the community. His awareness that the average Spaniard's character was as distant from a sense of social responsibility as the nation's culture was from European advances in science and learning gave him, of course, a special vantage point, a heightened sensitivity to the weight of the past, the burden of tradition so proverbial in Spain. Like other contemporary intellectuals and writers from such peripheral areas as Russia, Scandinavia, Ireland, and even Italy, he felt a gnawing hunger to be abreast of the best minds at work in the laboratories, universities, cafés, and ateliers of the major European cities, and his central mission became the translation of that ferment into his native language and culture.

In analyzing the development of Ortega's notion of modernity, however, we must note his crucial critique of that very concept, for he was at pains to distinguish what he called the "modern age" from his own period of the early twentieth century, for which he wanted a new designation. He wished to dissociate his time semantically from the long post-Renaissance period often called "modern" or "early modern." Briefly, Ortega held that the modern period properly so called had begun with Galileo and Descartes and was principally characterized by the pursuit of scientific and mathematical reason. In 1923, in *El tema de nuestro tiempo* (The Theme of Our Time, misleadingly published in translation—given Ortega's attempt to distance himself from the Cartesian modern age—under the title *The Modern Theme*), he announced definitively the death of the old philosophical faith and the birth of a new one for which he saw himself as a midwife in "our time." The modern age as sketched there covered roughly three centuries of European intellectual history from about 1600 to 1900. During that time physics had become the new queen of the sciences. Under its sway men believed that nature and human life itself could be exhaustively understood through scientific paradigms. This powerful mode of envisioning reality had elevated a certain kind of reason to the status of absolute truth during the very period in which Spain suffered the dramatic decline of its empire and became the paladin of Counter-Reformation Catholicism. The nation that experienced only a minor, derivative Enlightenment in the seventeen hundreds, became during those centuries a lesser province of the cultural area it had once gloriously dominated. The myth of dark, backward, and mysterious Spain, cultivated so richly by nineteenth- and twentieth-century romantics, was established in the Western mind during this period of isolation and withdrawal. Similarly, the earlier Black Legend, created by Protestant historians of Europe in sympathy with resistance to Spanish imperialism in the Netherlands and elsewhere, had portrayed Spain as the obscurantist and fanatical land of the Inquisition, a nation that imposed its conquering faith through the dark workings of the dreaded tribunal. Throughout much of Europe and even North America after the sixteenth century this picture of a cruel and tyrannical Catholic empire, bastion of the Counter-Reformation and homeland of the scheming Jesuit, came to overlie the complex history of Spain's extrapeninsular ventures.

From this modern periphery of Europe Ortega's voice became preeminent in a chorus of national reassessment running from the Revolution of 1868 to the birth of the Second Republic in 1931. Being philosophically more sophisticated than any of his predecessors or peers, Ortega managed to link his campaign to reintegrate Spain into the historical European community with his announcement of a new era in European philosophy: the end of the modern age of Cartesian reason brought together, that is, the birth of a new Spain and of a new stage of European thought. Ortega deployed the notion of a dual cultural watershed as a strategy for introducting his ambitious projects of reform at home. However, despite the force of a rhetoric that bound Spain's future to that of Europe, he never supposed that his nation contained within herself the driving energy of regeneration; rather, he hoped to infuse her with the vitality of his own writings and those of the foremost Continental thinkers of the day.

In *El tema de nuestro tiempo* Ortega argued that the moribund Cartesian paradigm of European culture was founded on the twin poles of rationalism and relativism. The former represented the reigning but declining culture, the scientific tradition initiated by Galileo, Descartes, and Newton; and the latter—an inadequate, contrapuntal "answer" to "physicomathematical reason"—affirmed the relativized truth of merely subjective experience. In one sense, relativism represented the claims of "life" against "culture"; but such claims were, in Ortega's view, vitiated by the difficulty of establishing truth value for the relativistic position. In attempting to counter the tyranny of earlier rationalism, relativists tended toward a solipsistic or mystical defense of individualized experience. The resultant fatal split between life and reason must needs be healed. Ortega's remedy was the synthetic vision of *la razón vital* (vital reason), a form of thought that would restore to each its proper relation to the other. Reason, he argued, was always rooted in life, understood as the organic basis of all existence and all consciousness. All that is known must be known through the circumstantially limited perception of the particular subject concerned. Even the truth of mathematical reason is accessible only in the complete context of a human life. Nor is such reason absolute in the sense that it elucidates laws existing independently of man's need to order his experience. The truth of the world is, finally, a composite of all the different perspectives on reality provided by the cumulative human record. One such perspective was that of Descartes; and though it had bulked inordinately large in the reasoning of succeeding generations, it was not ultimately privileged as a viewpoint on life.

Just over a decade after the publication of *El tema de nuestro tiempo*, Ortega deepened and extended his vision by proclaiming the dawn of *la razón histórica* (historical reason) in *Man and Crisis* (*En torno a Galileo*, 1933), a series of lectures commemorating the 300th anniversary of the appearance of Galileo before the tribunal of the Italian Inquisition. There Ortega made more explicit his definition of the modern age and argued that his new doctrine of historical reason would require man to understand himself as a pilgrim on an unending road that followed the turnings of successive philosophical answers to the dilemmas of civilized life. In this light, the crisis of the twentieth century was simply one more in an ongoing series of crises that had periodically forced Western man to reorient himself in the world. Since the Cartesian or Galilean solution to his questions no longer obtained, he must now see himself as the inveterately historical and historicized creature he truly was and had always been, understanding his present situation in terms of former patterns of existence that were no longer viable. To understand the imperative of one's time was, thus, to understand the past, and vice versa. Man was the being who could not abide with a single and absolute version of the ends of culture. There were no "eternal" answers to the question of what it meant to be human.

Well before *El tema de nuestro tiempo*, Ortega had published a short but seminal essay foreshadowing his more extensive analysis of the modern period as that which the European intellectual vanguard had to transcend. In 1916, in "Nada 'moderno' y 'muy siglo XX'" (Not at All Modern and Very Much Twentieth-Century), he had established the crucial distinction between a merely modish subjection to time-bound taste and an allegiance to the most advanced ideas of twentieth-century European culture. While declining to ride on the merry-go-round of shifting intellectual fashion—the trivial form of trying to be up-to-date in every detail—he nonetheless allied himself solidly with the new priorities being established in contemporary scholarship, art, philosophy, and science. In this paradoxical perspective, the "modern" was whatever would quickly become outmoded, whatever was old hat almost as soon as it was new. This view of modernity also made clear Ortega's intention to oppose the nineteenth century as a residual, even retrograde presence in the lives of twentieth-century men and women. The recent past was the real enemy, what had just been modern and was now moribund. He who would be "muy siglo XX" must define his life over against the dying, whose deeds and modes of thought pressed upon him still. In fact, the preceding century had been, Ortega argued, the age that dubbed itself preeminently "modern," making that epithet its battle slogan. Hence, men of the new century must achieve their own form of modernity by denying the previous version of it, which had been proclaimed in positivist and progressivist terms. In sum, nineteenth-century culture, like the modern age as a whole, had committed the folly of trying to make permanent its own particular version of modernity. But all such cultural paradigms were subject to change and decay. Since an order of culture was simply man's tentative attempt to cope with life, neither Cartesian reason nor nineteenth-century positivism could pretend to be a kind of Hegelian fulfillment of history. History moves on, and the best way to be modern is to be fully of one's own time, living its problems in search of the new answers they demand.

In one sense, Ortega was, in much of his work, trying to put the shibboleth of the modern behind him; but in another, he was driven by modernity and its discontents, for despite his acute awareness of the modishness of the need to be modern, he could not avoid a deep fascination with the timely features of cultural innovation in his day. When he dismissed the modern age that was presumably drawing to a close during his youth, he simply exchanged a static notion of what it was to be modern for a fluid one. Cultural modernism (not to be confused with the Spanish literary movement of *modernismo*) and sociocultural modernization would continue to engage him and to provide him with his role as Spain's guide toward the future. Like many other modern Western intellectuals, Ortega understood this role in terms of the polarities of culture and politics, thought and action, philosophy and concrete reform. A man of many talents in an acutely needy country, he restlessly built a variegated career as a philosopher, a man of letters, and a popular educator. All these activities implied the task of creating and instructing a significant public, for Ortega understood better than most intellectuals the radical dependence of the thinker upon his audience and his readers. In different ways, the following chapters comment on this task—in terms of his generational consciousness, his place in the history of Spanish culture, and his relationship to modernity.

The general conditions required for an intellectual vocation— critical distance combined with a passionate concern for ultimate values—combined with Ortega's biographical circumstances to place him in tension between culture and politics. He lived on the boundary between these two realms of activity, deriving from his liminal location much of the wonderful bite and urgency of his writing. Despite the apparent certainty with which he outlined programs for the modernization of Spanish culture and society, despite his vivid sense of what constituted the creative peaks of his own epoch, he came intimately to know uncertainty, to which he alluded in the middle of the Second Spanish Republic (1933) as "periods of crisis in which one does not really know what each man is because in point of fact he is not anything with any decisiveness."[4]

If ambivalence about the intellectual's proper place in the world loomed in Ortega's mind on numerous occasions, much of the reason lay in the political turbulence of his period and in the resultant complexity of the many "boundary situations" he experienced. From 1910 to 1933, he lived in tension between allegiance to high culture and philosophical thought on the one hand and an urgent, ambitious sense of political vocation on the other. But, as we have noted, he also stood between Spain and Europe, Madrid and Marburg, modernity and tradition, past and future, liberalism and conservatism, philosophy and letters, the study and the newspaper, criticism and affirmation, center and periphery, metropolis and province. The significance of these polarities will emerge as the tale is told.

In response to these multiple tensions, Ortega sought to ground his intellectual career in fidelity to his circumstances and to the perspective they imposed—most concretely, to the vantage point on Spain, Europe, and the rest of the world formed by the Castilian capital of Madrid in the first decades of this century. Thus loyalty to this native locale informed his theoretical writings on man's historicity. What man has already done and been, he argued, tells us all we can know of "human nature." What we may become depends upon the destinies we come into by shaping our individual life-projects out of our individual encounters with our circumstances. Thus, any authentic existence must include an element of personal "provincialism"—the primacy of immediate circumstances—together with one's aspirations to a larger, more cosmopolitan world. This interplay of the local and familiar with the cosmopolitan and exotic is fundamental in the lives of modern Western people, who cannot live simply within the ethos of the "tribe" or the "hometown."

For Ortega, the Spanish cultural center—Madrid—and Spain's central province—Castile—were by accident of birth his own centers.[5] But beyond Spain, as we have seen, the cities, universities, and intellectual institutions (museums, libraries, publishing houses, laboratories) of Western Europe constituted the larger composite "center" from which he took his bearings; and like many of his peers in other

European countries, he saw the need to transcend the merely local as part of a general process of modernization affecting intellectuals around the world. However important their ties to nationalistic and populistic traditions, they could not, Ortega realized, entirely fulfill themselves without a cosmopolitan awareness of the value of other cultures and traditions. Inherent in the fulfillment of their vocations must be what has been called the "solvent effect" of cultural modernization as it flows in upon local mores and ideas.[6]

More thoroughly and systematically perhaps than any European intellectual generation before it, that of 1914 understood that culture has no national boundaries though its origins must always remain closely bound to local circumstances. Of course, that same generation included some who became passionate defenders of the mystique of native soil, men who feared the erosion of the more intimate sources of culture located in the mores and modes of life of a given locale. In general terms, it may be said that intellectuals are, by the very nature of their vocation, bound to rebel against provinciality, as they are often the first members of a society of identify it and to feel the onus it imposes. It has been argued that this kind of "advanced" consciousness stems from the intellectual's intense concern with the human spirit and with the "sacred" sources of cultural creation and social organization. He is, presumably, more concerned than others with the mores and the ethos of his people and, by extension, of other peoples around the world. In this regard, he is by definition antiprovincial:

> Whereas a businessman or a craftsman or a farmer can be content with being a fish of whatever size in a small pond, the intellectual's realm, by his very engagement in intellectual activities, is oceanic. The more comprehensive and more open sensitivity which prior selection finds and which training elicits in the intellectual, and the need to place his productions on a scale which refers to achievements everywhere, inevitably put the intellectual into a network, the standards of which he cannot lightly disregard or deny. His wide-ranging sensitivity commits him to self-assessments based on achievements in a race in which his colleagues throughout the world compete.[7]

This is not to say that the intellectual never defends the provinces, the common people, or the periphery, but if he does so he will seek to give his allegiance to the lowly or the local a general, potentially universal significance that reaches beyond the immediate time and place. One might say that the true intellectual seeks either to bring every periphery into close touch with a center or, failing that, to make new centers of the former peripheries. His vocation makes him incapable of any simple allegiance to a particular set of folkways. And he must be understood not only in relation to a central metropolitan culture (or several such cultures) but also in relation to a place in history—the role he has defined for himself in a generation, an era, or a cultural moment. One may speak of a person's "entrance" into his own time as that crucial moment when he defines his vocation through a serious assessment of the world around him. Ortega's own debut, as we shall see, was in 1914, when he gave the speech "Old and New Politics" and published his first book, *Meditations on Quixote*.

Two years after that, the Spanish painter Joaquín Sorolla portrayed the young thinker whose rapid rise was impressing men of the preceding generation like Unamuno, Antonio Machado, and Azorín. Sorolla shows us Ortega, age thirty-three, seated at a desk—a figure intensely alive in every detail of posture and look. Beside him is a stack of volumes; before him, an open text. Behind him, in his study, some furniture looms vaguely. Dominating the canvas is the stocky body of the man, who is tastefully dressed in a dark suit, white shirt and tie, handkerchief in the coat pocket—modest, correct, but with a certain flair as well. His right hand supports his cheek and jaw in the classic thinker's pose: looking up from study for a moment's deliberation, perhaps to pose us a question. His left hand, holding a cigarette, rests on the edge of the desk at a tensely alert angle. His body leans angularly to one side, supported on his right elbow. The electric energy of this alert, nimble-witted young man from the cultural backwater of *fin de siècle* Spain is evident. And what he pursues here is "study" in its root sense of passion, agitation, excitement (*studium*). Ortega was immersed in German philosophical scholarship, but he loved the racy colloquial speech of Madrid. He turned to Plato, Aristotle, Kant, and Husserl, but he was also stirred by art and poetry, by the human comedy, by women, and by the astonishing beauty of the visible world. He insisted that the philosopher's main obligation is to keep *looking* at everything and everybody. And the gaze that comes straight toward us from Sorolla's canvas does exactly that—we feel an intense scrutiny enriched by philosophical curiosity.

There was a temperamental and somatic base to the vitality so evident in this portrait, but there was a larger historical one as well, for the "young meditator," as Antonio Machado called him, was already known in 1916 as the leader of those who would turn Spain toward the rest of Europe. Since in the Spain he confronted there existed relatively little institutional basis for such a task, his vocation was necessarily political as well as intellectual. Before him, the struggle for cultural and educational reform had begun in the middle of the nineteenth century with the Spanish Krausists (of whom more later), led by Julián Sanz del Río (1814–1869). Their work was continued by Francisco Giner de los Ríos's (1839–1915) Institución Libre de Enseñanza (1876–1936), a secular alternative or "free" school that formed a number of the nation's most distinguished cultural leaders. Both the Krausists and Giner had responded to the dominant force of Catholic traditionalism in Spanish education. Initiating a turn toward European models of thought and pedagogy, they in turn influenced the Generation of 1898, and were ultimately responsible for the major educational reforms undertaken by the Junta para Ampliación de Estudios e Investigaciones Científicas, established in 1910 under the Liberal government of José Canalejas. The Junta, with which Ortega was closely associated, became an administratively autonomous umbrella institution for numerous experiments in higher education, including the prestigious Centro de Estudios Históricos (where the influence of the latest German scholarship was evident), the Instituto de Ciencias Físico-Naturales and the Residencia de Estudiantes, all also established in 1910. The various activities carried on under these auspices posed as never before in Spain a secular and liberal alternative in native educational circles.

Since the Junta also awarded travel grants for study abroad (and in 1912 established, through the Centro de Estudios Históricos, the first summer course for foreign students in Spain), it directly furthered the cause of Europeanization. By the turn of the century, native attitudes toward the "problem of Spain" had tended to polarize around the *hispanizantes* and the *europeizantes*. The former included many educators who espoused the nativist traditions rooted in Catholic thought and doctrine, but prominent intellectual leaders like Unamuno and the journalist Ramiro de Maeztu (1874–1936) also turned in that direction in their later careers, after more youthful involvement with a wide range of European literature and thought. (Unamuno, who read avidly in Nietzsche, Kierkegaard, Bergson,

William James, the English romantics, and the whole range of nineteenth-century German thought, eventually came to belive that all Western learning must be seen *sub specie hispanitatis*. He turned his wide learning to eccentric personal uses from a solitary vanatge point on the high Castilian plateau, where he was rector and professor of Greek at the University of Salamanca.)

Aiming to send the nation to school north of the Pyrenees, the *europeizantes* drew, in Ortega's case often tacitly, on the Krausist, Ginerian "*institucionista*," and Junta models and on the massive scholarly work of Joaquín Costa (1844–1911) in agricultural history, folk culture, and studies of law and society. Thus, despite the relatively bleak condition of Spanish social thought, historiography, and philosophy in the nineteenth and early twentieth centuries, there were indeed precedents for Ortega's early dedication to the cause of Europeanization. Perhaps to dramatize his mission, however, he often spoke as if his generation—and even he alone— were breaking radically new ground, for he and his like-minded contemporaries at least *felt* that they brought to the critique of Spanish culture an incisiveness, a breadth of intellectual preparation, and a vision of systematic reform exceedingly rare among earlier Spanish intellectuals. In retrospect, this judgment seems essentially accurate.

On the subtle issue of Europeanization, however, Ortega in fact never took a doctrinaire position, though his polemical correspondence with Unamuno as early as 1904 pressed the younger man to develop an emphatic "open door" policy in reaction against Unamuno's movement toward a mystique of Spanish uniqueness. For the young Ortega, Spain urgently needed to take stock of its modest position in the world and eschew grandiose dreams of former greatness. His project of cultural modernization aimed ultimately to promote the nation's cultural autonomy, but he insisted that this could be achieved and maintained only through constant discourse with the seminal sources of contemporary European culture in the broadest sense. In his view, this issue claimed priority for the simple reason that Spain's existing cultural structures failed to provide an adequate base for a vigorous intellectual life: secondary schools and universities were still steeped in formalism, despite efforts at reform; libraries were sharply limited and often inaccessible; scholarly research, even with the work of the Junta, was exiguous; travel abroad remained a rare privilege for a fortunate few; and important translations from other major languages were infrequent and often poor. If Spanish intellectuals did not confront these problems, they could have no ground for their work and no educated public to whom it might be addressed. Hence, when Ortega began to write and lecture in the first years of this century, his own cosmopolitan spirit, shaped by a privileged education, was tempered by his sense of the duties Spanish citizenship placed upon him; and in nothing was he more Spanish and more of his time than in his manner of pursuing these issues.

We may perhaps best characterize Ortega as a charismatic culture-bearer who sought to introduce new forms of thought and art into a society that was only tentatively and unevenly beginning to undergo various forms of modernization. This essay presents his work neither as a chapter in the history of philosophy nor as a body of thought or a system in itself. It considers instead his social role as defined by the public he sought and the purposes he espoused, for Ortega's career poses in exemplary fashion the problem of the thinker's influence on the public—an issue to which Western intellectuals have been especially sensitive since early in the nineteenth century. Ortega was faced with the task of enlightening the diverse and intellectually ill-prepared public whose "massification" was a major consequence of Spain's accelerating rate of entry into the modern West after roughly 1900—precisely the public to which he later pointed in *The Revolt of the Masses* (1930). The responsive audiences, readers, and peers he sought were essential to the fulfillment of his pedagogical goal; and these supporters, excited to find a native son who seemed a peer of Europe's most distinguished thinkers, heightened the élan with which he thrust philosophy into the public domain.

Ortega understood as few other modern thinkers the subtle interplay between the prosperity or impoverishment of one's thought and the disposition of its recipients. Consequently, he quarreled with the powerful Platonic, Neoplatonic, and Judeo-Christian elements in Western intellectual history which have asserted that philosophy is first of all the quest for transcendental and enduring truths to be contemplated in solitude or in ecstatic union with God. For him, philosophy was nourished in active commerce with the world. Formulated and developed in solitude it certainly was, but it would be, he felt, a trivial affair indeed if it forgot its experiential origin and its destiny in a world that each person shares with others. He also understood that the small, basically ill-educated Spanish middle-class public, recalcitrant as it was before difficult philosophical questions, needed a "good show" in order to begin to think larger thoughts. His preference for an impressionistic, metaphorical, and even anecdotal treatment of serious ideas was also temperamental, and may point to his feeling that he was, as he said of himself once, a "cocky little fellow from Madrid who has been through Kant."[8] In any case, he became both the perfect mentor for a philosophically naive middle-class audience in Madrid and the leader of more select reforms carried out in his university teaching and through the *Revista de Occidente*, founded in 1923.

In his diverse efforts to create an educated Spanish public, Ortega often seemed to overextend himself. Dividing his prodigious energies among journalism, teaching, editing, and political work as well as philosophical writing, he was widely regarded a freelance "thinker" rather than the major systematic philosopher he so fervently wished to be in his later years. The great diversity of his mission *in partibus infidelium*, as he put it, in a land where few pursued philosophy, of course means that he cannot properly be judged if his work is seen solely as a contribution to the Western philosophical tradition. As we shall see, he was indeed a philosopher, but he was also one of that rare breed of writers who take the whole of a culture's thought and literary expression as their province.

Whatever perspective one assumes on Ortega, it is evident that the predominant forms of his work are the essay and the lecture series rather than the systematic monograph. This stylistic predilection was even more evident in the Generation of 1898, where it perhaps indicated a certain resistance to science and scholarship, a preference for the belletristic *aperçu* and the intuitive judgment. But Ortega managed brilliantly to fuse great learning and intellectual rigor with the quick grace and colloquial tone of which he became a master. In this way, he wooed his Spanish public by deftly making accessible the most difficult philosophical issues. Yet, by announcing major themes as if they had never previously been considered—his broader public was quite unaware of the source of so many of his ideas in the neo-Kantian and the phenomenological schools of German thought[9]—he pretended time and again to "expose" questions presumably neglected or incompletely treated by others before him, thus making his audience feel that it was part of an informed elite or vanguard. This hyperbolic turn was at once a function of his ambition to be a philosophical innovator and of the need of an increasing Spanish public for cultural "news" from beyond its own frontiers. Hence, broadly speaking, much was taken for new in his work that was in fact not so. (Recently, those scholars who have thoroughly investigated the matter of Ortega's philosophical sources have established the essential justice of his claims to brilliant innovation.) Because of his personal charisma, the controversial nature of his career, and the vastly diverse impact of his work in Spain, students of his work have been slow to disentangle and interpret the sprawling body of his writings, many of which have appeared posthumously and often piecemeal, only later being incorporated in the essentially misnamed *Obras completas*. Thus a thorough picture of his significance as a thinker and a public figure has been exceedingly difficult to achieve.

To many literate but philosophically ignorant Spaniards of his day, Ortega appeared on their personal horizons as a great sun, a dazzling eminence. In attempting to write philosophy for this public, Ortega encountered the typical dilemma of the gifted writer in a culturally underdeveloped setting. Obliged to court his public, the Spanish or Latin American philosopher must disguise the rigors of philosophical work. As Ortega's Argentine colleague Francisco Romero had noted:

> The general orientation of his thought, his themes, the peculiar nuance they assume in him, concord ... with Western circumstances. But in the economy of his work, in its ordering and distribution, one must give their due to local circumstances. In cultural areas more avid of learning than ours, those of our language, the author knows he will somehow be understood; the appropriative effort falls to the audience. In Ortega the tone, the proximate and persuasive expression, can deceive the unprepared reader; the rich intellectual contribution of many of his pages, even those of the freshest novelty, strike us as familiar matters, and the ultimate gravity of the questions is veiled by a wise pedagogy that suppresses all distance between the writer and the reader.[10]

Similarly, Romero observes, Ortega was not always free to follow his most intimate intellectual promptings:

> The tranquillity with which the thinker chooses his proper theme and resigns himself to leaving the rest aside, depends principally on his sensing

about him a community of work, a plural and continued labor assuring the successive study of all the aspects of the theme. And this condition—it is all too clear—does not yet obtain in the world of our language. Resolved that once and for all one might philosophize in Spanish, Ortega was obliged to confront almost alone the task that normally should have corresponded to a generation of philosophers. And beyond strict philosophical work, he has had to devote himself to more trivial duties, indispensable in order to impose and make possible what on another occasion I have called "philosophical normality." [11]

Ortega more than once indicated the massive difficulties of purveying his material in such a cultural atmosphere. Chiding the audience of his lecture series "What Is Philosophy?" (1929), he remarked that the danger of their misunderstanding his point arose not so much from the definitions he gave as

> from the manner in which we men, especially those of the warm races, are accustomed to read and to listen. After a quarter of a century of production in the realm of ideas ... I have lost all illusion, all hope that either Spaniards or Argentinians will, with rare exceptions, understand the act of reading or of listening as more than a slipping along from the spontaneous or impressionistic sense of one word to another, from the simplest meaning of one phrase to that of the next. [12]

And in a prologue to the 1932 edition of his *Obras* he wrote, defending his choice to devote much of his energy to journalism for the general literate middle class in Spain:

> Our people do not accept the faraway and the solemn. What reigns there [in Spain] is the purely everyday and common. The man who wishes to create something—and all creation is aristocracy—must succeed in being an aristocrat in the public square. This is why, submitting to circumstance, I have caused my work to appear in the intellectual public square represented by the newspaper. [13]

Compared with the work of other modern thinkers like Croce, Karl Jaspers, Heidegger, or Sartre, Ortega's shows relatively little trace of the long meditative talk with oneself and with earlier texts that traditionally forms the ground of philosophical speculation. He steeped himself as much as they in the major philosophical traditions, but the broadly public pedagogical use to which he put them meant that his learning could not be obtrusive nor his vocabulary highly technical. The distinctly colloquial tone running throughout his work reflects his constant, almost sensual need to feel in touch with inter- locutors and audiences. The happiest result of this need was an animated prose of sparkling clarity. A less felicitous effect was his ten- dency toward pleonasm and an elaborateness he himself recognized as "baroque." Generally, however, Ortega drew in his writing upon the main currents of spoken Castilian, rich with rhetorical and pro- verbial resources. Unlike Heidegger, for example, he rarely resorted to abstruse neologisms. In that sense, his prose was conservative, but it was also adventurous in its aim to establish serious philosophical discourse in Spanish for the first time since the seventeenth century and so to bring to the language a speculative and analytical spirit all too rare in its modern history.

Setting himself against the separatist and traditionalist tendencies in his culture, Ortega was devoted to integration or "wholeness"— psychological for the individual Spaniard; social and political for the nation he described as "invertebrate"; cultural, philosophical, and scientific for those Spaniards who wished to be full-fledged Euro- peans. Chapter 1 of this essay establishes the wider European and Spanish background for this effort in terms of generational member- ship and intellectual awareness of the concept of "generation." Chapter 2 traces Ortega's search for these multiple integrations as a member of the Spanish generation that came to maturity around 1914. Chapters 3 and 4 follow his career through the Spanish political crisis of 1917 and into the years under the dictator General Miguel Primo de Rivera. Chapters 5 and 6 focus on the "high period" of his philosophical development and political activism, encompassing the fall of Primo, the brief life of the Second Republic, and the outbreak of the Spanish Civil War, an event that irrevocably redefined the lives of all Spaniards, intellectuals and nonintellectuals alike. For many of the former, the ensuing diaspora, which cast them abroad from the Peninsula, was the "sea change" that obliged them to reconceive their calling.[14] Ortega became one of their number in 1936. The story of his exile and his dislocated "second" career after the war is told in chapter 7, which runs from 1936 through to his residence in Lisbon in the mid-1940s and the composition of his major postwar book on Leibniz and deductive theory. Chapter 8 deals with the final seven years of Ortega's life, when he simultaneously failed to establish a firm base for work in Spain and became an internationally known repre- sentative of European culture. With the collapse of the Republic,

Ortega had lost a vast personal web of commitments and achievements and was forced to live with the pain of that loss and the hostility of the new regime in Madrid. His not very satisfactory solution was to become a nomadic intellectual-at-large, a kind of man without a country. Finally, the epilogue offers a brief review of his accomplishments and of his enduring influence.

1

FATHERS AND SONS: THE SPANISH AND THE EUROPEAN SCENES

> A generation is fashion: but there is more to history
> than costume and jargon. The people of an era must
> either carry the burden of change assigned to their
> time or die under its weight in the wilderness.
> —Harold Rosenberg, *The Tradition of the New*

As I have already suggested, Ortega's mission in Spain was integrally tied to an acute sense of his own place in the successive waves of Spanish literary and intellectual generations. In fact, his dedication to the cultural modernization of his country led him to a heightened sense of generational periodization and membership; for in good part, though not always explicitly, he defined the new message of the Generation of 1914 in relation to and often over against the perspectives of earlier generational leaders such as Unamuno and Giner de los Ríos. This awareness of distinct generations and their respective destinies did not, of course, simply spring to Ortega's mind as a convenient rhetorical strategy: much of nineteenth-century European history had prepared him and other early twentieth-century thinkers to place their work in such a conceptual framework. This chapter will sketch the background of this decision.

In particular during the *fin de siècle* period in many European societies, the perception of extraordinarily rapid change both in ideas and in the material forms of life was linked with a heightened awareness of generational differences. Discontinuity in the respective experience of fathers and sons seemed the order of the day. Freud's theory of the oedipal conflict was only one sign of the widespread conviction that to achieve authenticity the young must revolt against the fathers. Sir James Frazer's account in *The Golden Bough* (1890) of the death of the king as a ritual of social regeneration cast the theme in a grand framework of age-old human patterns. Implicit in the idea of revolt against the world of the fathers was a growing discomfort with the past understood as the weight of received ideas and customs. Writers, philosophers, artists, and critics in many European capitals shared the increasingly powerful idea that "modernity"—what Ortega would come to call living at "the level of the times"—could be achieved only through radical revision or even rejection of "tradition," a term of newly problematic semantic density. Coming to stand for a whole congeries of older, established ways of living and thinking, the word became associated with the older generations, who imposed their order of life upon the "sons."

These generational terms were, of course, relative and eluded exact definition, for the sons of one moment were destined to become the fathers of the next as ever more nuanced shifts in life-styles and the rhetoric supporting them became the distinguishing marks of generational identity. The notion of such identity itself rose to new prominence as European intellectuals and artists attempted to articulate a pervasive sense of being swept along in a stream of rapid historical change. A good part of the feeling that the turn of the century represented a turning point in European cultural history—a feeling later confirmed in political experience by the Great War—stemmed from the rhetoric of generational rebellion and the closely associated cult of youth that grew in many parts of Europe in the two decades or so before 1914. While "the young" were often literally that, the term also was loosely used to refer to all those, of whatever age, who shared the spirit of opposition to an older cultural or social style. Thus, for example, Ortega's early call for the revitalization of Spanish culture through a program of self-criticism and Europeanization caused him to extend the term, as Robert Wohl remarks, "to the educated elite among the middle and upper classes." [1] Ortega later made a similar appeal to an initiated elite when, in *The Dehumanization of Art* (1925), he urged the appreciation of the "young art" of Cézanne, Braque, Picasso, and other postimpressionist innovators.

In the attempt to invoke a rising generation who would both discern and help to establish the *Zeitgeist*, Ortega may be compared to such European peers as Maurice Barrès, Charles Péguy, Valéry,

Croce, Giovanni Papini, Karl Mannheim, Eduard Spranger, and, in England, Wilfred Owen, Siegfried Sassoon, and other poets whose careers were shaped by the outbreak of war in 1914. While these are only a few of the names invoked in Wohl's story of the trans-European Generation of 1914 and though the differences in their experience are as great, perhaps, as the similarities, one may note in all of them a common desire to gather the young behind their respective causes. This aim indicated their sense that a new world was theirs to make over, against the work of the preceding generations.

Characteristic as this pattern was of turn-of-the-century Europe, marked by a sense of simultaneous death and rebirth of culture, it was not in fact a new one, for already at the turn of the previous century the struggle of each new human wave to "make it new" had been established as a central feature of modern Western history. Among the many profound effects of the romantic age in Europe must be counted the appearance of generational self-consciousness as such. As never before, artists and men of letters at that time expressed the idea that a new human generation implied a new stance in the world. This notion developed first and most acutely in those cultures where the romantic passion was most intense and productive, England and Germany; it came of age a bit later in France. In Germany, Goethe quite consciously saw his work as ushering in a new age in the national letters. He aspired to and succeeded in giving his time its unique cast by marking it with his poetic voice. In England, Wordsworth perceived the French Revolution as a watershed event in human history, dramatically separating his experience from that of prerevolutionary generations. His famous notion of "spots of time"—epiphanic moments of truth broken out of the temporal flow—arose in part from his feeling that modern history had, as it were, broken in two in 1789. In France, the Revolution and the subsequent Napoleonic period produced a world dramatically removed from that of the ancien régime. Tocqueville, Stendhal, Daumier, Delacroix, and other observant spirits of the age recorded their sense of a precipitately vanished past replaced by the tumult of postrevolutionary politics and the corresponding social changes. The effects of the Industrial Revolution throughout Europe and, later, in America as well heightened the growing feeling that a son could grow up in a world dramatically unlike his father's. The transformation of daily life by rapid political and technological change was further intensified by the romantics'

charting of the inner world of the individual psyche. As autobiographical self-consciousness led to passionate exploration of ultimately ineffable personal worlds, the problematic nature of personal
identity became increasingly salient.

The roots of the modern concern with generational membership
and generational mission reach back into patterns of life dating from
the latter part of the eighteenth century. As nationalism burgeoned in
Europe after the French Revolution, many intellectuals and artists
sought to delineate the particular color and tone of their nations'
cultural lives. Increasingly conscious of the idea of a *Zeitgeist*, they
sought to express the spirit of the age in painting, poetry, and philosophy. In a period newly conscious of historical time, they saw their
moment on the stage of history as a challenge to distinguish themselves from those who had preceded or would follow them. The broad
current of historicist thought which marked that period emphasized
the idea that each people made its unique contribution to the history
of humankind, and it was not a long step from there to the conviction
that each generation must do something unique. In an age that
witnessed an unprecedented proliferation of movements and manifestos, spokesmen for and critics of the times sprang up on every side. It
became clear that both a man's ideas and his intellectual style were
in good part "products" of the time and place in which he lived. To
distinguish one's voice (or the collective voice of one's generation)
from those of earlier men became imperative. During the first decades
of the nineteenth century, romantic writers sought to overthrow the
classical models, while political liberals fought against traditionalists
and reactionaries who supported the restoration of monarchy and
controls on the popular will.

A major feature of the new mentality was the development of
autobiography as a distinct literary genre. Its roots were in
Rousseau's *Confessions* (1764–1770) and Goethe's *Dichtung und Wahr-
heit* (1810–1832), but its full flowering took place throughout the
nineteenth century. Together with the *Bildungsroman*, which traced
the character development and peregrinations of its heroes in several
European languages, autobiography represented the growing desire
to record or create a life history reflecting the particular world in
which it had taken shape. From approximately 1800 onward, historical consciousness affected both men's public deeds as self-conscious
members of generational peer groups and their more personal rumin-

ations as chroniclers of the individual self. The century was the great age of personal journals and diaries as well, and this increased men's recognition of the extraordinary diversity of human experience. To be human now meant less to exemplify certain generic traits of the species than to express a way of being never entirely seen before. As one historian of autobiography writes: "[T]his outlook [historicism, broadly speaking] places immense value on the specific goodness of each individually specified expression of the human experience.... Each style of life has its own intrinsic justification; each has the right to be understood in its own terms."[2]

Romantic thought fostered this valorization of the unique and particular, for central among its tenets was the rejection of the earlier neoclassical idea of a general human nature. The effort of successive nineteenth-century generations to define their own styles of living and forms of belief was part of that rejection writ large. Just as the range of human expression was enlarged and redefined by the emergence of the modern "individual," so it was extended and diversified by political and artistic vanguards seeking to define the novel viewpoint of each new generation (the *Sturm und Drang* and the later romantic writers in Germany, the Benthamites and two generations of romantics in England, the pan-European generation of young liberal intellectuals in the 1820s, the *Carbonari* in Italy and other protonationalist circles elsewhere in Europe, the Decembrists in Russia, the Concord Transcendentalists in America, and so forth). Membership in such movements or circles gave the individual a formative context; but the innovative group, intent on defining the mandate of the times, often felt isolated in its "advanced" consciousness, as was remarked of the Decembrists, "a generation without fathers and without sons."[3]

Despite the appearance of a heightened sense of generational isolation, however, each new generation was more aware than ever— if only antagonistically—of those who came before and those who would follow. The nineteenth century was, in fact, the period *par excellence* of fathers and sons, as Turgenev suggested in the title of his representative novel. Shot through with a sense of the father's overbearing power and the son's consequent struggle for his own distinct identity, generational succession seemed fraught with psychological problems. As Bruce Mazlish, speaking inclusively of the period, notes in his study of James Mill and John Stuart Mill, "A

relationship expressing an eternal biological aspect of development...
now became shifting, dubious, and open to critical reflection."[4]
To the sons, faced with the fathers' power, fell the task of proclaiming the discontinuity of outlook and experience—an early version
of our "generation gap"—that served to increase their need of
generational membership. The sons, of course, became fathers in
turn, perpetuating a dialectic of cultural change cast in psychological
terms.

As young men who were heirs to the romantic discovery of psychic
"innerness" came of age on the 1820s and 1830s, they encountered
powerful new political and social patterns not of their own making:
novel occupations generated by industrial and urban expansion;
increasing social and geographical mobility; and population growth,
dramatically evident in several European countries. As the idea of
progress was accepted as a principle of history and, simultaneously,
the nuclear family began to replace the older model of extended kinship in middle-class circles, sons felt challenged to experience the
world differently from their fathers. The latter were not, in fact,
always overbearingly dominant in the nineteenth century: the oedipal
pattern developed as much from the sons' changing perceptions of the
old ways they rejected as from any paternal tyranny. Claiming the
romantic legacy of introspection and self-cultivation, each younger
generation tended rather to *displace* than to *replace* the elder.[5] The
conviction that the ineffable individual was called to establish a "new
world" through the unfolding of his personality found its most famous
exemplar in Goethe. After him, the romantic idea of the artist as
hero—a conqueror of new psychic territories—took powerful hold in
the European mind. The stage was set for increasingly complicated
struggles between fathers and sons that caused as much a crisis of
"generativity" (Erik Erikson's term for the acceptance of "paternal"
responsibility for the world one has made) in the older generation as
a search for identity in the new one.[6]

These broad structural changes promoted a heightened rhetoric of
vanguardism. The more virulent was the urge to distinguish oneself
from one's cultural forebears, the more oppositional became the
vision of historical dynamism. The need to be modern implied rivalry
with those who had gone before. Consequently, they had to be
portrayed as more antiquated and inadequate, more sunk in the past
and in outmoded traditions, than was in fact the case. In Spain, it was
to Ortega's advantage as one who aspired to be the spiritual chief of

the Generation of 1914 to demarcate it sharply from the preceding Generation of 1898, to which, as we will see, he was in fact indebted for his programs of modernization and Europeanization. Unamuno, for one, had anticipated the cry for Spanish cultural renewal while Ortega was still a schoolboy; his cosmopolitan curiosity about other cultures should not be obscured by the later countercurrent in his thought of a kind of mystical nativism that invoked the *intrahistoria* (intrahistory) of the Spanish people, an "inner" or invisible history unaffected by superficial movements of social and political change.

Too often Ortega's devotion to Europe as Spain's historical legacy and future goal has been neatly counterposed to Unamuno's call for the "hispanization" of Europe, but the subtle and richly varied thought of these two great modern Spaniards, whose views on national reform were markedly influenced by each other's work, cannot be reduced to such a facile dichotomy. It is not just to cast Ortega simply as the consummate cosmopolitan man, the Europeanized Spaniard come home from Germany to wake his people from their cultural slumber. While his most ardent defenders like to see him as an enlightened liberator, few have adequately probed the provincial bias in his grand program for a new Spain. After all, according to the cliché, it was Unamuno who remained the obstinate provincial in the sleepy university town of Salamanca. It was he who often scorned the urban culture of Madrid, and who celebrated the metaphor of eternity he saw in the "sea" of the Castilian plains and the unchanging rhythms of Spanish village life. In the widely popular view, Unamuno often becomes the quasi-mystical traditionalist who uttered the cry "Let them in Europe invent, we have St. Teresa and St. John of the Cross!" But this simplistic portrayal of the man ignores the fecund restlessness of his dialectical and self-combative thought, as well as his remarkable openness to developments in European and American letters.

Writing from a perspective outside Spain, the historian Salvador de Madariaga, a resident of England after the Spanish Civil War, has seen the other side of both coins:

> Ortega and Unamuno...are the protagonists of the two trends of thought which the Generation of 1898 brings to light: one [Unamuno] stands for the salvation of Spain within her own substance; the other for her renovation by European influence and example. In a sense, Spain... has in these two men a pair similar to...: Dostoyevsky and Turgeniev, the one intensely Russian and indifferent, if not hostile, to Europe,

the other a convinced European and critical of Russia as such; but the case of the two Spaniards is even more complicated. Unamuno, in his unchecked spontaneity, is a voracious consumer of European values and shows readiness to assume every kind of tendency...; this ever-ready curiosity for things human, combined with the permanent appeal of his main theme, make him, while intensely Spanish, a universal author. Ortega, on the other hand, more exacting and intellectualized, shows a far less hospitable mind; there is, moreover, in his temperament a curious imperviousness to the Anglo-Saxon world; and these limitations, combined with his tendency to ride on top of the wave of fashion, make him less universal though more abstract and general in his thought than Unamuno.[7]

It is no answer to Madariaga's portrait of the two men to point out that Ortega carried out his mature work in the large, relatively progressive city of Madrid and had studied the latest philosophy in what were, in his student years, the best German schools, while Unamuno took his degree in the traditional discipline of classical Greek and spent most of his productive years in a provincial town that afforded him no peers. There is still truth in the charge that Ortega had a provincial side and Unamuno a universal one. On one hand, the intellectual and social life of Madrid just after the turn of the century often failed to offer Ortega the genuinely cosmopolitan stimulus he so much needed. Unamuno, on the other hand, freer than Ortega from the goad of "timeliness" and given over to the profound routine of his cloistered ruminations, could read the world's literature in peace and follow a vigilant, prolific career as a commentator on whatever caught his fancy. Both men wrote extensively on politics, books, travel, and cultural movements abroad; but by comparison, Ortega's work often seems more single-mindedly programmatic in its need to measure all things European for their relevance to Spain's modernization. Less systematic in his quest for European "science," toward which he developed in his later work a complex ambivalence, Unamuno may indeed have shown a more spontaneous hunger for Europe than his younger peer, who set out so systematically to conquer the culture of the Continent.

But Unamuno was only one—if perhaps the most famous—of the Generation of 1898, which also included novelist Pío Baroja (1872–1956), poet Antonio Machado (1875–1939), novelist-essayist Azorín (the pen name of José Martínez Ruiz, 1873–1967), novelist

Ramón del Valle-Inclán (1866–1936), playwright Jacinto Benavente (1866–1954), journalist Ramiro de Maeztu (1875–1936), and, by some accounts, essayist Ángel Ganivet (1865–1898) and even the influential Nicaraguan poet Rubén Darío (1867–1916). In a broad context this gifted group of writers, acutely conscious of one another as peers, may be seen as the Spanish contingent of the European intellectual vanguard that shaped certain modernist attitudes throughout the Continent. As one critic remarks (somewhat hyperbolically) of the Generation of 1898:

> Their lasting importance lies in the fact that they were the first unified group in modern Western literature to explore systematically the collapse of belief and existential confidence which has been a major theme for writers and thinkers ever since. Nowhere else in Europe or the Americas in the early twentieth century can we find a similarly compact body of writers whose work illustrates so consistently the critical moment of transition from the relative stability and optimism, already hollow as it was, of the preceding period, to the philosophical and spiritual impasse in which the main part of our culture finds itself today.[8]

While this perspective neglects abundant earlier evidence of similar ideas in many European and some American writers, it has the virtue of signalizing in Ortega's immediate predecessors the distinctly secular and existentialist currents of thought that would play so prominent a role in his own view of man as the maker of life's meaning. The same critic asserts about the 1898 writers that "however underdeveloped Spain was in other ways at the turn of the century, she was in the forefront of modern cultural development."[9] Such a judgment at once rescues the Generation from a narrow role in the history of Spanish letters and reminds us that Ortega did not emerge *ex nihilo* from centuries of Spanish cultural backwardness. Too little has been said of the native roots of his passion for the regeneration of his culture. But to place Spain "in the forefront of modern cultural development" is to exaggerate. Seeking to correct earlier stereotypes of backwardness, perpetuated by Spaniards and outsiders alike, this view fails to consider the very real burden of traditionalism faced by Ortega and his "fathers" in the Generation of 1898; and, in suggesting that Spain was "underdeveloped ... in other ways" (presumably in social and economic ways), it misstates the checkered, uneven quality of Spanish cultural life at the turn of the century.

A more accurate statement would place Spain somewhere between the extremes of cultural forefront and cultural desert. The latter picture, indeed, was largely developed by the writers of 1898, who responded to the nation's defeat in the Spanish-American War by creating a myth of Spain in desperate isolation from the modern world. Like most such cultural myths, that one contained an important truth. But Spanish backwardness was not in fact unique: other areas of Europe shared a sense of removal from the centers of cultural innovation in England, France, Germany, Austria, and elsewhere. What distinguished Spain from other "peripheral" European areas was, in Wohl's terms,

> the wound of its lost empire, the unrelenting obscurantism of its reactionary Catholics, the equally dogmatic anticlericalism of its progressives, the tradition of military intervention in public affairs, and the bizarre fact that it was the most dynamic and industrialized sectors of the country that were questioning the doctrine of the unitary and indivisible nation.[10]

Spain's remembered greatness, her fall from a high place, and her peculiarly sclerotic reaction to this historical fate gave to her culture a distinctly antimodernist cast that emphasized the nation's distance from the world in which she had once reigned so majestically. A sense of historical alienation is, in such a case, the result of actual and perceived separation. The fact of Spain's imperial decline and progressive isolation from transmontane Europe after roughly 1600 supported the growing perception by sensitive Spaniards throughout the nineteenth century that their country was a kind of lonely *finis terrae*. Numerous foreign visitors too, from Washington Irving to Théophile Gautier, Richard Ford, and George Borrow, found Spain an exotic land beyond the frontiers of familiar cultural forms. Alexandre Dumas's bon mot that Africa began at the Pyrenees gained wide currency, encouraging the image of Spain as a land of barbarism and romance in the minds of Spaniards and non-Spaniards alike.

This legacy, a blend of fact and fancy, weighed on Ortega when he traveled to Germany in 1905; he smarted to see how provincial his native land looked even from a little German city like Marburg. It does not seem strange, then, for him to have embraced the idea that Spain languished in intellectual darkness. Doubtless to highlight the special charge of his generation and, more specifically, his own sense of mission, he said relatively little about the native predecessors who had also espoused the cause of Europeanization for as much as half a century before him. If he did not overtly promote, neither did he reject the notion that he was destined to be the first genuine philosopher to appear in Spain since Francisco Suárez (1548–1617), whose *Disputationes Metaphysicae* (1597) marked the high point of Counter-Reformation Scholasticism and later became an influential system of thought in European universities and schools.

While such a notion appears at first excessive, it is true that in Spain the period between the zenith of Scholasticism and the beginnings of this century was strikingly barren of real philosophical innovation. Though those three hundred years were not without periodic intellectual ferment and important efforts—especially under Charles III in the eighteenth century—to open channels of cultural exchange with the rest of Europe, nonetheless the relative paucity of serious philosophical thought outside the confines of Christian theology is undeniable. In the eighteenth century such writers as Padre Benito Jerónimo Feijóo, José Cadalso, and Gaspar Melchor de Jovellanos cultivated the critical essay as a means of publicizing Spain's need for cultural and political reform. In the early nineteenth century Mariano José de Larra portrayed Spanish mores with a cutting critical sense, but one historian's summary of Spain in the nineteenth century seems generally true:

> The century produced no outstanding philosopher, and, toward the close, only one great critic, and a single historian of importance. Little original work was done in the natural sciences; little in the study of foreign languages and literatures. But much was accomplished by Spaniards in the study of their own literature.[11]

Ortega himself was not far from a judgment something like this, for he tended to see nineteenth-century Europe, in the culture of which he was well versed, as a period to be *overcome*, as much in art, music, and politics as in what he termed the moribund philosophical legacy of Cartesian reason. That view was a highly polemical one, of course, fired by the need to "make it new," in Ezra Pound's phrase. Nevertheless, apart from his numerous references to nineteenth-century French literature and his youthful immersion in the writings of Nietzsche, one cannot easily discover in Ortega's published work either positive appraisals of the preceding century or specific references to the tradition of Spanish political liberalism dating from the Cortes of

Cadiz in 1812, nor to the reformist movement initiated by Julián Sanz del Río and the Spanish Krausists. More clearly present in his work are the examples of Joaquín Costa, to whom he paid explicit tribute, and of the Generation of 1898.

Although much of the thematic content of Ortega's mature philosophical work came from outside Spain and must be seen within the larger history of European neo-Kantianism, phenomenology, and existentialism, his early work and his lifelong concern for the condition of Spain cannot be understood without reference to major Spanish reformists of the later nineteenth ceutury. Although even earlier writers such as Feijóo and Jovellanos seem comparable to Ortega in the most general way, he never referred to their work as an inspiration for his own. Nevertheless, it is important to note that the original model for the essay of social criticism came into Spain from the French Enlightenment and the *philosophes*, of whom Feijóo and Jovellanos were Spanish counterparts. It was the *philosophes* who provided the more distant historical precedent for the kind of far-ranging essay writing that Ortega was ultimately to refine in his modern Spanish prose. It is also among the *philosophes* that we find an early source of modern historicist philosophy—the assertion that man lives in time with no guarantee of a beginning or a destiny beyond this world. Out of that period came the modern concern with progress through the organization of society and the moral betterment of men, for the *philosophes* began to see that past and future were deeply interdependent: their criticizing of the past so as not to prolong its mistakes implied concern with moral progress. One may indeed argue that the real watershed between the modern and premodern worlds came with the Enlightenment. It was in that period that acute thinkers sought literary forms for thought which departed from those of the great philosophical systems of the seventeenth century: the new impulse took a wide variety of guises in Montesquieu, Voltaire, Diderot, d'Alembert, and Rousseau. In this broader view, it is possible to consider Ortega a latter-day *philosophe*, despite his very considerable indebtedness to various German thinkers of the late nineteenth and early twentieth centuries and, as we shall see, to nineteenth-century reformist currents in his own country.

Unlike his eighteenth-century predecessors in France, Ortega did not attack the Church, the monarchy, and the aristocracy in the name of enlightenment. Instead, as his work matured, he projected the *philosophes*' bugaboo of dogmatic mindlessness upon a certain type of modern man (not a social class as such) who worshipped the power of scientific knowledge and gloried in his own half-educated opinions. In the so-called "mass man," victimized by specialism, devoted to technique, and possessed of a notion of mind reduced to physico-mathematical reason, Ortega found the enemy who opposed modern enlightenment. Yet in the end it was not so much this specter, so memorably evoked in *The Revolt of the Masses*, who broke Ortega's later dream of a republic of intellectuals as it was the reactionary forces of order, authority, and tradition, the enduring power of which he surely underestimated in his hope for a vital new Spain that was to arise from the ashes of the Restoration monarchy. Indeed, had Ortega been more of a *philosophe* in the classic French style, he might have read better than he did the power of retrograde forces in the culture that arose under Franco's leadership in 1936. But all of that belongs to a later phase of his life: we are here concerned with the buoyant young Madrid intellectual who took up the banner of cultural modernization in the early years of this century. For no matter how dark Ortega's youthful rhetoric of a benighted "official" Spain mired in the "old politics" of the Restoration—a rhetoric directly indebted to the Generation of 1898—the dominant note from his earliest essays affirmed a bright future.

As mentioned above, the reformist tradition that set the stage for this conviction, though largely unacknowledged by Ortega, began with Spanish Krausism, his debt to which is noted in some detail in Julián Marías's treatment of his teacher's early career.[12] The founder of this movement, Julián Sanz del Río, rejected French literary culture in favor of German "science"—as Ortega would several decades later—thus setting the example for other Spaniards' intellectual quests during the *fin de siècle* and Restoration period. After obtaining a doctorate in canon law from the University of Granada in 1836, Sanz went to Madrid in 1838 and took his doctorate in civil jurisprudence in 1841. He was appointed by royal decree in June 1843 to the newly established chair in the history of philosophy at the Central University of Madrid, on condition that he would devote two years to the study of this subject in Germany. This plan was drawn up by Minister of the Interior Pedro Gómez de la Serna, who envisioned for the first time in Spain's history a full-scale, university-level School of Philosophy, separated from the School of Theology and empowered to grant both the *licenciatura* and the doctorate. Previously in Spain one had studied philosophy as an extension of secondary education, to prepare to enter the *facultades mayores* (professional schools) of law, medicine, and theology. For political reasons the plan was not fully realized until the Law of Public Instruction of 1857 established the six degree-granting schools of theology, philosophy and letters, law, science, medicine, and pharmacy. In the fall of that same year, Sanz gave his now-famous inaugural lecture on the principles of the Krausist philosophy, adapted from the relatively obscure Kantian philosopher Karl Christian Friedrich Krause (1781–1832), of whose work Sanz first learned through the book *Cour de Droit* of the German jurist Heinrich Ahrens at the University of Brussels.

Under the conditions of his grant, the first given to a Spaniard for formal study abroad, Sanz went first to Paris, where he spoke with the popular philosopher Victor Cousin in the summer of 1843, then on to Brussels, where Ahrens advised him to study in Heidelberg under the Krausists Karl David Röder and Hermann Karl Leonhardi. He remained in the German university town until the end of 1844, when he returned to Madrid, only to refuse his university appointment on the grounds that he was still unprepared to discharge his duties effectively. Sanz then retired to a life of study in the little town of Illescas, near Toledo, where, in monastic seclusion, he proceeded to think through Krause's writings. Returning to Madrid a full decade later (1854), he took up his academic duties and rapidly formed a circle of disciples, who helped him launch the career of Spanish Krausism in earnest.

The long hiatus in Sanz's career is perhaps not surprising in view of the actual condition of Spanish universities at the time. A centralized university in Madrid was mandated by the Spanish Cortes in June 1821, during the brief period of renewal of the Constitution of 1812, but the plan to transfer the waning remnants of the university at Alcalá de Henares to the capital was not realized until 1836–1837, when a makeshift institution was assembled in an old building of the Salesian Order. "In 1852," writes Juan López-Morillas in his seminal study of Spanish Krausism, "an improvised Faculty of Philosophy was given university status. By means of the quick and easy procedure known as 'a stroke of the pen,' the youth of Spain was to be given suitable instruments for intellectual work." A flurry of reformist plans followed, but they were merely "plans of study that might perhaps

have been useful had university studies in fact existed. But there were
none. There were no competent professors, no libraries, no laboratories." In support of this portrait, López-Morillas quotes the harsh
verdict on the situation of the polymath historian Marcelino Menéndez Pelayo (1856–1912):

> No one thought of studying. . . . Instruction was pure farce, a tacit agree-
> ment between teachers and pupils founded on mutual ignorance, slovenli-
> ness, and almost criminal neglect. The experimental sciences had been
> forgotten; physics was studied without ever seeing a machine or a piece of
> apparatus. . . . If anything was left of the old order of things it was lack of
> discipline, disorder, the bribery involved in voting and the provision of
> chairs by examination.[13]

Such as it was, then, the new Central University existed more as a
pious hope than a functioning reality when Sanz del Río was appointed to its faculty. Thus his withdrawal from active status during
the decade in Illescas obliquely reflected, in the admirable mirror of
his personal integrity, the sorry state of higher learning in the Spain
of Isabella II.

Yet the germ of a radically different future lay in these first
uncertain attempts to establish the serious study of philosophy on
independent secular terms, a legacy from which Ortega himself was
to profit some half a century later. For Spain, the idea of separating
intellectual endeavor from the direct control of the Church was a
novel and important one, which called into question the traditional
role of theology in the culture. In the broader picture of the development of nineteenth-century universities throughout the West, Spain
presents a particularly dramatic instance of the long struggle for the
professionalization of academic life and its separation from outside
controls. In Spain, Krausism provided a path toward such transformation by offering a highly idealistic and universalistic ethical doctrine
that naturally appealed to liberal Catholics and apostates alike, who
sought to teach and think in independence of Catholic orthodoxy and
to establish a philosophical basis for their reformist programs. Out of
Sanz's meditations on Krause's works, particularly *Das Urbild der
Menscheit* (1811), which he translated into Spanish as *Ideal de la
humanidad* (1860), grew a current of personal and social reform of
exemplary significance, if slight institutional permanence. Thus, in-
appropriate as the work of Krause seems in retrospect for any attempt

to bring Spain philosophically up to date, Sanz's choice of this German mentor may have been wiser than those critics think who have contented themselves with puzzling over the curious success in Spain of an obscure German metaphysician all but forgotten in his own land and language.

Krause saw reality as a dualistic system combining Nature and Spirit. To the first realm belonged the body; to the second, the realm of reason, belonged the human mind and spirit. Both realms found their absolute ground in God, whose perfect essence harmonized the two spheres. Such was the metaphysical basis for Krause's vision (comparable to Kant's theses in "Idea for a Universal History") of a united humanity as the end of history. Each man, capable of perfection in the image of God, must seek his Creator through an ultimately religious cultivation of the tasks given him in his time and place, through educational self-improvement, and through progressive adherence to the imperative of universal solidarity with all other men. The proper development of one's mind and a healthy respect for one's body must lead beyond merely personal preoccupations to concern for the welfare of the family, the nation, the arts and sciences, and religion. Thus, ultimately, the fate of all men is bound up in that of each one. In this dictum one sees the utopian-religious quality of Krause's teaching, which stood against secularized atomistic individualism and in favor of community as the bond that heals one's alienation from one's fellows. Like Hermann Cohen and the Marburg neo-Kantians with whom Ortega later studied, Krause elaborated the humanitarian social consciousness present in Kant's hope for a single brotherhood of man.

Calling his system "Panentheism" to mark his effort to mediate between pantheism and transcendent theism, Krause sought to make God one, though not coterminous, with the world. Just as for his American contemporary Emerson the individual soul was sustained and united to all else by its participation in the Over Soul, so for Krause each individual, properly an end in himself, joined an ideal League of Humanity through membership in a spiritual whole. God, the unifying principle of all that existed, was known to man through spiritual intuition. Men were enjoined by Krause to strive to imitate God in both their inner lives and their social organizations. While a kind of pietistic union with the Deity formed the basis of individual goodness, it remained unfulfilled until individuals fulfilled themselves morally through membership in the various communities of family, city, region, nation, and—ultimately—world. By working to transcend local and national allegiances, men learned to see themselves as citizens of the universe.

This consmopolitan and ecumenical vision of human destiny, rooted in the German Protestant and pietistic tradition, appealed to Sanz del Río in its rationalistic, liberal, and clearly ethical implications. A potentially revolutionary program in its devotion to intellectual freedom, Krausism provided Spanish reformers with a form of "natural religion" that affirmed the possibility of direct intuitive knowledge of Absolute Being as the ground of all knowledge. As a version of the Kantian notion of religion within the limits of reason alone—an instance of the way German idealism provided a secularized philosophical alternative to the waning power of revealed religion—Sanz's adaptation of Krause was particularly well suited to a select circle of educated Spaniards who sought a rational, humane and socially just alternative to the doctrines of the Church.

In the late 1860s, Sanz del Río, together with Fernando de Castro (1814–1874), Manuel de la Revilla (1846–1881), and Emilio Castelar (1832–1899), founded a philosophical circle for the cultivation and diffusion of Krausist ideas. This influential group came to include key figures like Francisco Giner de los Ríos, Gumersindo de Azcárate (1840–1917), Nicolás Salmerón (1838–1908), and others among those who supported cultural and educational reform in Spain after the Revolution of 1868. In the main, their work was carried out through teaching and writing, though the personal example of their conduct was fully as important as the impact of their words. Men of the Krausist persuasion sought to make themselves models of enlightened rational behavior and of a personalistic ethics devoted ultimately to uplifting mankind as a whole. The ethical thrust of Krausism in Spanish intellectual history is well summarized by López-Morillas:

> First in Krause, as afterwards in Schopenhauer, Nietzsche, and Bergson, this inquisitive and fickle Spaniard [the type attracted to Krausism] sought ... more than anything an anodyne for his ethical inquietude. From Sanz del Río to Ortega, from Fernando de Castro to Unamuno, from Francisco Giner to Antonio Machado, this unmistakable preoccupation persists, the fruit of an instinctive apprehension of the primacy of man over ideas.[14]

Although strictly speaking Ortega cannot be considered a direct descendant of the Krausist movement, its central if diffuse influence upon reformist currents of thought in late nineteenth-century Spain makes him necessarily a legatee of a tradition that runs from Krause through Giner de los Ríos into the early twentieth century, most clearly in Giner's Institución Libre de Enseñanza, the primary institutional fruit of Krausist teachings on educational reform. Giner's own voluminous writings on literature, law, and social and pedagogical reform inherited from Sanz's teachings an often complicated and abstruse conceptual structure largely uncongenial to the young Ortega, who quite rightly chose to study German philosophy in its more contemporary neo-Kantian form in Marburg. But, despite his philosophical distance from Giner, Ortega recognized the importance of the older man's work as a precedent for the reformist goals of the Generation of 1914. Moreover, he corresponded frequently with Giner until the latter's death in 1915, and thereafter helped to promote the several institutions that developed from the example set by the Institución Libre. It was, then, clearly Giner's work, more than that of anyone in the preceding Krausist generation, that provided Ortega with the key native model of a liberal, Europeanized approach to pedagogy. While Sanz del Río had set the example for studies abroad in Germany rather than France, Giner, a genuinely cosmopolitan man by comparison, exemplified a catholic receptivity to French literature, German philosophical ideas, and English schooling, with its emphasis upon sports and the small residential college unit. In touch with the new trans-European sensitivity to the child's need for direct experience of nature, art, and life in society, Giner did for Spain the kind of pioneering work carried out by Johann Pestalozzi in Switzerland, Friedrich Froebel in Germany, Ellen Key in Sweden, and Maria Montessori in Italy.

Francisco Giner de los Ríos was born in Ronda, in the province of Malaga, on October 10, 1839. After obtaining his law degree at the University of Granada in 1859, he moved to Madrid in 1863 to seek a professorship at the Central University. There he met Sanz and quickly became one of the master's most devout philosophical disciples. Sanz's Krausist teachings furthered Giner's move away from the Catholic training of his childhood. The Vatican Syllabus of 1864, which condemned liberalism, rationalism, pantheism, and related doctrines, confirmed his decision to be a Christian outside the precincts of the Church. With the help of his uncle Antonio de los Ríos Rosas, Giner obtained the university's chair of philosophy of law and international law in 1867. Before he could begin teaching, however, the government of General Ramón María Narváez (1799–1868) established mandatory loyalty oaths for all secondary teachers and university professors. When Sanz was dismissed from his professorship for refusing to sign, Giner, Salmerón, and others among the master's circle resigned their posts in protest. Reinstated with the Revolution of 1868, Giner vowed to devote himself to educational and constitutional reforms. When the First Spanish Republic gave way to the Bourbon Restoration in December 1874, reactionary politics again placed Giner in jeopardy. He was jailed briefly in the fortress of Santa Catalina in Cadiz in 1875 for refusing to comply with government regulations governing the doctrinal content of university courses. When he was freed after forty-eight hours because of health problems, he determined to establish an alternative to the system of state-controlled education. Thus in 1876 was born the Institución Libre, originally planned as a center for pre-university and university studies.

After the first two years, Giner saw the acute need to reach students in their very early formative years, and by 1881 the Institución had dropped its higher-level courses and assumed its permanent form as a school devoted to a new kind of primary education. While traditionalist forces held sway in most of Spain's other primary and secondary schools, the Institución continued to keep alive many of the Krausist ideas, now coupled with Giner's emphasis on the development of the "whole child." Together with his disciple Manuel Bartolomé Cossío (1858–1935), Giner stressed personal contact between teacher and student in small classes where a form of Socratic dialogue was often practiced. Personal conduct and the formation of ethical norms were central, though religion was taught only in a broad cultural and historical context rather than catechistically. Taking cues from English schooling, Giner believed that character formation was an integral part of all pedagogy. Classroom activities were supplemented by workshops and laboratories and by frequent field trips to art museums, scientific institutions, and the Spanish countryside. Practical experience and personal hygiene were deemed as important as books and lessons, and traditional annual examinations were replaced by general ones held at the end of a five- or six-year period of study. In essence, Giner worked to form a moral elite that would

slowly transform Spanish culture. His doctrine is summarized by one
of his best students and later secretary of the Junta, José Castillejo:
"The only real aristocracy is talent and, as a consequence, the
greatest force in modern society is the school." [15]

Toward the turn of the century, more politically active supporters
of the Institución spirit, like Salmerón Azcárate, and Canalejas,
worked to extend its influenced through reformist legislation. These
efforts led eventually to the creation of the Junta para Ampliación de
Estudios e Investigaciones Científicas, a body that might never have
existed without the long struggle for educational autonomy begun in
the mid-1860s by the Krausists and continued in the work of Giner
and Cossío after 1876. Established by royal decree in 1907 (although
it did not begin to function until 1910, after the fall of the government
of Antonio Maura), the Junta was a bold new departure in Spanish
higher education. Although it was nominally under the Ministry of
Public Education and dependent on funding from the Spanish
Cortes, the Junta in fact enjoyed almost complete independence
under the guidance of its secretary José Castillejo and a board of
directors headed by the renowned histologist Santiago Ramón y
Cajal and including Costa, Azcárate, Menéndez Pelayo, and the
painter Joaquín Sorolla. Overall, the membership of the board represented friends of the Institución Libre in good number. A primary
purpose of the new council was to disburse grants for study abroad, a
priority early identified by Giner.

Further plans were quickly laid for the creation of laboratories and
research institutes under the Junta's purview. Thus the Centro de
Estudios Históricos was created in March 1910, and was followed in
October by the new Residencia de Estudiantes, an English-style
college residence for students from the University of Madrid. (The
story of this illustrious experiment, which expanded in 1915 to include a Residencia de Señoritas under Ortega's former student María
de Maeztu, Ramiro's sister, belongs primarily to the following decade and is given in more detail below, in our treatment of Madrid
during the 1920s.) There followed soon after the Instituto Cajal de
Histología and the Instituto de Física y Química, and in 1915 the
Instituto Escuela, a "laboratory" school on the secondary level. In
addition, the Junta sponsored publications of its own, many of them
the result of research undertaken by its grantees. The various research
organizations that grew under its auspices were designed to support

the continuing work of grantees and to upgrade the general level of study and research already being conducted in Spain. The establishment of the Junta was a dramatic step toward implementing Giner's dream of having the most gifted young Spaniards bring new ideas from abroad to advance cosmopolitanization; and the many educational and research facilities that rapidly developed under its auspices allowed Spanish educators, scientists, and intellectuals to pursue their academic interests free from Church and governmental pressures.[16]

Although Ortega referred to Giner only in passing in his early writings, he was surrounded by *institucionistas* in his youth and was clearly indebted to the innovations promoted by the Junta. In later years he moved often in the distinctly lay circles that grew up around it, the Residencia, and the Instituto Escuela, to which in time he sent his own children. Nonetheless, these brave experiments could not alone effect the grand transformation that he sought after his return from Marburg in 1911. Indeed, if we are to account for the pessimism of Unamuno's judgment in 1906 that Spanish culture was "shamefully coarse and decrepit" and for Ortega's scorning of cultural emptiness in many of his early essays, we must acknowledge that the various reforms just after the turn of the century were not sufficient evidence for Ortega's generation that the nation had overcome its cultural stagnation. In this regard, the judgment of the English historian Raymond Carr on the work of the earlier Krausists and Giner—"A heroic minority cannot hope to change an intolerant society by quiet persuasion"—is not unjust, though it understates the stimulus that such work provided for both the Generation of 1898 and the younger men of Ortega's day.[17]

There is little doubt that as creators of a national literature, certain writers of the enormously influential Generation of the Disaster (1898)—Unamuno, Baroja, Machado, Maeztu, and Azorín—gave definitive literary form to the myth of a fallen and degenerate Spain, providing a language and an ideology to which Ortega was bound to respond in his first essays, beginning in 1902. Although other more "scientific" writers of the same period (e.g., Costa, Ángel Ganivet, Rafael Altamira, and Ricardo Macías Picavea) pursued the question of national crisis in sociological and historical terms, the former group created the literary and stylistic "horizon" Ortega confronted as a young intellectual determined to tackle the perennial "problem" of

Spain. Discussion and definition of the Generation of 1898 and its impact on Spanish intellectual life has been prolific throughout the course of twentieth-century Spanish letters and in the literary history written by non-Spaniards as well. Though I cannot hope to review such a vast field here, some mention must later be made of Ortega's relations with those to whom he felt most closely tied (Unamuno and Maeztu, a childhood friend of Ortega's) and with those whose work he criticized at length (Baroja and Azorín). My primary focus for the rest of this chapter, however, will be on the matter of generational periodization as a theme in Spanish literary historiography. For Ortega's search for his intellectual vocation was, in part, a function of his attitude toward his literary "fathers" in the preceding generation and of their sense that they divided the decadent Spain of the Bourbon Restoration from the Spain that had to be made anew. His writing up to and including *Meditations on Quixote* in 1914—often seen as his intellectual declaration of independence—gathered up the concerns that exercised the older men and gave them a new, philosophically more sophisticated turn.

The effort to understand modern Spanish cultural and intellectual history by means of its "generations" is not of course an isolated phenomenon, for the very impulse to name the reformist writers of the *fin de siècle* the "Generation of 1898," like that of Ortega and his contemporaries to call themselves the "Generation of 1914," was a consequence of the growing generational consciousness to which we have referred.[18] Ortega eventually took up the question of generations in full in *The Modern Theme* (1923), *Man and Crisis* (1933), and *Man and People*, first delivered as a lecture series in 1949–1950; but he had already touched upon this issue in the years just before the Great War, when he was simply one more of the myriad European voices responding to the identity crisis felt by many writers and intellectuals of the period. At about this same time the notion of a "Generation of 1898" was formally established, first by the historian and politician Gabriel Maura in 1908 and later by Azorín in 1913.[19] Their statements mark what Ricardo Gullón has called the "invention" of the Generation.[20]

As a device, the naming of generations is bound to have about it something factitious and even dubious, for no self-conscious elite group stands in such clear separation from the past as it imagines. Unamuno, for example, is probably the best-known member of the

Generation of 1898, yet his early works fall within the last Restoration years. And the biographies of figures like Ganivet and Costa, usually seen as precursors of the 1898 group, belong solidly within that period. Costa is a special case, for, as indicated, he shared the Krausist concerns with institutional reform and their view of the central importance of education. Ganivet, by contrast, is clearly a predecessor of the 1898 group in his emphasis on the spiritual dilemma of Spain as a land without what he called *ideas madres*, or central guiding ideals.

In his influential *Idearium español* (1896), Ganivet set the tone for much of the culture criticism of the 1898 group. His was the primary example of a turning away from the apparently hopeless dilemma of specific social, political, and economic reforms toward the notion of a Spain sick in soul. In this sense his work is an example of what the historian Fritz Stern has called "the politics of cultural despair," an attitude exemplified by Stern's portrait of three minor German intellectuals of the late nineteenth century (Paul de Lagarde, Julius Langbehn, and Arthur Moeller van den Bruck), who substituted "sociological or cultural analyses for political criticism."[21] Stern sees this same penchant at work in thinkers like Charles Maurras, Barrès, D'Annunzio, Knut Hamsun, and Unamuno, all of whom felt alienated from modern urban life and found in a kind of mystical "metapolitics" an ideology to sanction their ambivalent feelings toward sociopolitical modernization. In Stern's argument, these men were examples of Julien Benda's "traitorous clerks," restless intellectuals and academics who espoused a *völkisch* definition of nationalism and a predominantly aesthetic treatment of politics. In Spain, a similar reaction to the challenge posed by political and economic modernization was a central part of Ganivet's cry for rediscovery of the Spanish *genio* or *alma*, which he felt had lost it sense of *autenticidad nacional*.[22]

In fact, "cultural despair" manifested as anxiety over the stresses imposed by modernity and modernization may be found in some form in all Western cultures of the period, if not earlier. Concern with the "national soul," closely related to the affirmation of folk and indigenous culture, spawned an enormous literature in the nineteenth century. The realization that nationalism itself threatened to break down and homogenize previously autonomous local cultures often particularized this concern, causing it to focus on the spirit of a region or provincial *pays*. Rapid urbanization and developments in international communication and transportation threatened to uproot men from their native ground. Immigration abroad, particularly to America, contributed to the growing sense of dislocation characteristic of the age. There was a widespread sense among artists and intellectuals, given unforgettable form in Henry Adams's *Education* (privately printed in 1907), that the world was hurtling toward a strange new century that would confound men's powers to understand and live securely in it.

This reaction may properly be called "antimodernism." It consisted of the desire to mitigate the threat of too rapid and widespread change in many spheres of life by reviving traditions that seemed to promise shelter and stability. Actually, these were often invented or elaborated to suit contemporary taste, as with much of romantic medievalism and the closely related cult of ruins that spread through Europe in the eighteenth and early nineteenth centuries. Antimodernist artistic taste combined eclectic sophistication with primitivism: one could turn away from the present by idealizing the innocence of life in the South Seas as well as by inhabiting a neo-Gothic mansion like Sir Walter Scott's Abbotsford. The quest for aesthetic alternatives to the ugliness of the newly industrialized and urbanized world stressed the beauty of earlier architecture—especially neoclassical and Gothic—and of the folk arts and handicrafts. In nationalistic historiography, a loosely populistic mystique of "the people" strengthened the idea that the characteristic virtues of a particular culture were to be found in the bosoms of country wives and the folkways of peasant farmers.

A cultural fabric of many strands, antimodernism was not solely an aesthetic or philosophical movement, nor just a manifestation of cultivated taste. As Stern remarks of its adherents, "They ignored—or maligned—the ideal aspirations of liberalism, its dedication to freedom, the hospitality to science, the rational, humane, tolerant view of man." [23] In several European countries around the turn of the century it became clear that a regressive mystique of nationalism could promote programs of national redemption with ominous political overtones:

> The Action Française and the anti-Dreyfusards, the Christian Socialists in Vienna under Karl Lueger, the pan-Germans and the anti-Semitic parties in Germany, and the Italian nationalists that emerged in 1903

—all of these attested the power and importance of the Ideology of Resentment.[24]

In Spain, the version of this ideology one finds in Ganivet or among some members of the Generation of 1898—and *not* among the earlier Krausists or the circle of Francisco Giner—seems relatively benign, but their search for the essence of Spain and "Spanishness" indeed foreshadowed the later, more virulent forms of *hispanidad* adduced in support of the Nationalist invasion in 1936 and the subsequent dictatorship. In Stern's comment that "[C]ultural discontent, Caesarism, and nationalist hope were the dominant sentiments of many Germans before the First World War," one is tempted to find parallels with a Spain humiliated by defeat in the Spanish-American War, caught in political stagnation, and in search of an "iron surgeon" who would restore the body politic to health.[25] In the inward turn of hispanocentrism (and in the related attempt to affirm "racial" and cultural ties with the peoples of Latin America, so-called *hispanismo*), some Spanish ideologues responded to Spain's diminished status in the world by separating their culture from the rest of Europe. In 1898, Ganivet, far from the outlook of the young Ortega only a few years later, posed the dilemma dichotomously:

> Either we submit ourselves absolutely to the demands and models of European life, or we return absolutely and work to form on our own soil an original conception of the national essence, capable of sustaining us in the struggle against exotic ideas. I reject all that would be submission and I have faith in the creative virtue of our land. But to create it is necessary for the nation, like the man, to meditate; and Spain must reconcentrate its efforts and abandon all sterile foreign commitments.[26]

For all its variety of outlook and of literary production in several genres, and the clear connection of some of its members with Giner's Institución Libre, the Generation of 1898 as a whole followed Ganivet's lead—including his essentially quietist injunction to meditate—in asserting that Spain's real problems were more to be conceived in terms of "national authenticity" than through specific political and economic analyses. Such, for example, was the case with Unamuno in his shift during the 1890s from youthful socialism to increasing preoccupation with *casticismo* (cultural and linguistic "purity") and the invisible *intrahistoria* of the silent majority of the Spanish people. Such also was the dilemma of Maeztu as he evolved from an early concern with guild socialism to his proto-Fascist defense of *Hispanidad* in 1934, just before his death at the hands of a Republican firing squad in October 1936, Azorín, for his part, gradually turned from youthful journalistic exposés of Spanish poverty and backwardness to an aesthetic savoring of the bewitching stasis to be found in the backwater corners of Spanish towns and distant Spanish history. Machado came of age as a poet with his unforgettable evocations of empty provincial plazas filled with the relentless dripping of water in old fountains. And Baroja's prodigious novelistic corpus aimed at the ideal of *ataraxia* or stoic acceptance of the way of the world.[27] Such a rapid review of these complex and prolific authors cannot do full justice to the variety of their work or the complexity of their varying intellectual development, but it is still essentially true that they provided no coherent political or economic program by which Spain might guide herself into the twentieth century.

In their particular response to cultural despair, the 1898 writers were representative of one major facet of the *Zeitgeist*. They were not trained as political and economic analysts; but, despite the antimodernist tendency in some facets of their work, they also experienced the crisis of European nationalism and the need to define themselves with the aid of wider, transnational ideas and feelings. In this sense, their example clearly prompted Ortega's similar but more frankly modernist and internationalist endeavor to make Spain culturally up-to-date. In his critical assault on the failures of the old political system, the young Ortega shared with members of the Generation of 1898 a greater concern for free-ranging cultural criticism than for a cogent political program. At the same time, it is equally clear that Ortega went beyond his immediate Spanish predecessors in his devotion to institutionalized political promotion and in his insistence on critical rigor and the systematic study of European cultural innovation. This advance justifies his claim that the Generation of 1914, of which he was the most articulate voice, had a more coherent program than the great figures of 1898.

The danger inherent in the search for clear generational groupings is similar to that encountered by any historian seeking to delimit an epoch, a movement, an intellectual age, or even the boundaries of a given event in the past: the more carefully one analyzes the historical issue in question, the more inaccurate seem the received forms of historical periodization. Thus while the Krausist generation of 1868 (which became influential in educational and political reform after the fall of Isabella II in that year) did not press upon Ortega with the same immediacy as the writers of 1898, those earlier men (Sanz del Río, Giner, Castro, Castelar, Azcárate, and Salmerón) established a vision of Spain which became the primary legacy of liberal reformist and regenerationist intellectuals for the next seventy years. This perspective enables one to counterbalance the almost obsessive attention given by some twentieth-century critics to the men of 1898, as if they were the sole important source of critical thought in *fin de siècle* Spain. The revisionist judgment is well exemplified by Carr's assessment of the earlier Krausist intellectuals:

> [I]t is to these years [the 1860s] that we must date a radical challenge to those accepted values in the realm of thought which the monarchy seemed to symbolize. It was to the fifties that Giner traced the intellectual and moral origins of modern Spain and it is against the members of the "generation of '68" rather than against the regenerationists of 1898 that the strictures of Catholic conservatives are most correctly directed. To arch-conservatives, experts in the paranoid style, it was these intellectual allies of Democrats and Progressive Freemasons who injected into the body of Spain those poisons which were only to be driven out in 1939.[28]

In this perspective, Ortega was as much a "grandson" of the liberals of 1868 (and of the later Giner) as a "son" of 1898. The larger liberal movement that began with the Krausists was, according to Hans Jeschke, "the most important spiritual current" of the nineteenth century, a current over against which the Catholic traditionalist position "influenced by containment and emendation, not by providing definitive norms but rather by subsisting within [a cultural atmosphere dominated by] the more powerful and fruitful liberal movement."[29] This characterization of the two broad camps of liberals and traditionalists should not, however, be taken simply to mean that only the intellectual liberals turned toward Europeanization while the traditionalists turned inward toward the Spanish past and the defense of Catholic orthodoxy, for as Jeschke points out, "both parties at bottom wished, in whatever fashion, to connect Spain once again with the mainstream of European thought."[30] The emphases and the particular choices of affiliation would, of course, be different, but the desire for reconnection ran from the radically liberal

Giner to the profoundly conservative Menéndez Pelayo. The latter
writer did more than anyone else of his time to awaken his people to
their own literary past, but he was equally influential in raising the
standard of required learning and in turning the attention of his
countrymen beyond national boundaries, particularly toward Germany. Though in his early career he defended "la ciencia española"
against European learning, his later writings exhibit a catholic taste
for all those elements of European culture that could illuminate
Spain. This later tendency is manifest, for example, in his joining the
original board of the Junta para Ampliación de Estudios e Investigaciones Científicas.[31]

Ortega's view of the years during which Menéndez Pelayo emerged as a central representative of Spanish scholarship was harshly
polemical and oversimplified, and ignored what Jeschke perceives
as a widespread yearning for reconnection with Europe. Eager to
differentiate his own generation from that of his father, José Ortega
Munilla, a respected journalist and man of letters, the young Ortega
declared in 1914, in the "Preliminary Meditation" of *Meditations on
Quixote*, that the Restoration years experienced a kind of spiritual
suffocation. Its sophistication, he believed, overcame the vital element necessary to any living culture. Even as subtle a writer and critic
of Spain as Juan Valera (1827–1905), who would receive kinder
treatment from Ortega later on, was seen by the young critic as the
archetype of erudition without perception and taste:

> During the Restoration the taste for anything really strong, excellent,
> whole, and profound was lost.... Greatness was no longer felt as great;
> purity did not move the heart; the quality of perfection and loftiness was
> invisible like an ultraviolet ray; and inevitably the mediocre and frivolous
> seemed to become more prevalent.... Study the literary criticism of the
> period, read carefully Menéndez Pelayo and Valera, and you will notice
> this lack of perspective. In good faith those men applauded mediocrity
> because they had no experience of the profound.[32]

This passage provides an example of the self-serving and frequently
careless historical periodization indulged in by writers and intellectuals who wish to accentuate the novelty of their message by asserting
that each new generation both confronts and creates a new reality.

In his judgments on the recent Spanish past, Ortega often spoke
with the voices of his older contemporaries of the 1898 group, most of

whose important works appeared at the same time as his early writing. Their stylistic critique of the Restoration rhetoric of Valera, Menéndez Pelayo, and Castelar coincided with Ortega's own reaction against the ornate, sonorous periodicity prominent in the prose of those years. Both the young Ortega and older writers like Unamuno, Baroja, Azorín, Valle-Inclán, and Rubén Darío opposed a native rhetorical tradition they deemed confining in its solemn bombast. They were joined in this revolution of taste by such *modernistas* as the poets Manuel Machado (1874–1947), Francisco Villaespesa (1877–1935), and Emilio Carrère (1881–1947), the playwright Eduardo Marquina (1879–1946), and the poet Juan Ramón Jiménez (1881–1958). Each of these writers began, in his own way, to open the language to new currents of thought and feeling. Writing about one of the chief iconoclasts, Baroja, Ortega early remarked on the rigidity of that literary Spanish that both he and Baroja deplored:

> The predominant manner of speaking in our books has customarily been of an aberrant complication: a paragraph was more difficult to build than a triumphal arch and, like the latter, was born of purely ornamental inspiration. Like horse-cloths gone almost stiff from their embroidery, like bishops' robes woven with metallic threads, literary forms cloaked the miserable little body of a timid and puerile psychology.... This vice in our past has not been, however, a fortuitous manifestation.... In all the other ethnic functions we have also suffered from this characteristic ornamental infirmity.... When strangers speak of us they always mention the "grandeur" of the Spaniard. But it turns out that that... is not the grandeur of the Spaniard, his magnanimity, splendor, or nobility, but rather the grandeur of the Spanish gesture.[33]

Ortega shared with the 1898 writers the sense that there was an authentic Spanish destiny to be rediscovered under the rubble of the Restoration. They all tended to feel that an analysis of the Spanish past was a vital national project. Not unlike Unamuno, who formulated Spain's "problems" through his gloss on Cervantes in *Vida de Don Quijote Sancho* (1905), Ortega, writing in *Meditations on Quixote* in 1914, nourished the hope that "[i]f one day someone were to come and reveal to us the profile of Cervantes's style, it would suffice for us to extend its line over our other collective problems and we would awaken to a new life. Then... the new Spanish experiment could be made in its purest form."[34] There was, it appeared, a "spirit" or

"style" of the race to be discerned, and though Ortega's own historical sense was too acute to accept Unamuno's quasi-mystical notion of
intrahistoria, the younger man seems in this passage to speak of something like an *intratexto*.

Ortega also shared with Ganivet, Unamuno, Azorín, and Maeztu
the sense that no compelling evidence pointed to a transcendent Being
as the source of our earthly existence. While he always refrained from
overt anticlericalism—another feature distinguishing him from the
Krausist reformers—Ortega was at heart an agnostic. In contrast with
agonized doubters like Ganivet and Unamuno, many of the Krausists
had treated the post-Kantian metaphysics of their German mentor as
an essentially religious doctrine that predicated the eventual unity of
mankind in one grand community. But most members of the Generation of 1898 faced at one point or another the anguish of religious
doubt and the threat of the loss of all absolutes.[35] Ortega met that
situation, so common to modern writers and intellectuals throughout the West, with less anguish than Unamuno and the others,
perhaps partly for temperamental reasons, and perhaps because he
replaced the Catholicism of his childhood with his ardor for learning,
his quest for cultural modernity, and his existentialist vision of *la
razón vital*.

Another link between the young Ortega and his immediate forerunners may be seen in their often immoderate hope that men of ideas
could affect the national life through their writings. The naïveté
implicit in their expectation that politics could somehow be directly
transformed by critical thought or philosophical principles was not, of
course, exclusively Spanish. It also appeared among intellectuals of
various persuasions in France, Germany, Italy, and other countries.

One instructive parallel from the cultural milieu in which Ortega
began to study philosophy is the case of Ernst Cassirer, who was, like
Ortega, a protégé of Cohen's in Marburg. Born about a decade before
Ortega, Cassirer was, in one historian's words, "the most gifted and
universal figure to emerge from the neo-Kantian ferment."[36] Yet,
like many another liberal intellectual of the Wilhelmine period, and
like his counterparts in Spain and elsewhere, Cassirer apparently
failed to foresee the difficulties that political and cultural elites would
encounter when they tried to shun or manipulate the unenfranchised
masses. For all his profound awareness of developments in modern
science, philosophy, and historiography, Cassirer seemed not to pon-

der the lessons of German history—the crisis of liberal humanism, the failure of the Weimar Republic, and the descent of his people into the maelstrom of Naziism—until very late in his life. Previously, in the face of growing evidence that the world was not run by reason and humane principle, he had asserted the continuity of Western culture in his superb studies of the Renaissance and the Enlightenment. To these he added his grand neo-Kantian vision (in *The Philosophy of Symbolic Forms*) of an enlarged reason that incorporated the "irrational" or prerational forms of myth, poetry and religion. This noble conception of the development of Western thought through the successive phases and patterns of symbolic form somewhat resembles Ortega's later notion of "historical reason," although Ortega did not believe as clearly as Cassirer in a melioristic view of mankind's intellectual evolution.

Only in his last work, *The Myth of the State*, finished just before his death in 1945, did Cassirer confront head-on the political naïveté characteristic of so many turn-of-the-century liberal intellectuals. There he examined the tragic resurgence of a political mythology (exemplified by Hegel and, more stridently, by Spengler in *The Decline of the West*) which helped promote the Nazi idea of a German state whose destiny was to rule the world. In a chastened, reflective mood, he wrote:

> It is beyond the power of philosophy to destroy the political myths. A myth is in a sense invulnerable.... All of us have been liable to underrate this strength. When we first heard of the political myths we found them so absurd and incongruous, so fantastic and ludicrous that we could hardly be prevailed upon to take them seriously. By now it has become clear to all of us that this was a great mistake.[37]

He drew for himself the bitter lesson that Ortega, too, would ponder after the defeat of the Second Spanish Republic: "What we have learned in the hard school of our modern political life," Cassirer continued,

> is the fact that human culture is by no means the firmly established thing that we once supposed it to be.... It seems ... that we have to look upon the great masterworks of human culture in a much humbler way. They are not eternal or unassailable.... We must always be prepared for violent concussions that may shake our cultural world and our social order to its very foundations.[38]

Well before these lessons of post-1914 European history, members of the Generation of 1898 had exemplified the tendency among intellectuals throughout Europe to rationalize politics as if it were simply an aspect of the history of ideas, their own internal dramas of thought writ large. Like many of their peers in other countries, those Spanish intellectuals from whom Ortega drew inspiration dramatized the ideas of national decadence and "crisis of values" in order to aggrandize their own social role as spokemen of the times; but none among them was able to offer as responsible and informed a program for economic reform as Costa proposed in *Colectivismo agrario en España* (1898) and *Oligarquía y caciquismo* (1901). In retrospect, their picture of the structure of society seems inadequate and, as Donald L. Shaw argues, "assumes a primacy of abstract, almost spiritual goals over concrete collective aspirations to (for example) material wellbeing."[39]

In the loss of the war with the United States, the writers of 1898 found a catalyst for the expression of their crises of faith, their sense of living in a moribund society, and their wish for a larger social role. As their own pains became fused with those of their country, they created the lasting rhetoric of "Spain as problem," as agony, as a cross to be borne—or, in Américo Castro's later memorable phrase, as *un vivir desviviéndose* (life as anxious quest). Uncertain though they were on a programmatic level, however, they, like the Krausists before them, turned toward Europe for intellectual stimulus. Unamuno learned Danish in order to read Ibsen and discovered Kierkegaard, who was virtually unknown in Spain at the time; Ganivet studied Sanskrit and modern European philosophy and was consul in Helsinki; Maeztu studied Fabianism in London and Kant in Marburg; and Baroja read a wide range of European literature in Spanish translation. In general, all the figures of 1898 were influenced by the work of Schopenhauer and Nietzsche; the poetry of Verlaine and other French symbolists, as well as the work of Darío; the political economy of Costa; and the ideas of Dostoyevsky, Tolstoy, Maxim Gorky, Ibsen, and D'Annunzio.[40] Resigned to inefficacy in practical politics, they became, as Pedro Laín Entralgo has so conclusively shown, the virtual creators for the Iberian Peninsula of a whole poetic landscape that has lasted into our own time.[41] Aware of the advanced thought and literature beyond the national frontiers and wrought up by their own helplessness as intellectuals, they devoted their energies to redefining the nation's destiny. As Jeschke has remarked, "the Generation of 1898, accepting and assimilating European literature, achieved spiritual unification in favor of the political postulate of 'Europeanization'."[42]

It should be clear, in this context, that placing Ortega in Spanish intellectual history is not a simple matter. He stood much closer to the 1898 group than is often admitted, yet he was at pains from early in his career to distinguish himself from them. In general, the generational method of approaching intellectual history poses major semantic problems in its proliferation of terms to classify artists, writers, schools, and movements. Consensus in such labeling may be achieved for a time, but later critics and historians, relying too heavily on established classifications, often fail to capture the complexity of career patterns as shaped by the formative experiences of a shared historical moment. Understanding such experiences, both individually and collectively, is fundamental to the method of generational placement presented in Karl Mannheim's seminal essay "The Problem of Generations" (1928–1929), in which the German sociologist developed the notion of "generational complexes" (*Generationszusammenhang*).[43] These arose, in Wohl's words, "when similarly [temporally] located individuals [i.e., those born at roughly the same time] shared a common destiny and participated actively and passively in the social and intellectual movements that were shaping and transforming the historical situation."[44]

In modern European history it was the Generation of 1914, to which Mannheim belonged with Ortega, which first fully and self-consciously grasped the meaning of generational complexes. In this way it became the archetypal modern generation, with its capacity to see itself as the harbinger of a new world waiting to be born. For many of its members, particularly outside Spain, which remained neutral in the Great War, the mission of forging fresh cultural forms was destroyed by the four years of international conflict. Those intellectuals, more obviously even than Ortega and his Spanish contemporaries, became what Wohl calls "wanderers between two worlds," generating profuse autobiographical testimony to the loss of the world of their youth. Spanish intellectuals of Ortega's generation, remaining as spectators and critics on the periphery of the war itself, responded by allying themselves either with Germany or with France and England. Despite their relative distance from the scene of the war, their knowledge of the European crisis combined with their acute awareness of Spanish decline to produce the sense of a destiny shared with foreign peers.

All across Europe the intellectuals of 1914 achieved a sense of generational identity which fits with Wohl's definition (itself based on Mannheim's earlier essay):

> What is essential to the formation of a generational consciousness is some common frame of reference that provides a sense of rupture with the past and that will later distinguish the members of the generation from those who follow them in time. . . . What allowed European intellectuals born between 1880 and 1900 to view themselves as a distinct generation was that their youth coincided with the opening of the twentieth century and their lives were then bifurcated by the Great War. Those who survived into the decade of the 1920's perceived their lives as being neatly divided into a before, a during and an after, categories most of them equated with the stages of life known as youth, young manhood, and maturity. What bound the generation of 1914 together was not just their experiences during the war, as many of them later came to believe, but the fact that they grew up and formulated their first ideas in the world from which the war issued, a world framed by two dates, 1900 and 1914. This world was the "vital horizon" [Ortega's term] within which they began conscious historical life.[45]

The war, of course, not only issued from that world but destroyed it as well, and the experience of traumatic separation from the political and social order of nineteenth-century Europe sent tremors through the work of many artists and writers of the period. Born in 1883, Ortega fits the chronological framework Wohl establishes, but Spain's relative distance from the war meant that he would define the Spanish "crisis" in terms rather different from those that preoccupied his generational peers north of the Pyrenees.

As a young man he inherited from the Generation of 1898 an awareness of the national disaster of Spain's defeat by the United States, but that event did not reverberate in his writing as it did in that of his older Spanish contemporaries, who felt the loss of the last vestiges of empire as a symbolic and epochal fact. Instead, his intellectual priorities as a young journalist and essayist were very much defined by the decline of the Bourbon monarchy and the parliamentary system established by Antonio Cánovas del Castillo in 1876, a political order destined to end in the military directorate of

General Primo de Rivera in 1923. In fact the magnitude of Spain's crisis became evident with the protests of army officers organized by the military Juntas de Defensa (Defense Committees) and a major nationwide strike in 1917; but well before that, men of Ortega's generation, in search of a distinct group profile, had proclaimed themselves more precise than their predecessors in the analysis of national ills and more practical in suggestions for remedial action. Rather than emphasize what Spain's allegedly unique "genius" could offer the world—a predilect theme for men like Ganivet and Unamuno—Ortega emphatically preferred to restate the theme of Europeanization, already evident in Sanz del Río; Giner; José del Perojo (1852–1908), the influential editor of the nineteenth-century *Revista Contemporanea*; and a number of other writers of the Restoration. For as Ortega and these predecessors saw, only a country enlightened by cultural commerce with its neighbors could confidently raise its voice in the concert of modern nations. Consequently, Ortega distrusted sentimental cant about the "spiritual values" that Spain might hold up to presumably secularized and materialistic civilizations elsewhere. Less like a major actor on the world stage than like a needy student, Spain did not so much incarnate an "eternal spirit" or *Volksgeist* that might set an example for other nations as manifest an urgent need of the qualities of tolerance, openness, and eagerness to learn.

The young Ortega had a very ambitious sense of the work to be done on native ground. His mission committed him to the posture of the vigilant cock returned from European high noon (the German universities) into Spanish darkness to proclaim the dawn breaking over the Pyrenees. Perhaps this role was simply the logical one for an intellectual from the cultural provinces of Europe and for a man solidly informed by a haut bourgeois liberal's sense of obligation to the betterment of his country. Ortega's origins in the two civic-minded and literary Spanish families of Ortega and Gasset partly explain the mixture in him of conservative nineteenth-century liberalism and a strong attraction toward cultural innovation from abroad. It was not unusual to find a similar blend among well-educated Spanish liberals, who shared the uneasy sense that their political creed would be severely tested in the twentieth century and the conviction, a form of noblesse oblige, that they must educate minorities capable of future leadership.

Even by the time Ortega first went to Germany as a student of philosophy at Leipzig (1905), a period of study abroad was still a rare event for a Spanish scholar; and his return with news of the latest European philosophical developments was welcomed with great excitement by the hungry few who listened for such news. Sophisticated polymath that he was by contrast with most of his countrymen, he was prompted in extreme moments to forecast Spain's complete intellectual bankruptcy: "The intellectual level is sinking so far and so rapidly at this point in our decadence, that shortly there will be neither academies nor theaters; rather we Spaniards will sit around enormous café tables and tell each other risqué stories." [46] Such judgments, which echoed the old theme of Spain's cultural emptiness, made him all the more prone to immoderate expectations in his pursuit of modernity. His resultant preoccupation with being at the leading edge of cultural innovation meant that he would continue to look toward the rest of Europe as a cultural community to which he had a historical right to belong, yet from which he was somehow disqualified for full membership. This painful sense of distance made him at once passionate in his study of foreign cultural innovation and unrelenting in his insistence that Spain "catch up" with the central models to the north. Indeed, the more Ortega and his peers measured Spain against international standards, the more she was found wanting and backward. Thus was the bright prospect of "modernity" (not to be confused with the preceding modern age of Cartesian reason) established on the generational horizon of the young prewar Spanish intellectuals, where it helped to define their sense of mission. At the same time, they exemplified the truth that one does not become a modernizer without a heightened perception of what seems archaic in one's surroundings. In dialectical terms, every thrust toward modernization judges exsiting mores, beliefs, and cultural processes not simply as old or traditional but as decadent and moribund.

Spain in the Restoration years following the failure of the First Republic was marked by strong currents of traditionalistic Catholic thought which sought to assert, through resistance to political and philosophical change, a faith in the absolute status of certain primary values. This movement among the "neo-Catholics," as they were labeled by the Krausists, was in essence a reactionary response to the "dangers" signaled by the Vatican Syllabus of 1864: pantheism, rationalism, secularism, liberalism, materialism, agnosticism, anticlericalism, and so forth. Prominent neo-Catholic voices like those of Antonio Aparisi y Guijarro and Juan Manuel Ortí y Lara defined Spain as a bulwark of Christian faith set against the relativistic paganism of modernity. As the clarions of what Carr calls the "recatholicization of Spanish upper-class society," they appealed to the ideal of a Spain that, they believed, had been and must again be, in Joseph Levenson's words on Confucian China, "a world itself, a world whose values were Value, whose civilization was Civilization."[47] With this powerful current, which represented the sentiments of a large portion of the nation's educated population, the Krausists and Giner's *institucionistas* had already joined battle and made significant advances; and though conservative and reactionary Catholicism was by no means a dead letter in the first years of the twentieth century, much of its ideological force seemed, for the time being at least, spent. In that moment of increased desire "to put a double lock on the tomb of the Cid," as Costa had said apropos of morbid traditionalism, the voices of those who would open doors to the outside world could now sound a definitive note.

2
THE YOUNG MEDITATOR:
1902–1916

Having sketched a broad national and international background for
Ortega's emergence as the intellectual leader of his generation, I will
now trace in greater detail the story of the first stage of his career,
during which he sought to define the mode of life and the model of
personality or character that would best prepare Spaniards for entry
into the modern world. While this stage is often said to conclude with
the obviously mature work *Meditations on Quixote* and the famous
speech of 1914 on the "old" and the "new" politics, I have found it
convenient to include in this chapter an account of the recently
translated *Psychological Investigations*, which, together with the *Meditations*, represents his encounter with Husserlian phenomenology. In
these two works Ortega took the measure of a central current in
contemporary German philosophy and established his own creden-
tials as a phenomenologist with roots in the neo-Kantian tradition he
had absorbed in Marburg.

At the time of his earliest writings, Ortega had not yet been to
Germany to study philosophy. Just after the turn of the century, he
was still searching for a theme, a method, and a style. His first essay,
"Glosas," appeared in the journal *Vida Nueva* in December 1902,
when he was nineteen. His theme was "personal criticism": in the
guise of the passionate warrior, he argued, the critic frees himself from
sterile objectivity. In this essay, Ortega voiced the earliest form of his
doctrine of "perspectivism," the idea he would later express in the
maxim "Each man is a point of view on the universe." In "Glosas" he
declared himself a journalist and a critic-at-large. In the immediately
following years, with a blend of the belletristic essay and political
commentary, he developed a highly individual viewpoint and a sense
of political responsibility. Later in his life he was to become known

outside Spain as an existentialist and historicist philosopher. Though the latter facet of his career requires attention somewhat independently of his criticism of Spanish culture, the two threads were intricately interwoven: with the years, the critic of Spanish mores whose vision of things was purposefully and insistently local became the broader philosopher of history and culture, and the philosopher in turn focused his theoretical lens on his native land. Concern with the condition of Spain, never far from Ortega's thought, underlay all his writings on history, society, culture, and human life.

By 1907, when he returned from his first philosophical studies under Cohen in Marburg, Ortega had published several more short essays, also probings of his country's cultural resources. He had written pessimistically in "La ciencia romántica" (Romantic Science, June 1906), "Our extreme race, our extreme climate, our unbridled souls are not the ones called to leave in history the memory of a continuous and reasonable form of life." [1] And, in August of the same year, writing what he called "barbarous criticism," he had turned his scrutiny on Spanish letters as a whole:

> I have read some books in contemporary Spanish literature and I continue to read them, even though most times it be only from patriotism. I confess that I usually open them full of a thirst for Spanishness, that I cut the pages almost religiously, and... that coming to the last pages I feel a heaviness in my heart and a spiritual dryness in my soul. [2]

Already this man of twenty-three, who would later call enthusiasm "the teeth with which one devours a culture," was turning sharply against the received and stultifying features of the society around him. Looking eclectically to classical Greece, Renaissance Italy, nineteenth-century England, and contemporary Germany, he noted Spain's need for "one of those epochs of affable and respectful intimacy, a familiar intimacy, preparatory of renaissances." [3] "Intimacy" was a key word for the young Ortega. It connoted at once a fuller knowledge of oneself, that is, a disposition toward creative introspection; an ability to establish deep and lasting interpersonal bonds; and a willingness to know what lay beyond one's immediate ken or contraverted one's convictions. A grain of this attitude, he felt, must become active in each Spaniard if the nation were truly to enter the modern world. Such was the "reform of character" to which he would later refer.

Ortega's critique of the Spanish psyche, however, focused from the start on the *intellectual* consequences of reform, for he was sharply at odds with the personalistic bias of certain members of the 1898 group and with the idea, often advanced by Giner, that a change in customs and manners was the road to reform. Sanz and Giner both had repeatedly invoked the concept of the "new man" who must arise in Spain, but their vision seemed often to rest more on deeds and conduct than on the new cast of mind so central to Ortega's outlook. Obviously, there was a philosophical and intellectual side to the Krausist and *institucionista* proposals. But Sanz's influence had worked as much through personal example—on the model of the inspired leader and his group of disciples—as through exposition of a system of thought; and Giner's effect was clearly dependent, despite his voluminous written work, on his almost saintly manner, which has been described as a kind of personal "priesthood." But the charismatic power of a single man or a few devoted followers was not, Ortega perceived, sufficient for the problems at hand. Spain needed new *ideas*, new methods and techniques of study, and practical reform, much as Costa had argued in regard to technology, industry, and the economy. As for the men of 1898, a clearly transmissible program for change was also missing from their work, which depended upon individual genius rather than a united front rooted in generational self-consciousness.

A particularly significant sign of Ortega's determination to do things differently appeared in an exchange of letters and published articles with his childhood friend Ramiro de Maeztu, beginning in 1908. Though Maeztu was only nine years Ortega's senior, his prolific journalism had brought him into close association with Unamuno, Azorín, and other members of the Generation of the Disaster. Nonetheless, his close connection with Ortega's intellectual development, which markedly influenced Maeztu's own thought between 1908 and 1915, makes the older man a kind of linking figure between the writers of 1898 and Ortega's generation.

The Conservative government of Antonio Maura (January 1907 to October 1909), brought down as a consequence of the "Tragic Week" of anticlerical protest and church burning in Barcelona in July 1909, was the clear stimulus for renewed concern among certain Spanish intellectuals with the political future of the country. Maura's hard-line refusal to cooperate with those members of the Liberal opposition who rejected his notion of "revolution from above" had rendered essentially inoperative the old *turno* system, established by Cánovas del Castillo in 1876, which was to guarantee the orderly alternation of Conservative and Liberal governments. In this situation of political impasse, Ortega and Maeztu shared an interest in liberal socialism as a future direction for national politics, but they differed significantly in their understanding of the proper means to proceed.

In opposition to Unamuno's famous 1909 diatribe in defense of the Spanish soul against European "invention"—"St. John of the Cross against Descartes"—Maeztu in fact seemed close to Ortega's insistence on the need for knowledge and fresh ideas. But as the polemic developed between these two old friends, Maeztu accused Ortega of being too intellectual to reach the average literate reader. Politics, argued the older man, must maintain its link with a charismatic leader capable of appealing to a broad public. Ortega replied that one's first concern must be with the political ideas that would form future leadership. Writing in *Faro*, in a series of three articles in June, August, and September 1908, Ortega answered Maeztu's accusation, made in the pages of *Nuevo Mundo*, that his young friend was slighting Spain's need for morally superior men. Both in the *Faro* series and in a private letter to Maeztu in July 1908, Ortega defended his belief in the primary relevance of science and scholarship. Finding that Maeztu suspected him of ignoring the moral dimension, Ortega publicly said that reform would come not from exhorting men to be better but by showing them how to think more precisely: "[T]here is no other road to the truth than knowledge: faith leads only to belief. Good intentions are a blessing for us, but we prefer good methods."[4] Against Maeztu's personalistic Christian faith in the exemplary role of good men, Ortega took a position closer to the thought of Costa:

> If there had been economists in Spain, there would have been less robbery. If there had been philosophers, religious materialism would not have erased from our innermost selves all noble aspirations; if there had been ethical knowledge about economics, the rigorous idea of democracy would not have perished.[5]

Privately, Ortega's letter to Maeztu echoed the same themes:

> I believe that a nation cannot live without a certain number of men who read Plato in Greek and comment on Kant and make inventions with

a rational mechanics and write treatises in biology and on cuneiform scriptures and reconstruct the first three centuries of Christianity.... You begin with the idea, as if it were an undeniable principle, that it is necessary to influence the majority, that there is no other useful, and therefore licit, work. In short, you want us all to be journalists. You do not admit the simultaneous possibility that Spain may need you to be a journalist and me not to be one.[6]

In a reply of July 14, Maeztu rebuked Ortega for his "cultural brahminism," adding, "We need high culture... but we also need mailmen who do not steal letters, teachers who can teach, good journalists, enthusiastic laborers, engineers who do not make crooked deals with contractors, etc."[7] These remarks were obviously incorporated in Ortega's "Sobre una apología de la inexactitud" (*Faro*, September 20, 1908), as quoted above ("If there had been economists ..."). At the end of September, Maeztu wrote that he had modified his own position more in accord with Ortega's insistence on the creation of culture; and from then until 1915, despite numerous qualifications of his viewpoint, Maeztu drew progressively closer to his younger friend's outlook. At the same time, both men affirmed the need for a wider "socialization" of culture somewhat in accord with Maeztu's earlier thoughts, themselves indebted to his contact with the English Fabians. Meanwhile, Ortega's own political trajectory through these years moved from membership in Alejandro Lerroux's Radical Republican party (1910) to active participation in the Reformist Republican party of Melquíades Álvarez and Azcárate (1912), and thence to a signal role in the founding of the Liga de Educación Política Española (Spanish League for Political Education) in 1913. This series of increasingly active political involvements seems to testify to the impact of Maeztu's chastisements of his colleague's earlier high-mindedness.

Both men defined their developing positions against the example of Unamuno's progressive retreat from Europe toward an irrational hispanocentrism, a trend that drew Ortega's fire in "Unamuno y Europa, fábula," published in the family paper, *El Imparcial*, on September 27, 1909. There, in response to Unamuno's chauvinistic promotion of the spirit of Spanish mysticism against that of European science, Ortega argued that being concerned with Europe was tantamount to eschewing the very kind of reckless, impressionistic intellectual play to which the rector of Salamanca was given. Had

Unamuno a serious concern for accuracy and truth, he would not content himself, Ortega argued, with facile thrusts against the "Europeanizers," a note Unamuno sounded again—stridently—toward the close of the classic *Del sentimiento trágico de la vida* (*The Tragic Sense of Life*) in 1912. Since Unamuno's word counted too much to be ignored, Ortega felt compelled to speak for the growing number of Spaniards who would replace the cult of personality with a concern for objective truth: "In the shipwreck of our national life, shipwreck in the turbulent waters of the passions, we calmly put forth a new cry, 'Let us save ourselves in things!' Morality, science, art, religion, and politics have ceased to be personal questions for us."[8] Unamuno had erred in his affiliation with an older, outworn intellectual style that Ortega's generation was eager to repudiate. Personalism understood as undue concern with artful wit or as pitched battle between symbolic personalities was declared a dead letter.

In April 1909 Ortega had declared his affinity with the French critic and historian Ernest Renan, whose ideas and literary style he had long admired: "Renan's books have accompanied me since childhood; on many occasions they have served me as a spiritual breviary, and more than once they have calmed certain metaphysical pains that assault youthful hearts made sensitive by solitude."[9] In this passionate skeptic and historian of the development of the human mind, Ortega discovered a kind of theology of culture which accorded with the attempt of Cohen, his Marburg teacher, to build a comprehensive neo-Kantian system that would incorporate all the faculties and activites of mind as made manifest in the unfolding of history. For all their differences, both Renan and Cohen were rational, nondogmatic humanists who believed that European culture should press toward the progressive enlightenment of all mankind. The Spanish Krausists, also nourished by the legacy of Kantian idealism, had believed something similar, but Renan and Cohen presented a more timely and engaging program for Ortega than the already obscure doctrine of Krausism. Renan, in seeing the world's goal as the development of mind, helped him to envision the creation of human culture as a noble spiritual process. If God were to be realized on earth, Renan believed, it would be in no other way than through the reign of reason and the pursuit of knowledge. Clearly, Ortega found in this historicist ex-Catholic, who had rejected the priesthood as a young man, a liberal spirit whose example was germane to his own youthful attempt to define his place in a predominantly Catholic culture long suspicious of modern learning and science.

While still a schoolboy, Ortega had conceived a passion for nineteenth-century French letters and read avidly the major writers of the culture to which politically liberal Spaniards had looked since the end of the eighteenth century. Julián Marías, who regards Chateaubriand, Barrès, and Renan as the three primary literary influences in Ortega's early career, quotes the following passage from Ortega's "Alemán, latín y griego" (published in *El Imparcial* in 1911), an analysis of French culture written in Marburg (where he was learning at first hand what German culture could bring to Spain):

> I hold a great affection for those French writers in whose works, for lack of native masters, we have learned to write. I believe that in the novel, as in painting, they have provided a new set of artistic techniques that, without them, might have taken another century to be discovered: the realism of Flaubert and the impressionism of Manet represent the most appropriate, vigorous, and worthy aesthetic stance men have up to now found. In lesser degree, one can find from Chateaubriand to Barrès and from Ingres to Cézanne many other laudable attempts to give suggestive and imperishable form to those human affairs which are passions and ideas.[10]

In this same article, however, Ortega laid bare the reasons for his disaffection from French culture, which he considered too decadent to serve as a model for Spain. In spite of his evident love of French letters, music, and art, he found the French nineteenth century politically conservative, "and entirely a growing reaction against the eighteenth century." The two French thinkers who had had "the most influence in the last forty years—Renan and Taine" had turned their backs on Voltaire, thus tacitly admitting that the evolution of "French originality" had reached a kind of conclusion late in the eighteenth century. Ortega construed this judgment to mean that "[t]he spiritual center of gravity had shifted toward the Germanic peoples." The deeper minds among the French admitted this, he argued, while the more frivolous ones occupied themselves with facile notions of reviving their cultural heritage and with creating a trivialized, formalistic image of the culture that had held sway so gloriously from the time of Louis XIV through the Revolutionary and Napoleonic periods. French writers and painters might indeed know how to give form to "passions and ideas," Ortega observed, but "culture is something more than that ... it is creation of new passion and new ideas." [11]

Over against France stood the great alternative, Germany. For Spain, "lacking ... cultural tradition, never yet having come to the exercise and the love of civil liberty," it was imperative to absorb German culture. But eventually, Spain and the rest of Europe would also have to transcend it:

> You can believe me when I say that probably no one has felt and will continue to feel greater spontaneous antipathy toward German culture than I. Protestant pathos, pedantry, impoverished intuition, insensitivity to literature and the plastic arts, and the political insensitivity of the average German keep me firm in my conviction that this is not a classic culture, that Germanism has to be overcome ... ; thus far it has not been. What has been is the so-called Latin culture. [12]

For all his apparent Germanophilia, Ortega early perceived that culture to be in decline. Not a "classic" culture, exemplifying time-tested standards, it was caught like all modern cultures in the movement of history. This meant that its innovations had become clichéd, that its great discoveries had ossified under the burden of systematization and scholarly appropriation, and, finally, that what Ortega called the "level of the times" (the blessing of the *Weltgeist* manifest in history) would eventually move on and be located elsewhere. But, for the moment, in philosophy, science, and humanistic scholarship, Germany set the cultural level Spain must reach. In fact, German thought provided Ortega with the preeminent modern instance of an intellectual vanguard, whose ideas he later conveyed to Spaniards by sponsoring and translating those German authors and theorists who best confirmed his own eclectic vision of modernity. [13]

Between 1918 and 1939, Ortega kept a close watch on the best of German intellectual life. But because his direct contact was limited to one brief visit (1934) during forty years of Germany's most turbulent history, he lacked the intimate sense of its cultural evolution which he might have gained by returning periodically to the haunts of his studenthood. Little wonder, perhaps, that throughout his adult life, despite his cosmopolitan concern for developments abroad, he remained attached to a picture of that nation as he had known it before

1914, when he had lived in its most venerable university towns and listened to its most distinguished scholars:

> I studied at Marburg, and at Leipzig and at Berlin. I studied deeply, orgiastically, and to the very limits of my being—for three years I was a pure Celtiberian flame burning, glittering with enthusiasm in German universities. I have argued Kant and Parmenides with Nicolai Hartmann, with Paul Scheffer, and with Heinz Heimsoeth, often late at night, on walks in snowy streets that ended at a railroad crossing while the monstrous Berlin express went by, its red lights tinging the virgin snow blood red. Then for years and years afterward I was enthralled by German science until I almost drowned.[14]

This reminiscence, filled with the ecstasy of youthful discovery, was actually intended for German readers, since it formed part of the prologue Ortega prepared in 1934 for a new German edition of *El tema de nuestro tiempo.*

Later in the same piece, he gave a slightly different version of his youthful hunger for things German:

> [A]t twenty I was totally immersed in the liquid element of French culture, and I went down so deep that I felt my feet touch bottom. I also felt that for the time being Spain could no longer derive nourishment from France. This made me turn to Germany, about which there was only the slightest knowledge in my country. The older generation had spent its life talking about "German mistiness." What *was* pure mist was their information about Germany. I realized that what Spain had to do was absorb German culture, swallow it whole—as a new, magnificent source of sustenance. The reader must not, therefore, imagine that my trip to Germany was the journey of a devout pilgrim who goes to Rome to kiss the Holy Pontiff's feet. On the contrary, it was a rapid predatory flight— the arrowlike dive of a hungry falcon on something fleshy and alive that his round, bright eye has discovered in the countryside below.[15]

As a student, Ortega had been moved on many levels by the spiritually rich Germany of the prewar years, particularly by its reverent attitude toward the past:

> In spite of appearances, the Germans have a virtue we lack: respect and love for the past. They have conservative, philological souls, and precisely from their philology and their grounding in what has gone before they derive the strength for daring in scientific or artistic thought.[16]

Those words were written in 1906. Approximately a decade later, the extraordinary cultural life of numerous German cities, together with the feverish richness of *fin de siècle* Vienna, would be shaken to its very roots. The First World War would by then seem to have made impossible any unambivalent reference to "the level of the times" in German-speaking Europe.

Early on, his way of reconciling the simultaneous disapprobation and admiration he felt toward different aspects of German life and culture was to establish, uncharacteristically, an artificial separation between culture and politics. In an open letter to Baroja dated "Marburg, September 4 [1911]" and published in *El Imparcial* three days after "Alemán, latín y griego," Ortega noted that it was "convenient to separate completely the political reality of present-day Germany from German culture," for it would be foolish not to see that "German imperialism will be tough, peremptory, and demanding in order to survive, just as all imperialisms past and to be have been so." [17]

That distinction was typical of many Spanish liberals before World War I who had been reared to admire the land of Goethe, Schiller, Heine, and Kant but were unable—like many of the German "mandarins" themselves—to reconcile Bismarckian imperialism with the great flowering of German letters and thought in the nineteenth century. Drawn to sympathy with the Germany of high culture, many of them supported the Allies in 1914 only with great difficulty. Certainly for Ortega there was no other path into cultural modernity except across the bridges of the Rhine—and this despite his remark about the "conservative, philological souls" of the Germans. Somehow, that is, he managed to embrace German conservatism (which apparently worked to nourish that nation's cultural growth) by exempting it from the stigma he applied to nineteenth-century French politics. The former presumably derived from a fruitful reverence for the past, while the latter was a reactionary turn against the radical spirit of the Enlightenment. Perhaps his dubious notion of distinguishing between German politics and German culture explains this apparent conflict, but why then had he not made a similar distinction for the case of France, where Flaubert, Rimbaud, Proust, and Cézanne were clearly as much pathbreakers in their crafts as anyone in Germany? In essence, since Ortega found German high culture clearly superior for his purposes to that of France, he seems to have constructed a sketchy, *ex post facto* rationale to explain the deep intellectual commitment he made during his periods of postgraduate study in Leipzig, Berlin, and Marburg.

Ortega's resultant program for cultural regeneration in Spain clearly echoed the patterns of Germanophilia and Gallophobia to be found in Spanish intellectual circles of the second half of the past century. On the one hand, it naively dismissed the spectacle of German imperial ambitions without asking how an admirable high culture might flourish in a problematic political atmosphere. On the other, it did not ponder the contradiction implicit in the flourishing of a lively French literature and art in the midst of an allegedly "devitalized" culture but only raised the question of what was missing in France that could be found in Germany. The answer was, presumably, philosophy and science, the two areas in which German work had entirely preempted the field. By "science," in the broad sense of *ciencia*, Ortega understood not only the natural or "hard" sciences but the budding social sciences and history as well. In these areas, Germany was unsurpassable.

France would continue to charm and astonish with painters like Cézanne and novelists like Flaubert, but she could not, in her supposed "decadence," administer the strong physic Spain needed. For all the lovely forms her greatest artists devised, France for Ortega was formalistic. And Spain, in looking to her, would be nothing, in his words, but "a dying man whom they propose to teach to dance." [18] As regarded innovation in philosophy and the criticism of culture, no modern French writer could offer Ortega an analysis comparable to what he found in Dilthey, Nietzsche, Simmel, Husserl, and Heidegger. Perhaps, in slighting the French novelists, essayists, and painters, Ortega revealed a split in his own personality between artistic imagination and systematic thought. The former was willfully subordinated to the latter when it was a question of national purpose, but the repressed impulse toward flourish and form found its way back into Ortega's writing throughout his career. Thus, while he cast France off with one hand, he accepted it back with the other, and his very choice to write more like a Montaignean essayist, a *philosophe*, or a kind of Spanish Renan than like a German professor underscored his complex allegiance to two very different cultural centers north of the Pyrenees.

Although French and German culture taken together account for most of Ortega's interest in modern European philosophy and letters (unlike Unamuno, he did not read a great deal of literature in English), his concern with the structure and restraints of civil society led him to admire the example of England as well. Following the lead of Giner de los Ríos, he lauded English schools and universities (particularly Oxford and Cambridge for their tradition of classical studies), as well as the English devotion to schoolboy sports and an ethic of "fair play," which seemed to him a sound basis for social responsibility. The "sportive" sense fostered by athletics coincided with his own predilect notion that all true culture had a playful, or as his friend the Dutch historian Johan Huizinga would put it, a "ludic" base. While London, Oxford, and Cambridge were never major sources of Ortega's intellectual orientation, like many Spanish liberals he fervently admired English society and culture from a distance. Precisely the absence of close cultural and political ties between the two countries made it particularly easy for Spaniards to yearn for the distant "green pastures" of the island people who appeared to have managed their civic life with such enviable good sense and political maturity.

Catholic as Ortega's errant curiosity was with respect to the cultural resources of other European countries, it did not distract him from the work to be done at home, where he had begun his teaching career with an appointment in 1908 to the chair of psychology, logic, and ethics in Madrid's Escuela Superior del Magisterio. This school had been established in 1907—although it opened formally only in the fall of 1909—for the training of master teachers (who would teach in Spain's normal schools), school inspectors, and high-level bureaucrats. While not directly a creation of the Ginerian *institucionistas*, the Escuela was close to the spirit of their ideas. It represented an effort to improve the professional status of teachers and to bridge the gap between the university and normal school education. It lasted until 1932, when its function was taken over by the new Department of Pedagogy in the University of Madrid's newly reorganized School of Philosophy and Letters. Ortega gave his opening lecture in the Escuela on October 20, 1909, an event we can recreate through the response of one of his most devoted students, María de Maeztu:

> It is nine o'clock in the morning. The classroom with a window looking toward the Retiro gardens is occupied by forty students, men and

women.... Ortega enters the room with a leather briefcase in hand, from
which he removes a little book. It is a dialogue of Plato.... The teacher's
words, clear, precise, elegant, produce a strange emotion. The students
try to write in their notebooks, but they remain absorbed instead, their
pens arrested on the paper before the wonder of that philosophical
exposition, clothed with a great richness of images and metaphors.[19]

In the fall of 1910 Ortega added to this already very influential
position the prize of the chair of metaphysics at the Central University of Madrid, left vacant by the death of the redoubtable Nicolás
Salmerón. (He agreed to continue without salary in his post at the
Escuela Superior, meanwhile postponing possession of the new university chair in order to complete futher studies in Marburg.) With
his appointment to these two major positions, Ortega had established
a firm and prominent institutional base for his dual role as leader of
his own generation and instructor of the one to come.

The year 1910, when he married Rosa Spottorno Topete, was a
very active one for the young professor of philosophy, who published
twenty-six essays and gave numerous lectures in and outside of classrooms. In March he delivered one of the two most seminal addresses
of his early career, before a liberal Basque audience in the El Sitio
society of Bilbao. Entitled "Social Pedagogy as a Political Program,"
it outlined a basic program for Spain's social regeneration. The
lecture marks the midpoint in Ortega's movement from an earlier
attraction to non-Marxist socialism toward an updated form of nineteenth-century liberalism, to which the deeper layers of his political
sense actually belonged. While Ortega, in agreement with the Fabi-
anized Ramiro de Maeztu, had all along rejected the notions of class
warfare and violent revolution, he had been drawn briefly to the
Spanish Socialist party, as when, writing in the midst of the long
Maura government (*El Imparcial*, September 26, 1908), he had
bemoaned "the political drought of this summer, a drying up of the
future more terrible than the present [which has] threatened to burn
out our last noble hopes." He added that a lecture of 1908 by
Unamuno in Bilbao's Socialist Club had renewed his conviction that
"the moral condition of Spain demands that socialism...rise up in
defense of culture" against "the citizen's ignorance and the priest's
cleverness."[20] At the same time, he cautioned those intellectuals
drawn to the political energy of the young Spanish Socialist party

(PSOE) under the leadership of the admirable Pablo Iglesias not to deprecate the somewhat rough-and-tumble atmosphere of this working-class movement. But Ortega was not moved to active participation in the party, and turned instead, like Giner and other liberals of the Restoration, to education as the most promising path toward the future he envisioned. Indeed, *no* organized political program ever held Ortega for long, and Iglesias's party was no exception to this rule. He had approached it in the idealistic-pedagogical spirit of the Comte de Saint-Simon, Auguste Comte, and the Marburg neo-Kantians, thinking perhaps to find there support for his own classically liberal goals.

A year and a half later, in Bilbao, he was able to articulate more fully his proper role as a teacher and writer in what he called the "socialization" of culture. By contrast with his pages on Renan, in which the term "culture" referred more to the ideal forms of law, art, and thought, and in which God realized Himself pantheistically through the moral and cultural progress of mankind, the address in Bilbao emphasized the praxis of constructing culture as an ongoing process comprehending all spheres of human activity: "In society no one who does not work can participate. This is the affirmation through which democracy is determined in socialism. To socialize man is to make of him a worker in the magnificent human task, in culture, where culture encompasses everything from digging in the earth to composing verses." [21] In emphasizing the labors of a community wherein the individual is fulfilled through participation in a larger social task—in this case, the rebuilding of Spain—Ortega was moving away from a more abstract, neo-Kantian language toward a concrete sense of the world: "Culture is labor, the production of human things: it is to do science, to make morals, to make art. When we speak of greater or lesser culture we mean greater or lesser capacity ... for work. Things, products, are the measure and the symptom of culture." [22] In this sense, the lecture marked a major step in Ortega's efforts to define man's "circumstances"—the term that would become central four years later to *Meditations on Quixote*—as both the cultural and the humble material world for which he must take responsibility.

The primary thrust of the talk in Bilbao was against self-concerned individualism, a bankrupt notion in that each man, as the Krausists too had taught, was a social being: personhood depended upon cooperative work with others. Thus, politics must become the instrument for "transforming the surrounding social reality." Education, of course, was a key part of a socially conscious politics, for "as the pedagogue enters into educative relation with his student, he finds... a social tapestry, not an individual." Like Plato, he continued, the modern pedagogue must first strive to educate the *polis*. Isolated each one in himself, Spaniards had lost that sense of culture which comes out of productive work and labor: "[S]hipwrecked by personalism, we need to grasp anything that in itself will make us float. This is what I have... expressed with a cry that issued from my aching Spanish innards: let us save ourselves in things!" The agonized rhetoric of this plea recalled the tone of Unamuno, but the stress on society, political activity, and "things" (institutions, schools, improved material conditions) departed from the tone of the older man. For Ortega, Spain needed objectivity, science, and lay education. Catholic schools, he felt, merely reinforced the Spaniard's unhealthy tendency toward subjectivism by encouraging the student to seek his own salvation. State schools founded on enlightened social consciousness were the only admissible path: "For an ideally socialized state, what is private does not exist; all is public, popular, and lay." [23]

During the summer of 1910 Ortega wrote his first major piece of aesthetic theory, a kind of philosophical sequel to the holistic sense of culture he had sketched out in Bilbao. In "Adán en el paraíso" he envisioned art as that form of culture which provides us with a model of an integrated world, a virtual form of the interdependency of all things. The artist achieves this effect through the development of a *perspective* that at once limits and liberates his vision. Adam in Paradise is everyman in his circumstances, surrounded by a world that is a world precisely because he "repeats" it in himself by taking a point of view on it. As Ortega put it, drawing upon the antimimetic aesthetic theory of Hermann Cohen and the constructivist epistemology of Cohen and Paul Natorp: "That supposedly immutable and sole reality with which to compare the content of artistic works does not... exist: there are as many realities as there are points of view. The point of view creates the panorama." [24]

As Julián Marías has argued, there may be in this early essay, which bears the stamp of the Marburg philosophy, a germ of Ortega's later philosophy of the subject's relationship to the circumstantial world. But in order to make this point Marías is obliged to quote a later passage, from one of Ortega's lectures in Buenos Aires in 1916, presumably applicable to Adam's discovery of the world about him as problem and preoccupation:

> The object and I are face to face but each outside the other, each inseparable from the other. The proper metaphor ... could be one from that pair of divinities ... that they call *Dei consentes* and also *Dei complices*, the gods in harmonious accord who had to be born and die together. In this fashion, the universe appears duplicated. We leave the eternal monotony of the "I," in which all appeared included, and before us appear objects in an infinite variety.[25]

In both the essay of 1910 and the passage of 1916, Ortega in fact seems more concerned with epistemological questions than directly with an incipient form of his more mature philosophy of "my life" as the radical reality. But quite consequent with his political concerns in "Social Pedagogy" is the philosophical critique of subjectivism and the "monotony" of egocentrism, signs of what he saw as the Spanish tendency toward atomistic individualism and a careless, indifferent attitude toward the world. In fact, his critique of such vices was the patriotic equivalent of his developing impatience with the philosophical legacy of subjectivism running from Descartes on into neo-Kantian thought. His interest, aesthetically and epistemologically, in the individualized perspective upon a circumstantial world was aimed ultimately at a new understanding of the person and of his place in society. The Spaniard of the future, rejecting the passionate, embattled ego of Unamuno's personalism and the self-absorbed sensualism of the man in the street, must instead become a modest participant in the total view of reality to be constructed from the multiple viewpoints of all men and women.

While these thoughts sprang from a fusion of Ortega's philosophical studies and his sense of civic duty, they were not without rough equivalents elsewhere in the culture of the age. As later historians of the early twentieth-century *Zeitgeist* have observed, a primary tenet in much of the vanguardistic thought and art of the period posited the disappearance of the notion of a privileged or absolute point of view on reality; no single perspective was superior to another; none revealed more truth than another. This shift from an ideology of absolute space and linear time to the new "multi-perspectivity" was echoed in Einsteinian physics, Husserlian "internal time-consciousness,"

modernist architecture (Wright, Gropius, Le Corbusier, et al.),
and cubist art, to cite a few prominent focal points.[26] Bergson's
understanding of "lived duration" in *Creative Evolution* (1907) deepened awareness of the subjective component of what had previously
seemed a shared objective experience of time and history. In fiction,
Henry James carried to exquisite refinement his understanding of
narrative point of view in his final three novels (*The Wings of the Dove*,
1902; *The Ambassadors*, 1903; and *The Golden Bowl*, 1904). With similar effect, Dorothy Richardson represented the world through the
consciousness of her heroine in *Pilgrimage* (first volume, 1915); Marcel
Proust portrayed the rhythms of lived time in *Swann's Way* (1913);
James Joyce made an epic of an ordinary Dublin day in *Ulysses*
(1922); and Virginia Woolf began with *Jacob's Room* (1922) the
technical experiments that would lead to *Mrs. Dalloway* (1925) and
To the Lighthouse (1927). In the year she published the latter, she
wrote in one of her essays, "Every moment is the centre and meeting place of an extraordinary number of perceptions which have
not yet been expressed." [27] In this remark, however, as in James's
irreconcilably separate points of view, there is almost a denial of the
integration of perspectives envisioned by Ortega for the double purposes of national recovery and philosophical order. In fact, "multi-
perspectivity" could as well purport solipsistic isolation as coordination
and completeness.

Many of Ortega's essays of the early period were, like those of the
1898 writers, literary criticism of a sort that encompassed broader
national problems. Thus, in "Una primera vista sobre Baroja" (A
First Look at Baroja, written in 1910 but published in 1915), he
remarked his older contemporary's tendency toward corrosive criticism of Spanish society, for which, in Ortega's judgment, he was to be
appreciated even more than for his fine novels:

> A glimpse of what really exists under the apparent camaraderie of Span-
> iards provokes us a bit. In reality, a terrible steel spring keeps them
> separated, ready, if it gives way, to throw themselves upon each other.
> Every conversation is on the verge of changing into mortal combat, every
> word, into the thrust of a lance, every gesture, into the gash of a knife.
> Each Spaniard is a center of ferocity that radiates hatred and scorn....
>
> And since life in community would be impossible if this were the
> substance of our existence, a mutual, tacit agreement binds each Span-
> iard within a mechanism of rigid customs. The forms of social relations are
> thus reduced to a minimal variety of categories.[28]

Similarly, in an early review of Azorín's *Lecturas españolas* (1912), Ortega praised the older writer for his attack on mindless patriotism and for his allegiance to a long line of critics (Cadalso, Larra, Costa, etc.) who had taught that a fresh study of national history would overturn received ideas about the past.

The notes on Baroja and Azorín reflected Ortega's intention to take his place in Spanish letters through a declaration of affinities and antagonisms. His dream was to build a republic of letters in which dialogue would replace diatribe among Spanish intellectuals. As part of this strategy, he helped found, in 1910, the second in a series of reviews and publishing enterprises that would bear his mark: the little magazine appropriately called *Europa*. Already in 1908 he had helped launch the short-lived *Faro*; *Europa* was a further attempt, also of brief duration, to establish a forum for reformist analyses of Spanish society. In fact, it was not until the founding in 1915 of the review *España*, in which Ortega again played a major role, that the maturing group of young critics in the Generation of 1914 would make a more lasting mark. One student of the period has noted the somewhat affected tone and limited public appeal of the earlier *Europa*, of which Ortega himself remarked, "*Europa* is not only a negation: it is a principle of methodological aggression against national bungling."[29] *España*, the official organ of the Liga de Educación Política Española, brought a more affirmative tone and inclusive scope than either *Faro* or *Europa* achieved. While many of *Europa*'s contributors would continue their work in the pages of the later review, the stress in *España*, reflecting Ortega's own development, shifted from a negative critique of Spanish culture to a design for its renewal.

Ortega's responses to important peers and forerunners were not solely ideological; the rich aesthetic strain in his nature also heightened his feeling of kinship with men like Azorín and Antonio Machado. Indeed, some of Ortega's early travel pieces might well have come from the pen of the former. In "Tierras de Castilla" (1911) and his later "De Madrid a Asturias," Ortega appears as a young meditator-poet wandering through the landscape of Castile. He seems destined rather to bright literary impressionism than to profound thought:

> It is a clean dawn over the roseate and dark purple tones of the town of Sigüenza. The last of the moon, soon to be reabsorbed by the sun, lingers in the sky. This death of the moon in full daylight is a scene of superior romanticism. The appearance of the sweet, musing heavenly body is

never tenderer. It is a tiny spot of milk on the polished brilliance of the sky, one of those white strawberries that some girls carry from birth on their breasts....

These early morning excursions through the rugged countryside have about them an air of erotic voluptuosity. It seems to us that we are the first to penetrate in our passing the air which hovers over the landscape, which seems to open to us with that bit of resistance necessary for us to realize that we are the ones who break open a path toward its heart.[30]

And, on another occasion, by train from Madrid to Asturias in the North, he wrote:

At the moment when night comes on, the waning moon appears half-way up the sky, like the pupil of an eye scanning the fields and now fixed full of astonishment. Out of the high wheatfield suddenly a laborer emerges with a scythe over his shoulder. One sees the moon on it, and the iron of the scythe seems to change into a moon as true as the one above. It is a moment of emulation and equivocation: both moons shine while traveling in opposite directions. But the train rolls on and leaves them both behind, without our finding out, in effect, which is the original one.[31]

In this predominantly aesthetic focus of a man who loved the contours, castles, and little towns of Old Castile, the politics, psychology, and history of Spain are all derived from a mystique of the landscape, Ortega's whole sense of Spanish culture seeming woven out of the very air and sun and colors of his native land.

The early travel pieces suggest abundant youthful energies moving between art and philosophy and trying for an intuitive blend of both. Out of his desire to restore to "theory" its root meaning of "vision" or "seeing," Ortega was eventually to build a mature prose style so compelling that it would divide his Spanish public into the two camps of adulators and detractors. The former were seduced into believing that what he put so well had never been said before; the latter refused to believe that one could write so gracefully and still tell the truth. Though not a member of either of those camps, the German literary historian and critic Ernst Robert Curtius, with whom Ortega developed a very warm friendship, captured something of his Spanish colleague's early power as a writer:

Ortega is a stylist of dazzling elegance and colorful profusion. Whether he is speaking of Andalusia or the Argentine woman, of the golf course in

Madrid or a restaurant in Biarritz—his sentences shoot off like arrows and hit the target squarely in the center. We feel that we are seeing all things for the first time and, what is more, seeing them in their true shape. Ortega's vibrant sentences trace clear profiles. The things of the world take on sharp contours, and in these contours they reveal their essence....

The works of Ortega's youth radiate a bright, virile enthusiasm. The profusion of life and world that they exhibit seems overwhelming. But the energy of the thought and the accurate handling of the language are equal to this abundance. The happiness of the spectator is a hunter's happiness. He stalks the game and brings it to bay. A festive luster plays about these books.[32]

One feels, however, that the youthful travel pieces are generally sentimental. The land and the villages are too attractive to have historical density. In this sense, Ortega's artistic bent probably complicated his development as a philosopher, for his rich sensibility combined with his commitments to political and cultural reform to further diversify an already complex vocation. As Marías has observed:

Many reasons, biographical, collective, philosophical, merely fortuitous, hindered him. To write a book requires having a somewhat more ascetic temperament than Ortega's, not asking so much from inspiration, being capable of writing without a full dream [*plena ilusión*], perhaps crossing rocky steppes. The voluptuosity of the themes, which Ortega felt in the most intense way and which made him not only an intellectual but a writer in the full sense of the term, too often distracted him toward incidental questions, and especially toward new projects, thus prejudicing the internal economy of ... his books. Before concluding them, he felt himself attracted and swept toward other themes. And, perhaps above all, his innovation in style and in the recreation of the minor literary genres—the article and the essay—absorbed his attention and his capacity during many years.[33]

The man who was so "hindered" in writing books would, of course, eventually forge the preeminent form of the philosophical essay in Spanish, using it to criticize and refine the fundamental insights of existential and phenomenological thought of the early twentieth century. Before Ortega's philosophical and literary vocation could come to maturity, however, his political one, spurred by the crisis in parliamentary politics made evident during the Maura government (1907–1909), demanded immediate attention. Seeking a comfortable alternative to his earlier interest in democratic socialism, Ortega joined the Reformist Republican party of Álvarez and Azcárate in 1912. In essence the Reformists were social democrats of a Fabian cast who, in the spirit of Costa, stressed agrarian reform, religious tolerance, parliamentary democracy, and lay education with emphasis on technical training. Critical of the monarchy, the party nonetheless supported it (except briefly in 1917) and lingered on as a minor political force until the beginning of Primo de Rivera's rule in 1923. In 1913, with a group of like-minded Reformist colleagues, Ortega founded the Liga de Educación Política Española, an intellectual vanguard concerned with many of the problems he had earlier identified in the "Social Pedagogy" of 1910.

On March 23, 1914, in Madrid's Teatro de la Comedia, he presented the now classic speech "Vieja y nueva política" (Old and New Politics) as the official inauguration of the League's activities. His central trope predicated the division of Spain into its "official" and its "vital" components:

> What I . . . affirm is that all those organisms of our society—that go from the Parliament to the press and from the rural school to the university— all that which, gathered under one name, we will call "official Spain," is the immense skeleton of an evaporated and faded organism which remains on its feet thanks to the material equilibrium of its bulk, as they say that elephants already dead remain standing.[34]

The strength of this speech lay in its sweeping exposure of the old system; more flawed, however, was the rhetoric of authenticity which posited a new Spain to be born of the present generation's self-discovery. This was clearly politics for intellectuals, who constituted the basic membership of the Liga. And so clearly did they see the enemy portrayed in Ortega's speech that they maintained, for a brief period, a collaborative front that could hardly last into their maturity. Ortega and Manuel Azaña, for example, openly at odds during the years of the Second Republic, cosigned the Liga's vague proposal "to investigate the reality of our native life."[35] This broad rubric easily included a wide spectrum of liberal and socialist reformers of good will who had not yet refined their political positions. Indeed, the list of supporters reads like a guide to Spanish culture in the ensuing quarter century: Salvador de Madariaga, Américo Castro, Federico de Onís, Manuel García Morente, Ramón Pérez de Ayala, Fernando de los Ríos, Antonio Machado, Ramiro de Maeztu, Enrique Díez-

Canedo, Tomás Navarro Tomás, Pedro Salinas, and some eighty more.[36]

Aiming to form the new political wave, Ortega's speech posited a sharp separation between the various programs of the older liberal republicans and members of his own generation, called to give rebirth to "the immense skeleton of a vanished organism" which Spain seemed to have become.[37] Departing explicitly from the critique of Costa, "who attributed the decline of Spain to the sins of the ruling classes," Ortega proclaimed a "total" politics: "An entire Spain— with its rulers and its ruled—is in its death throes."[38] It was not only, he continued, the Spanish state that was sick unto death, but "the race, the national substance" itself. "National vitality" was the living water overflowing the old streambeds of political forms, states, parliaments, and heads of government. The time had come to kill off the ridiculous sham of the seesaw parliamentary system, which oscillated during the Restoration between like-minded Liberals and Conservatives, who divided the spoils while the state suffered rigor mortis.

But the Liga, as the loose affiliation of its membership suggested, had no real program. Instead, sympathetic men were called to confirm the exhaustion of the old programs and to work toward "a new structure of political ideas and passions."[39] They must eschew allegiance to the alternatives of the Restoration and the nineteenth century, "which," Ortega observed, "is for us as far in the past as the tenth century." Both monarchism and republicanism, they believed, were invalidated by received conventions, which left Ortega to assume an "experimental posture," asserting that "the generic, eternal ideals of democracy are the only immutable, indispensable thing remaining."[40] In fact, Ortega envisioned a nationwide organization rising above partisan causes to educate the Spanish masses politically, for "a nation is not made simply with a poem, an argument, or a paragraph that comes to the orator's mind. It is a task for each day, for each instant"—in short, what Renan had called a "daily plebiscite."[41] The result would be a properly articulated Spain, structured in terms of the needs of the nation as a whole. Yet here again one can only guess at the detailed implications of this clarion call. Ortega's vision of the informed minorities of this new Spain was very like that sketched out later in *Invertebrate Spain* and *The Revolt of the Masses*. He called for a "liberalism" apart from any past or present institution or party, envisioning, for his "national" and nonideological program, a kind of politics above politics. This, of course, could easily become ideologized in turn, as became clear when this very terminology was taken up by José Antonio Primo de Rivera (son of Miguel Primo de Rivera) and the Spanish Falangists for their own purposes later on.[42]

Raising numerous unresolved questions, "Vieja y nueva política," with its hortatory tone, carried unmistakable marks of the Generation of 1898. Yet Ortega clearly sought in it to establish his generation as a distinctly new wave:

> [Ours is] a generation, perhaps the first, that has never negotiated with the topics of patriotism and that ... upon hearing the word "Spain" does not recall Calderón and Lepanto, does not think of the victories of the Cross, does not suggest the image of a blue sky with splendor below, but rather merely feels, and what it feels is pain.[43]

In fact, the emphasis on "pain" as a mark of a deeper patriotism was a well-worked trope of the time, and often included a romantic sense of mission toward the hinterland, as Ortega's use of it does further on in the speech:

> We will flood the most remote corners of Spain with our curiosity and our enthusiasm. We intend to see Spain and to sow in it love and indignation. We will roam the countryside with apostolic cries, living in the villages, listening to the desperate complaints there where they arise. We will first be the friends of those for whom we will later be guides.[44]

The populistic note in this passage, exemplifying the intellectual's tendency to evoke a *Volksgemeinschaft* even while calling for a purge of outworn traditions, prompted the later Catalan historian Jaime Vicens Vives to write:

> Neither Miguel de Unamuno nor José Ortega y Gasset turned to history; both approached the Castilian through an experience that was very personal and simultaneously, eternal. From this approach emerged an unreal Castile that has been perpetuated up until now by all the men of that earlier generation and, even more, by their followers.[45]

Ironically, the Spanish writers of the time who were most critical of the dead weight of tradition often incorporated in their work a nostalgic attitude toward the land and people. Thus divided in themselves, they criticized those patterns of national life of which they disapproved, while celebrating those others that pleased their fancy or suited their particular version of regeneration.

Four months after the speech in the Teatro de la Comedia, only days before the outbreak of World War I, Ortega's first book, *Meditations on Quixote*, was published by the Residencia de Estudiantes in Madrid. A firm friend and supporter of the Residencia since its founding in 1910, Ortega had for some time been wont to come for a *tertulia* in its gardens after his university classes and before the midday meal. His *Meditationes* was the second in a series of publications sponsored by the Residencia, beginning with an edition of Gonzalo de Berceo's *El Sacrificio de la Misa* in 1913 and running through twenty-two titles by Spanish authors (in fields as diverse as history, philosophy, musicology, and physics) until the final publication in 1935 of Jesus Bal y Gay's *Treinta Canciones de Lope de Vega*.[46] The slim volume that appeared in Madrid bookstores during the late summer of 1914 proposed the exploration of Spanish reality through the refractory glass of Cervantes's great novel, itself an intricate texture of diverse viewpoints on the world. Ortega's first major work was distinctly literary in its graceful turns of thought, an elegant essay that nicely complemented his earlier criticism, political journalism, and the handful of more technical philosophical essays he had published before 1914. Much of the *Meditations* had been composed in a room overlooking the monastery of El Escorial in the foothills of the Guadarrama range north of Madrid, and in the gardens of Philip II's grand palace-retreat-mausoleum. Ortega had temporarily moved his family from their residence in Madrid to an apartment earlier leased by his father on the actual grounds of the monastery. In this sober and tranquil setting, he found the concentration necessary to finish a book that opens with a meditation on the forest and its purling streams, both features of the landscape surrounding the little mountain town.

The handful of short pieces that compose the volume, referring only obliquely to *Don Quijote*, sounded the same urgent note of renewal to be found in the slightly earlier "Old and New Politics." In the book's "Preliminary Meditation" Ortega, describing criticism as a form of higher patriotism, employed a rhetoric of purgation which posited a depth of experience covered over by the detritus of custom, usage, and ordinary politics. Although he would talk in later writing of the *fondo insobornable* of the psyche—the incorruptible depth in which personal authenticity is achieved—here he preferred to emphasize its political counterpart:

> We forget that, in the last analysis, each race is an experiment in a new sensibility.... Occasionally, external causes may turn aside from its ideal course this movement of creative organization...and the result is the most monstrous and lamentable that can be imagined. Each step forward in that diversionary process buries more deeply the original intention, gradually encasing it in the lifeless crust of abortive, faulty, and inferior products. That people becomes every day less and less what it was meant to be....
>
> [T]his is the case with Spain.... Is it not a cruel sarcasm that after three and a half centuries of misguided wandering, we are asked to follow the national tradition? Tradition! The traditional reality in Spain has actually consisted in the gradual annihilation of Spain as a possibility. No, we cannot follow tradition.... [O]n the contrary, we must go against tradition, beyond tradition. From the traditional debris we save the primary substance of the race, the Hispanic core.... In one huge painful bonfire we ought to burn the inert traditional mask, the Spain that has been, and then, among the well-sifted ashes, we shall find the iridescent gemlike Spain that could have been.[47]

This declaration of new departures recalled Unamuno's invocation in *En torno al casticismo* (1895) of the eternal depths of *intrahistoria*, and Ganivet's appeal to the "genius" of the race in *Idearium español* (1896). In fact, all three writers were exploring the meaning of *casticismo*, ethnic or cultural "purity" conceived as the basis of a "true" or living tradition. The term had received its initial modern definition in Unamuno's essay, which denounced the tendency to derive a superficial version of the national character from the vicissitudes of history. Instead, his concept of an "eternal tradition" would ground the "chastity" of the Spanish folk in what was universally human. Attacking the abuse of the notion of *Volksgeist* as employed to "explain" so-called Spanish pride, egocentrism, passion, and so on, Unamuno cut through these putative national characteristics to imagine a *castizo* (chaste, pure) spirit in the depth of the nation's life. A key concept in the turn-of-the-century search for a national identity, *casticismo* found numerous echoes in Ortega's *Meditations*:

> In the expanse of the globe, in the midst of innumerable peoples, lost in limitless yesterdays and endless tomorrows, below the immense, cosmic

chill of starshine, what is this Spain, this spiritual promontory of Europe, this prow of the continental soul? Tell me, where is there a single, clear, radiant word that can satisfy an honest heart and a fine mind, a word that will illuminate the destiny of Spain? Unhappy is the people that does not pause at the crossroads before continuing the journey, that does not feel the heroic need to justify its destiny, to cast clearly its mission in history! The individual can orient himself in the universe only through his people, for he is caught up in them like the raindrop in the scudding cloud.[48]

Ortega too was wary of a topical psychology of Spanish virtues and vices. Instead, he argued that an adequate grasp of "the style of Cervantes, the Cervantine way of approaching things," would lay bare the national condition. This same point of departure had earlier appeared in Unamuno's *Vida de Don Quijote y Sancho* and Azorín's *La ruta de Don Quijote* (both 1905). Ganivet and Antonio Machado had also embraced Cervantes and his hero for their own purposes of cultural criticism. Turning to that high point of late Renaissance culture in Spain, they marked the beginning of Spain's decline from her golden age about the time *Don Quijote* was published. A rereading of that classic seemed a way both to recover the national patrimony and to celebrate Spain's cultural awakening from a long slumber.

Philosophically speaking, the *Meditations* laid down the basis for Ortega's two interrelated ideas of perspective and circumstance. A man was, he argued, both himself and his circumstances: neither made sense without the other. The self without a surrounding world was a phantom inheritance of Cartesian and Germanic idealism, while the world without a point of view to constitute it was no world at all but merely an inchoate cluster of matter and energy. Things and objects came forth into order only with the intentional perspective of a purposeful being who gave coherent shape to his surroundings, thus making culture from the raw material of mere impressions and wresting meaning from the brute, resistant force of circumstances. Pointing toward this position, much of Ortega's early work had attempted to establish a relationship between the limited individual ego and its necessary social and cultural context. Culturally, he saw, the Spanish form of individualism played a divisive and isolating role, leaving each person stranded in himself, deprived alike of community and environment. In philosophical terms, the separation of the person from community and world could be seen as the late fruit of the Cartesian division of the world into *res cogitans* and *res extensa*.

Philip Silver has shown that the *Meditations* actually constitutes clear evidence that Ortega had already completed by 1914, if not before, a critique of early Husserlian phenomenology, with its stress on the transcendental reduction enacted in consciousness. Based on his readings of Scheler, Brentano, and, through Brentano, Aristotle, Ortega was seeking what Silver calls a "mundane phenomenology" that would avoid the Husserlian error of supposing, first, that one could entirely suspend the "natural attitude" through the phenomenological *epochē* and, second, that "consciousness of" the perceived world was the result of that suspension. Like William James in the essays in "radical empiricism" (1905–1907) and the later Maurice Merleau-Ponty, whose *Phenomenology of Perception* (1945) he remarkably anticipated in his early work, Ortega saw that the irreducible reality of corporeal human life meant that we never simply had "consciousness of" anything. Rather, we always *were* prephilosophically in the world as sentient beings, just as the world always *was* present to and toward us. In a sense, it intended us as much as we intended it, and no phenomenological reduction could miraculously remove us from our intimate entanglement with it. Ortega early intuited the excessively "mentalistic" bias of Husserl's original position. Over thirty years later, in a lengthy footnote to his book on Leibniz (written in 1947), Ortega made explicit the insight he had already developed before the 1914 *Meditations* and in its pages as well. The explication of this remarkable act of philosophical originality in a man only recently finished with his studies in Germany is intricate and difficult, and the reader is best referred to Silver's pages for the entire argument.[49] However, the later footnote, probably composed in Portugal in 1947, lays out the essential critique:

> Since 1914 (see my *Meditaciones del Quijote*, Vol. 1) *the basis of all my philosophical work* has been the *intuition* of the phenomenon "human life" [Silver's italics]. At that time I formulated it—in order to explain Husserl's phenomenology in several university courses—, correcting especially his description of the phenomenon "consciousness of..." which, as is well known, is in its turn the basis of his doctrine.... [Some years later Ortega summarized his objections to Husserl's doctrine to his assistant, Eugene Fink, in the following terms:] Consciousness in its character as phenomenon is thetic ("*Setzend*"), something which Husserl recognizes and calls the "natural attitude of consciousness." Phenomenology consists in describing this phenomenon of natural consciousness from the vantage

point of a reflexive consciousness which looks upon natural consciousness "without taking it seriously," without its positings (*"Setzungen"*), but suspending its executant quality (*"ejecutividad"*) [in an *epoche*]. To this I object on two counts: (1) that to suspend what I have called the executant character (*vollziehender Character*) of consciousness, its thetic or actualizing character, is to eliminate what is most basic to it and hence to *all consciousness*; (2) that we suspend the executant character of one from the vantage point of another, the reflexive consciousness, which Husserl calls "phenomenological reduction," without its having any superior right to invalidate the primary consciousness reflected upon; (3) on the other hand, the reflexive consciousness is allowed to retain *its* executant character, and to posit the primary consciousness as *absolute being*, which is called *Erlebnis* or *vivencia* ("lived-x"). This shows precisely that every consciousness has executant validity and it makes no sense for one consciousness to invalidate the other. We can discount an act of our consciousness with a subsequent thought, as always happens when we correct an error; as, for example, an optical illusion: but if we counterpoise, without intermediate thought, the "deluded" consciousness and the "normal" consciousness, the latter does not invalidate the former. Hallucination and perception have as such inherently equal rights.

The consequence of these objections was that from 1914 on, I set forth the description of the phenomenon "consciousness of...," pointing out, *against all idealism* [Silver's italics], that it is a hypothesis and not pure description to say that an act of consciousness is real while its object is *merely* intentional; therefore, unreal. A description that attended strictly to the phenomenon—I said then—would state that in a phenomenon of consciousness like perception we discover the *coexistence of myself and some thing*, that, therefore, the coexistence is not ideality or intentionality, but very reality. So that in the "fact" of perception what we have is: on the one hand, myself, "being-to" the thing perceived, and on the other, the thing "being-to" me; that is to say, there *is* no phenomenon "consciousness of..." as a general form of the mind. Instead there is a reality that I am, opening out on, and undergoing, the reality that my surroundings are; and the supposed doctrine of the phenomenon "consciousness" becomes description of the phenomenon "real human life" as the coexistence of myself and the things around me or my circumstances. *The result, therefore, is that there "is not" this consciousness as phenomenon, and that consciousness is a hypothesis, the very one we inherited from Descartes.* This is why Husserl turns back to Descartes.[50]

All this was not explicit in the *Meditations*—and its development in 1947 was almost certainly an amplification and extension of what

Ortega actually thought in 1914—but it was implicit, for example, in his call in the "Preliminary Meditation" for renewed attention to the Spaniard's "Mediterranean" awareness of the sensuous surface of life. Ortega believed heightened sensitivity to the phenomenal surface of the world to be characteristic of the peoples of the Mediterranean basin, in which he included, perhaps questionably, all Spaniards. Taking issue in 1914 with Menéndez Pelayo's famous distinction between "Germanic mists" and "Latin clarity," Ortega replaced "Latin" with "Mediterranean" and proclaimed that the peoples of northern and southern Europe simply differed in the kind of clarity of which they were capable. Read aright, he argued, the Germans showed themselves clear in the depths, in their systematic conceptualization of reality; while Spaniards and other peoples of the South achieved clarity through the immediate impressions of the senses, though they suffered confusion upon trying to think, to conceptualize things. The answer to this problem was to reenvision Spain as part of Europe and to claim for the Spaniard his rightful "Germanic inheritance." [51] The North offered the depth of ideas and concepts; the South, the glaring clarity of "the sun-drenched coast" or the sweeping *meseta*. The road toward integral culture meant that each people, uniquely valuable as a particular point of view on the world, must contribute its part to European culture as a whole, while drawing from it what national or local cultures could not offer.

By virtue of falling outside the mainstreams of European thought in the modern age (1600–1900), Ortega argued, Spaniards had lost touch with the best aspects of their Mediterranean nature. Through a kind of degenerate, uncritical splitting of self from circumstance, the self-aware "I" of each one had become isolated in his atomistic individualism, while the world of *res extensa* was abandoned, despite the Latin "impressionism" of Spaniards, to shameful neglect. To overcome this schism was not only the imperative of national cultural reform, but the primary task of post-Kantian philosophy in its phenomenological turn. And if Husserl still retained the idealistic bias, it might be the very miserable condition of Spain herself that would prompt a young native meditator to develop a more satisfactory philosophy of human life in the guise of a mundane phenomenology.

While, in Ortega's view, each Spaniard was castled in his own formidable ego, the nation's history could be seen as a centrifugal torrent of energies turned everywhere outside itself, particularly during the great imperial period from the early sixteenth until the mid–seventeenth century. But exploration, conquest, and domination had not, it seemed, taught Spaniards any genuine altruism, understood as the concern to know and care for what one conquers. Spain, Ortega felt, had hurled herself into world history with abandon, only to fall back exhausted and unreflective by the late seventeenth century. In this sense, her history was paradigmatic of the consequences of action without thought, or the exercise of political and military power without that "intimacy" that was peculiarly a product of the modern bourgeois centuries Spain had missed:

> Spain is a country ready to realize deeds and missions not incumbent upon it—like casting out the Jews, conquering America, dominating Flanders and Italy, combating the Reformation, supporting the temporal power of the Popes; a country, on the other hand, which, with incomprehensible tenacity, leaves unfulfilled the clearest and most elemental mission proposed to her by history: thus, the Europeanization of Africa from Tunis to the Canaries and the Sahara.[52]

In this view, Spaniards of Ortega's day were the heirs of a long, misconceived crusade, living in a dry, vapidly rhetorical culture, the men as parched and blasted as the land surrounding Madrid:

> Look upon this poverty-stricken, tormented countryside in which one expects only to see some man lying flat in dusty clothes, his bloody face against the earth. These are cursed fields, fields bought with the handful of coins that suggest only an act of betrayal or some unappealing crime. Thus we *madrileños* find ourselves among the fiercest and most hostile beings on earth. Spaniards tend to flee from the countryside as soon as they can, for in solitude they have no one to attack or annihilate.[53]

For Ortega, the Spanish soul needed, as much as the land required irrigation and reforestation, the primary lesson of philosophy: to see unity in all things. This was another way of stating the need to unite mind with body, spirit with matter, or ordering concept with diversity of sense impressions. Ortega's bywords for this effort were generosity and curiosity. One's mind and eye, he felt, must fall in love with the world, seeing it as the object of cultivation and care. The visual sense had constituted the basis for philosophical metaphors of understanding since the ancient Greeks, and Ortega frequently recalled that a Platonic term for the philosopher was *philotheamon*, "a friend of looking." His own example, inspired by the essays of Azorín and Unamuno, the novels of Gabriel Miró, and the poetry of Antonio Machado, set a standard of aesthetic sensitivity for twentieth-century Spaniards. Most of his countrymen he found deficient in visual alertness and aesthetic taste. They seemed blind to the very landscape itself; and as if in return, the harsh, deforested, and irregularly cultivated land—especially in Castile—proclaimed its abandonment.[54] Lack of feeling for the natural world—a deficiency more obvious in Spanish literature than in that of England or the United States—found its corresponding psychic form in the Spaniard's lack of personal "innerness" and sensitivity to intersubjective relations. These, Ortega suggested, would all follow from a greater cultivation of *amor intellectualis*, or cognitive love, which seeks to lift things into their fullness and link them with all else. This was the method of "salvations" of reality he announced in *Meditations*.

Amor intellectualis would teach Spaniards to cultivate curiosity and altruism. These forms of caring for the world and for others in turn required what Ortega would later call *ensimismamiento*, "turning inward." That is, the "I" cannot really "be" without meeting and absorbing its circumstances, and these in turn are rendered shapeless and centerless unless the "I" turns to them—*is* to them—with loving attention to their structure and detail. As Ortega summarized it apothegmatically in the central statement of the *Meditations*, "I am myself plus my circumstance, and if I do not save it, I cannot save myself."[55] This deceptively simple statement was rich in implications. It provided, for example, a rationale for the study of folklore and local customs. Although Ortega did not fulfill his announced intentions in these pages, he suggested the scope aspired to by a mundane phenomenology:

> Besides glorious affairs, one very frequently speaks in these Meditations about the most insignificant things. One attends to details of the Spanish landscape, to the laborer's way of conversing, to the turn of popular songs and dances, to the colors and styles of dress and utensils, to the peculiarities of the language, and, in general, to the minute manifestations in which a people's intimacy reveals itself.[56]

Understood in context, the central motto of the *Meditations* also illuminated Ortega's passion for what was right under his countrymen's noses:

The circumstance! *Circum-stantia*! Mute things that are round about us! Very near, very near us they lift up their tacit faces in a gesture of humility and yearning, as if needy that we accept their offering and at once ashamed of the apparent simplicity of their gift. And blind toward them, we march amongst them, our look fixed on distant enterprises, projected toward the conquest of far-away schematic cities.[57]

What kept Spaniards from taking responsibility for their circumstances was the allegedly typical vice of *soberbia* (pride). Prone to rhetorical exaltation of their "Spanishness," they could achieve philosophical and cultural maturity only through a modest awareness of the hierarchical nature of things: "Let us learn in Spain to be second, third, last. Perhaps the deepest lesson given by contact with real things...is that life is worth the trouble of living even though we are not great men."[58] In that statement Ortega acknowledged Spain's dilemma as the least advanced and enlightened of the major European nations. To accept and learn from this perception, Spaniards would be obliged to relinquish their arrogant notion of being the chosen people of the Christian world, and embrace a more distinctly secular vision of things. On the level of high culture and scholarship, they would begin by studying modern European science, philosophy, psychology, and history; on a more ordinary and day-to-day level, they would confront the sorry state of their railroads, their agricultural methods, their libraries, and their civic institutions.

Culture and philosophical concepts, Ortega made clear in his "Preliminary Meditation," were essential for saving men from chaotic immersion in the raw impressionism that particularly threatened Spaniards. By presenting philosophy as "the general science of love," Ortega offered his people a basis for the structuring of experience. Reality is given to us in depth, he argued, when we grasp it through the concept, which catches and orders our circumstances, making them in fact a world:

> The mission of the concept, then, is not to displace the intuition, the real impression. Reason cannot and should not aim at replacing life. This very opposition between reason and life...is in itself open to suspicion. As if reason were not a vital and spontaneous function, of the same kind as seeing or touching.[59]

In rooting reason in individual, embodied human life, Ortega laid the ground for his mundane phenomenology, to be fully developed in

the later writings. This was the tonic he would administer to Spain,
which still had in 1914 a "wild culture...a frontier culture." [60] To
transcend its limitations, he reminded the reader that Spaniards
could claim an ethnic and a cultural connection with the peoples to
the north:

> Do not force me to be only a Spaniard if by Spaniard is meant only a man
> of the sun-drenched coast. Do not introduce civil wars into my heart; do
> not incite the Iberian within me with his harsh, wild passions, against the
> blonde man of Germanic heritage, meditative and sentimental, who
> breathes in the twilight zone of my soul. [61]

The aim was to integrate clarity of conceptual understanding with
intensity of sensory awareness:

> On the moral map of Europe we Spaniards represent the extreme pre-
> dominance of impressions. Concepts have never been our forte. There is
> no doubt that we should be unfaithful to our destiny if we should abandon
> the energetic affirmation of impressionism lying in our past. I do not
> propose abandonment, but the opposite: an integration. Genuine tradi-
> tion cannot be, in the best sense, anything but a supporting ground for
> individual vacillation—a *terra firma* for the spirit. This, our culture can
> never be if it does not base and organize its sensism upon the cultivation
> of meditation. [62]

As regards Ortega's program for Spain, the *Meditations* must be
related to themes developing out of his earlier writings and continuing, shortly after, in two publications in 1916: the essays collected as
Personas, obras, cosas and the first volume of his series *El espectador.*
Ortega's fundamental view of Spanish character, as reflected in these
three works, had in fact changed little since his earliest journalism. In
pieces like those on Renan and on Costa ("Observaciones," 1911), he
had aready opposed *amor intellectualis* to what he saw as the Spaniard's
characteristically "monadic" individualism. [63] Nonetheless, *Meditations on Quixote* should be seen as the true beginning of his philosophical career. It contains and sums up what he had written in the years
before 1914; at the same time, most of the fundamental themes of his
mature work after that date are announced *in nuce* in its fragmentary
pages. [64]

In the fall of 1915 and the first three months of 1916, Ortega
extended his dialogue with Husserl's work in a course he gave at the

Centro de Estudios Históricos in Madrid. The fifteen lessons, which took up numerous themes already explored in the *Meditations*, would not appear in print until 1982, when they were published as *Investigaciones psicológicas* (*Psychological Investigations*)[65]. The title, chosen by Paulino Garagorri, echoes Husserl's *Logische Untersuchungen* (*Logical Investigations*) of 1900–1901, the text that clearly stands behind Ortega's attempt at a philosophy of perception. In fact, no other of Ortega's writings makes clearer than this series of lectures his indebtedness to the founder of phenomenology, who had preceded him in rejecting the legacy of nineteenth-century "psychologism" and in revising the neo-Kantian philosophy of constructivism. The former entailed the claim that philosophical inquiry must base its search for truth on the subjectivistic process of self-observation (or introspection), thus making psychology the fundamental philosophical discipline; the latter, as represented by the Marburg School (Cohen and Natorp), argued that the validity of science, ethics, and aesthetics must be based not on psychological conditions but rather on laws proper to those sciences. Neither position seemed to Ortega to provide a philosophically sound account of perception as it arose in the interplay of mind and world, or self and circumstance.

Psychologism was suspect as a part of the subjectivistic legacy of Cartesian thought, while the Marburgian philosophy posited a clarity about the objects of thought which was rendered dubious by the discovery of new problems in research that threw into question the unstated presuppositions of various fields. These "domestic explosions," as Ortega termed them, in disciplines like mathematics, physics, and biology, gave rise to "nodal problems" (*problemas nodales*). Rightly understood, these implied a crisis of method that would eventually lead to what we now call "paradigm shifts" in entire areas of thought. In the largest sense, he observed in concluding his first lecture, nodal problems reflected the fact that European culture had entered a period of pervasive uncertainty and was undergoing a veritable "changing of the gods." Such a situation called into question the most fundamental assumptions concerning man and the world; and precisely in mathematics and the sciences—the pride of the modern age—one could best assess the epistemological consequences of a crisis of belief affecting Western civilization as a whole. The resultant dilemma gave philosophy an imperative role in the establishment of new theoretical bases for scientific research. Like

Husserl, Ortega believed that only a phenomenological investigation could bracket the working assumptions of a given discipline in order to clarify its root assumptions. More pointedly, in psychology, vitiated by a blend of subjectivism and ad hoc experimentalism, philosophical analysis must pose the fundamental question of truth above and beyond the relativized and conflicting truths of individual experience. As the American translator of the *Psychological Investigations* remarks,

> [T]he psychologistic or positivistic reduction of reality (i.e., of reality as experienced) to mental content and ultimately to sensation is tantamount either to making science impracticable or to declaring it impossible. Following Husserl, we can fully grasp the absurdity of this conclusion once we note that its formulation does away with science as the systematic pursuit of truth, and thereby ... with psychological inquiry as well.[66]

Faced with this challenge, Ortega undertook, first, a redefinition of mental phenomena from a broadly phenomenological viewpoint. His conclusion was that subject and object "are inseparable and identical *qua* phenomena" and that though "the mental and the physical are given to us as different kinds of phenomena at the same level of immediacy," neither sphere can be reduced to the other, for the reduction of mental to physical leads to sheer sensationalism, while the opposite process results in some form of idealism.[67] The position he established here was at once an extension of the notion of "I and my circumstances" as developed in *Meditations on Quixote* and an anticipation of the dual critique of idealism and vitalism which he would state more explicitly in *The Modern Theme* (*El tema de nuestro tiempo*) in 1923.

The remaining lectures cover a wide range of themes. Central to them is the effort to establish psychology as an empirical science, while the role of "first and fundamental science" is reserved for philosophy in its quest for "truth as one," above and beyond the particular conflicting truths of individual experience. Taking issue with the skeptical position that we can have no certainty of the existence of truth, Ortega argues that the very reference to "truth"—even in the assertion that we cannot know whether or not it exists—implies a notion of what it is. Genuine doubt, as distinguished from a complacent skepticism, is seen as a sign of the ongoing quest for clarification. (Hence the appearance of "nodal problems" in the sciences is a healthy sign.) The possibility of doubt arises from our belief "in a realm containing literally an infinite number of truths," namely, a world in which each individual person's perception makes the claim that things are as he believes them to be.[68] But this is a different matter from the position of absolute skepticism, which is tantamount to the outright denial of truth. The search for truth in psychology, then, means the effort to determine to what extent the thought content of a proposition or belief coincides with reality.[69] Truth itself, Ortega argues, is not relativistic, although that portion of reality which each person is able to illuminate with his focus of attention is necessarily so in the sense that "[e]very individual is a perceptual organ which can apprehend something that escapes the rest of mankind, and is like an extended arm which alone reaches into certain depths of the universe that remain unknown to others." This fact provides the fundamental challenge to all psychological inquiry, for "[w]hile other disciplines are engaged in the orderly gathering of truths about the world ... psychology turns its back on such truths and on the world, and devotes itself to the study of the mechanism and structure of each subjective consciousness." [70]

Thus far Ortega arrived, along a circuitous route with many digressions, in his attempt to overcome psychologism and lay the foundation of a phenomenologically informed science of psychology. Many of the problems raised in this series of lectures were left just barely sketched out, but the central issue of relativism, as posed by the ineluctable fact of the "radical solitude" in which each human life is rooted, would surface repeatedly in his later work. The *Investigations* are sketchy and rough-hewn at many points, and several of the lectures as preserved consist of little more than telegraphic jottings; but they are nonetheless a significant contribution to the psychology of perception and a bold application of Husserlian phenomenology to a fledgling science badly in need of clarification.

3

A MATURING VOCATION:
1916–1923

This chapter traces Ortega's deepening involvement in domestic politics, the maturation of his journalistic carreer as he began to write for the distinguished liberal daily *El Sol*, and the publication of his next two major works, *Invertebrate Spain* (*España invertebrada*, 1921) and *The Modern Theme* (*El tema de nuestro tiempo*, 1923), both of which appeared first as series of essays in *El Sol*. The first of these represents his analysis of the historical conditions that he believed explained the nation's political crisis during the last years of the Bourbon monarchy; the second provides the first full treatment of his central concept of *la razón vital* (vital reason), his answer to the fatal split in the Cartesian tradition between mind and world.

The troublous years that would terminate with the fall of the Spanish monarchy coincided with the outbreak of the First World War, which began very shortly after the appearance of "Vieja y nueva política" and *Meditations on Quixote*. Although Spain's mounting political crisis took place at some distance from the collapse of the old order occasioned by the Great War throughout much of Europe, the nation's brief economic boom and bust, directly linked to wartime needs north of the Pyrenees, helped to sharpen the cry for reform at home. Spanish intellectuals, viewing the war from the vantage point of Spain's neutrality, were predominantly behind the Allies, and the great majority of those who had joined the Liga de Educación Política Española were liberals who favored the cause of England and France. But it was not a propitious time for new domestic political programs, and the Liga dissolved for all practical purposes after the inaugural speech by Ortega. The influence of its original sponsors was, however, to be felt in many areas of education, politics, and scholarship during the ensuing years, which were turbulent ones for Spain. The remains of the old Restoration parliamentary system continued to operate in feeble oscillation between Liberal and Conservative governments under a monarch who seemed unable to offer new political direction to the country. The First World War itself brought Spain a rush of prosperity as a neutral supplier of goods for both sides, but the economic collapse that was inevitable came in 1918, on the heels of an internal crisis in 1917. The crisis was caused by renewed pressure for Catalan autonomy; a syndicalist protest by lower-ranking army officers, who required more pay and greater evenhandedness in the system for promotions; a major strike in large cities and industrial districts in August of that year; and increasing agitation for a republican alternative to the decrepit parliamentary monarchy. Altogether the war wrought great changes in Spain, despite her nonparticipation. It forced her to a greater consciousness of contemporary European history; it involved her in international trade, mediating diplomacy, and traffic with spies, financiers, and foreign ideas; and it brought into clearer public view a group of intellectuals who sharpened their ideological swords on the whetstone of the European conflict.

Although for some Spanish observers the spectacle of the Great War seemed only to heighten the sense that Spain, provincial and isolationist, remained on the sidelines of modern history, the general effect was to accelerate political and intellectual processes toward crisis and showdown. The years immediately after 1918 brought to Spain what Raymond Carr calls "two complementary stresses: postwar labour troubles and the return of the generals to politics." A series of revolutionary strikes between 1919 and 1923 was brought on by falling prices and unemployment, themselves worsened by the postwar contraction of the European market. Many Asturian mines were closed, and shipbuilding, initially stimulated by the war, decreased notably. Steel mills curtailed production, and, Carr notes, "[l]andowners, who had brought marginal land under cultivation, allowed it to revert to scrub pasture. Thus agricultural under-employment aggravated unemployment in the town." [1] The countryside and peasant life, though stirred by currents of revolutionary unrest from the Russian Revolution of 1917, remained by and large caught in the traditional patterns of absentee ownership and a semifeudal organization. Technical and social innovations were present in only a few major Spanish cities, where the most radical social criticism also burgeoned. In Madrid and Barcelona, and to a lesser extent in smaller cities like Bilbao and Valencia, people were becoming accustomed to material improvements characteristic of many other European cities: streetcars, electric lighting, telephones, and an expanding rail network began to change the average urban Spaniard's sense of life. Literary and artistic modernism also was becoming prominent, particularly in the country's two largest cities.

The year 1917 was portentous both for Spain and for the young philosopher whose political vocation brought him into ever closer contact with national events. In June the Juntas de Defensa were formed by young army officers who banded together to protest low pay, poor administration, and declining morale. At issue too was the worsening situation in Morocco, where Spain was attempting, with little success, to occupy and pacify the protectorate it had shared with France since 1913. The Juntas became the spearhead of wider agitation for renovation and reform, inspiring the organization of groups of civil servants, labor leaders, Catalan nationalists, and socialist and republican politicians. Representatives of these groups met in Barcelona in July 1917, and the seventy-odd diverse delegates called for a constituent assembly to revise the constitution. A series of industrial strikes throughout the summer came to a head in a nationwide strike called for August 10, 1917, by the socialist and the anarcho-syndicalist unions, the UGT and the CNT. But the August strike was quickly broken as the army, loyal under the threat of a proletarian rising, turned against workers and their organizers. Following this crisis, the Juntas continued to agitate for military reform, and further strikes disrupted the Spanish economy over the next few years. The entire process was steadily undermining the credibility and effectiveness of the tottering constitutional monarchy.

Ortega, who had been a regular contributor to the moderate liberal daily *El Imparcial*, had for some time been at odds with the paper's support of the defunct parliamentary system. On June 13, 1917, he announced his break with the family organ in an article entitled "Bajo el arco en ruinas" (Under the Ruined Arch). Recognizing the Juntas as the manifestation of a new level of protest against the legal status quo, he pointed out that they had the gravest exemplary significance for other organized groups, and in fact the general strike of August confirmed his insight. There was, in Ortega's view, only one solution: an assembly that would immediately "reconstitute the constitution."[2] This declaration was too strong for the directors of *El Imparcial*. Shortly thereafter, Ortega left their pages entirely and, in December 1917, began to publish in the newly founded *El Sol*, which became almost from its inception Spain's greatest liberal daily, of a distinctly bolder political cast than *El Imparcial*. For a short period Ortega's friend and the principal financial engineer of *El Sol*, Nicolás María de Urgoiti, had attempted to buy out *El Imparcial* and begin his own daily with its resources. That transaction came near completion, but collapsed at the last moment when the Gasset family regained control of the enterprise. Urgoiti, accompanied by Ortega, was obliged to strike out independently: *El Sol* was born on December 1, 1917. As chief intellectual architect of its critical position toward the Restoration political system, Ortega was immediately a dominant voice in the new paper, which quickly attracted many of the country's best writers and journalists. From the first, its pages were of extraordinary literary quality, as much in matters of art, culture, and social commentary as in political and economic news. For many middle-class families around the country it soon became daily fare.[3]

In the next three years Ortega wrote frequently in the columns of his new forum. Many of the articles appeared as unsigned editorial comment, but an equal number bore his signature. Throughout this period he took the Junta movement as a dangerous but ultimately salutary sign that the "vital" Spain he had invoked in "Vieja y nueva política" was soon to triumph over the old system. He hammered at this point repeatedly in some one hundred articles and editorials between the summer of 1917 and the end of 1920.[4] Repeating the bon mot of Mariano José de Larra at the beginning of the past century, he spoke of a politics of "cuasi," of nothing quite adequate to the situation.[5] He inveighed against the fatal durability of political institutions, warned of their folly those who ignored the plight of the workers, chronicled the failure of Antonio Maura's compromise "national government" of 1918, and called for a Spain open to the postwar world. He foresaw the growing desire in Spain for a dictator who would set things aright, and cautioned against the extremism that polarized around revolution or repression. As the monarchy staggered on through a series of inept and helpless cabinets, Ortega was by turns pessimistic and hopeful about its inevitable end. He still remained a man without party affiliations, for he nurtured the dream that a new politics of national concern would emerge at the hands of the liberal intelligentsia.

With *El Sol* solidly established, Urgoiti sought extensions of its distinguished model. In 1918 he proposed the formation of a new publishing house to be called "Calpe," and by July 1919 the paper announced the beginning Calpe's first venture. The Colección Universal, to be directed by Ortega's colleague the philosopher Manuel García Morente, would provide inexpensive and reputable editions of classic works in literature, history, travel, philosophy, and other fields.[6] The Colección's distinguished career ran from 1918 to 1938, when the civil war interrupted its operation. During those years, it offered an expanding educated minority 308 works in 563 volumes. The great majority of these were translations, though sixty-one outstanding Spanish authors were also represented. With Urgoiti's financial backing, the new enterprise could afford excellent translations. Eventually the Colección Universal was incorporated in the large Austral series of paperbacks, founded in 1937. This later and larger venture, born of the early projects of Urgoiti and Ortega, incorporated numerous other early series undertaken by the Calpe house: a collection on biology and medicine established in October 1920, one on technical studies for engineers established in December of the same year, and, in 1921, the series of Obras Contemporaneas and two other collections, Los Humoristas and Los Poetas, as well as works on geography, history, travel, pedagogy, agriculture and animal husbandry, and jurisprudence. In 1922, under the same auspices, Ortega instituted and directed the series Biblioteca de Ideas del Siglo XX, comprising select translations of the best European works of science and philosophy.[7] In May 1922 the rapidly expanding Calpe enterprise joined with the Catalan house of Espasa to form the new concern of Espasa-Calpe, S. A. By the end of 1922 this most brilliant project in Spanish-language publishing could claim nine collections of the best works in science and letters directed by the country's outstanding scholars and thinkers.

All the while, Ortega continued his observations on the political situation. In general, for the liberal *aliadófilo* (pro-Allies) intellectuals the period of Spanish neutrality between 1914 and 1918 was charged with a heady sense of urgency. In one critic's words, "For many of those men [members of the Spanish League for Political Education] neutrality was a new 'ninety-eight' which revealed the incurable apathy of the people and the decrepitude of political policy."[8] Marked as it was by military syndicalism, economic crisis, and broad social unrest, the period seemed to open the way to precisely that "vital

Spain" that Ortega had seen struggling up through the crust of officialdom and tradition. The domestic crisis combined with the war abroad to confirm for him and other Spanish writers the "heroic" cast of their efforts to bring forth a new world at home. This new self-consciousness on the part of intellectuals gave rise to numbers of small magazines and *tertulia* circles, which sprang up during that time as points of contact for men of ideas and places in which they debated the meaning of their social role.[9] The issue of Spain's "Europeanization" gained new currency. Many of the *aliadófilos* would have been inclined to favor Germany had it not been so clear to them that England and France represented the cause of political liberalism.[10] The complex split that drew them toward one side in politics and the other in high culture raised the level of debate on this question.

Feeling utterly disillusioned with party politics and lacking an adequate liberal hero among the political figures of the day, the intellectuals of Ortega's persuasion (by and large those who had signed the Liga's manifesto) sought to discredit the ailing parliamentary system in any way possible. Thus they united in criticism of the campaign in Morocco; against the government of Antonio Maura; in support of Unamuno when he was removed as rector at Salamanca in 1914; and in sympathetic response to the protests of the Juntas de Defensa in 1917.[11] Most of all, though, they scored the backwardness and recalcitrance to change of the petite bourgeoisie and the status quo political conservatives. Among them, they argued, one found the "implacable" Spaniards whom Ortega observed calmly going about their business amid headlines of the holocaust in Europe.[12]

The lesson such men should have been gleaning from the conflict was made clear by Ortega in a banquet speech (November 18, 1918) honoring the armistice. Saluting the allies for having "brought to the world this peace without precedent in history," he hailed the end of the war as marking the collapse of all that was decayed in the warring nations:

> Only that which is pure, youthful, and possible in the future remains standing.... [t]his means ... that the liquidation in these days of an entire past is being carried out—who knows, not merely of a whole century but even of an entire epoch, of the entire broad age leading from the Renaissance to our time.

Touched by the apparent power of ideas in history, he proclaimed that things are more what our sensibility makes of them than what they may be in themselves. Hence a change of heart would effect a change of world. The New Age was upon men, and a new Spain, moved by "a yearning for justice and the imperative of free modernity," must go forth to meet it.[13] This was after-dinner talk, to be sure, but it underscored Ortega's conception of the prophetic intellectual as the harbinger of modernization.

Politics did not wholly preoccupy Ortega in those years just after *Meditations on Quixote*. In pursuit of his philosophical vocation, for example, he traveled in 1916 with his father, José Ortega Munilla, to lecture in Argentina at the invitation of the Institución Cultural Española, created under the Junta para Ampliación de Estudios in 1914. In the same year the Institución had established a Menéndez Pelayo lecture chair for outstanding Spanish writers and scholars who would visit Argentina. Following the historian-philologist Ramón Menéndez Pidal, Ortega y Gasset was the second Spaniard to accept the invitation. The trip signified a major extension of his pedagogical career, for Argentina would become the principal early recipient of his influence overseas, both directly through his own writing and indirectly through the European thought he introduced there in translation. Ortega visited the country on two further occasions: in 1928 and from 1939 to 1942, during his exile from Spain after the outbreak of civil war in 1936. Although he wrote extensively on Argentine themes, Ortega had remarkably little to say for and to the rest of the vast South American continent. He visited Chile briefly in 1928 and addressed the parliament in Santiago, but was never in any other Latin American country.

Ortega's excursion in 1916 to the most "European" of the Spanish-speaking nations in the New World was consistent with a long European tradition of viewing the American peoples, both white and Indian, as varieties of noble savage. The Argentine population included almost no Indians, and consisted mainly of descendants of the original Spaniards, with a large admixture of German, Italian, English, and eastern European immigrants. This made it more accessible for Ortega's purposes than any of the so-called "Indian" countries— Bolivia, Paraguay, Peru, Ecuador, Colombia, and so on—where large segments of the population spoke little or no Spanish. Further, no other Latin American capital offered him such cosmopolitan variety as Buenos Aires, which, despite its undeniable provincialism, was more like a European capital than Lima, Quito, Santiago de Chile, or even Mexico City.

The Argentine visit of the Ortegas, father and son, was one of a growing number of cultural missions from Spain to Latin America in the early years of this century. The former colonies were still culturally distant, but citizens on both sides of the sea were increasingly aware of possible cooperative efforts toward a larger Spanish-speaking community. There was a movement in several Latin American countries to turn away from the traditional portrayal of the Spanish conquest as cruel, oppressive, and exploitative. The atmosphere Ortega encountered in 1916 was thus more receptive than it might have been twenty or thirty years earlier, when Spain was still something of a colonial power in Cuba.

Ortega brought to this first excursion a centralist viewpoint on the relation of the former colonies to the mother country. Much as he viewed Castile as the compelling center of the Peninsula, so he viewed the Peninsula as the seat of the spiritual force that had brought civilization to the New World. This attitude was typical of many Castilian intellectuals of the late nineteenth and early twentieth centuries, who believed that Spain still had an uplifting and civilizing role to play in Latin America. Their conviction that their region on the high *meseta* of central Spain was the cultural center of the entire Spanish-speaking world defined other parts of Spain and the countries of Latin America as peripheral. Both nationally and across the seas, many of these intellectuals employed the closely related ideologies of *hispanismo* and *hispanidad*, two versions of the idea that Spain was a world-historical culture that had discharged a noble civilizing role during its high imperial age and that still could impart to the world a superior normative vision.

Indeed, for the Spanish philologist Manuel Rodríguez Navas (1848–1922), writing in 1914, enlightened Spaniards could be instrumental in preventing social revolution in Latin America:

> In [Spanish] America the danger of social revolution is greater than elsewhere because of the materialism and lust for wealth of the peoples who have emigrated there. This danger in America is indeed grave unless a vivifying spiritualism comes to the nations of the new continent to compensate for the disequilibrium resulting from excessive materialism.... Spain can supply this spiritualism because it still represents the fine arts, the secular humanist tradition, and chivalry.... Without Spain, [Spanish] America would be an immense portion of the planet dedicated exclusively to material pursuits, without art, ideals, spirituality, that is to say, without a human end or destiny.[14]

The self-important pretension of this declaration indicates the burdensome sense of proprietorship many "enlightened" Spaniards felt toward their "benighted" brothers. Spain's civilizing work, they felt, was obviously not finished, though Rodríguez Navas's inflated rhetoric suggests that many Spaniards sublimated their own poverty and powerlessness, turning it into a "selfless" missionary drive. Ortega, in accord with his own liberal notion that gifted minorities must raise the cultural level of the masses through education rather than immediate concern for improved living conditions, appealed to a culture-hunger in those Latin Americans who could afford to listen. Speaking in a tradition of pan-Hispanic cultural custodianship exemplified by Valera, Menéndez Pelayo, and Unamuno before him, he gave himself over at times to arrogant pronouncements reminiscent of Nietzsche at his worst. In an essay published in the review *Sur* in 1937, Ortega took certain Argentines to task for unscrupulous publishing practices, charging that Latin Americans:

> carry in the deepest confines of their collective soul a source of immorality. Let us not discuss now how that source was formed. The fact is that it exists, and as long as it is not cast out and replaced with an energetic repertoire of moral reactions which will function automatically on every decisive occasion, they cannot dream of ascending to the rank of select peoples, even if one of their countries, like Argentina, has not a few of the rarest gifts needed for such a claim.[15]

The geographical and cultural distance of these peoples from the exemplary centers of European civilization presumably provided a means of ranking them in a hierarchy that made the project of cultural regeneration—ascent "to the rank of select peoples"—coincide with the attainment of moral superiority. In addition, Ortega shared the general Spanish assumption that the Indian cultures and Indian "blood" were inferior to that introduced by Spain. He noted of the peoples indigenous to Latin America that "[i]n their culture they were so far inferior to the colonizers that it was as if they did not exist except as exploitable items."[16]

This brief background sketch in cultural history must be held in mind over against the grand success of Ortega's first tour of Buenos Aires and the Argentine provinces. When he addressed himself to Latin American readers and audiences, he spoke with the double authority of the Spaniard and the European, as one who came both from the seat of the old empire and from the sophisticated cultural terrain of the Old World. His person would doubtless have been less charismatic for Argentine audiences had he been merely another man of letters out of Madrid; but his Latin American public saw him also as the bearer of the latest developments in German phenomenology and one who was thoroughly conversant with contemporary European learning. In Europe, as a young man from a marginal country who had gone north to find the bases of Spanish cultural regeneration beyond the Pyrenees, Ortega was merely the student of a superior intellectual tradition. But when he turned to Latin America, particularly during his first and second Argentine visits, he immediately became a cosmopolitan intellectual mentor who prescribed cultural remedies for the Creoles similar to those he recommended to his own provincial countrymen during the decades preceding the Spanish Civil War.

While the extension of Ortega's influence into Latin America was a perfectly natural process in light of his talent as a writer and his ability to whet the desire of literate minorities in Buenos Aires, Montevideo, and Santiago de Chile to "escape" from the cultural provinces, what especially animated his enthusiastic cultivation of that public was the realization that there in the New World he could be welcomed as an unparalleled cultural authority. Latin America provided him with an arena in which he could dispense with the doubts that troubled him when he measured his own work against that of men like Cohen, Natorp, Husserl, or Scheler. In fact, if the impact of such thinkers reached the Latin American public at all in the early decades of this century, it was generally through the ministrations of Ortega, who, in addition to his role as a harbinger of philosophical "news" from Europe, was producing work of his own which gave Latin American readers the opportunity to see their native tongue superbly employed for philosophical disquisition.

The predominant note of Ortega's Argentine visit in 1916 was, not surprisingly, a mutually celebratory one: he delighted in being touted and toured about as the visiting philosopher, and his public responded eagerly to his numerous and well-publicized lectures. Perhaps the tour was greatly enhanced by the fact that Argentines were watching a father-son team, for both Ortegas received warm reviews on almost every occasion. As a distinguished journalist and novelist, José Ortega Munilla gave several readings on his own. But the public was ultimately more impressed by his philosopher son. He taught them to think, they said, and had reached those who were "missing Plato among so many Durham steer."[17] Young José was the social lion of Buenos Aires from June to December of 1916. Newspaper clippings—with reports of German submarines and European battlefields on the reverse side—recount the round of banquets and speeches that marked his visit. Ortega did not limit himself to the more properly professional series of lectures he delivered on *The Critique of Pure Reason*—in itself an unusual event for Argentine audiences—but also established himself as a cultural mentor by his remarks on the "American soul," the philosophy of travel, and the civilization of the pampas.

Argentina, and especially Buenos Aires, was destined to become the major Latin American extension of Ortega's intellectual horizon, the main location below the Rio Grande where his work was avidly read and discussed. This work of cultural diffusion was eventually promoted by Argentine figures like the novelist Eduardo Mallea, the philosophers Francisco Romero and Coriolano Alberini, and the editor Victoria Ocampo, who established the review *Sur* in 1931. (After the Spanish Civil War, of course, Ortega's influence was extended by Francisco Ayala and other prominent Spanish émigrés who came to live in Buenos Aires.) Clearly, from as early as 1916, Ocampo became Ortega's major connection in the Argentine capital. Born in 1890, she was a spirited upper-class feminist, essayist, and publisher, descended from a long, illustrious line of political and military leaders in Argentina.[18] She grew up with great material comforts, while learning, like other wealthy young Creole ladies, French and English from tutors and governesses. An avid reader from her earliest years, she traveled to Europe at the age of six and became cosmopolitan in a fashion characteristic of those sophisticated Argentines who wished to keep what was then called the "Gran Aldea" (Big Village) of Buenos Aires in touch with the great world across the seas. By the time she met Ortega at a dinner party during his lecture tour of 1916, Ocampo was intensely unhappy in a confining marriage and eager to enter a wider world of learning and thought. The Spanish philosopher, so obviously gifted as a speaker and a public personality, naturally attracted the artistically gifted young woman, who had never heard Spanish spoken with the verve and elegance Ortega displayed. She realized with a shock that she had lived her entire literary and imaginative life within the worlds of French and English literature, while the language native to her own country was almost alien to her. In short, Ocampo saw, under Ortega's influence, that to claim her native culture for the first time as her own would require a linguistic and intellectual reorientation.

For his part, Ortega was flattered by the attention of this tall, striking, highly educated woman. Dining with her on several occasions, he began to envision Ocampo as one of those who would constitute the spiritual aristocracy he sought to form. Drawn to her as a woman, he expected her to be charmed by his brilliant personality. In his attitude toward women, even the most intellectual ones, Ortega was what would today be termed a "male chauvinist," though he had, characteristically, elaborated a theory to defend his views. As in his later *Estudios sobre el amor*, so throughout his life he believed in the Stendhalian and Proustian notion that love is a process of crystallization, in which the lover "creates" that image of the beloved he wishes to see. At the same time, perhaps contradictorally, he believed that nature dictated the relations of man and woman. In this, he was influenced by various literary and philosophical sources, among them Otto Weininger's *Sex and Character* (1903), which offered an archetypal and polarized vision of man and woman as the eternal opposites who must complement each other. Man, in this scheme, was the active principle, while woman was the object, the passive receptive field of his creative drive. As Nelson Orringer has shown, Ortega was also influenced, in his understanding of the creative, imaginative nature of love, by the work of Emil Lucka, particularly *Die drei Stufen der Erotik* (The Three Stages of Eroticism, 1913), which included a consideration of the courtly love tradition and its impact on later Western civilization.[19]

Perhaps Ortega fancied himself something of a courtier or a honey-tongued troubadour in his conversational and epistolary overtures to Ocampo in 1916 and in later years, for she eventually became one of his predilect correspondents; and though she modestly rebuffed the frankly erotic aspect of his first attentions to her, she ultimately wished to retain the friendship and admiration of this magnetic man. Their relationship gradually took a Platonic-literary form, in which Ocampo became one of Ortega's "discoveries" for the *Revista de Occidente*. In 1924 he published her study of Dante, *De Francesca a Beatrice*, adding to it a lengthy epilogue saluting Ocampo and several of her Argentine women friends as contemporary examples of the civilizing female presence that had first demanded of men, in the courtly love tradition, devotion, measure, and grace. Drawing upon the work of Lucka and other sources in his vast reading, Ortega turned his Argentine friend into a latter-day Provençal princess. In more general terms, he announced that woman's highest destiny was to demand perfection of man, uplifting his vision and refining his sensibility. Man, of course, remained the actor, while woman, demanding and aloof, called forth from him his full creative potential: "Manly excellence is rooted . . . in *doing*, that of the woman in *being* [*ser*] and *being there* [*estar*]; or, in other words, man is worthy for what he *does*, woman for what she *is*." [20] Faced with more demanding, high-minded women,

> the hearts of men will begin to beat with a new rhythm, unexpected ideas will awaken in their minds, new ambitions, projects, undertakings will furrow vital spaces, all of existence will march to a rising rhythm, and in the fortunate country where that femininity appears, a historic springtime will burst forth triumphantly, a whole new life—*vita nuova!*[21]

This high-flown rhetoric of organic renewal is echoed contrapuntally at the conclusion of Ortega's epilogue by his invocation of the end of an age that, following in the tradition of Dante, exalted the spirit at the expense of the body and sought to replace life with ideas. The time had come, he suggested in the closing pages, to restore the body to a more vital place in our civilization, for Dante and the whole Christian Middle Ages had bequeathed us a legacy of depreciation of our corporeal existence. There was a flaw in the overly idealistic concentration on the spirit or the soul:

> Once discovered, the life of the soul is too easy because it is imaginary. Nietzsche said "that it is very easy to think things, but very difficult to be them." The body signifies an imperative of fulfillment which presents itself to the spirit. Even more, the body is the reality of the spirit. Without your gestures, Señora [referring to Ocampo], I would know nothing of the golden mystery that is your soul.[22]

Hence a new age of *la razón vital* and of human life as the radical reality was the demand of the day. It was the decline of the spiritualist and the idealistic traditions that Ortega seemed to refer when he remarked:

We are in an hour of universal twilight. An entire moribund orb is sinking, surrounded by the splendid festival of its agony. Even now the fiery disk brushes the cold, green edge of its restless sepulcher. There remains still a bit of daylight.[23]

This somewhat enigmatic image, alluding apparently to a verse from the *Purgatorio* and as well to the twilight of a fading cultural order, may also have alluded to Ortega's view of Spain during the early period of Primo de Rivera's dictatorship. But in the most general terms it was part of his elaborate language of decline and renewal: Spain and the West were ready to give birth to a new era, for which Ortega would be the midwife.

Ocampo was not pleased with what she felt to be the patronizing tone of Ortega's salute. Previously irked by what she judged an offensive remark of his to her in 1916, she had broken off all correspondence with Ortega, a silence that lasted until his second Argentine visit in 1928. Not until three years after that, in 1931, did she finally answer the epilogue of 1924, agreeing with his views on the body and the soul but stressing that a relationship of "mutual respect and mutual independence" between men and women could best promote the desired changes.[24] Ocampo's feminist sensibility had been wounded by Ortega's chauvinistic pride and vanity, which fed on his supposition that she could do what he felt so few women could—understand him. But she was cautious in expressing her pique. In an article of 1933 she took issue with an article of Ortega's of a decade earlier, a piece in his series *El espectador* (The Spectator), which had praised the French poet Anna de Noailles for being an exception to the rule that women's souls were incapable of sincerity:

What I gather to be on the tip of the Spectator's pen does not seem to me to have the indestructible force of conviction. This is not because I doubt for a moment the power of the scrutinizing glance that Ortega casts over the most diverse kinds of topics, but in this particular case, isn't he at a slight disadvantage? In the first place, because he's a man, and secondly, because, although he may be a European by virtue of his privileged intelligence and a citizen of the world by virtue of his roots, he is Spanish by instinct. Thus, to the fatalities of his sex are added those of his nationality. Let's not forget that there are motives behind the Spanish expression: "A queen of Spain must not look out the window." ... I fear that, in a certain sense, all women are, for him, queens of Spain.[25]

Ortega was deeply offended by these charges, and Ocampo agreed to delete them when a version of her article on Madame de Noailles was published, as part of a collection of essays, by the *Revista de Occidente* in 1935.[26]

The relationship with Ocampo was one of the liveliest aspects of Ortega's first visit to Argentina. He later directly influenced and supported Ocampo's review *Sur* (the name was suggested by Ortega), which was modeled in part on the *Revista* in Madrid. He would reach the South American public in other ways as well. The publishing house of Espasa-Calpe, which he had earlier helped to found in Madrid, opened a branch in Buenos Aires in the 1920s, further extending the distribution of titles promulgated by him, many of them translations of major European philosophers and essayists. Meanwhile, there remained missions to pursue back on home ground. Upon returning to Spain in January 1917, Ortega continued to cultivate his intellectual vocation in *El espectador* (The Spectator), a series of free-ranging essays on literary, artistic, and philosophical matters which he had begun to write in the spring of 1916. The second volume appeared in 1917. In all, the ambitious project was to run sporadically through eight volumes between 1916 and 1934. Today many of its pages still seem among the most spirited and felicitous Ortega ever wrote. In these loose collections of work done at a distinct remove from his more occasional journalism, he hoped to find a select public for whom philosophy as literature would be welcome. It was an experiment less democratic than his writing in the editorial pages of *El Sol* and more open, more public, than the intimate circle of his university seminars in philosophy. In pursuing this kind of "intellectual journalism," Ortega was again following the distant example of the French encyclopedists and *philosophes*. Closer to home, the same form had been cultivated by earlier Spanish essayistic *pensadores* like Feijóo, Jovellanos, Larra, Clarín (the pen name of Leopoldo Alas), Ganivet, and Unamuno, but Ortega refined and deepened the literary essay of ideas as no previous Spanish writer had.

From the first, *El espectador* was intended for the leisurely reader. These pieces, "written in a low voice," roved wherever their author chose. Yet, aware of their unevenness, he too modestly announced in the first number:

> There will be issues that may suffer from mental aridity. The writer, no doubt, passes through spiritual zones where no idea arises. Sometimes this

sterile situation endures for months. During them, the reader will have to be content with a "spectator" who reads, extracts, and copies. Other issues will carry a piece of my soul.

The potential reader had to expect as much:

This is an intimate work for readers with intimacy, which neither aspires to nor desires the public at large, which ought, strictly speaking, to appear a manuscript. In these pages, ideas, theories, and commentaries are presented with the character of personal wanderings and adventures of the authors.[27]

A major portion of the first *Spectator* volume was devoted to a critique of Ortega's old friend Pío Baroja.[28] The bulk of the essay is a consideration of Baroja's novel *El árbol de la ciencia* and its protagonist Andrés Hurtado, in whom Ortega divined the writer's rejection of the florid posturing and insincerity of Restoration Spain.[29] This negativism, ultimately boring for the sensitive reader, was nonetheless a dialectically necessary step toward the positive reconstructive attitude Ortega deemed characteristic of his own generation of younger writers. Thus Baroja's "confused babble" was saluted by Ortega, who recognized him, Unamuno, Benavente, Valle-Inclán, Maeztu, and Azorín as the "interior barbarians"—writers who had sprung up around the turn of the century from "the very center of the national mythology," like a new "epicenter" to counter the force of Old Spain, which "continues orbiting around that old center as a dead star rotates upon its core."[30]

Ortega's early study of Baroja was also a semiconfessional stock-taking by the young spectator—as much a definition of his own intellectual vocation as an assessment of Baroja's fiction. In considering the suicide of Andrés Hurtado, Ortega was actually developing a theory of happiness. It was inactivity, he claimed, *accidie* (sloth), and indifference to the world, which opened rifts in our being, leaving us vulnerable to disillusionment and despair. Hyperbole was often Ortega's method, but he was quite in earnest when he held that Baroja's protagonist, morbidly introspective and inactive, was the late, sickly fruit of Spanish indifference toward the everyday world. Ortega's psychic vigor stood in contrast to the infirm melancholoy of Baroja's nonhero, a man incapable of love and work. For Ortega, the point was to learn to love one's condition, to cultivate an *amor fati* without overtones of determinism:

We have to seek out our circumstance, such as it is, precisely in what it has of limitation, of peculiarity, the proper spot in the immense perspective of the world. . . . In short, the reabsorption of circumstance is the concrete destiny of man. The sense of life is, then, nothing other than each one's accepting it, converting it into a creation of ours. Man is the being condemned to translate necessity into liberty.[31]

The turbulent shapelessness of life as Andrés Hurtado perceived it was the sign of being lost in one's circumstances. Baroja's character was suffering the *surmenage* of the romantic aspiration to limitlessness. What he needed instead, Ortega argued, was a salutary sense of the life given to him to live. That was the groundwork of happiness.

Baroja's work was for Ortega a valuable cultural indicator, but he felt it far too prolix and unpruned to constitute an unqualifiedly laudable addition to Spanish letters. If, he argued, there had existed a competent literary criticism in Spain, Baroja would have deepened and disciplined his talent rather than publish a new novel each spring and fall, with all the regularity of a "zodiacal rhythm." The vacuum where responsive criticism should have been was a primary sign of Spain's cultural malaise. Although Ortega felt that the older man deserved praise for his freedom from virtually all rhetorical pre-tension—a rare distinction among Spanish writers—his novelistic dialogue depended too heavily on interjection and contemptuous reproach (*improperios*). Ortega viewed this stylistic tendency as a "na-tional symptom," which revealed the "hysterical" subsoil of Spanish character, reliant as it was on "roguishness, flamenquism, bragga-docio, exaggeration, [and] the pun"—all forms of bravado which covered for insecurity and weakness of character. Baroja's characters cried out as Spaniards did, hysterically, and Baroja himself became "a superior manifestation of Spanish hysteria."[32] This critique pointed to Ortega's own standards of rationality, order, and clarity as opposed to the turgid emotions and theatrical posturing he so re-sented in his countrymen. In fact, he was not himself entirely free of those qualities; but in his work they were tastefully controlled by intellectual rigor. Ortega had from the first the performer's sense of public presence and the particularly Castilian feeling for the drama of man-to-man encounter and public speech, yet he rejected in Baroja's characters the florid forms of these traits. Sobriety, learning, and thoughtfulness were his watchwords: Spain had languished long enough in a surfeit of grand gestures, what he called "phrase making" (*fraseología*).

In the second volume to *El Espectador* (1917), Ortega continued his criticism of literary contemporaries with a long essay on the essayist Azorín.[33] He had already contrasted Baroja and Azorín in the previous volume, finding in the latter the very essence of refinement and delicacy by contrast to the former's rough directness. Azorín's subtle penetration into everyday life and his care for minutiae awakened the sentimental poet in Ortega:

> The philosophy of history gives a rational interpretation of life, but the vital text remains outside it: the vital text is composed of the dilations and contractions of my cordial organ—it is this sensation of radical solitude that now sounds in me like a cry in an infinite empty space—it is that sudden illumination in which the world seemed to float when, among the murmurs of the fiesta, the beloved voice, the voice that was a silver thread, released the essence of a word in my ear.... The philosophy of history concerns itself with nothing of this; it passes, imperturbable, over my heart and yours, reader, and over so many others, like an elephant over the trembling daisies of the field. Ah! And this immediate life, these feelings of each man are, for him, the first thing in the universe.[34]

A genuine sense of history began at home; respect for one's personal history was the cornerstone of concern for the national and collective past. Again, Spaniards needed more of the sensibility stemming from self-exploration. But Ortega found Azorín "quite the contrary of a philosopher of history." He seemed, rather, "a senser [*un sensitivo*] of history," one who cut through the surface of a time, below the sweeping characterizations that allow men to divide the world into high and low, progressive and decadent, illustrious and unfortunate epochs.[35] This quality in the exquisite essayist of Spanish customs and scenes endeared him to the young philosopher. The limpid tranquility so attractive in Azorín came from what Ortega, perhaps in sympathetic identification, called his "aristocratic" posture. One of the elect central to Ortega's dream of a reformed Spain, Azorín provided a rare tonic for the arid imaginative life of the nation, "a morally ill country," divided between "two irreducible ways of thinking about life and things: that of the few intelligent ones and that of the innumerable dull ones." [36]

As on other occasions, Ortega interspersed with his appreciation of

Azorín his own rhetoric of anguish over Spain's intellectual vacuity:

> In Spain, hatred of intellectual work is traditional, inveterate, and
> centuries-old.... The Spain of recent centuries is, apparently, sourly
> hostile to the life of the spirit. Almost a century has passed since Larra, in
> some superb pages that the eight or ten people who today in Spain are
> dedicated to pure literary passion cannot read without... emotion, gave
> a cry of desperation: "To write in Madrid is to weep...." Save some
> points on the periphery, Spain offers to the visitor the spectacle of a dying
> gesture still not done with. Spain is a vast ruin stretched from sea to sea,
> between Maladeta and Calpe.[37]

Travel in other lands, he continued, showed that life elsewhere was
more organized and functioned better than in Spain: the walls of
houses were in good repair; doors closed smoothly on their hinges;
windows slid in their grooves. Ortega's mounting list of material
malfunction pointed as well toward the scrap pile of calcified ideas or
mere topics upon which Spanish minds were accustomed to feed.
Azorín brought this dilemma to the fore because his books were
steeped in melancholy, decay, and ruins: decrepit palaces, bookish
men in isolated country towns, forgotten books discovered in second-
hand kiosks. His was a doleful, dirgelike recitation of national en-
feeblement in a key that had been in vogue with a select literary
public in Spain since the end of the nineteenth century. Antonio
Machado had caught the strain perfectly in his phrase, in *Campos de
Castilla* (1917), "Castilla miserable, ayer dominadora." Azorín made
the same sad music in the richly evocative prose of his own *Castilla*, of
which Ortega noted:

> In this book there arises a slow, paralytic world, towns that live in a coma,
> immobilized fields, pools of hardly stirring water encircled by lofty elms
> with leaves that barely tremble. It is a quiet and unchanging life, like that
> of the wise lizards on the blackish green garden stones gazing at the solar
> grandness with fine, shining little bead-eyes. Read *Castilla* or *Lecturas
> españolas* and you will feel something like a cosmic inertia.[38]

For Ortega, Azorín rightly preferred to portray the "vulgar" or
ordinary life over the poetic and heroic. He chronicled the daily
habits and quirks of the national life, the endless repetitions of which
contributed to its "thickening." With characteristic sympathy,
Ortega composed his piece on Azorín in a setting ideally suited to the

latter's temper: the courtyard of the Escorial, Philip II's great monastery-mausoleum. Closing his remarks on Azorín's relentlessly quotidian tone, Ortega was interrupted by the cloister bell: "It is eleven o'clock. The guard asks me to leave the garden shimmering with sun. It is the hour in which the friars descend from their cells and proceed to stroll as they did a century, two centuries, three centuries ago." [39] Azorín, whose Nietzschean phrase for that kind of experience was "To live to see things return," attracted Ortega by his power to discern beyond the surface record of custom and local tradition the substratum of "the power of persistence and monotony which in his [Azorín's] opinion represents the world's ultimate substance." [40] But for the younger man such repetition boded ill for the nation:

> We [Spaniards] still live in the forms of the Middle Ages, and of those the profoundest is the lack of individual personality. Life runs on in typical, not individual, variety. The businessman, professor, congressman, or soldier lives as a type, but exceedingly rare is the man who imposes upon our society his individual destiny, who lives in his own fashion. The narrowness of our environment does not permit one to exceed the moulds of normalized and corporative life. [41]

In addition to Ortega's multiple publishing ventures, including continued production of *El espectador*, he furthered his career during the years just after the Great War as one of the nation's leading political journalists. While he did not neglect philosophical and literary themes during this period, there was a stretch of nine years between *Meditations on Quixote* and the next major philosophical publication, *El tema de nuestro tiempo* (1923). In 1921 he published the third volume of *El espectador* and the timely essay *España invertebrada* (*Invertebrate Spain*, a portion of which was published in English, together with several brief essays by Ortega, in 1937; a complete English translation of which appeared in 1974); and in July 1923 the first number of what would quickly become the best monthly review in the language, the *Revista de Occidente*.

Like a number of Ortega's works, *Invertebrate Spain* first appeared as a series of articles in *El Sol*, in 1920. Composed, as he remarked, under the duress of Spain's prolonged political crisis, it was a brilliant but cavalier work that presented a compelling argument built upon the flimsy base of mere historical intuition. In a prologue to the fourth edition of the book (June 1934), Ortega announced that he had never properly intended to write a book on the theme. Had there been, he argued, more adequate historical research on the Spanish past, he would not have undertaken such an impressionistic essay; but as there was not, he stepped into the breach in a role for which he was ill prepared. Here, as elsewhere, he advanced his bold interpretatons in an impromptu manner, pointing to Spain's troubles and the press of time to justify his temperamental preference for the journalistic sketch or *aperçu* as against scholarly, systematic development:

> Life is quite the contrary of the Greek Kalendas. Life is haste. I needed without fail or delay to clarify a little for myself the direction of my country, in order to avoid in my conduct at least the great stupidities. Someone in the middle of the desert feels ill, desperately ill. What will he do? He is simply a poor man from whom life is escaping. What will he do? He writes these ... to whoever has the unusual capacity to feel himself, in full health, dying and, for that reason, ever disposed to be reborn.[42]

This book was the first major statement of Ortega's growing preoccupation with the massive egalitarian rejection of cultural and political authority in the modern age. It may be read as a prologue to the theses he would develop more insistently in *La rebelión de las masas* (*The Revolt of the Masses*, 1930) and in numerous shorter works. In the simplest terms, it argued that Spaniards preferred an anarchic separatist individualism to organic, structured communities based on the proper relationship between the leaders and the led. Even though the book was seriously hampered by the bravado of statements like "Spain is a thing made by Castile, and there are reasons for suspecting that ... only Castilian heads have organs capable of perceiving the great problem of Spain as a whole," in it Ortega gave cogent attention to continuing national problems.[43]

He argued, preliminarily, that a nation is forged and prospers only when there is a shared "project" that draws men together in the service of an envisioned future. Castile had been the historical home of this program and, in her union with Aragon, had given Europe its first properly national state. This achievement was ill starred, however, for rather than indicating a superior will to integration, it sprang, Ortega argued, from the overcivilized weakness of the early Visigothic invaders of Spain. While France had been shaped by the powerful feudalism of the younger, more vigorous Franks, Spain had been settled by a people who no longer had the strength to establish powerful feudal dominions. Had there been true lords and vassals, the Christian Reconquest of the Peninsula, which lasted eight centuries, could have been carried out more efficiently. Therefore, Spain had suffered since medieval times from disintegrative "particularism." Her political golden age was achieved prematurely under Ferdinand and Isabella and lasted only until the end of the sixteenth century. Since then her history had been one of centrifugal breakdown: after a brief period as the Roman Empire of modern history, she lost her claims in Austria, Italy, and the Low Countries; then her overseas colonies; and finally, in the twentieth century, her centralist control over the uneasily integrated national peripheries—the Basque country, Catalonia, the Levante, Galicia, and even Andalusia. Ortega summarized his deft, impressionistic analysis in metaphorical terms: "All this [tendency toward separatism] is like the sad spectacle of an autumn centuries long, which is marked periodically by gusts of wind that tear whole armfuls of yellow leaves from the tired tree."[44]

Castile had presumably made Spain a nation, and now was to blame for unmaking her. Just as the mass of men needed a vigorous, genuine aristocracy to feel comfortable in their station, the country needed a forceful, centralizing will to power in order to overcome its tendency toward regionalized disintegration. Lacking a national enterprise, Spain had become brittle and desiccated. She had none of the "social elasticity" that allows distinct groups and professions to work cooperatively, transcending local vested interests. This drama was being played out on the three levels of the nation, the social class, and the individual. Invertebration (or lack of hierarchical social structure) was exacerbated, too, by the appearance in all groups—but particularly among the middle and upper classes—of the "mass man," who refused to recognize authority and leadership. The old cry that Spain lacked proper men to lead really meant, Ortega believed, that there were no masses willing to be led. Taking a less sympathetic view of the army Juntas than he had espoused in 1917, he cited them as an example of how groups inspired by self-interest could turn national problems to their own end. As the social fabric was weakened by each such assault, particularism was bound to result in *pronunciamientos* or "direct action."

In Ortega's analysis of the aberrant relationship between the Spanish masses and their would-be leaders, it is sometimes difficult to know where the trouble really lies. On the one hand, he argued that it was the common people who, for lack of distinguished leadership, had shouldered all Spain's historic enterprises. On the other hand, great men were lacking in Spain because the people had refused to lend them sufficient support. Granted, "the people" seemed to have turned into a rebellious "mass" in modern times and would no longer be disposed to honor a potential leader, but one cannot decide whether Ortega thought Spain had all along lacked great men, or whether the people had been from the beginning resistant to their guidance. In spite of his attempt to give a historical analysis of this problem, Ortega fell back finally on an ahistorical idea of national character, which controlled what a people made of itself: "A people cannot choose between various modes of life—either they live in their own fashion, or they do not live. It is useless to hope that an ostrich which is unable to run will fly like an eagle." [45] Presumably the people as a whole would follow their collectively destined path in any case, but with proper leadership Ortega believed them able to build a lasting civilization.

Since neither individuals nor traditional classes nor the professions could be counted on for the nation's future, Ortega sought the formation of elite groups to be drawn from the various social classes. These vanguard "cells" would break up old vested interests and class alignments. Otherwise, troubled by self-centered regionalism and the obstinate rejection of standards of critical authority, Spain would be rent asunder in the struggle for local autonomy. Further, in order for the nation to profit from examples of cultural excellence from other European countries, she required a coherent sense of her own internal goals. Thus Ortega's plan to bring Spain up to the level attained elsewhere implied the need for a single national program of modernization in culture, politics, education, and social life. The Achilles' heel of this vision, as Ortega was doubtless aware, was the historical weakness of the Spanish bourgeoisie, from which he must draw his support. Both before and after *Invertebrate Spain*, his grand plan was doomed to languish for lack of a substantial public whose interests could be truly addressed in the glowing rhetoric of national "renewal" and the promise of cadres of middle-class, professional leadership.

In the final portions of the book, which clearly point toward *The Revolt of the Masses*, Ortega gave himself to rash overstatement. He was hardly willing to grant Spain the status of an organized society.

Both "exemplariness" and "docility" had disappeared in the dust of Spanish history. His historical arguments were weakest in these later chapters, which were riddled with strident pronouncements: for example, the statement "We are forced to the conclusion that except for a few fleeting moments, the whole of Spanish history has been the history of a long decay," or the claim that Spanish history was "fellah-ized" and moved at the changeless pace of North Africa.[46] But Ortega's lack of historical scholarship was not really the point at issue, for he meant to convert the national past into a storehouse of suggestive metaphors for his own critical purposes.

Until the early 1920s, the great bulk of Ortega's writing had been concerned with Spanish politics and culture. But he returned to philosophy with *El tema de nuestro tiempo*, presented first as a course at the University of Madrid during the winter of 1921–1922. Ernst Robert Curtius, reviewing both *España invertebrada* and the new book in 1924, felt Ortega's work belonged "to that genre of sociological-intellectual analysis that is so abundantly represented in France (Taine, Renan, Barrès, Maurras) and that is all but undeveloped in Germany."[47] Yet, finding a national basis in his friend's writing, Curtius averred that Ortega's "perspectivism" came quite logically from the pen of a Spaniard:

> Spain is geographically and mentally the eccentric country. It provides an excellent observation post for a spectator of Europe. Undisturbed by rivalry, by hatred, or by egocentricity, he will grasp the movement of the various national mentalities more clearly than they can themselves.[48]

In *El tema de nuestro tiempo* Ortega vouched for the acuity of Curtius's insight by making the Spanish political crisis emblematic of the state of European culture as a whole. Even his call for renovation in philosophy—to heal the split between "reason" and "life"—was connected in this book to his feeling that Spain lay in coma, as if this stasis dictated an intellectual mission toward which all Europe was leaning, waiting for Ortega to recognize it as "the theme of our time." Generalizing from the case of Spain, he remarked:

> I believe that in all of Europe, but most especially in Spain, the present generation is one of . . . deserters. Few times have men lived less clearly with themselves, and perhaps never has humanity borne so docilely forms that are not akin to it, holdovers from other generations that do not respond to its intimate beat. From this derives apathy, so characteristic of

our time, for example, in politics and art. Our institutions, like our spectacles, are stiffened residues of another age.[49]

Spain lay in the shoals of the sea of history, unable to go forward or back. Clinging to the tatters of tradition, Spaniards had abandoned themselves to living with a potpourri of outworn and formalistic ideas and styles of life. The result was a nation of men and women acting out the parts of their grandfathers, seeming to illustrate the truth of Marx's observation, in *The Eighteenth Brumaire of Louis Bonaparte,* that the second appearance of historical events is farce rather than tragedy.

The first chapter of *El tema de nuestro tempo,* a sketch of Ortega's "theory of generations," provided the theoretical basis for his idea that the men of his generation were destined to break this stasis. Employing a dubious arithmetical scheme based on the classical generational unit of fifteen years, he sought a "scientific" foundation for the idea that each generation represented a certain historical level or "height" (*altura*) that mandated a fresh imperative for each new human "wave." On this assumption, he posited as the philosophical imperative for his generation the task of overcoming the inherited di- chotomy between devitalized rationalism and a mindless vitalism, the latter a legacy of Nietzsche's brilliant attack on the ossified forms of European thought and culture. The Scylla and Charybdis confront- ing Ortega's generation could also be expressed, he noted, in terms of "relativism" and "rationalism." The former, concerned to recognize the enormous variety of life, ended in a thoroughgoing skepticism toward objective values; while the latter suppressed life's varied creative energies in the interest of an unduly formalized order. Think- ing and living had become tragically opposed; but true thought was a "vital necessity for the individual . . . ruled by the law of subjective utility," helping him make an "adjustment to things" which re- spected "the objective law of truth."[50] Cultural renewal could come about only through a continuous interplay between the grounding of thought in the elemental creative force of life and the objective truths to be discerned in art, morality, law, science—in a word, culture. Human life as *natura naturans* (to employ the language of Spinoza) reaches constantly beyond its subjectively experienced and elemental biological basis toward an orderly structure (*natura naturata*). Only thus can the estranged poles of biology and spirit be reunited, life disciplined, and culture pruned of what Nietzsche had called its "Alexandrian" excesses.

In this critique Ortega made his clearest break thus far with the tradition of German idealist thought and its neo-Kantian inheritors in Marburg:

> We have seen with terrible evidence in the evolution of Germany to what extent it is illusory to wish to isolate from life certain organic functions that are given the mystical term "spiritual." As the Frenchman of the eighteenth century was a "progressivist," the nineteenth-century German has been "culturalist." All the high German thought from Kant until 1900 can be gathered under the rubric "philosophy of culture." Immediately upon entering it, we see its formal resemblance to Medieval theology. There has been a supplanting of entities, and where the old Christian thinker said "God," the contemporary German says "Idea" (Hegel), "Primacy of Practical Reason" (Kant-Fichte), or "Culture" (Cohen, Windelband, Rickert). That illusory divinization of certain vital energies at the expense of the rest, that disintegration of what can only exist together—knowledge and breath, morality and sexuality, justice and a healthy endocrine system—brings with it the great organic failures, the enormous collapses.[51]

This critique of the term "spiritual" as applied to human energies rooted in earthly and bodily existence—a sign of Ortega's movement toward the later proclamation of "my life" as the "radical reality" (1929)—points up his increasing distance from the texts upon which he had cut his teeth in Germany and clarifies his intention to be "nada moderno" (not at all modern) but "muy siglo veinte" (very much of the twentieth century). Concern with spiritual matters should be left to theologians, and their incorporation within the lexicon of neo-Kantian thought explains his remark in *El tema de nuestro tiempo* that "[c]ulturalism is a Christianity without God."[52] As exemplified in Cohen, Rickert, and others, the devotion to culture as the form of mankind's highest self-realization divorced "spiritual" values from their roots in life. A rationalized Christianity (or, in Cohen's case, Judaism) tended toward the deification of goodness, truth, and beauty in themselves. But, Ortega realized, since the unhoused religious impulse responsible for this transfer was itself an emanation of man's "vital" energies, the culturalist construct of neo-Kantianism must be corrected. The worship of culture (or its correlates: progress, the future, utopianism) caused men to lose touch with "the initial act of culture," which was "the choice of a point of view" in order to impose shape on the relative chaos of undisciplined spontaneous energy.[53] It was precisely in "that strange activity of our spirit that we call 'preferring' " that life made its connection with culture: "preferring" gives to desire and impulse a focus that not only constructs culture but de-constructs it in the spirit of jovial "play" which Ortega saw as the source of all significant human creation. Just as art, morality, law, and philosophy itself must transcend both any abstract sense of duty and any demand of sheer necessity alone, so the "sportive" excess of human energy, unexhausted by the immediate tasks of living, must assert its freedom to revoke or overturn the forms of its earlier design that threaten to entrap it. Such was the import of what, in the slightly earlier essay "El *Quijote* en la escuela," Ortega had called "vida ascendente" (a concept drawn from Nietzsche), the idea that the end of life is *to live*, but in such a way that one's energies reach buoyantly outward toward others and toward the constant recreation of the world. This "adventure" of life must affirm itself as "more life" without falling into an irrational moil of whirling passions and animal desires. In this regard, as Pedro Cerezo Galán has recently argued, earlier critics of *El tema de nuestro tiempo* like José Ferrater Mora, J. H. Walgrave, and Ciriaco Morón Arroyo were wrong to claim that Ortega's concept of "life" was still unformed and merely "biologistic" in 1923.[54]

In the final chapter of *El tema*, "La doctrina del punto de vista," Ortega asserts that each man, each people, and each era must come into the truth in his or its own fashion. Since there is neither a single preestablished path nor any transcendental objective truth to be known independently of the knowing subject, each vital project reveals yet another facet of the total truth, which can finally be known only through the juxtaposition of all perspectives. This sum total would be God, who "enjoys all the points of view and in His limitless vitality gathers up and harmonizes all of our horizons." Thus God "sees things through men, men are the visual organs of the divinity."[55]

Ortega's attempt in this book to revitalize reason participated in a long tradition reaching back to the period of the late Enlightenment. Rousseau's critique of the social contract was only the most salient manifestation of a broad critique of rationalistic concepts of man and culture. The romantics in Germany and England were redefining man's psychic life by exploring the power of feeling and intuition. In philosophy, Schopenhauer, Schelling, and Kierkegaard posed the challenge to Hegelian rationalism. The poetic and philosophical exploration of subjectivity, by intensifying the sense of an estranged "inner" world separate from the extended outer one, helped bring the tradition of Cartesian dualism to crisis. The more one journeyed into the "interior," as it were, the more urgent it became to salvage the abandoned world of ordinary experience. Such was the ground upon which *Lebensphilosophie* would eventually lay down the rudiments of understanding what later came to be called "the life-world." In response to the subjectivization of art and thought, and also to an objective world dominated by politics, industry, and material growth, the idea of "life" underwent semantic transformation throughout the nineteenth century. The development of modern biology gave the term an unprecedented scientific complexity, but in philosophy and literature too its meanings shifted and were diversified. Sometimes scientific and philosophical ideas overlapped, as in Bergson's concept of "creative evolution" or, more thoroughly, in the interplay between William James's research in *The Principles of Psychology* and his later philosophical explorations of what he termed "the world of life." In the second half of the past century, the notion of a "life force," surging forth from its organic and unconscious roots, was found across a wide spectrum of Western thought. The sources of life, like its refinements in enlightened self-awareness, came to seem grand and mysterious. Man's conscious mind—the intellect, the ego —was often perceived as arising from great depths and aspiring to distant heights.

One historian of the period remarks:

As early as 1866, E. S. Dallas [whose *Gay Science* helped establish the idea of the artist as a high priest, a "whole man" called to save others from excessive civilization and overstrained consciousness] had observed that "outside consciousness there rolls a vast tide of life, which is, perhaps, even more important to us than the little isle of our thoughts which lies within our ken." At the end of the century the theme was being sounded more and more frequently: life is something which *transcends* the intellect and which is largely inaccessible to empirical inductive reasoning; there are vast areas of truth not known by man.[56]

As if in response to the waning of traditional religious faith and the new stresses and anxieties of modern life after the Industrial Revolution, this sentiment of unplumbed human powers issue around the end of the century in works like Richard Maurice Bucke's *Cosmic Consciousness* (1898) and James's *Varieties of Religious Experience* (1902). The entire preceding century was marked by ecstatic expression of life's possibilities and dangers. Nietzsche's injunction to "live dangerously," like Melville's idea that we all live as if in a whaling dory bent on the chase, expressed the conviction that men must break through, in risk and excess, to the deeper springs of their existence.

Vitalism, aestheticism, irrationalism, organicism, and the proto-existentialist thought of Kierkegaard, Dostoyevsky, and Nietzsche—all contributed to the sense that the very living of life was a kind of sacred, perilous, and uniquely distinguished drama. Novelists and poets, often concentrating on the wonder of the lived moment, saw life as an art and a new form of religion. This ecstatic celebration of life's wondrous immediacy and depth was a revolt against both positivist and idealist conceptions of reason; but the larger aim was often to restore validity to reason by connecting it to newly explored realms of emotion, intuition, and subconscious awareness. Mind and life, often opposed in extreme forms of vitalism, needed to be remarried—or perhaps married truly for the first time. In Ortega's view of the nineteenth century, the legacy of Cartesian reason was undergoing a prolonged crisis. His philosophy of culture, influenced by biological models and by Spengler's *Decline of the West*, stressed the organic rhythm of history, within which cultures waxed and waned. In this perspective, the nineteenth century was the late autumn of the Age of Reason.

But the natural analogy breaks down, for, as he himself proclaimed, the autumn was already shot through with signs of spring: claims for the renewal of life burgeoned along with alarums of its decline. Many analysts and artists of the era perceived this drama in terms of an authentic or "real" life pitted against bourgeois routine and the stultifying forms of civilization. While modern novelists dissected the falsity and pretense of much modern life, other enlightened spirits sought in art, poetry, and mystical forms of religion an antidote to what Hegel had forecast as the "Age of Prose." Despair of culture led dialectically to an intensified self-cultivation and a corresponding cult of "life" celebrated for its very "quickness" by the representative voice of D. H. Lawrence early in our century. On both sides of the turn of the century, "life" took on what C. S. Lewis has called a "semantic halo," suggesting variously an uprush of spontaneous energy, a stern duty, a high calling, and a holy devotion for the communicant. In England, Thomas Carlyle, Matthew Arnold, Walter Pater, and John Henry Newman enjoined passionate seriousness in what Ralph Waldo Emerson, on the other side of the Atlantic, had called "the conduct of life." In Germany, the ideal of *Bildung* extolled the development of character as man's highest end. In Spain, Krausist visions of a "new man" combined with the restless work of writers like Ganivet, Unamuno, and Baroja to challenge orthodox Catholic doctrine on human nature and behavior. In the midst of this widespread questioning, the sheer fact of living itself—beyond any ideal of living correctly or wisely—took on a peculiar value.

But the valuation of life in its precious, one-time-only immediacy revealed a concomitant preoccupation with mortality, for the more life one had, the more death one faced. As the wish to seize and hold the day intensified, so too did the anxiety (or *Angst*) over its loss. Celebrants of life for its own sake seemed to say that nothing stood between man and death except life itself—a truism, to be sure, yet a key reflection of the disappearance of faith in a loving God who records the fall of every sparrow. In the cry "life is real, life is earnest," one heard the perplexity over what to do with life. An abiding crisis of confidence was evident. To speak, as so many English Victorian sages did, of "living life" produced a curious tautology. In earlier times life had been seen as at the service of a cultural ideal or a transcendental faith, the value of which sometimes required the sacrifice of life itself. Now, throughout Europe, if perhaps somewhat less in Spain, the valorization of sheer living implied a morbid undercurrent, a sense that human existence was somehow "dehumanized" by the discontents of civilization.

The burden of refined culture in increasingly complex industrialized societies seemed to impel men to strike through the mask toward a pure vein of experience. In so thinking, philosophers and poets from Kierkegaard and Nietzsche to Rilke and Stefan George forged a new vocabulary of life. Prominent in it was a fascination with the daily and "ordinary" facts of human existence, later given formal status in *Lebensphilosophie* and phenomenology. The greatly weakened Christian sacramental understanding of the world brought progressive secularization, obliging the sensitive soul to "save" the world by

dignifying what before had been considered merely prosaic or insig-
nificant. But the impulse to scrutinize (and sometimes to exalt) the
ordinary entailed the risk that it, like unaided or undirected life, could
not bear the resultant intensity of expectation. Speaking of the modern intellectual revolution that "reduced the stature of the symbol to
the merely symbolic," the contemporary critic Erich Heller has summarized the dilemma: "Reality, freed from its commitments to the
symbol, became more real than before. The hand of man, reaching
out for his reality, was no longer unsteadied by the awe and fear of the
symbolic mystery.... As reality became more real, so the symbol
became more symbolic and art more artistic." And he adds:

> The portraitist of this situation is Van Gogh. He painted the tree of
> Rilke's [first Duino] elegy, the sunflower, the chair and the boots that are
> the chance receptacles of all the homeless energy of the spirit which had
> once its lawful house with Giotto's angels and madonnas.... This bough
> of almond blossom ... this chair ... get much more than their due of the
> spirit, almost bursting with its superfluity. It is a mere moment of explo-
> sion that separates Van Gogh's objects from the distorted fragments of
> surrealism.... [In sum, the situation testifies to] the absence from our lives
> of commonly accepted symbols to represent and house our deepest feel-
> ings. And so these invade the empty shells of fragmentary memories,
> hermit-crabs in a sea of uncertain meaning.[57]

In a related manner, certain modern philosophers responded to
the crisis of the previously overarching symbolic order by seeking to
understand the components of the human life-world. Whether in
Kierkegaard's autobiographical personae, in Dilthey's patterns of
cultural experience, James's "radical empiricism," or Scheler's and
Husserl's phenomenological analyses, the search continued. The later
existentialist revision of this quest was carried out most systematically
in Heidegger's *Sein und Zeit* (1927), but in a looser, though perhaps
clearer, more pungent way, Ortega had realized by 1914 that human
life, self-evidently present to each of us at every moment, embraces
and annuls the intellectualized dichotomy of self and world. His call
in *Meditations on Quixote* to embrace the humble presence of those dear,
mute things from and among which we make our lives—not unlike
Gerard Manley Hopkins's beautiful line "There lives the dearest
freshness deep down things"—combined with his sense of the passion
of reason in *El tema de nuestro tiempo* to ground all intellection in an

earthly human condition. At the same time, the mind remained essentially unlimited in its imaginative reach. Thought, never simply the activity of a separate, self-affirming "consciousness" or a Kantian transcendental subject, is always linked to the pre- and extra-conceptual priorities of one's life. By 1923, the concept of *la razón vital*, though still sketchy and somewhat abstract, was beginning to emerge as the rubric under which Ortega would seek to complete the renewal of human reason—a renewal toward which so many of his predecessors, including the greatest iconoclast, Nietzsche, had worked.

4

PRAECEPTOR HISPANIAE:
1923–1929

During almost six and a half years (from September 13, 1923, to January 1, 1930) Spain was ruled by the military dictator General Miguel Primo de Rivera y Orbaneja (1870–1930), whose regime will be described later in this chapter. Despite the fact that hostility soon developed between the dictator and many of the nation's leading intellectuals and that he later sought to quash student protests against some of his policies by closing the universities, Spain under his command was rich in cultural and intellectual development. Ortega, piqued by the spectacle of what he considered a crude "mass man" as head of state, bent his own energies all the more passionately to the task of cultural modernization. A scant two months before Primo assumed power, Ortega had founded the first journal to be truly his own, the monthly *Revista de Occidente* (Review of the West). By turns pessimistic and optimistic about the future of Spanish culture— which he believed could prosper in spite of the politically unstable situation created by King Alfonso XIII's departure—he invoked in the first number of the *Revista* (July) a select public ready, he assumed, for "thoughtful news" of intellectual events beyond its own national frontiers:

> There exists a large number of persons in Spain and Spanish America who take pleasure in a joyous and serene contemplation of ideas and art. It interests them as well to receive from time to time clear and thoughtful news of what is felt, done, and suffered in the world; neither the inert report of the facts nor the impassioned and superficial interpretation offered by the newspaper fits with their desire. This curiosity ... is, behind its appearance of dispersion and lack of discipline, quite natural. ... It is the vital curiosity that the individual of alert nerves feels for the vast germination of life around him, and it is the desire to live face to face with deep contemporary reality.[1]

The first issue of the *Revista* featured a story by Pío Baroja and articles by Ortega, Georg Simmel, and Adolf Schulten (the archaeologist who was seeking the "lost" city of Tartessos in Andalusia). Also included were shorter notes and reviews by old friends and collaborators like Fernando Vela, Antonio Espina, Alfonso Reyes, and Antonio Marichalar. This gathering of the faithful was a primary *modus operandi* of the review, as its historian Evelyne López-Campillo has observed:

> Ortega is forty years old; he is at the height of his powers; his hopes of playing a role in the transformation of Spanish culture are being realized. He had prepared a group of very qualified collaborators (among others, those of the Calpe house, of *El Sol*, of *La Voz*, the evening paper published by *El Sol*); he had been gathering, since the foundation of Calpe, a great quantity of information in all fields; and he had established relations, national and international, that permitted him to undertake the organization of a review.[2]

The *Revista* reached a relatively restricted public (its press run was three thousand copies per issue between 1923 and 1936), but it was clearly, after *El Sol*, the most influential of Ortega's projects. In the review, he could turn away from the elusive immediacy of Spanish politics toward what he felt were more enduring themes worthy of slowly matured treatment. Exceptionally sensitive to recent innovations in physics, art, ethics, history, and other fields, Ortega saw a whole horizon of new concepts in the West around 1900. He surveyed them as an omnivorous and eclectic reader who strove to be and to appear *au courant* with the latest developments. Rarely afraid to pronounce on countries, writers, and areas of study which he knew only as a brilliant spectator, he developed a penchant for short, impressionistic articles on every subject. His self-appointed role as a harbinger of the best work being done elsewhere was and remains typical of gifted intellectuals located in marginal or "underdeveloped" countries.

As a brilliant attempt to combat Spain's cultural isolation, the *Revista* projected Ortega's view of modern European culture as it had developed over the last few decades. He intended the review to rescue the general literate public from the threat of intellectual and spiritual chaos he discerned in the postwar period. The *Revista* would speak for and to the entire "West," as its title suggested, for the idea of the unity and hegemony of Western culture—more precisely, *European* culture—was still very much in force for Ortega. Europe, he believed, must reaffirm its role as the historic crucible of a great humanistic and scientific civilization. In this sense, the *Revista* was also a response to Spengler's influential *Decline of the West* (published in Germany between 1918 and 1922), of which Ortega early promoted the Spanish translation. The *Revista*'s affirmative tone announced that instead of twilight, the West was actually experiencing the sunrise of a new day.

The greatest strengths of the magazine were the extensive variety of its subject matter and the high quality of its contributors. It provided the best and most exciting forum in Spain for aspiring young intellectuals concerned with the fate of high culture. Its frequently remarked lack of concern for contemporary Spanish politics and society did, however, indicate a real limitation on its range of inquiry. The *Revista* seemed to prefer to ignore the old truth that an apolitical outlook in itself implies a covert ideological position. As Manuel Tuñon de Lara suggests, it very skillfully perpetuated Ortega's vision of a select group of charismatic men of ideas who would awaken their more benighted countrymen. In fact, such would-be leaders were isolated from the bulk of the population both by their taste and by their assumptions about the power of knowledge in the world. In Tuñon's words:

> There is . . . a level . . . on which Ortega's influence has been fundamental: that of two university generations shaped in the spirit of . . . the negation of the leading role of the multitudes. . . . Spanish intellectuals of the first order, who turned toward very diverse attitudes and works, began from a common repertory of Orteguian attitudes and ideas carried to the various fields of philosophy, law, sociology, history, the essay, and, without doubt, politics. The desire to *see clearly* and "to be more intelligent," outlined by Ortega through the channels of *El Sol* and *Revista de Occidente*, together . . . with the elitist spirit, with sidereal distancing . . . from simple men and women, from the stuff of which the nation is made—has created a whole cultural current in Spain.[3]

Tuñon's Marxian critique is not unjust. Nonetheless, the *Revista* was a remarkable achievement. From the very start, it established in Madrid a native product fully worthy of comparison—in quality if not in viewpoint—with Croce's *La Critica* in Italy, T. S. Eliot's *Criterion* in England, the *Nouvelle Revue Française* in France, the *Neue*

Deutsche Rundschau in Germany, and, slightly later, the *Partisan Review* in the United States. The *Revista's* express preference for material from the best European writers and theorists reflected Ortega's sense of intellectual priorities and his impatience with the poverty of much national scholarship. Unconcerned finally with Tuñon's "simple men and women" who were the putative salt of the Spanish earth, Ortega revealed here, as elsewhere, something of the elitist tendency that marked his role as a cultural innovator and popularizer. In choosing a medium and an intellectual level that restricted his public impact, and by developing a rhetoric of "deep reality," to which thinkers like himself and readers of the *Revista* had privileged access, he compensated for his growing sense of political ineffectiveness in the 1920s.

Although Ortega was not solely responsible for its editorial policy, the general tendencies of the magazine constituted a kind of cultural topography of Europe as he perceived it. Perhaps most notably, the particular currents within psychology which the journal emphasized reflected his assessments of the field. For example, the *Revista* encouraged contributions on what López-Campillo classifies as "characterology," "typology," and "phenomenology of the feelings"— which coincided closely with favorite themes in Ortega's own work— from such authors as Simmel (whose work Ortega greatly admired), Carl Jung, and the Spanish endocrinologist and man of letters Gregorio Marañón.[4] Similarly, the review's ambivalence toward Freud's work, which may be inferred from the fact that it published no texts by the father of psychoanalysis, was doubtless a reflection of Ortega's own reservations, and perhaps as well those of his first managing editor, Manuel García Morente. There were, in the first two years of publication, several reviews of books by Freud, but these were generally marked by an underlying discomfort with his claims to scientific status for his work. Significantly, the year in which Freud's name last figures as a subject in the *Revista*, 1925, is the first in which Jung appears in its pages; he was a regular contributor thereafter. Ortega, as a philosopher and an informal student of the history of religions and mythology, doubtless found the work of Freud's greatest disciple more attractive than that of the original master. Jung provided a more open framework for speculative play, his work being characterized by an explicitly philosophical and religious tendency as contrasted with Freud's aspirations to rigorous science.

Ortega had first critically questioned the claims of Freudian psychoanalysis to be a science in an essay entitled "Psychoanalysis, Problematic Science" (1911). Later he provided a foreword for the Spanish translation of the complete works of Freud, published in 1922 by Biblioteca Nueva of Madrid. In this piece he saluted Freud's pioneering work in the unknown territories of the erotic and libidinal, but also cautioned, albeit briefly, that the Viennese doctor was often frankly speculative, presenting as science what was in fact inspired guesswork or tentative hypothesis.[5] Ortega's reservations were, however, mild compared to those of other educated Spaniards, for the traditional culture, with its confessional Catholic base and the very resistance to "intimacy" which Ortega had early signaled, provided strong defenses against a secular technique for the cure of souls. Consequently, psychoanalysis made almost no inroads in Spain before the civil war (and has in fact developed only very haltingly there since that time).

The *Revista*, however, did play a major role in fostering a general interest in psychology among vanguardistic Spanish circles in the 1920s. As López-Campillo says of the period beginning with the early twenties:

> Certain problems that before were customarily considered exclusively from an economic or political angle (principally the ills of Spain) acquire a supplementary dimension thanks to consideration of the psychology of individuals, the sexes, and crowd behavior. One can hardly weight too much in this shift the importance of the world war.[6]

Even so, the magazine's promotion of psychology was not unaffected by the backward Spanish culture that it generally opposed. For example, in Marañón, whose contributions to the *Revista* emphasized the study of sexual types and roles, there was a marked traditionalism. According to López-Campillo:

> He considers pathological all those who are not guided by the most traditional morality: the superiority of the monogamous family, the praise of work, the authority of the mature male, the softness and resignation of woman, etc. The success of Marañón's theories [among the Spanish intellectual elite]...shows how rooted was the traditional morality in cultured circles.[7]

Ortega, like most of his predecessors in the Generation of 1898, essentially subscribed to Marañón's sexual typology, which corresponded as well to Jung's tendency to see woman as the more passive and animalistic of the two sexes.

As in the the case of modern psychology, Ortega's taste was reflected in the *Revista*'s abundant attention to European history and sociological theory (the latter a distinctly new item for Spanish readers), its censorious critique of surrealism, its praise of modern abstract art, and its vigilant awareness of literary developments in several languages. In philosophy the review published less than one might have expected, although the appearance there in Spanish translation of Simmel, Scheler, Russell, Whitehead, and others clearly opened new frontiers for Spaniards and for a select readership in Latin America. Beginning in 1929, a new, younger group of contributors (including Xavier Zubiri, María Zambrano, Julián Marías, and José Gaos) brought increased attention to metaphysical and ontological questions. Schelerian phenomenology also figured prominently during this period of publication, probably because it offered a prestigious alternative concern for those Spanish intellectuals who preferred the study of philosophical anthropology to preoccupation with more immediately pressing social and political issues.[8]

Theoretical and also more empirical studies of society played a major role in the magazine, accounting for some fifty articles between 1923 and 1936.[9] Since there was at that time no other Spanish journal specializing in such issues, the *Revista* offered its readers a unique service. The writings, or reviews of the writings, of Werner Sombart, Spengler, Karl Mannheim, and Max Weber—not to mention important native contributors—all appeared in its pages during those years. (All the while, the new Revista press was bringing out a steady line of works in translation, running the gamut of the intellectual life of Germany.) With one or two exceptions, very little attention was given to Spanish society during the entire first period of publication (1923–1936). Russia, by contrast, received extensive attention throughout the twenties and into the early thirties. One may also note, particularly after the world economic crisis of 1929, a gradual turn of interest away from Russia and the Orient (China and Japan) toward the problems of the industrialized West (prominently including the United States).[10] In May, June, and September of 1931, the *Revista* did turn its attention to Spain in connection with the beginning of the Second Republic. At this time, Ortega was particularly responsive to those members of the student syndicate Federación Universitaria Escolar (FUE) who sought the support of the liberal intellectuals in their protests against government censorship of academic freedom. Eager to act as an inspiration to the young, he departed briefly from the *Revista*'s pattern of devotion to high culture and theory in order to include commentary by Antonio Marichalar and Fernando Vela on the role of university students in politics, the prospects for agrarian reform in Spain, and other timely topics.[11]

Ortega's own sociological contributions to the magazine gave particular attention to the social role of the intellectual, a theme of growing import for him in the years of Primo's government. His failure to find a wider public among the Spanish bourgeoisie, which remained relatively small and politically ineffective in this period, contributed to this preoccupation. Picking up themes developed by Julien Benda and Paul Valéry in France and by Mannheim in Germany, Ortega published two essays (in 1924 and 1926, respectively) deemphasizing the intellectual's obligation to transform the entire society and focusing instead on the mission of preserving intelligence in the world.[12]

In the first, "Cosmopolitismo" (December 1924), he recognized the growth of an international community of intellectuals. Over the preceding fifty years, he argued, European intellectual life had been unduly nationalized, hence restricted to concerns on native grounds. (This judgment seems more applicable to Spanish intellectual history than to that of some other European nations.) The only intellectuals to escape this confinement had been those in mathematics and the sciences; men of letters had been especially parochial. But in the 1920s, according to Ortega, the cosmopolitan spirit was being fostered by a select group of writers and thinkers whose concerns transcended all local allegiances. (These were, in fact, members of the trans-European Generation of 1914, who experienced the "shock of recognition" in each other's thoughts and works.) These men alone, Ortega said, understood the gravity of the cultural crisis of Europe, which was marked by the fact that "[n]ormative principles of every sort—in science, in art, in politics— have ceased to be in force."[13] The resulting hiatus—a kind of cultural interregnum—meant that intellectuals could not expect to impose new principles upon the masses:

> Intelligence must not aspire to command, not even to influence and save, men.... It is not by advancing to the front rank of society in the manner of

the politician, the warrior, or the priest that it will best fulfill its destiny, but, on the contrary, by concealing and covering itself.[14]

History had chastened Ortega's earlier immoderate expectations for the direct effect of ideas upon the daily life of a people.

In the second, related essay, "Reforma de la inteligencia" (January 1926), Ortega launched a defense of theory as the "lovely and serene contemplation of the universe."[15] While theory eventually fostered the growth of an applied technology, it would be an error, he argued, for intellectuals to muddy their vision by immersion in worldly affairs. Yet, between 1750 and 1900 in Europe, according to Ortega, intellectuals had made precisely that mistake. Intoxicated by the power of ideas, they had sought to remake society in their own image. Witness, for example, their salient role in the French Revolution and, thereafter, in the whole development of nineteenth-century political theory. This hunger for a more wordly role had led many intellectuals to abandon what Ortega, waxing lyrical, now deemed the thinker's true vocation:

> What a delight for intelligence to see itself exonerated of the heavy duties it frivolously took upon itself! What pleasure not to be taken seriously and to attend freely to its refined needs! In this manner it could again return unto itself, on the margin of worldly affairs, feeling no haste to provide premature solutions for anything, allowing problems to expand according to their own elastic radius. What a delight to allow everyone to step ahead—the soldier, the priest, the captain of industry, the soccer player—and from time to time to launch upon them a magnificent, exact, well ripened idea glowing with light![16]

The genuine thinker, called to "radical solitude," found his highest activity in contemplation—sportive, disinterested, quasi-divine. The only "technique" to pursue was that of the authentic life.

In affirming the classical tradition of thought as free from necessity or practical purpose, Ortega joined a long line of thinkers who had defended the autonomous life of the intellect. Platonic, Aristotelian, and Thomistic threads ran through this tradition, accentuating wonder, contemplation, and man's need to know for its own sake. But there were other, more modern traditions, which stressed the pragmatic, historicist, and existentialist orientation of thought; and to this line Ortega also belonged in his emphasis on the "vital" function of thought in the world. In this vein, side by side with his commitment to high theory, he recognized man's need to "reabsorb" his circumstances, to come to terms with a world that thrusts challenges and problems upon him. Life, he was wont to say, comes at us "point blank," demanding immediate response. In this, Ortega was closer to William James and John Dewey than to Plato, Leibniz, or Kant. The pragmatic turn to his thought was heightened by his image of the intellectual as a kind of spiritual chief charged with the mission of transforming the surrounding culture. As, by turns, his faith in this role waxed and waned, his portrayal of the intellectual's duty changed correspondingly.

Finally, regarding the *Revista*'s publications on history and historiography, López-Campillo notes a marked emphasis on premodern times and on philosophical speculation, suggesting a turn away from the present and "a crisis in history as a science," which seemed "emptied of a part of its substance in favor of other parts of the human sciences such as philosophy, sociology or psychology."[17] To be sure, the names of Bachofen, Frobenius, Schulten, Burckhardt, Weber, and Huizinga appeared in the review, but their emphasis was distinctly upon classical or medieval themes. Various Spanish scholars, such as Claudio Sánchez Albornoz, Ramón Carande, Emilio García Gómez, and Luis Asín Palacios, also presented studies of the Middle Ages and of the Muslim period in Spanish history. In sum, the historical contributions gathered together

> Spanish collaborators whose work and training are within the framework of certain organizations inspired directly by the Institución Libre de Enseñanza such as the Junta para Ampliación de Estudios and the Centro de Estudios Históricos, particularly as regards the Middle Ages and Hebraic and Arabic studies; and foreign collaborators, the majority of them German, whose contributions are in the fields of ethnology, prehistory and antiquity.[18]

As a result, the *Revista* of the first period published almost nothing about European history after the French Revolution. López-Campillo's conclusion that this tendency represented a contemporary crisis in the study of Spanish history seems exaggerated—Ortega, after all, remained deeply committed to the idea that the present could be understood only from its deepest roots in the past. Nonetheless, it remains true that little native work was being done in the study of Spanish history beyond the medieval period, and the contents of the *Revista* in those years indeed reflect that fact.

In retrospect, we may see the wisdom in Ortega's editorial direction, for the *Revista* stands as his finest institutional creation. Even today, both the monthly review, which was renewed after 1963, and the Revista press continue to serve a significant public in the entire Spanish-speaking world. However limiting appears Ortega's choice to ignore the immediate political and social issues of his day, the *Revista* gave a minority of his countrymen a vastly expanded picture of modern scholarship and thought. In this regard, it had no peer in prewar Spain. When it was founded, Manuel Azaña's *La Pluma* (1920–1923), a more exclusively literary review, had just ceased publication. *Residencia*, put out by the Residencia de Estudiantes from 1926 to 1934, bore some resemblance to Ortega's journal, though its overall quality was hardly comparable. In January of 1927, *La Gaceta Literaria*, concerned with native literary matters, appeared under the direction of the eccentric literary intellectual Ernesto Giménez Caballero, who had already published in the *Revista*. López-Campillo notes of *La Gaceta*:

> During the ... existence of the *Revista de Occidente*, the appearance of *La Gaceta Literaria* is the first indication of a restructuring of the different intellectual currents that had until then collaborated in an apolitical, universalist and cultural perspective, but which at a certain moment find themselves obliged to forge an organ capable of gathering up their new aspirations. It will be necessary to await the first years of the Second Republic for the new tendencies sketched in *La Gaceta Literaria* to crystallize in three principal directions: the creation of the political weekly of Ramiro Ledesma Ramos [a young fascist theorist] *La Conquista del Estado*, that of *Cruz y Raya*, and that of *Octubre*.[19]

The three latter magazines, representing more limited and politically committed views than Ortega ever permitted for the *Revista*, were respectively fascist, leftist Catholic, and communist. This progressive sharpening of ideological viewpoints among the various reviews was furthered some years later by the founding, in May 1934, of the radical left socialist *Leviatán*, while extreme rightist Catholics gathered around their own *Acción Española*. Here, however, we anticipate the later history of Ortega's review, when, during the early 1930s, it was often criticized for failing to take a clear stand on the events surrounding the end of the monarchy and the beginning of the Second Republic. The *Revista*'s alleged refusal to make clear its tacit ideological slant suggests that all along this was subtler and more complex than that of the more militant magazines that arose in the time of political crisis.

Not content with the immediately successful monthly review, Ortega, drawing on the example of Espasa-Calpe, chose to expand its scope through a Revista de Occidente press. The new house published its first book in April 1924, and followed with some 225 titles before its temporary interruption during the civil war.[20] It brought an extraordinary influx of new names and new ideas into Spain throughout the 1920s and early 1930s. Thanks to the monthly review and the press, much of the work of Husserl, for example, was translated into Spanish at a time when it was very scantily known anywhere else outside Germany. The titles of the press's prewar activity read like an anthology of the intellectual elite of Europe: philosophy, physics, psychology, sociology, history, literature, archaeology, geography, economics—there is almost no field neglected. A thorough reading or the press's output would have been tantamount to a liberal education in central concepts of postwar European culture, and even a cursory glance at the monthly review gave the reader a sense of the intellectual ferment Ortega had signalized in the first number when he spoke of the "vast germination of life" that he called "deep contemporary reality."

With the creation of the *Revista* and with Ortega's growing reputation not only at home but in the Spanish-speaking world generally, he might well have felt by the mid-1920s some satisfaction with his work as a modernizer of Spanish culture. But his social role was not a simple one, and he continued to experience a sense of conflict between his more theoretical vocation and the temptation to engage himself in immediate political issues. This conflict was complicated by his need, like that felt by many intellectuals in culturally underdeveloped countries, to work simultaneously on several fronts—institutional, journalistic, pedagogical, and political—in order to bring his culture into parity with the models he had chosen. To his final credit, he never resolved the issue of the intellectual's political responsibility but rather lived out both sides of the question. Nonetheless, from the founding of the *Revista de Occidente* onward, he tended, like Julien Benda in *La trahison des clercs*, to distrust the partisan blindness occasioned by *engagé* commitments.

A scant two months after the first number of the *Revista* appeared, Miguel Primo de Rivera, Captain General of Catalonia, issued a *pronunciamiento* and, with the covert cooperation of of Alfonso XIII, assumed the head of a military directorate, which put an end to the parliamentary government. In 1925 Primo was to replace the military with a civilian directorate, but he remained solidly in power as dictator until his fall in January 1930. The interregnum, carried out in the old style of nineteenth-century Spanish putsches, constituted a death blow to the Restoration system, which had functioned for almost fifty years. Primo suspended the Constitution of 1876 and with it much enlightened legislation for civil liberties. While the arbitrarily repressive and flagrantly illegal conduct of the dictator was soon to alienate many of the country's leading scholars and intellectuals, Primo was at first welcomed by some of those who would become his enemies. Among them Ortega's voice was prominent, for initially the dictatorship looked like a clean "surgical" stroke that had swept away the rotten system of "old politics" against which Ortega had cried since 1914. Indeed, the nationwide, single-party Unión Patriótica, founded by Primo in 1924, seemed at first a conceivable fulfillment of Ortega's repeated calls for a nonpartisan organization that would put the social regeneration of the entire nation above the vested interests of old party loyalties and regional politics. While Ortega was quickly disabused of any vague notions that Primo might be the true "iron surgeon" for whom Costa had earlier called, both the dictator and, later, his son the Falangist leader José Antonio Primo de Rivera found support for their ideas in Ortega's well-known assaults on the old system. Ironically, Antonio Maura, the very incarnation of the decrepit parliamentary system and the man Ortega had bitterly criticized for years, stood in the elder Primo's mind as a model for the "revolution from above" that he planned to bring to Spain.[21]

The period of almost six and a half years of dictatorship was an economically prosperous one for the Spanish middle and upper classes, albeit the lives of the workers and peasants remained largely unimproved. Although Primo's style of governing combined elements of *caciquismo* (bossism) with sentimental impulsiveness, and could hardly be called politically enlightened, under his loose guidance Spain gained a modern highway system, women's suffrage, an improved plan for irrigation and dam building, a prosperous domestic economy (with emphasis on the nationalization of industry), widespread rural electrification, and an improved railway network. During the twenties Madrid became a strikingly more cosmopolitan city,

leaving behind some of the manners and the pace of the period before
World War I. But Primo's greatest achievement was the successful
conclusion of the nation's costly, frustrating involvement in Morocco.
Under his bold leadership, Spain and France cooperated to defeat the
rebel forces under Abd El Krim, and by 1927 the Spanish protectorate there was pacified.

For all his personal charm, his military fame, and his devotion to
certain domestic improvements, Primo was not long able to command the support of the major pressure groups—the old-guard
Liberals and Conservatives, the Church, the army, and the bourgeois
entrepreneurs like Francesco Cambó of Barcelona. While his first
years were marked by the flush of success and unwonted prosperity,
he quickly ran into growing opposition and unrest. Of increasing
significance throughout the 1920s was the opposition of the liberal
intelligentsia. Many Spanish intellectuals turned sharply against
Primo when Unamuno was dismissed as rector at Salamanca in 1924,
after a personal letter in which he attacked the dictator was published
without Unamuno's permission in *La Nación* of Buenos Aires. From
that time they began to perceive the dictator as an almost comical
anachronism whose proposed "brief parenthesis" in the legal functioning of the state might endure indefinitely. One of them, Salvador
de Madariaga, remarked of the general:

He believed himself to be the leader of a new Spanish order, but he was
representative not of the 'old regime,' i.e., of the Restoration, but of the
'very old regime,' i.e., the era of pronunciamientos, which covers practi-
cally the middle third of the nineteenth century.[22]

And Primo indeed seemed backward in his haphazard, anti-
intellectual policy of press censorship, and in his decision in 1925 to
close the venerable Ateneo of Madrid, a distinguished forum for
liberal and critical thought since early in the nineteenth century. He
foolishly chose to censor the intellectuals, the universities, and the
students just as Spain was entering a period of great literary, artistic,
and political ferment. Political opposition to the regime was perforce
muted and clandestine, but the general upwelling that was excited by
the breakdown of the old parliamentary monarchy found indirect
expression in the development of Spanish artistic modernism. As with
roughly comparable situations in other European countries—the
final years of czarist Russia, Weimar Germany, or *fin de siècle* Vienna

—political turmoil was accompanied by an efflorescence of creative energies.

For many writers, artists, and musicians in Madrid during the 1920s, the political situation was, of course, a background fact not bearing immediately on their lives. When young men like Rafael Alberti, Federico García Lorca, Salvador Dalí, Luis Buñuel, and Jorge Guillén gathered to talk of art and poetry in the gardens of the Residencia de Estudiantes on a lovely hill at the outskirts of the city, they were hardly concerned with the portly, mustachioed general who kept the trains running on time and fomented the development of hydroelectric power. But the feeling that Spain aspired to enter the twentieth century through the modernization of her economy, her highways, and her rail system echoed and indirectly supported vanguardist experimentation in prose, poetry, the visual arts, and even philosophical thought. Though it is impossible to say just how much a pervasive sense of political unrest and cultural ferment accounts for the frequent frissons one senses in the prose of Ortega's most spirited essays, it seems obvious that such background conditions sharpened his perception of life as an ever-shifting drama.

Ortega was clearly the most prominent and charismatic spokesman for the process of Spanish cultural modernization so evident in the twenties. It was in the pages of the *Revista de Occidente*, for example, that several members of the poetic Generation of 1927 (sometimes known as the Generation of 1925, or of "the dictatorship") and numerous vanguardist prose stylists of the decade made early appearances. The poets of 1927, whose work came to maturity during the decade, constituted a second wave (after older poets like Antonio Machado, Unamuno, and Juan Ramón Jiménez) of what has been called the Silver Age of Spanish poetry. They are generally thought to include Federico García Lorca, Jorge Guillén, Rafael Alberti, Pedro Salinas, Gerardo Diego, Dámaso Alonso, Vicente Aleixandre, Emilio Prados, Luis Cernuda, and Manuel Altolaguirre. The innovative prose writers who benefited from the *Revista*'s sponsorship included Francisco Ayala, Ernesto Giménez Caballero, Benjamín Jarnés, Antonio Espina, Max Aub, Ramón Gómez de la Serna, and Rosa Chacel, among others.

The Generation of 1927 took its name from the passionate interest many of its members showed in the poetry of the great baroque writer from Córdoba, Luis de Argote y Góngora (1561–1627), the tricentenary of whose death was celebrated in that year. Mixing the complex style known as *culteranismo* (culteranism or cultism) with a passionate interest in the popular music and balladry of his native Andalusia, Góngora strongly attracted poets of Andalusian origin like Lorca and Alberti; but other members of the modern generation as well found his work a model of poetic freedom from the rules of linguistic convention and the obligation to verisimilitude in literature. Largely unconcerned with social and political issues of the decade, the poets of 1927 hailed Góngora for his ability to create a poetic world independent of the "real" one of everyday life. The Ortega of "The Dehumanization of Art" was sympathetic to the form of poetic license that freed the poet from sheer mimetic activity, although he was not himself an admirer of Góngora nor even entirely comfortable with the way poetry "hid" the world of things through periphrasis and metaphorical invention. Nonetheless, the *Revista* not only sought out the brilliant young poets of the mid-1920s but even published, on the occasion of the tricentenary, an edition of Góngora's *Soledades*, a collection of the popular *romances* (ballads) from which he drew inspiration, and an *Antología poética en honor de Góngora*. Toward the end of the decade the Revista press initiated a collection called *Los Poetas*, which featured major works of Guillén (*Cántico*), Salinas (*Seguro azar*), Alberti (*Cal y canto*), and García Lorca (*Romancero gitano* and *Canciones*).

If Ortega did not share the feeling of many members of this generation for the rich suggestiveness of Góngora's work, there is little doubt that he influenced their thinking about literary art and generally impressed them as the leading intellectual model of the day. Undoubtedly too, his mature prose style, in which gravity of tone combined with a spirit of inventive play, showed many younger writers the superb effects to be achieved in Spanish nonfictional prose. Before Ortega, few educated Spaniards would have expected philosophy to seem as interesting and as rooted in the writer's temperament and daily existence as it appeared to be in Ortega's most felicitous essays.

It may also be argued that Ortega, for his part, was drawn to the work of poets like García Lorca, Alberti, and Guillén because he felt he shared with them a literary vocation that in his case had long before been subordinated to a theoretical and pedagogical mission. He had chosen above all else to be a writer of discursive prose; yet, if in nothing more than in his love of metaphor (which he cultivated despite his sense that poets often used it to excess), Ortega could see himself, perhaps a bit vainly, as the natural mentor for the poets whose work appeared in the *Revista* during the years of Primo de Rivera's dictatorship.

One poet-critic of the Generation of 1927, Luis Cernuda, in fact noted rather sharply Ortega's fascination with metaphor:

> In the image there is a greater poetic creation than in the metaphor. In the first, imagination intervenes more than *ingenio* [wit]; in the second, *ingenio* more than imagination. The metaphor quickly seduces the Spanish reader, and readers and critics based themselves especially on it in discerning preeminence in the new poets of 1925. The metaphor was in fashion, so much so that Ortega y Gasset, with his strange ignorance in poetic matters, at that time defined poetry as "the superior algebra of metaphors." [23]

But Cernuda's appraisal does not do justice to most of Ortega's work, for though he may have fancied himself a kind of hybrid of poet and philosopher, Ortega's primary allegiance remained to philosophical prose and criticism. His repeated conviction that all great intellectual themes require ample explication—the credo of the discursive writer—counterbalanced his penchant for what he called the "algebra," or shorthand, of metaphor.

In his chair of metaphysics at the University of Madrid Ortega was the animator and central figure of a philosophical renaissance that included the work of colleagues and disciples like Xavier Zubiri, Manuel García Morente, and José Gaos. By the twenties, the university's School of Philosophy and Letters had become the most outstanding academic center of humanistic thought the country had known in modern times. Here, as well as in the quality and diversity of literary production, Spain was bidding fair to catch up with France and Germany. One could begin to see Madrid as a cultural capital not unworthy of comparison with Paris and Berlin in the 1920s. Much as the First World War had helped to catalyze a self-conscious group of intellectuals who sought to play a crucial role in political and cultural modernization, so the Primo regime sharpened—by opposition—the critical edge of a younger generation of writers and thinkers whose work was concentrated in the *Revista* and, slightly later, in *La Gaceta Literaria*.

In his political commentary for those years, Ortega continued to agitate for a return to parliamentary government, but not of the old style. In essays written in the mid-1920s he was developing his vision of a parliament more responsive to the people, free of the traditional drag of *caciquismo*, and elected on a regional rather than a local and municipal basis. The government, once appointed, would be sufficiently dissociated from the "waves" of shifting parliamentary politics to achieve some continuity of action. To supplement the necessary reorganization of the state, he called upon the young—writers, students, critics of society—to "form your teams" and to "hunt down the petit bourgeois," whose timid, unimaginative habits constituted a block to radical change in social mores.[24] In a playful and celebratory tone, he envisioned a new Spain arising out of the ruins of the dictatorship, much as he had seen it coming beyond the war years of 1914–1918.

On the other front of "cultural politics" Ortega continued in his role as an interpreter of the new times with two seminal essays published as a single volume in 1925, "La deshumanización del arte" and "Ideas sobre la novela" ("The Dehumanization of Art" and "Notes on the Novel"). Manifestos of sorts, both pieces described the new cultural epoch of the early twentieth century. The greater and longer of the two pieces, "Dehumanization," gave to the Spanish artistic and literary vanguard of the 1920s a kind of generational self-consciousness. In writing it to and for the rising generation, Ortega sought to assume their point of view in his crucial separation of "art" from "life" (as the latter term was understood by naturalists and programmatic realists). The two essays were linked by his assertion that in visual art and the novel the traditional humanistic emphasis on man as the measure of all things (and thereby the proper focus of art) was exhausted. Such a view, he argued, could now produce only cant and repetitious sentimentality. It had depended upon an essentially narrative mode that permitted the viewer or the reader to incorporate the artwork into the story of his own life, thereby failing to see anything in it which did not immediately mirror and comment upon him. The new painting solved the problem by eschewing representational images; the experimental novel did so by reducing the narrative element to an absolute minimum. In both arts the point was to take away anything that could lead to extrinsic or extra-artistic concerns.

Though curiously at odds with the existentialist humanism and the vitalization of culture evident in much of Ortega's other work, "Dehumanization" typified his self-conception as a herald or prophet of the new, a role that often led him to immoderate pronouncements. Written at the very moment when the modernist and surrealist poets of the Generation of 1927 were first appearing in print and when Dalí was beginning his career in Madrid, "Dehumanization" sought to be at the leading edge of contemporary art criticism. When Ortega extolled the "young art," he addressed himself particularly to young poets like García Lorca, Alberti, Guillén, and Dámaso Alonso. (Closely associated figures like Cernuda and Vicente Aleixandre had not yet appeared in print.) This seminal essay fell toward the beginning of an extraordinarily productive period for Ortega, spanning the years from 1921 to 1935.[25] In these years—and most pointedly from the presentation of the course "¿Qué es filosofía?" in 1929—he achieved the full maturity of his prose style and his thematic range as a philosopher and political critic. Arising out of the cultural ferment so characteristic of Madrid in those years, the now-classic essay on art appeared, in its simplest guise, to be an apology for the radically new European art that grew out of symbolism, cubism, futurism, surrealism, and the whole revolt—already implicit in French impressionism—against representational realism in painting.

A closer reading, however, shows that Ortega was not an unqualified panegyrist of this composite movement, despite his felt obligation to announce its historical importance to the Spanish public. For all the brilliance of this piece, it seemed that Ortega's heart was neither in it nor in the art it heralded. Indeed, he repeatedly stated that his purpose, like the surgeon's, was merely to lay bare the principles and assumptions of the new art. It called for just such an approach, he argued, because earlier art, which he considered excessively romantic, programmatic, and sentimental, had always attached its public to the world rather than, as he thought proper, to the artist's *idea* of the world. Since, he added in a Husserlian turn, all we can ever really have of the world is the ideas we form of it, it was idle for art to cling to overt representations of man and nature. Why not then take the cleansing, purgative step toward the full freedom of the artist's idea, toward an art that daringly proclaimed itself just art? This need not be a variation on the formula of art for art's sake, since he considered the new works as much "for" man and culture as the preceding art, perhaps even more so. In its naked openness—not cloaked with familiar, stirring, or comforting imagery—postimpressionistic art supposedly brought men closer to their own ideational processes.

In writing the essay from the assumed point of view of young people, Ortega presumably suspended his own aesthetic judgment, thus allowing himself to pose as the disinterested chronicler of the innovations introduced by what he deemed the artistic elite of the time. This "surgical" operation on the body of culture lent his voice a quasi-scientific tone. Faced with this assumption of authority, one has to remind oneself that some of his claims about nineteenth-century art—that it was all programmatic, for example—are patently ridiculous. But Ortega was more concerned with the polemical thrust of the piece—more concerned with promoting the new art and, thereby, his own role as a voice of the times—than his cool, expository approach might suggest.

If "Dehumanization," despite Ortega's avowed suspension of feeling, was indeed skillful polemic, yet he was ambivalent in his aesthetic response to the new art, then what drove this essay? What was the source of its implicit fervor? The answer to that question lies right on the surface in the opening pages, where Ortega declared the hallmark of the new art to be its manifest unpopularity. That is what separated the mass of people moved by the sentimentality of "humanized" representational art from the refined few capable of hailing the new work of Debussy, Mallarmé, Stravinsky, Picasso, Pirandello, and Proust. Such an irrefutable principle of separation—against which the ignorant herd of museum-goers was quite helpless—would force the "masses" back into place, "compelling the people to recognize itself for what it is: a component among others of the social structure, inert matter of the historical process, a secondary factor in the cosmos of spiritual life." Simultaneously, appreciation for the new art aided the elite in its self-definition over against "the drab mass of society," thus helping the former "to learn their mission, which consists in being few and holding their own against the many." [26] What Ortega called "artistic art" enabled him to assert sub rosa an essentially political notion in the guise of aesthetic theory. Hence he took the new art as a sign of potential return to sanity, from which democratized mass society had departed since sometime around the French Revolution:

> A time must come in which society, from politics to art, reorganizes itself into two orders or ranks: the illustrious and the vulgar. That chaotic,

shapeless, and undifferentiated state without discipline and social structure in which Europe has lived these hundred and fifty years cannot go on. Behind all contemporary life lurks the provoking and profound injustice of the assumption that men are actually equal.[27]

Here, as in the later *Revolt of the Masses*, his vision of a hierarchically organized society was monolithic: there were only two groups across the board, and they were to be distinguished solely by the preference of the elite for high culture and self-transcendence, and of the mass for conventional sentiment and vulgar self-satisfaction.

If this distinction between the leaders of society and its inert mass membership points to the affective heart of the essay on art, the simplistic binary model of a society of leaders and led, shepherd and flock, also suggests a central tension in Ortega's political outlook: on the one hand, he was clearly a liberal in his devotion to education and to individual self-realization; but on the other, he feared the invasive force of mass taste, which, he believed, threatened to reduce all models of excellence to its own base level. With the noblesse oblige of the liberal who is not at heart a democrat, he seemed at once committed to raising men's sights and fearful that success in this effort might ultimately elude him and the elite leadership of which he dreamed. Ideally, elite taste would define the center of the reordered society Ortega envisioned for the future of Europe. In this scheme, debased mass taste—once divested of its hostility to the new art—would presumably take its respectful, subservient place on the sidelines, content to receive an aesthetic education from those in the know. What would actually happen to popular culture in its massive and astonishingly rapid development in this century Ortega neither knew nor, from our current perspective, could have dreamed. By invoking a new educated sensibility, he sought to curtail the insurgency of unrefined demotic taste. The effect was like trying to turn back the clock to a time before the common people had appeared on the stage of history, back to the world of the ancien régime.

The catalytic force of the "young art" ("young" in being produced by and appealing to youth, and also in being in itself youthful, zesty, challenging) called forth the response of the initiates in the form of a leap into authentic connection. Thus Ortega could characterize avant-garde art as "an art of privilege, of nobility of nerves, of instinctive aristocracy."[28] The sportive, vitalistic criterion pointed toward a kind of athletics of culture in which the spiritually stronger would establish their heroism by raising themselves above all those who, no matter what their likes and dislikes, could not *understand* Stravinsky or Picasso. This profoundly irrational vision of "instinctive" excellence was closely akin to Nietzsche's idea of the *Übermensch*, whose choice to "live dangerously" was the sign of his capacity for self-transcendence. Similarly for Ortega, breaking into the inner sanctum of developing cultural modernism became a daring balancing act, an acrobatics of intellect.

The authentic art of the vanguard was dehumanized, non-natural, antisentimental, and (though Ortega might not admit it) antisocial. It did not simply separate the sheep from the goats, it set them at war with each other. In a little section of the essay entitled "Negative Influence of the Past," Ortega noted the essentially antagonistic spirit of all vanguardist art, which could not but be self-conscious precisely of the dependence of its novelty upon a rejection of immediately preceding works and styles. Being new, after all, requires calling something else old or outmoded, and the immediate past (as well, perhaps, as the past in general) hence becomes the radically inauthentic realm. Self-proclaimed authenticity tends to de-authenticate all that against which it takes its stand. As the pull of the future becomes increasingly powerful, the new, the up-to-date, and the modern become compelling cultural imperatives, which may go so far as to promote the "agonic" or self-sacrificing urge of an artist or art movement to "perish" into the next apotheosis of "the modern." [29] Vanguardist art is thus infused with the notion of development or progress, though not toward any clear or socially useful end, and its authenticity is achieved through a "murderous" domination over the past which allows it—even obliges it—to kill off its historical antecedents. [30]

Ortega understood that a "negative mood of mocking aggressiveness" was a basic feature of the vanguardist impulse, that from the time of Baudelaire on, "the successive styles contain an ever increasing dose of derision and disparagement until in our day the new art consists almost exclusively of protests against the old." [31] He saw this phenomenon as a part of the larger "futuristic instinct" characteristic of Europe as opposed to the Orient, and suggested that the new art was only the latest manifestation of a long-standing Western fascination with the metaphors of development, evolution, and progress.

Nevertheless, the vanguardist assault on previous art was, he argued, equivalent to turning "against Art itself," and an attack on Art implied "hatred of science, hatred of State, hatred, in sum, of civilization as a whole." Such a prospect, almost stumbled upon in the strange turns of this essay, could only have been deeply alarming to Ortega. Insofar as he believed, with other modern theorists, that cultural renewal required periodic assaults on the accreted forms and manners of civilized life, he was enthusiastic about the artistic revolt of the early twentieth century.[32] But in his deep commitment to a liberal political order and to the progressive enlightenment of the general populace, he could not unambivalently affirm the possibility "that modern Western man bears a rankling grudge against his own historical essence." [33] By raising this thought in "Dehumanization," he was working out his own critique of the burden of civilized life so strikingly assessed by his older contemporary Freud but already salient in the writings of the German and English romantics. Indeed, Ortega's misgivings about an unquestioning devotion to any established order—artistic, learned, or political—could easily echo Coleridge's observation that

> civilization is itself but a mixed good, if not far more a corrupting influence, the hectic of disease, not the bloom of health, and a nation so distinguished more fitly to be called a varnished than a polished people, where this civilization is not grounded in cultivation, in the harmonious development of those qualities and faculties that characterize our humanity.[34]

In his explication of a viewpoint that conceived of the past as a "negative influence," Ortega was manifesting a form of that deeply ambivalent attitude toward the past characteristic of many artists and intellectuals since the later years of the eighteenth century. This outlook was fostered most pointedly by the French Enlightenment, together with the beginnings of German historicism and the rise, throughout Europe, of romanticism in literature and the visual arts. In simple terms, it has consisted in the sense that the past is a shackle or burden to be thrown off and that, simultaneously, we are through and through historical beings, owing even our distrust of the past to certain aspects of our recent history. Since the late 1700s, then, many writers and artists have turned nostalgically toward the past, even as they have decried its burdensome presence. Important for our purposes is the figure who affirms the significance of the past while standing critically apart from it and looking forward toward the fulfillment of his "vital project." No one is a better representative of this Janus-faced stance than Ortega, who believed that history had at once made man what he was and condemned him not to repeat his previous solutions to the problem of living. One sought a sense of the past, then, in order to sharpen and clarify the need for choice in the present, so that each generation and each individual would choose its destiny and add to the expanding repertoire of ways of being human. This thoroughly historicized manner of seeing the past at once invoked it and criticized it by elaborating a new style of life appropriate to one's own moment and generation.

A distinct but not unrelated position was the modernist one that pitted the latest incarnation of the vanguardist spirit against the past and against tradition as the "mechanism" that perpetuated it. In "Dehumanization," Ortega's historicist outlook was affected by this polemical spirit, which he adopted from "the young," whose viewpoint seemed to him to have carried the day:

> No doubt, Europe is entering upon an era of youthfulness. Nor need this fact surprise us. History moves in long biological rhythms whose chief phases necessarily are brought about not by secondary cause relating to details but by fundamental factors and primary forces of a cosmic nature. It is inconceivable that the major and, as it were, polar differences inherent in the living organism—sex and age—should not decisively mold the profile of the times. Indeed, it can be easily observed that history is rhythmically swinging back and forth between these two ploes, stressing the masculine qualities in some epics and the feminine in others, or exalting now a youthful deportment and then again maturity and old age.[35]

What Ortega here attempts to make a general "law" of human life was much more conditioned than he realized by the history of his own time. He had come to maturity at a moment—just before World War I—when youth and youthfulness were extolled as rarely before in European history. "Biological rhythms" seemed a more salient, visible aspect of history, at least of intellectual history, than they had seemed a century or two before, though one could not so easily infer from that a structural principle applicable over long periods of time. As with many of his pronouncements on the theory of generations, this assertion that youth commanded importance had not a little self-interest, for Ortega founded much of his legitimacy as an interpreter of modernity on his supposed ability to keep pace with the breaking edge of the future as it rolled into the present moment. In "Dehumanization," he was caught, like many another modern prophet of cultural crisis, in the anxious stance of hailing without really welcoming the corrosive modernist attack on earlier traditions. Toward the end of the essay he turned abruptly, perhaps with relief, to the ironic mode of perception. Under the heading "Doomed to Irony," he noted, "I very much doubt that any young person of our time can be impressed by a poem, a painting, or a piece of music that is not flavored with a dash of irony." [36] It was the ironic note—in his own viewpoint and in the art he heralded—which allowed him to find a *modus vivendi* with artistic modernity.

Elsewhere in his writings, Ortega was wise enough to know that the "authentic" and the "new" did not constitute identical categories, but in "Dehumanization" the two indeed coincided—at least from the point of view he assumed: that the humanized art of the past had sunk under its own weight of "meaning" to a debased, fraudulent condition. Perhaps, more accurately, it had been thrust into that inauthentic position by the audacious vigor of the new art. With his own notion that culture was born in the superfluous energies of play, Ortega found much to admire (and, on a deeper level, to distrust) in the stunning irreverence of the makers and appreciators of this art "of no consequence." One can take as paradigmatic his pose of apparent detachment from the artistic assault on the past. It was, once again, a mark of his self-appointed mission to comprehend and announce the *Zeitgeist*.

Less ideologically charged than "Dehumanization," "Notes on the Novel" arose from a polemic with Pío Baroja, whose work Ortega took to represent a defense of "adventures" in old-fashioned narrative sequence. Baroja, for his part, rejected Ortega's emphasis on the "function" and "form" of the novel over against the "substance" of its stories. Displeased with Baroja's fast-paced, episodic tales, Ortega cited the genius of Dostoyevsky, a writer whose stories and characters, he believed, were subservient to a superb philosophical gift for revealing "the form of life." [37] The novel, however, could not go as far as painting toward radical dehumanization, for it must retain at least a minimal thread of narrative structure not to be lost in floating contemplation of the sort Ortega objected to (but was also fascinated by) in Proust, who seemed to have suspended action so far in *A la recherche du temps perdu* as to cast the reader into a kind of bewitched stasis. The painter, by contrast, was presumably freer to recreate the rhythms and contours of his consciousness without concern for that referential link with the world which language seemed to demand. Despite his caveat regarding Proust, however, Ortega defended the "imperviousness" of the modern novel (its quality of being a complete world unto itself and thus free from mimetic obligations that would limit the writer's invention) and its movement away from the realist narrative tradition toward a mixture of lyricism and psychological analysis. In such works, thick description and penetrating analysis of character would count much more than narrative flow and plot development. These vanguardistic qualities of the modern novel in fact linked it very closely with visual art: "Imperviousness is but the special form taken on in the novel by the generic imperative of art: to be without transcending consequence." [38] Consequently novels of the future must eschew "philosophical, political, sociological or moral ideas." [39]

Both "Dehumanization" and "Notes on the Novel" were in essence polemical and normative treatises (despite Ortega's disclaimers) from the pen of a man frankly acknowledged by the young writers of the 1920s as *the* outstanding mentor for their work. They heeded his dicta, attended his lectures, hoped to be asked to his *tertulias*, and delighted in publishing their work under his auspices. Not only did several of the best poets of the Generation of 1927 and young prose writers of the twenties appear early in the pages of the *Revista de Occidente*, but experimental novels by Pedro Salinas, Benjamin Jarnés, and Antonio Espina were launched by the Revista publishing house. Ortega also promoted, through the *Revista* and the Colección Austral of Espasa-Calpe, a series of highly inventive biographies of nineteenth-century Spaniards by writers like Jarnés, Espina, Antonio Marichalar, and Juan Chabás. This project sprang not only from his conviction that the absence of a strong biographical tradition in Spain kept the nation ignorant of its own culture but from his perception that an inventive biography—akin in its poetic license to the novel—provided perhaps the finest concrete example of the interdependence of the individual "I" and its circumstances. To the evident displeasure of Baroja and other writers who, even more than he, still honored the realist tradition of Emile Zola and Benito Pérez Galdós, Ortega counseled the young Spanish prose writers of the period to downplay the older narrative in favor of free invention and fantasy. Exemplifying in some of his own early descriptive prose— "Notas de andar y ver," "Temas de viaje," and "Notas del vago estío"—the sensibility of a novelist of clear vanguardist bent, Ortega not only led but participated with the upcoming writers in the movement toward a densely evocative poetic prose and a rich play of metaphor. Indeed, more than once he referred to his "abandoned" early vocation as a writer of fiction, and Luis Araquistain, remembering Ortega's remark in Marburg concerning a novel unfinished in his drawer, has written, "I heard him say just before the First World War... [that] for his own pleasure he would continue to write novels ... but there were no philosophers in Spain and it was necessary for her mental health to have them." [40]

In promoting the latest artistic developments in narrative prose, Ortega suggested that the finest hour of the novel might yet come in the midst of its departure from everything that had fundamentally defined it up to his time. Neither for visual art nor for literature did he feel he was writing an epitaph, though both forms of expression seemed afloat in uncharted seas. They must get their bearings, he believed, by learning to pretend to less, to delight in beautiful form rather than labor to tell the truth or teach the reader or viewer about the world. In fact, he concluded his essay on the novel with a boldly affirmative prognosis: "The possibility of constructing human souls is perhaps the major asset of future novels.... Not in the invention of plots but in the invention of interesting characters lies the best hope of the novel." [41] The prospect for the visual arts was less clear, prompting him only to the vague affirmation that "whatever their shortcomings, the young artists have to be granted one point: there is no turning back." [42] Perhaps that same lesson was the one Ortega meant to apply to the political hopes of the liberal intelligentsia and their judgment of the Primo regime, for it was to become clear shortly to those who did not already see the point that after Primo there would be no turning back to the parliamentary monarchy of the days before 1923. The dash with which Ortega saluted the ventures of young artists who could hardly have satisfied the more conservative side of his temperament seemed to echo the rhetoric that he had employed for years against the old politics.

Madrid in the 1920s was certainly not turning back either. Under the stimulus of the economic prosperity that came with Primo's rule and ended with the worldwide depression at the close of the decade, the Spanish capital boomed into something resembling what one historian has called "an old-world Buenos Aires."[43] The city was moving rapidly away from the slow-paced life in which the well-to-do found the charm of the capital during the *belle époque* of the Restoration years. As Éléna de la Souchère remarks, Madrid in 1880 was "provincial and old-fashioned" and "still had the skeleton given it by Charles III at the end of the eighteenth century."[44] Within that framework the even older city represented by the narrow, irregular streets around the Plaza Mayor was still clearly visible. Around that nucleus a neoclassical urban plan was developed and determined the city's form until the late nineteenth century. Then rapid expansion began, as "rectilinear avenues sprang up from the peneplain in the rim of old Madrid" and outlying towns fell within the reach of the burgeoning metropolis.[45] The first Spanish "skyscrapers" appeared in the years following the war, when the Gran Vía struck diagonally through the eastern edge of downtown toward the Plaza de Cibeles.

The forms of daily life of course changed with the modern urbanization of the city. New fashions were introduced, automobile traffic increased dramatically, and modern daily newspapers changed the *madrileño's* sense of pace and his awareness of the world within and outside the national borders. Yet withal, much of Madrid life was still linked to the nineteenth century by literary *tertulias*, young ladies chaperoned in public, and the night watchmen (*serenos*) who unlocked the heavy, grilled doors at street level. The uneven, checkered quality of modernization in the social life of the capital repeated the paradoxical political and cultural situation in which a general ruled in distinctly premodern fashion while artists dallied with surrealism and "ultraism" and a writer like Ortega announced the latest discoveries in physics and phenomenology.

In spite of the hurly-burly of urban transformation which marked the third decade of this century in Madrid, the city under Primo de Rivera appears to have been one of the most attractive in Europe. For those who could afford it, the capital provided leisurely, pleasant living. The long boulevard running north and south by the Prado, the central post office and the elegant residences and embassies of "La Castellana" was a continous delight of fountains, flower gardens, and groves of shade trees. There were spacious outdoor cafés for the few clement months of the year and endless coffee houses, bars, and restaurants for winter conviviality. One had easy access to the surrounding countryside and the historical and architectural riches of Castilian towns like Toledo, Segovia, Ávila, El Escorial, and Alacalá de Henares. Fresh winds blew down from the Guadarrama, and by February the sun grew warm as the almonds and mimosas blossomed. Such a setting naturally encouraged bohemians and solid citizens alike to stroll and talk the day away. Although automobiles had begun to alter the urban landscape of the rapidly developing capital, they were still such a novelty in the 1920s that Ortega could jab at the local *señoritos* who drove their expensive vehicles round and round the same few blocks, as if to show off a new suit of clothes. But he bought a roadster himself in those years and set to prowling the forgotten small towns and austere contours of his beloved Old Castile, which he clearly preferred to the lands stretching south of Madrid. Pastrana, for example, a scant forty or fifty kilometers from the capital, contained some of the finest tapestries in Europe, but it was then—and is today—a tiny village through which the flocks were driven each evening at dusk. The outer limits of Madrid, far short of their present sprawl, opened directly into the countryside. The Residencia de Estudiantes, for example, on its lovely hill above the north end of La Castellana, commanded an unobstructed view of the plains and mountains to the north.

"What a delight it is," Ortega wrote at one point, "to roll aong the byways of Castile!" Bringing to the landscape something of the painter's eye, so evident in travel pieces like "Notas del vago estío," Ortega, like the writers of 1898 before him, explored the byways of his native culture and the physical features of its ecology with a driver and frequent companions. Many family photographs from the period portray him standing before a ruined castle or gazing across a stretch of sere, rolling countryside toward the horizon. He marveled at the way a people's character seemed to be stamped on the land it inhabited. He loved to record the intricate unfolding of vistas viewed from the automobile or the donkey's back as he entered villages without paved streets, electricity, or telephones, where old men and women sunned themselves against adobe walls and housewives scrubbed their clothes on rocks at the riverbank. Life in these places, picturesque for the cultured visitor if ordinary for their denizens, moved in slow, ritual patterns, the evolution of which was invisible to all but the most astute observer. The sun-cracked faces of the Castilian peasantry mirrored the parched surface of the soil of the *meseta*, broken only by tiny clusters of humble dwellings and laced with dusty, poplar-lined roadways. Before Ortega, the writers of 1898 had explored such settings often from the windows of railway coaches, in their quest for a fresh concept of the national soul. If, as Pedro Laín Entralgo has noted, they virtually "invented" a national landscape in their pages, bringing to the public eye scenes and customs previously ignored by much of the educated public, younger writers like Ortega, Marañón, and Gabriel Miró continued in their work the evocation of "lost corners" of the country begun by Azorín, Unamuno, and Antonio Machado. Ortega's own acquaintance with rural Spain had begun during youthful summers spent on the *fincas* of his maternal uncles outside Madrid and the provincial town of Guadalajara. There too he learned to hunt—an avocation he pursued in later life—with as much pleasure in the trek itself as in the kill. (Much later, in the 1940s, he would celebate the metaphor of hunting in his superb prologue to his field companion Count Eduardo Yebes's *Veinte años de caza mayor* [Twenty Years of Hunting Big Game].)

As for Madrid itself, despite the bustle of material development under Primo de Rivera, the city still seemed something of a village metropolis where one met everybody one knew in the street, at the café or club, or strolling in the Retiro gardens. The abundant literary *tertulias* were closely-knit but often open groups, and the cafés were packed with regular gatherings of friends. Men of letters easily encountered their peers, if not as intimates at least as colleagues at a banquet or a social gathering. It was not unusual for Ortega to run across Baroja or Azorín on Alcalá Street or in the Retiro, and Ramón Gómez de la Serna could write of observing the wanderings of Valle-Inclán at the library or offer a dinner for Ortega at the Pombo Café, a modest establishment just off the Puerta del Sol which Ramón had claimed as his private literary fiefdom. Such images, of course, represent the brightest and most charming face of the capital, for there remained the less visible life of the poor and forgotten, whose miserable lot was sought out and immortalized in the great novels of Benito Pérez Galdós (1843–1920). And it was the "low," popular Madrid that an observant, gifted young English traveler named V. S. Pritchett saw when he stepped off the night train from the north in 1924:

> My first impressions of the city were gloomy.... The people in the street, all in black, walked about with a look of long mourning about their

persons: the place seemed shut in some pinched and backward period of the nineteenth century, the "modern" itself being long out of date and sad. The cafés were feebly lit, the shops were small and dim. There was the sour smell of charcoal in the doorways, for most people cooked on charcoal or ground olive stones; and, even so, in their shawls or coats and with their knees tucked under heavy tablecloths for warmth.... Barefooted children ran coughing their lungs out and poor women screamed out the names of newspapers and sold lottery tickets in the wet. One passed enormous cold churches, their huge jawlike doors open, and inside lit only by the altar candles: they seemed to me like warehouses of melancholy and death.

Madrid had little industry: the place was packed with government employees, most of them obliged to do two or three jobs to keep alive. Delay was the only serious labor. The first two words one heard in Spain were, of course, *mañana* and the shrugging *nada*—the nearest to the Russian *nichevo* in Europe, uttered in all shades of meaning, but rooted in indifference to all ego except the speaker's own.[46]

Pritchett's sketch illuminates the "subterranean" city never portrayed in the *Revista de Occidente* and shows us the larger condition of the society that Ortega wished to bring to general cultural parity with the more advanced ones of northern Europe.

The social and cultural life of the city, as Pritchett notes, was centered in the government, the university, the presses and bookstores, and the cafés and *tertulias*. In contrast to the industrial and commercial life of Barcelona, Madrid was literary and diplomatic, lacking alike a genuine bourgeois class of entrepreneurs and the petit bourgeois merchants and shopkeepers. The expansion of these groups in Barcelona from the late nineteenth century onward put the Catalan metropolis closer to other European cities than to its own national capital. Indeed, the difference between the two cities in temperament, productivity, and class structure was a principal root of the long-standing and vexing "Catalan question" (part of the polemic over regional autonomy), central as this question was to the perennial struggle for power between Castile and certain particularly centrifugal regions on the edges of the Peninsula. The struggle between separatism and centralism had been with Spain at least since Ferdinand and Isabella joined their respective reigns to make of the union Castile-Aragon a kingdom strong enough to command allegiance from lesser potentates. The creation of the Trastamara dynasty established a tension between the administrative center and the provinces whose coastlines and centers of trade and industry

(Barcelona, Bilbao, Valencia) turned them toward other horizons. As Ortega showed in *Invertebrate Spain*, the issues surrounding the struggle for local autonomy had not changed essentially since the fifteenth century.

A grasp on the dramatically different styles of Madrid and Barcelona is also necessary for understanding the rise in the Catalan capital of the anarchosyndicalism, fierce anticlerical sentiment, and diffuse urban violence that made Barcelona, early in this century, a center of radicalism that had no parallel in Madrid. By contrast, the national capital, for all its concentration of vanguardist literary talent, remained in much of its tempo, taste, and appearance a slow-paced nineteenth-century metropolis far from the rest of Europe. One benefit of this more traditional life was relative civic order, for Madrid had far fewer street crimes and political murders than Barcelona during the four decades preceding 1931.[47] Public security, leisure, and conventional moral restraint were its hallmarks. It had, however, enough vitality to help two or three generations of artists and writers toward an extraordinary productivity. Though the majority of those men were not native *madrileños* (as Ortega decidedly was), they found Madrid their necessary center of stimulus and exchange. They came, in fact, from all corners of Spain to spend at least some time in the historic center: Dalí from Catalonia; Valle-Inclán from Galicia; Falla, García Lorca, Machado, Alberti, and Cernuda from Andalusia; and Unamuno and Baroja from the Basque country.

Even as late as 1930, the obvious hub of Spanish cultural life was not really a city on the scale of London, Paris, Berlin, or New York; and by European standards, Madrid was not very old. When Philip II designated it the capital of Spain in 1561, it was an obscure hamlet on the severe Castilian plateau. Though its growth was accelerated by the establishment of the royal court there, it was, even into modern times, never characterized by the middle-class expanison that had made Paris, London, Berlin, and other cities of the world such sprawling gatherings of humanity. In fact, the Spanish term *clases medias* as applied to Madrid may best be translated "intermediary classes," that is, men who occupied government and professional posts between the working class (traditionally small in Madrid) and the nobility or court and diplomatic figures. The *clases medias*, not a truly bourgeois group, had few ties either to property or to industrial expansion and capital investment. The petit bourgeois merchants, the servant class, and those in menial service occupations (boot-blacks, barbers, doormen, cabdrivers, and night watchmen) de-pended on the *class medias* and the aristocracy for their livelihood, having few alternatives, for example, in factory work or the building trades. And then, so many people seemed not to work at all! They sat for hours on end in the grand old cafés, mixing business and idle conversation. It was in this atmosphere—as well as in Primo de Rivera himself—that Ortega doubtless found models for his portrait of the mass man in *The Revolt of the Masses*—the brash, opinionated "generalist" who foolishly trusted his own uninformed opinion, ready to pronounce point-blank on anything. Though he himself was an ardent friend of the *tertulia*, Ortega was not unambivalent about that national institution:

> Whenever in France or Germany I have attended a gathering where a person of outstanding intelligence was present, I have noted that the rest have attempted to raise themselves to his level.... On the contrary, I have often noted with dread that in Spanish *tertulias*—and I refer to the higher classes, especially to the haute bourgeoisie, which has always set the tone for our national life—the very opposite occurred. When by chance an intelligent man came to those gatherings, I noted that he ended by not knowing how to come forward, as if ashamed of himself. Those bourgeois ladies and gentlemen put forth their continuous foolishness with such firmness and indubitability, they were so solidly installed in their inex-pugnable ignorance, that the slightest clever, precise, or even elegant word sounded like something absurd and even discourteous.[48]

Out of that verbiage, Ortega's work rose as an exemplary criticism of rhetorical excess. In the Madrid of the 1920s, amid the still reigning literary eminences of the 1898 group, a brilliant concentration of poetic talent, and a profusion of experimental magazines, Ortega deserves, according to his contemporary the critic Guillermo de Torre, special distinction:

> No doubt...about the outstanding personality of Ortega as essayist. That he has been wholeheartedly and perfectly. We could even affirm, in fact, that the author of *El espectador* is the true creator of the genre in our language.[49]

Ortega was also an indefatigable walker of his city's streets and a devotee, even in serious essays, of Madrid's colloquial speech. He would not forsake his love of everyday speech in order to model his work on the example of nineteenth-century German thinkers. He felt instinctively that Kant, Hegel, and the neo-Kantians (Natorp and Cohen, under whom he had studied at Marburg) were too distant in their prose from the Socratic example of live verbal play in the *agora* or marketplace, and although Ortega's attachment to good talk and to the podium was distinctly theatrical, it was never mere showmanship. Indeed, newspaper coverage of his public lectures, particularly after the civil war, often highlighted their "social" character. Whatever other subtle qualities they had or lacked, they were always grand events of the cultural season.

While Ortega's written work became widely known during the twenties in the pages of *El Sol* and the *Revista de Occidente*, as well as in volumes of *El espectador* and other publications, his public presence was most prominently felt in the two key institutions of the School of Philosophy and Letters at the University of Madrid and the Residencia de Estudiantes, relocated on what Juan Ramón Jiménez dubbed "the hill of poplars." In this period, the university, not yet a century old, became a center of learning worthy of comparison with many of its counterparts elsewhere in Europe. The School of Philosophy and Letters was its special glory, including not only the distinguished faculty of philosphy led by Ortega but also outstanding men in history, philology, and Arabic studies. But across town, on what was called "Los Altos del Hipódromo," the Residencia had developed by 1920 into something like a mini-university in its own right.

Closely tied to the university both because it housed many of its brightest students and because the intellectual aristocracy of the city fostered many of its cultural activities, the Residencia, in many ways the most interesting institution in Spain during the twenties, was a direct offspring of Giner's Institución Libre. The Residencia, founded in 1910 in a peak moment of educational reform, began modestly, with seventeen students housed in a former hotel at number 14 Calle Fortuny. Envisioned on the model of the university colleges of Oxford and Cambridge, it was from the start much more than a mere dormitory. Its first and sole director was the young Alberto Jiménez Fraud, recommended for the position by his former teacher Giner. Jiménez Fraud quickly became an exemplary leader of youth in a project dedicated "to the moral life, to the formation of character, to general culture, to hygiene ... and ... to the ennoblement of university youth.''⁵⁰ He had married the daughter of Giner's close disciple Manuel Bartolomé Cossío, and together the elegant and attractive couple animated the activities of this latest fruit of Giner's dreams of a new Spain. Between 1911 and 1914, the Residencia acquired new properties in the Calle Fortuny, and in 1915 moved to the first three of the beautiful new buildings being constructed on the hill at the end of the Calle Pinar. Meanwhile, beginning in the summer of 1912, under the auspices of the Centro de Estudios Históricos, its dormitories had been used to house the first summer courses for foreign students in Spain, many of them from England and the United States. In 1913 it began the series of publications in which Ortega's *Meditations on Quixote* was the second volume. From the start, Ortega, a member of the original board of directors, saluted the venture as one of the noblest efforts of the reformers with whom he made common cause. Together with many of the nation's outstanding scholars, scientists, and men of letters, he frequently visited the lovely grounds of the poplar-lined hill and helped to organize the diverse cultural activities that made the Residencia perhaps the outstanding example of the enclaves of cultural leadership he hoped eventually to see created throughout Spain.

During the early years of the Residencia Juan Ramón Jiménez, the painter-poet José Moreno Villa, and the sculptor and art critic Ricardo Orueta lodged there regularly, serving as informal tutors, and Unamuno and Antonio Machado were frequent visitors. Other cultural luminaries, like Santiago Ramón y Cajal, Ramón Menéndez Pidal, Gregorio Marañón, Américo Castro, Manuel García Morente (dean of the School of Philosophy and Letters in the twenties) and the physicist Blas Cabrera were also close supporters of the new cultural center. Among the young residents during the twenties were Federico García Lorca, Rafael Alberti, Salvador Dalí, and Luis Buñuel, who often met and entertained each other with poems, songs, and stories in the pleasant gardens (including one, The Garden of the Poets, designed and planted by Juan Ramón Jiménez) with their view of the mountains. Lorca, having first arrived in Madrid from Granada in 1918, lived intermittently in the Residencia until 1928, then occasionally during the summers until 1934. There he directed the university theater group "La Barraca," founded by the government in 1931 to bring versions of the classics of Spanish theater (Calderón, Lope de Vega, Tirso de Molina, et al.) to provincial cities around the country. Often skillfully abridging the works under his direction, Lorca learned stagecraft and sharpened his own tools as a playwright. On many evenings in residence he discussed poetry with Alberti, Moreno Villa, and others and also entertained his friends with renditions of old Spanish *tonadillas* and *coplas*, which he accompanied on the piano or guitar. Alberti, in his own memoir of the period, *La arboleda perdida* (The Lost Grove, written in exile in Buenos Aires many years later), recalls the wonderfully effervescent atmsophere of literary Madrid at the time, particularly at the Residencia, where the halls and lounges of the capacious buildings seemed constantly abuzz with good humor and animated discussion.

The range of programs associated with this cultural center grew steadily during the decade. In addition to the small but distinguished line of publications bearing its imprint, there appeared in 1926 the magazine *Residencia*, which ran through twenty numbers before its discontinuation in 1934. A primary source for assessing the broader cultural milieu in which Ortega moved, *Residencia* published news of activities on the hill, scholarly and literary pieces, and, in many cases, the texts of programs presented under the auspices of the institution's Sociedad de Cursos y Conferencias. Founded in 1924 and supported materially by certain members of the enlightened aristocracy (the Duke of Alba, the Count and Countess of Yebes, et al.), the Sociedad brought to the Residencia lecture hall many of Europe's outstanding writers and scientists: Leo Frobenius, who presented the first program with three lectures in March 1924; Paul Valéry, Louis Aragon, Paul Claudel, and Georges Duhamel in 1925; Max Jacob and Count Keyserling in 1926; and Francis Poulenc, Maurice Ravel, Maurice de Broglie, and Madame Curie in 1931. Einstein himself had lectured there in 1923, with Ortega as his interpreter, and in 1928 the Sociedad sponsored a series of talks on modern architecture by Le Corbusier, Gropius, and others. Ortega, of course, was instrumental in identifying appropriate speakers, many of whose contributions appeared in either *Residencia* or the *Revista de Occidente*.

Although for our purposes, the Residencia's humanistic programs are the most germane, it should be added that the steady development of facilities on the hill made it also the site of some of the finest laboratories and centers of scientific research in the Spain of the day. Even while the fledgling institution was still at number 14 Calle Fortuny, it had included rudimentary laboratories of microscopic anatomy and general chemistry. After the move to new quarters in

1915, facilities were developed for physiological chemistry, physiology and anatomy of the nervous system, serology and bacteriology, and general physiology, all of them directed by outstanding Spanish scientists in the respective fields. A major step forward was taken in 1926 when the Rockefeller Foundation donated funds for construction next to the dormitories, of the new Instituto Nacional de Química y Física.

Throughout the course of its existence (1910–1936), the Residencia generally enjoyed an excellent reputation. Under the leadership of Jiménez Fraud, the conduct of the students (approximately 150 in residence at any one time) was correct and even gentlemanly, perhaps harking back to the somewhat puritanical personal model established by Giner and, before him, by the original Krausists themselves. Alfonso XIII had visited the early building in Fortuny in 1911 and clearly approved of what he saw, but trouble arose with the start of the government of Primo de Rivera in 1923, when more reactionary vioces spoke out against the whole reformist tradition in education. At that point, the Duke of Alba and other friends of the institution came to its defense, forestalling any contrary action by the dictator. Also the formation of the Comité Hispano-Inglés in 1923 by the British ambassador Sir Esme Howard, Alba, and others served to protect the Residencia from adverse criticism by accentuating its ties with the college system of Oxford and Cambridge, establishing grants for exchange students, and bringing to Madrid leading figures of English cultural circles. Thus, in addition to the distinguished visitors to the hilltop from France, Germany, and elsewhere, the Residencia would welcome H. G. Wells, Walter Starkie, G. K. Chesterton, John M. Keynes, General Bruce (explorer of the Himalayas), Sir Arthur Eddington, and others.[51] The work of the Comité confirmed the observation of the English musicologist and hispanist J. B. Trend, an enthusiastic visitor, that the Residencia was "Oxford and Cambridge in Madrid." With determined and diplomatic support from many sides, it continued to prosper through the Primo period and became a vital model for pedagogical reform when the Second Republic arrived in 1931. During the early 1930s, many students from the "Resi" did volunteer work in summer camps for poor children, collaborated in the founding of new schools by the Institución Libre, and joined in the Misiones Pedagógicas, organized under Cossío in 1931 to bring books and cultural programs to forgotten corners of the country. Many years after the Spanish Civil War, during which the Residencia buildings became a combination of barracks and hospital, Ortega would often lament the disappearance of that grand experiment, which was, he sadly noted to his son Miguel, "a lost paradise." [52]

If Primo de Rivera was in fact won over to the cause of the Residencia by the late twenties, his regime certainly did not win the support of the liberal intellectuals, at whom he was accustomed to take potshots. As the decade went on, Ortega's political criticism focused increasingly on the faults of the dictatorship. His growing disillusionment with Primo stemmed not so much from the man's domestic policies as from his generally arrogant and unenlightened cultural views and his troglodytic behavior—a spectacle not likely to make a favorable impression upon the rest of the world. Ortega, after all, was struggling to bring Spain to the level of the times, while Primo often seemed—at least to the intellectuals whose scorn he had quickly earned—to be dragging it down into anachronism, back to the old Spanish vice of valuing personal impulse more than sound knowledge and mental discipline. While in fact Spanish intellectuals were far freer under the capricious rule of Primo than they were later to be under the hand of General Francisco Franco, Ortega could hardly accept Spain's deprecation in the world's eyes as Alfonso XIII appeared to be every day more the prisoner of the very man he had helped to seize power. [53]

In the midst of his mature career in the mid-1920s, as he was becoming increasingly influential as a teacher, editor, and political critic, Ortega perceived with alarm the nation's political stasis. In 1927 his growing pessimism was evident in the essay "Mirabeau, or the Politician" (first sketched out in *El Sol* in February) and in a series of five articles he published under the heading "Social Power" (appearing in *El Sol* during October and November). The piece on Mirabeau is a convenient summary of Ortega's view of the social power of intellectuals as he conceived of it in the middle of the Primo period. Although he saw that power to be very limited, he argued that men of ideas should be given greater influence without being obliged to enter the lists of partisan politics. Action, Ortega declared with respect to Mirabeau, was the domain of the politician, while the intellectual's highest work was "to think the truth and, once thought, to speak it, be it as it may, even though he is quartered for it. This is the maxim of action that falls to the intellectual." [54] In stressing the primacy of honest speech rather than direct action, he revealed how far he had come from his earlier idea that critical thought could more directly effect change in the world. By 1927 he could say:

> The discrete thing, in any case, is not to delude oneself, for the very reason that in politics it is so easy to do so. I sometimes manage to convince myself that I am Napoleon, because like him I don't have more than sixty pulse beats a minute. The confusion in my case is not so serious, for I am only a writer. [55]

He had already affirmed this position three years before in the essay on "cosmopolitanism," where he had appeared to resolve his uncertainty over the intellectual's social role. In context, that earlier statement, curiously at odds with Ortega's repeated conviction that intelligence must help men to live in the public as well as the personal world, appears to represent only one side of a dialogue with himself which he never finished. The sharp lament of the essays on social power reveals that he was far from settled in his previous choice of a sotto voce role for the intellect. In those five short pieces he argued that the optimum social power is that granted a man by an entire society. In modern Spain, Ortega claimed, politicians had in fact enjoyed a social power greatly disproportionate to their intrinsic worth. The Spanish politician's pretense was more ridiculous than ever if one applied to it Ortega's assumption that the parliamentary monarchy and its traditional parties were politically exhausted. As for the Spanish clergy, he argued that they *appeared* to have great social power, but in fact exercised it within a relatively limited sphere. Several years later, in 1931, he observed:

> We consider it an error of historical optics, but very general among the Spanish left, to suppose that the Church and the religious orders have a great social power in Spain. In our judgment this optical error proceeds from confounding the social power that the Church might have by itself with that which comes to it through the state, the organisms of which it in large measure managed. Once this favor of public power for the Church is suppressed and reduced to its exclusive social power, we believe that it will represent in Spain a force considerably less than it may have even in the most lay country of Europe. [56]

Not suprisingly, though paradoxically in view of his growing eminence, Ortega found the Spanish writer to be at the bottom of the scale of social power. The writer, he contended, faced a largely obdurate and uninterested public, while the politician's manipulative control of the populace was thoroughly established and, in normal times, was guaranteed continuity. Cultural projects were always more fragile than political ones, but particularly so in Spain: "I don't believe," he noted, "there exists...any nation less docile to intellectual influence than ours."[57] From this lamentable condition derived what he termed the "bitter, violent, gross tone that dominates our literary production." The gravity of the situation suggested to Ortega that "Spain is coming to a historical turning in which she can be saved politically only with the serious collaboration of the intellectuals."[58] This extraordinary expectation, quite the opposite of his conclusion in the Mirabeau essay a few months earlier, was immediately followed by the contradictory counsel that intellectuals should not believe too much in themselves. The pessimism of this 44-year-old professor of metaphysics, heightened perhaps by wounded pride, was essentially accurate, for he realized his dilemma as a kind of cultural missionary who could not escape the burden of working *in partibus infidelium*. As with his predecessors in the Generation of 1898—Unamuno's famous cry was "me duele España" (Spain aches within me)—Ortega, in the essays on social power, saw how much remained to be done and how limited were his resources for doing it. He realized that his project of transforming his compatriots' standards of cultural excellence actually existed on a little island of enlightenment surrounded by the stubbornly resistant mores of traditional society and the clearly anti-intellectual bias of many of Primo's supporters. Connected in his imagination to Marburg, Berlin, Paris, Oxford, and other centers of European culture and learning, Ortega felt ever more compelled to declare himself a "European."

Although his hopes for a major public role would rise briefly with the beginning of the Second Republic, Ortega's increasing awareness during the 1920s of the fragility of his real social base caused him to pin his hopes on the cultivation of intimate circles of loyal followers and carefully chosen peers. Such, for example, was the purpose of his lavish attention to the traditional Spanish institution of the *tertulia*, or literary salon. Ortega's daily *tertulias* at the offices of the *Revista de Occidente* in Madrid's Gran Vía were, in fact, the most brilliant of many such gatherings in a city whose intellectual life seemed to rest as much on bright conversation as on reading or study.[59] In his prodigiously eccentric autobiography, *Automoribundia*, Ramón Gómez de la Serna caught this aspect of his friend Ortega's life by casting the salon as an enchanted undersea kingdom presided over by a benevolent wizard:

> The *tertulia* was the presbytery of the magazine, and both people and texts were selected there.... It was neither hasty nor anxious. It had a sofa and a number of armchairs.... Don José Ortega y Gasset was accustomed to arrive at 7:30 in the evening.... Only at 8 o'clock the salon, with its rather submarine decor, was opened.... Ortega, who applies his compass-nose to each conversation while he sniffs at the far horizons for the distant hunt, offers pastry with thoughts for shortening and the pine-nut seed of a kindly phrase. And in that blueish medium, conversation is agile, and we wish to remember afterwards what we have said, favored by that agility which propitiatory water gives to one's movements and to the frantic stretchings of the imagination. Only a great man who possesses the keys of the marvellous grottoes can allow us that delight of levitation.... Rarely is there silence in the *tertulia*, but when one of those pauses came, it was an ineradicable silence, a silence of the cathedral.
>
> The young poets arrived a bit rattled and vainglorious. Ortega was kind and friendly with them. García Lorca came there with his first manuscript of verses, and the *Revista* published them without more ado; they were one of its chief successes.
>
> The *Revista de Occidente* seemed like the eternal home, and the captain with his compass pointed toward the West carried us along under the sun which had not begun its decline, following its leap on the horizon and never falling behind in some valley.[60]

In view of the importance of live dialogue in Ortega's life, the English historian Raymond Carr's curt judgment of prewar Madrid culture seems deficient: "This emphasis on conversational exchange and journalism was one of the main weaknesses of Spanish intellectual life: conversation was the essential foundation of Ortega y Gasset's work."[61] Carr is certainly right in one sense, precisely as Ortega's portrait of mediocre salons indicates; but when those endless conversations bore fruit, the result was the provocative, polished, and quasi-colloquial essay at which Ortega became a master.

Outside the intimate circle of the *tertulia*, Ortega of course continued his work in the pages of *El Sol* and the *Revista*, as well as in the chair of metaphysics at the university, for which a new campus on the west side of the city was begun in 1927. As before, he realized that the creation of a Spanish intellectual elite required the creation of progressively wider circles of readers, teachers, and students who could spread throughout the body politic the new ideas he championed. In many ways, the Spanish bourgeoisie of the time, still relatively small and characterized by a certain thinness of cultural preparation, justified his bouts of pessimism. And although the Central University of Madrid was coming into its own and that of Barcelona was also vigorous, outside the two major cities the university system as a whole was feeble, libraries and booksellers were few, opportunities for travel abroad were limited, and the Church continued to exert a strong conservative influence at all levels of education. Perhaps, then, as a means of extending his reach and of finding a fresh public, Ortega made a second trip to Argentina in the summer and fall of 1928. At the University of Buenos Aires he gave a short course entitled "Hegel y la historiología" and a series of talks before the association of Amigos del Arte, which had invited him to make the trip.[62] This second visit heightened his sense of connection to the Argentine capital, where he had been so warmly welcomed in 1916. In 1917 he had written "a few words to the subscribers" for volume 2 of *El espectador*:

> The select spirits of this peninsula who are working to augment Spanish culture ought to cross the Atlantic in order to be comforted.... For a writer, a poet or a scientist the political separations of states are nonexistent when linguistic identity ... flows beneath them. The point of the pen or the tremulous air of the voice will move alike the nerves of men who belong to very diverse states. A Spanish writer, then, ought not to feel himself further from Buenos Aires than from Madrid.

In this spirit, Ortega could envision a greater Hispanic unity emerging from the postwar world, in which "over the last century and thanks to the independence of the Central and South American countries, a new ingredient has become prepared to act in the history of the planet: the Spanish race, a greater Spain, of which our peninsula is only a province." [63]

When he addressed the Argentine public, Ortega was at times generously eulogistic of future intellectual life in what he called the "pre-historic" continent.[64] In his "Letter to a Young Argentine Studying Philosophy" (1924), he revealed his greatest expectations for Latin America and congratulated the young man on his *docta ignorantia* and his openness to the curious wonder that was the starting point of genuine philosophy. He also gave him direction and warning:

> One must turn to things, one must turn to things without delay. The American, my friend, ... tends toward narcissism and what you call "parade." When he looks at things, he does not release his gaze upon them but tends to use them as a mirror in which to contemplate himself. That is why, instead of penetrating their interior, he stands almost always before the surface, busy representing himself and making scenes. But science and letters do not consist in posturing before things, but rather in bursting feverishly into them, thanks to a virile appetite for penetration.[65]

At times it was impossible for Ortega to avoid a tone of condescension toward the American peoples. Although he came from a European country whose modern history was one of decline and impoverishment, he brought with him when he addressed the Argentine public a sense of cultural custodianship and the valuable, if bitter, perspective of a people wounded by their own history. Beside Spain, Argentina seemed to Ortega hardly to have begun its history. It was this innocent condition, he argued, which gave Argentines (and other Americans, North and South) the vital energies of youth. Ortega admired this vitality but characterized it as "primitive" and "prehistoric." Assuming a sympathetic distance, he became the cultural analyst for the South American continent; and for all his efforts to avoid premature judgment, he spoke to the Argentines as a prophet of their national destiny. His movement in this role between humility and proud certainty gave piquance to his reflections on Latin Americans, particularly in playful and coquettish pieces like "Meditación del pueblo joven" (Meditation on the Young Country) and "Meditación de la criolla" (Meditation on the Creole Woman).

Latin Americans could not, Ortega believed, rapidly overcome their cultural distance from Europe. But this condition provided them with a basis for reflection on the problem of learning from the Old World:

> You [Argentines] are more sensitive than precise, and as long as this does not change, you will depend integrally on Europe in intellectual matters.... Because, being sensitive, the fine receptor that is your organism will be moved, like it or not, by every lively and fertile idea produced in Europe. But when you wish to react to the received idea—to judge it,

refute it, evaluate it, or oppose another to it—you will find within
yourselves an impression, a vagueness...a lack of certain and firm
criterion sure of itself, which is obtained only through rigorous
discipline.[66]

Nevertheless, Ortega hoped that the pristine sensibility of young
Argentines would remain free of undue seriousness. Let them not
dedicate their best energies to the prosaic business of politics,
economics, and cattle raising. Their abundant natural resources all
too clearly tempted them to emphasize material development to the
neglect of cultural refinement. He urged more truly creative activities, especially "pure science" and art. In short, Argentina needed
theory more than praxis, which would come in time as the fruit of
free-ranging intellectual exploration. In the pragmatic New World
setting, Ortega was the European intellectual committed to the
"play" theory of culture. On one hand, he characterized politics,
industry, law, and economics as "serious occupation, ... pure formalism and, as such, sad, grey, without inner sufficiency."[67] Philosophy,
on the other hand, was the noble *gaia scienza* born in the "sportive"
atmosphere of the gymnasium or the plaza and presided over by
smiling old wise men. The picture was charming, though perhaps
neither consoling nor readily applicable for many of his Argentine
readers.

Ortega's assumptions about the general Latin American public's
response to his work point to his low estimation of the continent's
intellectual life beyond one or two select centers like Buenos Aires or
Santiago de Chile. In a footnote to the 1922 article "Themes of
Travel" he bluntly summarized his harshest judgment on the matter:

> In the Spanish-American world the majority of the writers are of such
> little weight intellectually, so little aware of things and so audacious in
> speaking of them, that the presence of people a bit more capable is
> dangerous. As among some barbarous peoples personal security has not
> yet been achieved, so among our [Spanish-speaking] peoples the same
> thing happens with intellectual traffic.[68]

Ortega's dismay was doubled by the tepid, uncritical Latin American
response to "books that I myself have had translated with the generous intention of amplifying the Spanish-American mind, so narrow,
so little generous, and so imprecise."[69] His pedagogical program of

bringing the best German and other European thinkers to the attention of American readers seemed to him too little appreciated.

The problem of the intellectual backwardness of Spanish-speaking peoples in modern times is present in some way in the work of every major essayist and cultural critic writing in Spanish in the last hundred years. In his cautionary notes to Argentines—kindly toward the young, mordant with the proud— Ortega added his part to this long chapter in cultural history, perhaps projecting on the Argentines the kind of criticism applied by others to Spain; for much of what he noted of the cultural debility, the personal posturing, and the defensive stance of the collective psyche of Argentines sounds curiously like the critique by northern Europeans of Spanish pride, cultural isolation, and so forth. Such criticisms, in both cases, were partially justifiable, although the European vision of Spain since the sixteenth century often merely repeated the received ideas of the "Black Legend" of Spanish history, created largely by northern European Protestant historians. In the case of Ortega's diagnosis of Argentina, the criticism arose from within the Hispanic world, illustrating perhaps what Freud has called "the narcissism of small differences."

Fancying that he was called to administer the therapy of blunt truth to the Argentine soul, Ortega made several declarations during his second visit that drew both hostile and affirmative responses. His analyses of the country's national character were unfortunately impressionistic. He had not studied Argentine history or society with any care, contenting himself instead with broad notions such as the superiority of the creole woman to her male counterpart. This idea was, characteristically, based on the admiring response to his work and his person from Victoria Ocampo and a small circle of her friends, all women of the Argentine upper class. Brilliant essayist that he was, Ortega failed to see the complexity of Argentina. His analysis of the landscape and the role it played in Argentine history, for example, was typical of a subjective, highly figurative literature of the national soul that already had an appreciable history in Spain and in other European countries. Rooted in the Hegelian and German romantic philosophy of history, this approach to cultural history sought to explain the collective psyche in terms of broad historical and geographical circumstances.

Working on the basis of this legacy, Ortega's very fine sense of cir-

cumstances did not save him from painting Argentina with too broad
a brush. In "The Pampa ... Promises," written in September of 1929
on the train from Buenos Aires to Mendoza, he imposed upon the
endless plains before him a whole theory of travel. Distinguishing it
from planned activity or mere tourism, he pictured the true traveler
as one who had the leisure and the largesse of soul simply to "be" in
the place where he was, to open his heart and his pores to its suggestive surroundings. Like the mature lover who is roused only by the
most select women, the mature traveler would not be moved by every
passing landscape. The romantic enthusiasm for exciting vistas had
indeed not been foreign to him in youth, Ortega admitted, but with
age and ripening he had learned to reserve his powers of appreciation
for the rare encounter. Now, on the westbound train through ex-
panses that seemed pure horizon, after what he termed years of
relative insensitivity to nature, he felt "the invasion of the Pampa." [70]
Such experiences, he continued, disturbed deep, settled areas of our
being, mobilizing dormant sides of our lives and releasing potential
we had forgotten we carried. These psychic layers corresponded to
the many lives we might have known had circumstances not inexorably pressed us to choose the path we ultimately took. When our
souls were bestirred by a profoundly moving ambience or spectacle,
we lived in imagination something of the "unborn" lives that wan-
dered within us like spectres of our unfulfilled multiple being:

> It is not a matter of abstract possibilities, but rather that each human
> being carries clustered about the nucleus of his effective existence a
> concrete, highly individual cast of other possible lives, his and his alone.
> And the strictly fated shape of our destiny appears sharp and clear only
> when highlighted against the background of these spectral biographies.
> Thus I will narrate my possible, unborn creole life. [71]

As with so many other themes that engaged his fecund imagination, this one was in fact "left for another time." But the pampas
themselves became the key symbol in Ortega's portrait of the Argentine soul, shaped as he felt it was by the sense of inexhaustible promise
so evident in the landscape. Employing his characteristic rhetoric of
fresh discovery, of themes never before broached, Ortega wrote of the
Argentine mind as holding a fascination with the promise of what one
was to become in some distant future. Yet, he felt, this scale was too
grand; it swallowed ordinary life in a maelstrom of ill-founded hope.

Watching the continual flights of birds and the huge, shifting Argentine skies, he felt that "[e]verything is a movement toward the beyond, an aspiring, an announcing that something is going to be. The pampa stretches away with gestures of promise." [72] The aura of expectation that Ortega divined in the geography implied, when transferred to the psyche, absenting oneself from one's actual life. The aged creole, he imagined, might well look back on his days to discover that he had lived them all with his eye on the miragelike future. The scale of the pampas provided no lesson in foregrounds, no sense of immediate or short-run goals: surrounded by this inebriating space, the typical Argentine could not attend to the tasks of the moment.

This disquieting expectation of fulfillment, which was constantly postponed, received further scrutiny in the more explicit companion essay, "El hombre a la defensiva" (Man on the Defensive, written in September 1929). Here Ortega explained the Argentine propensity for narcissism and posturing as a function of the lack of firm character at the core. Dreaming of inflated, grandiose accomplishments, the Argentine man (for creole women were generally exempt from these charges) covered his sense of insufficiency with bravado and arrogance. Much as he was "all future" in his sense of life, he was all surface in his personal conduct. Nor could he find support from his culture, which had been created in an almost improvisational way, or from the great wealth that outran the intrinsic cultural and intellectual resources of the nation. Speaking as a European, Ortega asserted that no country could build its spiritual strength in haste, and Argentina seemed a clear case of a "boom" phenomenon that would have to catch up with itself gradually. Much of its daily functioning he found makeshift, uncommitted, and incompetent; and he sought, despite the bluntness of his critique, to redirect the still "youthful" energies of that enormous land. Such change would require the Argentine to break his narcissistic shell, abandoning glorified images of himself and his nation.

These criticisms of what Ortega, in sanguine moments, considered his second homeland understandably alienated much of his Argentine audience; but he won the frank admiration of an intellectual minority that included Ocampo, Eduardo Mallea, and Ezequiel Martínez Estrada. The two latter writers shortly published books echoing Ortega's linking of landscape and psyche, a linking based upon his central idea that the "I" or ego is partially constituted by its circumstances. In fact, this Orteguian valuation of circumstances helped Latin American writers and thinkers, particularly in Argentina and Mexico, to affirm their own national experience as a source for philosophical reflection, artistic creation, and historial narrative.

Thus Mallea's *Historia de una pasión argentina* (1935) very likely borrowed from Ortega the distinction between a "visible" and an 'invisible" Argentina.[73] Another influence on Mallea was undoubtedly the American writer Waldo Frank, who gave a very successful series of lectures in various Argentine cities in 1929. In *America Hispana* (1931) Frank showed how artistic intuition and a poetic sense of geography and culture could produce brilliant insights into the cultures of a region that suffered an inferiority complex toward Europe and North America. Mallea, Frank's translator, obviously learned from his work, but the highly charged poetic prose of *Historia de una pasión argentina* seemed more clearly indebted to the example Ortega had provided for the passionate evocation of national temperament. Likewise, Martínez Estrada's *Radiografía de la pampa* (1933) developed, perhaps under Ortega's influence, a bitter yet prodigiously inventive picture of Argentina as isolated from the rest of the world, turned in upon its own history, and lost in the vast solitude of the pampas. This searching essay reached back in the long, basically romantic tradition of tracing intimate connections between the sensitive soul and its natural surroundings. In fact, Ortega too had incorporated in his Argentine sketches of a poetic geography a constellation of received ideas about the influence of landscape upon the psyche. In the case of Argentina, his perception of the land had long before been beautifully stated in W. H. Hudson's *The Purple Land* (1885) and his autobiographical *Far Away and Long Ago* (1918); and much before that the great Argentine writer and statesman Domingo Faustino Sarmiento (1811–1888) had unforgettably portrayed the overwhelming power of space in the national life in his classic study *Facundo* (1845).

Ortega's visit to Argentina in 1928 strengthened his ties with a select group of the country's literary intellectuals, but others, like Jorge Luís Borges, did not take kindly to his critique of Argentina, and many of his audiences were taken aback by Ortega's presumptuous judgments of their culture. In his writings to Argentines and about Argentina, Ortega revealed the weakness in his claim to penetrate to the heart of things. His almost obsessive concern in those pieces with the absence of genuine dialogue in Argentina must be seen as much as a sign of his own failure to judge wisely and communicate well as of the lack of cultural exchange among Spanish-speaking intellectuals. Yet, in the larger picture, Ortega's three visits to Argentina and the work of his disciples there and elsewhere in Latin America did much to revitalize both Spanish and Spanish-American culture through the affirmation of a transatlantic linguistic and historical community. His impact as a self-appointed ambassador of culture seems clearly preferable, for example, to that expressed in the hackneyed rhetoric of *hispanidad* which underlay Primo de Rivera's promotion of an increased Spanish presence in diplomatic and commercial circles of Latin America. Ortega's response to the New World was quick with sympathy and intuitive insight by comparison to Ramiro de Maeztu's mystique of a pan-Hispanic Catholic community, or to the later postwar ideology of the Franco regime's cultural and economic panhispanism. Cavalier as he sometimes was in his assertion of the ties between the mother country and her former colonies, Ortega rarely rang as hollow or as illiberal as the lesser rhetoricians of *hispanidad*.

5

THE LEVEL OF THE TIMES:
1929–1930

Ortega returned to Spain, after a busy fall in Buenos Aires, in January 1929, toward the end of a decade in which his nation had advanced rapidly into the modern material world. By this time the dictator who had held the nation in a kind of political stasis, even as many areas of Spanish life were being deeply transformed, had lost much of his earlier support. In fact, Primo's resignation was just a year away, and the atmosphere in Madrid, for prescient observers, was one of heightened expectation and a heady feeling that anything might be possible once the old order was gone; for the dictatorship, it would soon become clear, was to be the last phase of a long political decline running from the end of the Restoration years (1875–1902) into the present. For Ortega, this historical moment, which appeared opportune for the political transformation he had long invoked, coincided with the full maturation of his philosophical thought and his political commentary. He was about to enter the great central period of his career precisely as the nation itself took one of the most decisive turns in its history. It is probably impossible to spell out fully the effect of events upon his writing, but it is certain that even the highest theoretical flights of works like *¿Qué es filosofía?* (lecture course of 1929; published in 1958; English translation *What is Philosophy?* published in 1960); *Unas lecciones de metafísica*, (lecture course of 1932–1933; published in 1966; English translation *Some Lessons in Metaphysics* published in 1969); and *En torno a Galileo* (lecture course of 1933; published in 1956; English translation *Man and Crisis* published in 1958) resonate with the drama of political change through which Spain was passing.

Immediately upon his return, Ortega found himself embroiled in

the uproar occasioned by Primo's audacious (and strategically foolish) attack on the university system and the Madrid Ateneo. Primo's
resignation and his abrupt departure for Paris was to come at the end
of January 1930, but the year preceding that date saw the death agony
of the failing dictatorship and a time of intellectual ferment and
increased political involvement for Ortega. Primo had actually been
troubled with student opposition to his regime almost since the
beginning. As Shlomo Ben Ami observes, "The years 1924–1931
witnessed a spectacular upsurge of political awareness in Spanish
universities. Leftist students and intellectuals played a major role in
fomenting opposition to the Dictatorship and to the Monarchy, and
in creating the nationwide protest that finally brought about the
downfall of both."[1] The nation's university system had expanded
dramatically as part of the economic and social modernization of the
decade, with the number of students doubling in the twelve Spanish
universities between 1923 and 1930.[2] Since January 1927, the dictator had been chivvied by increasingly determined resistance from
the liberal student syndicate FUE (Federación Universitaria Escolar), formed in that month with support from republican and leftist
professors and intellectuals. Its first nationwide strike, in March 1928,
was a dramatic manifestation of what had become a general loss of
confidence in Primo's policies—or lack of them. When a government
decree of May 19, 1928, conferred degree-granting status on the two
confessional colleges of Deusto (Jesuits) and El Escorial (Augustines),
seeming thus to have established a rival tribunal of authority in higher
education, unrest grew quickly among both students and teachers. At
both the secondary and university levels, Primo had consistently
attacked those teachers and intellectuals who, in the long struggle
begun by the Krausists, stood for autonomy from state and church
control. The general had taken several steps to support clerical control
of education, prominent among them the legalization of uniform
textbooks for use in secondary schools. In opposing a state control
closely tied to traditional Catholic morality, the FUE was openly
republican in many of its sentiments and was encouraged by pro-
republican professors like Unamuno, Marañón, and Luis Jiménez de
Asua, who hoped for a wide-ranging change in the nation's moral and
intellectual climate. Indeed, the syndicate's democratic orientation,
Ben Ami writes,

was inextricably tied up with the rejection of old moralities and traditional values, sympathy toward occasional demands for free love and praise for nudism, a greater interest in politics and a growing literary sensitiveness at a period when "rebellious" authors like García Lorca, Salinas, and Alberti were making their appearance and Ortega's *Revista de Occidente* was sponsoring the "new wave." [3]

When initial protests against the new decree favoring the clerical colleges had failed, the FUE declared a nationwide university strike on March 7, 1929. Trouble broke out in a number of cities (Madrid, Barcelona, Seville, Granada, Valencia, and Valladolid), and Primo closed the University of Madrid from March 16 to May 30, 1929. In protest against this high-handed exercise of state power, Ortega resigned his professorial chair along with his colleagues Luis Jiménez de Asua, Fernando de los Ríos, and Felipe Sánchez Román. All four were reinstated on February 1, 1930, under the government formed by General Dámaso Berenguer, which followed Primo's resignation on January 28 of that year; but the breach between the university and the state had been opened wide, and students and faculty alike had learned something of the tactics of political pressure groups. Certain of the leaders of FUE had drawn close to Ortega and to other faculty who, in marked defiance of Primo's order, had agreed to hold informal interim classes in their homes and offices during the closure.

In February 1929 Ortega had begun a course at the University of Madrid entitled "¿Qué es filosofía?," portions of which he had already presented in Buenos Aires the preceding fall; but the closure of the university and his own resignation obliged him to continue it extramurally, first in the Sala Rex and then, as the audience unexpectedly swelled, in the Infanta Beatriz theater, both in downtown Madrid.[4] He was not quite taking philosophy into the streets, but the varied and enthusiastic crowd listened to him both as a symbol of resistance to the failing regime and as an exponent of the philosphical "news" of the day. The complete text of the lectures, essentially unchanged in style and format, was published only posthumously in 1958. As they stand today, notes Ortega's American translator Mildred Adams, "they read like ... Ortega's spoken Spanish, and in the movement of the prose one can see the eyebrows peak up, the forefinger come down, the mobile face change, the shoulders present the coming paradox in anticipation of the words." [5] Although fragments of the course were published during Ortega's lifetime (including the first three "lessons" in *La Nación* of Buenos Aires in August, September, and November 1930), his apparent decision to leave the course as a whole in manuscript may indicate that he was uncertain of having achieved the new philosophical "level" that he repeatedly announced to his audience between February and May of that spring. Whatever his motives, however, the public occasion, coming in the midst of the university crisis, was unprecedented, as the editors of his *Obras completas* have observed:

> This was the first course in pure philosophy given in Spain outside a university, before the most heterogeneous public one can imagine, made up not only of "initiates" and students of philosophy and *dilletanti* of spiritual pleasures, but also in large number by uneducated men whose enthusiasm for such themes could hardly be suspected.... As was written [by Fernando Vela] at its conclusion: "The social phenomenon has been surprising.... Obscure men from obscure towns are requesting copies of the newspaper which extensively reviewed the lessons." It was "the almost magical revelation of a Spanish reality different from that which has fed our pessimism and our indolence." One might say that Ortega had wanted to carry out an experiment, seeking for the purpose the conditions of failure: a matriculation fee... an abstruse theme, ten long, full, and difficult talks.[6]

In recent Ortega scholarship, *What Is Philosophy?* has been seen as the beginning of Ortega's fully mature philosophical period and, at the same time, as a skillful if often tangled adaptation of ideas from various German sources, principally Scheler, Heidegger, Dilthey, Husserl, and Nicolai Hartmann.[7] The essential judgment is that he managed in these lectures to incorporate into his own vision and lexicon crucial aspects of Heidegger's *Sein und Zeit* (1927), which he read carefully shortly after its appearance. Thus the key earlier idea that "yo soy yo y mi circunstancia" ("I am I and my circumstances," first enunciated in the *Meditations* of 1914) reaches a kind of plenitude through crucial transformations in the 1929 course and in the later 1933 course on metaphysics. In the former ("¿Qué es filosofía?"), other key terms—notably *ser* (to be), *vivir* (to live), *vida* (life), *mundo* (world), and *razón vital*—undergo a similar semantic development, culminating in the last lecture (the eleventh) in the four "categories of my life," Ortega's own version of what Heidegger calls "existentials" (fundamental categories of human existence).

The four categories are, in Nelson Orringer's summary, "life as transparency to itself; life as finding itself in the world; life as decision; and the category of the circumstances."[8] The first, in keeping with Ortega's long struggle to overcome philosophical idealism, is a radical revision of the Cartesian *cogito*; for if Descartes believed he had discovered an indubitable reality in finding himself thinking, Ortega asserts by contrast that what we most obviously find when we turn to ourselves is the basic reality of "our life," understood always as the "my life" of each one of us. We are transparent to ourselves in the sense that nothing could be more patent, though it is that very patency that renders thought about this "radical reality" so difficult. Nonetheless, to live, if nothing else, is to feel oneself living. The second category, an adaptation of Heidegger's *Dasein* and *Befindlichkeit* as well as a refinement of earlier Orteguian insights, refers back to its roots in the "natural attitude" (previous to any phenomenological epoche) of Husserl's *Ideen* of 1913. Ortega had previously understood life in the world as the imperative to confront one's circumstances and to "save" onself by saving them—that is, rendering them meaningful in a determined perspective—but Heidegger presses him at this moment to connect the fact of being-occupied-with-the-world to self-awareness and to decision, the third category. Here particularly, in Ortega's splendidly dramatic sense that the press of our circumstances forces us to decide at each moment what to do, one observes the humanistic and "anthropological" cast of Ortega's existentialistic understanding of the Heideggerian analysis of *Dasein*. For Ortega, being—truly known only in the concreteness of "my life"—is understood as a constant process of deciding how to continue living. Faced with the world as a repertory of facilities and impediments, of opportunities and constraints, man asserts his freedom by choosing what he is going to be. Orringer, who sees a distant reference in the third category to an earlier doctrine of Hermann Cohen "which teaches that life is the problem of individualization," makes clear how Heidegger's work helped Ortega to find his own distinct voice:

> Heidegger writes that the being of *Dasein* lies in its existence, and a decision must always be made how to possess that being, whether in an authentic or an inauthentic mode.... Likewise Ortega sees life as our being, not predetermined being, but being decided by us.... Heidegger helps Ortega establish a clear relationship between the category of finding oneself in the world and the category of decision, an outgrowth of the idea of life the problem.[9]

The fourth category, that of circumstances, had been in Ortega's thought since 1914. Enriched by later influences from Scheler, Bergson, and Dilthey (whom Ortega began to read, prompted by Heidegger, in 1929), it comes to full flower in *What Is Philosophy?* and leads into an analysis of "destiny" as a combination of "freedom and fatality." As Ortega puts it toward the end of this text:

> Life always finds itself amid certain circumstances, in an arrangement surrounding it, filled with things and other people. One does not live in a world which is vague; constitutionally the vital world is circumstance, the things and the people about one, this world, here and now. And circumstance is something determined, closed, but at the same time open and with internal latitude, with space or emptiness in which to move about and to make one's decisions; circumstance is a riverbed which life goes on cutting within a valley from which it cannot escape. To live is to live here, now; the here and the now are specific, not to be exchanged for others, but they are ample.[10]

Incorporating the categories of finding oneself in the world and of decision, this understanding of circumstances is greatly evolved from Ortega's first use of the term fifteen years earlier. If not clearly in *Meditations on Quixote*, then certainly by 1916 in his lectures in Buenos Aires, Ortega had understood that the split between mind and world in idealism must be overcome in terms of the radical interdependence of the "I" and its surrounding world. He had expressed this in Buenos Aires in the metaphor of the *Dei consentes* or *Dei complices*, the harmonious gods that must be born and must die together.[11] Although he had at that point already learned from Husserl that the world comes to us in a flow of mental states reciprocal to our intentional address to it, Ortega (and for that matter Husserl himself) was still a long way from the highly concrete understanding—as quoted just above—of circumstances in their relation to self-aware self-encounter in the world, to decision, and to destiny. Carried by Heidegger's work toward a greater refinement and clarification of his ideas in 1929, he was simultaneously grateful and anxious, for *Sein und Zeit* was a more fully achieved work than anything Ortega had ever attempted. It caused him to review his own work critically, but also to suggest, at various points in the lectures of 1929, that certain of his own earlier ideas could rightfully claim chronological priority over those of Heidegger as expounded in 1927. Thus he noted in the penultimate lesson of *What Is Philosophy?*:

These common words—*finding oneself, world, being occupied*—are now technical words in this new philosophy. One could talk a long time about every one of them, but I will limit myself to observing that this definition, "to live is to find oneself in a world," like all the principal ideas in these lectures, can be found elsewhere in my published work. It is important to me to mention this, especially with regard to the idea of existence, for which I claim ideological priority. For that very reason, I am glad to recognize that the man who has gone deepest into the analysis of life is the German philosopher, Martin Heidegger.[12]

If Heidegger had indeed, in some sense, gone deeper, the paths of the two men, who would not meet face to face until 1951, had been and would continue to be separate. What Ortega shared with or took from Heidegger would be progressively transformed after 1929 not only into a distinct idiom (clearly less technical than Heidegger's, more accessible to the common reader) but into a temperamentally different vision of life. Unconcerned with the search for Being itself yet not antimetaphysical, Ortega sought precisely to construct a new metaphysics of human life. Less abstract than Heidegger, he defined being as the "radical reality" (a term he first used in 1929) of "my life," a concrete point of departure that allowed him to develop a compact and exceptionally vivid account of his own metaphysics by 1932–1933. What Pedro Cerezo Galán calls the "playful/heroic character" of Ortega stood in clear contrast to the "tragic/heroic" one of his German colleague. Asserting the "jovial" side of his nature, Ortega eliminated from his own analysis of existence the key Heideggerian concepts of "Being-towards-death" and of "not-Being," and he gave to "anguish" (*Angst*) only a relative role, insisting on the equal importance of life as venturesome undertaking (*empresa*). "Hence," Cerezo writes, "faced with the severe moral heroism of 'resolution' (Heidegger), Ortega prefers, in very Nietzschean fashion, the gay heroism of the artist who dances."[13] Over against the German thinker's rebarbative coinages and genius for sounding the depths, Ortega triumphantly crafted his own prose in a language (i.e., Spanish) almost wholly devoid of any live philosophical tradition. Defending Ortega against the charge that he was merely a pale Spanish imitation of Heidegger, Cerezo writes:

> His expression has an insuperable plasticity. What it loses in analytic power with respect to Heidegger, it gains on the other hand with abun-

dance in power of suggestion and dramatic force. His turns of thought are like globed medallions; they sculpt more than they define. Finally the rhetoric, the good rhetoric, wins out over the analysis. The formulas [of Ortega] aim more to call for awareness of life than analytically to describe its condition. The pedagogical will, and the rhetorical talent that serves it, never fail in Ortega. There is in his writings a permanent humanistic call, a pathos of enthusiasm, which contrast with Heidegger's cold, severe energy, and, above all, a will to the clarity of high noon which dissipates all the mists.[14]

Reinstated in his university chair at the beginning of February 1930, only days after Primo's resignation and following a student strike on January 20, Ortega spoke before the FUE on "The Mission of the University"; the remarks were published under that title later in the year. As his ties with the student movement became closer, he felt a mounting sense that intellectuals would be called upon to guide public policy in the last days of the dictator's reign. The original pamphlet edition of "Mission of the University," published by the Revista press and carrying a (later omitted) dedication to the FUE, was cast in a hasty, telegraphic style suggestive of the pressure of events that prompted it.[15] The term "mission" employed in the essay's title was pregnant, for Ortega, with connotations of destiny. Feeling the moment propitious for a redefinition of student life, universities, and the meaning of European culture, he showed in this piece his gift for grafting large, diachronic themes onto occasional concerns. Seizing the opportunity provided by release from Primo's censorship, he could reconsider the whole direction of institutionalized higher learning.

"University reform," he argued, "cannot be reduced to, nor even principally consist in, the correction of abuses. Reform is always the creation of new customs [*usos*]."[16] His statement did not, of course, imply any move toward a purist, hispanocentric definition of education; parochialism was anathema to the genuine university. Nor, he knew, would it benefit Spain thoughtlessly to ape English or German models, for an effective university must be founded both on the needs of a given society and in accord with the widest cultural imperatives of the world-historical moment. Spanish universities had, Ortega felt, split themselves between training for "the intellectual professions" (law, medicine, pedagogy, economy, public administration) and the promotion of scientific research. To this traditional dual mission must now be added the central task of the "transmission of culture." By that phrase he expressly did not mean to support the travesty of "general culture" handed out in capsulized doses to add polish to the student's otherwise specialized preparation. Indeed, the *contradictio in adjecto* of "general" culture merely indicated how drastically denatured was that more comprehensive part of the university's true mission, for culture, always specific and historical, had to be at the heart of men's decisions on how to live.

In another sense, of course, any true culture *was* general, in giving to life a comprehensive order. As Ortega had always seen, culture was the form men made to discipline and fulfill their urgent need for direction and choice. It had nothing to do with the disconnected smatterings of knowledge which gave mere social polish, nor should it be confused with the extreme specialization characteristic of advanced research. Like their peers in many other parts of the West, Spanish students threatened to become the half-educated "new barbarians" of whom Ortega was soon to write in *The Revolt of the Masses*. These were men who knew a great deal in a fragmented way about a particular field, but were unable to grasp the larger shape and import of the culture whose norms they pretended to define and judge. Unless they were put in touch with the most advanced concepts in their several fields of study and given a coherent picture of culture itself, they could only, Ortega feared, "progress" further into incommunicable corners of learning and technique.

For the modern university, Ortega proposed, in addition to continued training for the professions and the pursuit of scholarly and scientific research, a School (*Facultad*) of Culture dedicated to the interdisciplinary study of the various modes of thought and branches of knowledge in their inter-relationship and distinct functions. Such a school would be at the center of the new university and serve all its members. Professional studies and advanced research would go on in more specialized "peripheral" parts of the university, while in the middle of all university activity, the integrative, holistic School of Culture would draw on research and professional learning to refine its evolving picture of culture. The reorganization would demand that each man reassess his proper calling and talents. Gifted secondary school teachers of languages, for example, would no longer aspire to be philologists, and lawyers would learn from jurists without envious pretensions to that career.

This quasi-utopian plan was clearly based on the principle that each man would fulfill the duties of his station. Europe's sickness—and particularly Spain's—was pretension. Modern men must be purged of their inflated desire to be more than they were:

> Europe is ill because he who before has not even tried to be one or two or three pretends as a matter of course to be ten. Destiny is the only soil where human life and all its aspirations can grow roots. The rest is falsified life, life in the air, without vital authenticity.[17]

And of destiny he remarked:

> If our existence were unlimited in possible forms and in duration, there would be no destiny. Young men, the authentic life consists in the joyous acceptance of inexorable destiny, of our inexchangeable limitation.[18]

As an analysis of the ailments of modern European culture, these hortatory passages do not go far, but they do fairly represent the charge to Spanish youth which underlay the "Mission" address, a charge quite in accord with Ortega's Spartan sense of learning and thought as brisk "athletic" activities. Further, his sense of solidarity with the rising generation, which would soon aspire to direct Spain's destiny (and many of whom would be brutally kept from that task by death in war or by exile), is evident throughout the speech:

> [W]e—isn't it so, young men?—are content that things be, for the moment, what they are and nothing more; we love their nudity. The cold and storms do not matter to us. We know that life is—especially is going to be—hard. We accept its rigor. We do not try to falsify destiny. Because it is hard, life does not cease to seem to us magnificent. On the contrary, if it is hard, it is solid, lean: tendon and nerve; above all, clean. We wish cleanliness in our dealing with things. That is why we strip them bare and ... wash them by looking upon them, by seeing what they are *in puris naturalibus*.[19]

This hyperbolic cry of "Excelsior!" did not, of course, aim to give much specific political advice. In fact, in its proximity to the heart of Ortega's philosophical teaching—the ideas that truth must be exhumed, the appearances "saved"—it was more a charismatic message from teacher to student than an appeal for concrete institutional reform.

Ortega's critique of the university system was complemented by

the publication in the same year of the work that, more than any
other, would make his name known to readers outside Spain—*The
Revolt of the Masses*. The volume collects a series of essays he had
published in *El Sol* in the last three months of 1929 and the first weeks
of 1930 under the heading "La rebelión de las masas"—a theme
patent in his work since *Invertebrate Spain*, alluded to repeatedly in his
political journalism, and present in two talks he had given in Buenos
Aires in 1928. The full-blown *El Sol* critique anticipated the end of
rule by the particular "mass man" who had crushed out the last, pale
vestiges of representative government in Spain.[20] In the tenth article
of the series (November 24, 1929), Ortega revealed his conviction
that the desired end of Primo's rule would move Spain toward the
level of the times:

> There is no hope for Europe unless its destiny is placed in the hands of men
> really "contemporaneous," men who feel palpitating beneath them the
> whole subsoil of history, who realize the present level of existence, and
> abhor every archaic and primitive attitude. We have need of history in its
> entirety, not to fall back into it, but to see if we can escape from it.[21]

While this essay was clearly a response to the political and intellectual "primitivism" of the dictatorship and to the garrulous,
banal café society that thrived in Madrid during the 1920s, on the
wider plane of Europe and the world Ortega's concern was with the
disappearance of hierarchical standards of cultural and intellectual
excellence. The future of elite intellectual leadership in Western
societies was at stake. The book has been read primarily as a description of the related phenomena of mass society and mass culture, and
for its description of the mass man himself. But what is often
overlooked in these readings is the pseudoaristocratic taste implicit in
Ortega's almost visceral discomfort with the spectacle of crowding
and of the depersonalized mass behavior increasingly prominent in
public places. He was himself "revolted" by the preponderance of
tastelessness and the growing domain of unenlightened public
opinion. Even more important, perhaps, is the testimony *Revolt* bore to
its author's disillusionment with the centers of European culture, for
the crowding and the "massification" of behavior so central to
Ortega's analysis were not happening in Spain as much as in the
urban centers of northern Europe and North America. This timely
but not essentially novel essay, which brought him renown beyond

Spain, was in fact a cry of distress and doubt about the very world toward which he wished to open the doors of Spain. Thus *Revolt* must be studied for what it suggests of Ortega's relationship to the rest of Europe and, more broadly, because it typifies the outlook of certain European critics of culture between the two world wars.

First we must establish a brief genealogy for this book, which coined and gave wide currency to the term "mass man" (*el hombre masa*).[22] Both Ortega's terminology and his conceptual perspective in *Revolt* reveal his allegiance to a tradition of social theory which developed after the French Revolution. The great line of modern theorists of society (Tocqueville, Marx, Durkheim, Weber, Simmel, Tönnies, et al.) sound in common a note of antagonism toward and profound distrust of the impersonal, collective, rationalized, and bureaucratic nature of modern society as *Gesellschaft*. In addition, writers like Nietzsche, Le Bon, Pareto, and Spengler stood behind Ortega's vision of mass society as an oddly classless, amorphous conglomeration based in the nature of mass man himself. One of the central myths employed by many of the thinkers we have mentioned was that of "the masses," about which Robert Nisbet has written:

> No rendering of the social landscape created by the two revolutions [the French and the Industrial] is commoner in the nineteenth century than that represented by the word *masses*. It has many synonyms: rabble, mob, crowd, hoi polloi, canaille, populace, people among them—all pointing to the large numbers of persons thrust suddenly, as it seemed, into prominence by the forces which had destroyed or weakened the fabric of the old, traditional, aristocratic order.[23]

In English, the social connotations of the term "mass" began to appear as early as the late seventeenth century, but the use of "the masses" to describe the great multitude of the common people did not become common until just before the middle of the nineteenth century.[24] Its use in the other major Western European languages follows a roughly comparable chronology. Thus it is, generally speaking, since the time of Tocqueville's *Democracy in America* (1838) that the vision of the common people alluded to by Nisbet has taken shape.

Later in the last century, the classic contrast of *Gemeinschaft* and *Gesellschaft* elaborated by Tönnies in 1887—the vision of community, which bound men together in shared ways, posed against the segregative and alienating control of society as collectivity—became the byword of German sociological romanticism. Somewhat before and certainly after Tönnies's formulation, "community" became, for many Western intellectuals, a self-evident good and a form of social organization assumed to have existed in the vast stretches of time lying on the nether side of the French and Industrial Revolutions. In turn, the search for lost community became closely linked with the critique of mass society. In one sense, Ortega did little more than give felicitous and memorable form to a perception of society with a considerable history before his time. But, from another viewpoint, *Revolt* was a key document of its own time and essential for understanding the modern liberal intellectual's sense of the extreme fragility of his social role in a world that appeared increasingly threatened by radical egalitarianism, mass democratization of taste, and the waning of hierarchical social structures.

Normally concomitant with the recognition and naming of "the masses" is the establishment, by liberal and conservative intellectuals alike, of a theory of elite leadership, which is asserted to be in extreme danger and to be forced to retrench in the face of incursions by the masses into those areas of cultural activity formerly reserved for the select groups alone. Ortega saw the incursions as deriving from two sources, neither of which, he insistently protested, must be confused with a particular social class, for he contended that the mass man could appear at any level and within any group or profession. The threat to cultural elites came, then, not so much from the masses considered as restive rabble or proletariat as from, first of all, the opinionated philistine, the "new barbarian," whose contempt for excellence and distinction made his brash self-assertion irreverently destructive. A second, similar threat to the older hierarchical order of culture and society came from the specialist—particularly the scientist or technician—whose intensified control of a particular field deluded him into supposing that he could judge broader social and cultural matters.

Much, however, as Ortega insisted that these two types did not belong predominantly to the lower classes, one feels that his notion of the masses constantly approaches the more conventional class distinction in which it is the poor and uneducated who constitute a good part of the "revolt" itself. In defense of Ortega's assertion, though, it may be argued that his youthful attraction to socialism, his disgust with the pretentious tone of the chatter in Madrid café society, and his intention to portray Primo as the mass man of the day, all suggest that in fact he did not think of the masses as simply the poor or the urban proletariat. Indeed, he speaks much more of "mass man" than of "the masses" as such, and the "revolt" is analyzed more in terms of a typology of individual personality than of traditional classes as such. The traditional notion of social classes inherited from nineteenth-century social thought is notably absent from the book, which divided society between cadres of elite leadership and the mass man who rejects them.

Ortega found many aspects of his critique of mass society available in the classic texts of nineteenth-century and early twentieth-century sociology, which affirmed both the romantic stress on the sacred powers of the individual and the paradoxical importance of *gemeinschaftliche* social groups. The affirmation of human diversity as a self-evident good became a fundamental tenet of nineteenth-century liberalism. As such, it found its way into Ortega's own stress on the inalienable perspective on life of each indispensable person in his unique circumstances. Out of this double stress upon community and diversity arose the later picture of the alienated "atomistic" individual set over against a society increasingly characterized by its destruction of the old ideals of *Volksgemeinschaft* and its devotion to rationalistic and bureaucratic organization. While the resulting social structures of industrialized and urbanized Western societies seemed in one sense more highly organized than ever before, the viewpoint that looked nostalgically back toward the idealized form of the lost community chose to stress the disorganization resulting from the wholesale destruction of earlier human ties. Thus, as Daniel Bell has noted,

> [b]ehind the theory of social disorganization lies a romantic notion of the past that sees society as having once been made up of small "organic," close-knit communities that were shattered by industrialism and modern life, and replaced by a large impersonal "atomistic" society which is unable to provide the basic gratifications and call for the loyalties that the older communities knew.[25]

The point of Ortega's adaptation of this perspective is that the preindustrial communities seemed to have offered a stable, relatively fixed hierarchical structure that left the business of high culture to aristocratic circles, court salons, and "men of knowledge" in their various scholarly and professional capacities. The claim to historical accuracy of this picture is doubtful. In essence, it is an ideal liberal vision of the function of intellectual leaders and tastemakers, sharing not a little with the thought of Tocqueville or John Stuart Mill. In his own time, Ortega was, despite his warnings about the barbarism of specialization and the unwillingness of the mass man to reach beyond himself toward the "noble life," something of an optimist in comparison to other theorists of mass society. Up to the collapse of the Spanish Republic, he continued to cherish the belief that a liberal intelligentsia would one day be heeded again.

Ortega's forceful but often clichéd indictment of the revolting mass man solidified his growing reputation as a major European thinker in the eyes of the public outside Spain. A felicitous stroke of the pen had produced a timely essay typical of the outlook of a number of intellectuals between the wars (Paul Valéry, Julien Benda, Karl Mannheim, T. S. Eliot, F. R. Leavis, Theodor Adorno, Max Horkheimer, and Erich Fromm, to name a few who cover the political spectrum). It is odd, nonetheless, that the piece that became a central text for the critique of mass society should have come from Madrid at the end of the 1920s, for there were surely other European centers—Berlin, Paris, London—where one could have experienced both the pressure of sheer numbers and the intrusion of the specialist and technician more acutely than in the Castilian capital.

The point, however, is not whether Ortega actually observed around him the increased incidence of human agglomerations which he announced as the most elementary fact of the day and which presumably constituted prima facie evidence of his thesis. While he alleged that everywhere one went—in cafés, movie theaters, hotels, doctors' waiting rooms—there were crowds of people eager to claim a place in society, his main concern was not so much with the mere spectacle of numbers as with the threat that the "intruders" would corrode traditional cultural standards. The emergence of mass man meant, in this analysis, that the masses were no longer willing to be "proper" masses, whose function was to be led, thus confirming their leader's charismatic power. Similarly, directing elites were either missing or denatured, just as the "true masses" were. Hence the individual type of mass man was really a creation of modern times and by no means a representative of the earlier masses who had been, presumably, *in illo tempore*, responsive to educated guidance from above. As Ortega conceived of him, the mass man was a descendant of Nietzsche's and Max Scheler's man of "ressentiment," who knew not how to make great demands upon himself and scorned those who did.

Yet there was much to be said for the pretensions of ordinary people to "the same 'vital repertory' which before characterized only the superior minorities," for the mass man gained his intrusive pretensions precisely because "the level of history has suddenly risen" and "human life taken as a whole has mounted higher." [26] The mass of men were being incorporated into society as never before, and their eagerness to enjoy the "vital repertory" of the elite few was an understandable function of this shift in level. Hence there was an optimistic note in Ortega's assertion that "the man of today feels that his life is more a life than any past one," that modern man "recognizes in nothing that is past any possible model or standard." [27] But the sense of plenitude also bred envy and ressentiment toward the few who had lived amply in the past, and the rejection of past standards threatened to extinguish wisdom itself. In this perspective, twentieth-century European man was, like Lear, out on the wild heath as a "bare, forked creature": "Any remains of the traditional spirit have evaporated.... The European stands alone, without any living ghosts by his side." [28] Such a situation was unlike that of any previous time and thus dubious in nature. How was one to assess its import if its uniqueness left it isolated in a present radically dissociated from the past?

Ortega's judgment of what he called "the increase of life" newly available to every man caused him distress and elation by turns. Through new modes of communication and travel "each individual habitually lives the life of the whole world.... This nearness of the faroff... has extended in fabulous proportions the horizon of each individual existence." [29] The upbeat note here, the same as the one heard in his statement of purpose for the first number of the *Revista de Occidente*, was as much a reflection of his cultural mission to bring the world to Spain and Spain into the world as it was a general sociological observation. Unfortunately, mass man was prepared only to abuse this heady prospect, which appeared to lay the world at his door: "Lord of all things, he is not lord of himself." [30] This sense of a rudderless life lived in the midst of abundance, of knowledge without wisdom, rationality without heart, technique without understanding, had often been voiced before Ortega, and has been a steady refrain among intellectuals and philosophers of culture ever since. Inert, self-satisfied, ungrateful, and spoiled, the mass man—like Huizinga's "puerile" *homo ludens* in his overextended adolescence—had to be brought to his senses and taught to play a constructive role in civilization.

The darkest passages of *Revolt* come in the long chapter appended to the initial series of *El Sol* articles— "Who Rules in the World?" Until a short time ago, Ortega tells us, the undisputed cultural ruler was Europe, but now European hegemony was in question. Europe's "spiritual power" and intrinsic authority had faded, perhaps never to be restored again. The spiritual weakness of Europe in turn invited the new nations of the world to assert their "nationality" as equal in importance to that of the truly historic nations of the West. With Europe—which meant France, England, and Germany—in the balance, the prospect loomed of a world without cultural standards. Ortega's insistence that the old centers—Paris, London, Berlin, perhaps also Rome and Madrid—could have no effective replacement indicated his adherence to a traditional cultural "map" and his inability to imagine the multicentered, pluralistic world in which we have lived since World War II. Moscow and New York, for example, "represent nothing new, relative to Europe." [31] Their pretensions to rule Ortega took as sheerest posturing: "[O]ne can assert . . . that Russia will require centuries before she can aspire to command." [32] Specifically, Spain, having long misconceived the whole matter of commanding and obeying, was prone to adapt itself to political irregularities rather than resist them. Primo's regime was implicated once again: "There can be no elastic vigor for the difficult task of retaining a worthy position in history in a society whose State, whose authority, is of its very nature a fraud." The resultant anomie created a situation in which "all imperatives, all commands, are in a state of suspension." [33] In assessing the state of Europe in general, Ortega was also invoking the hoped-for end of illegitimacy at home. Ten months after Primo's fall, in the midst of the interim government under General Berenguer, he would make his argument (echoing the elder Cato's "Delenda est Carthago") into a political battle cry: "Delenda est monarchia" ("The monarchy must be destroyed"). [34]

Revolt projected the grave illness of Spain's body politic into Europe and the West as a whole. As Spaniards must rise to the "historic level" of the times, European man must work for the political, economic, and cultural unification of Europe, thereby bringing "the effective capacities that life has come to acquire in each European individual" in line with transpersonal and transnational programs.[35] The nationalistic ethos had run its course in history. Europe itself must become the new "national idea." Otherwise, the "demoralization of Europe" would perpetuate confusion concerning the cultural level men should seek: "There is no longer a 'plenitude of the times,' for this supposes a clear, prefixed, unambiguous future, as was that of the XIXth century."[36] Caught in the doldrums between past and future, "life today is the fruit of an interregnum." Plenitude must be forged on a much larger scale than Europeans, especially Spaniards, had been used to.[37] Otherwise, fascism and bolshevism would seize the day.

Ortega was not alone among his European peers in construing the social landscape of the early twentieth century as dotted with upstart marauders surging out of the previously quiescent multitudes. Nor was he the only one who felt that the intellectuals themselves had contributed to the demise of their own leadership. Thomas Mann's *Magic Mountain* (1924) had dramatized the schism in postwar European culure through the endless contentions of Naphta and Settembrini. Julien Benda, in *La trahison des clercs* (1927), had excoriated his fellow *clercs* for whorishly putting their minds in the service of narrow partisan causes. Karl Mannheim, in his *Ideology and Utopia* (1929), had protrayed the intellectual as the free-floating critic of entrenched ideologies and the catalytic agent of utopian projections. Karl Jaspers advanced a philosophical analysis of mass society in *Man in the Modern Age* in 1931.

But temperamentally closer, perhaps, than all these to Ortega was Paul Valéry, who was in those same years writing the lucid little pieces that set European civilizaton on trial for its life. In much the same vein as Ortega, Valéry signaled the erosion of cultural standards in art, philosophy, and scholarship. In "The Outlook for Intelligence" (1935), he sounded if anything more pessimistic than Ortega in *Revolt*. "We can no longer deduce from what we know," wrote Valéry, "any notion of the future to which we can give the slightest credence.... *Man is now assailed by questions that no man before had imagined*, whether philosopher, scientist or layman; everyone has somehow been taken unawares."[38] Modern Western men were witnessing, by his account, an unprecedented predominance of innovation over an increasingly attenuated body of tradition:

> Hence that general sense of helplessness and incoherence that pervades
> our minds, keeping us on the alert, in a state of anxiety to which we can
> neither become accustomed nor foresee any end. On the one hand is the
> past that can neither be abolished nor forgotten, but from which we can
> derive almost nothing that will orient us in the present or help us to
> imagine the future. On the other hand, there is the future without the
> least shape. Every day we are at the mercy of some invention, some
> accident, either practical or intellectual.[39]

Mind was adrift in the world; the outlook for intelligence, as Valéry so
augustly put it, was bleak: "I say that modern life affects the mind in
such a way that we may reasonably feel great anxiety for the survival
of all intellectual values."[40] The rapidity of change of all sorts, the
frenzied consumption of energy, the fabrication of a taste for the
meretricious—all these features of modern European life led to a
destruction of the sensibility which feeds intelligence, "which is actually its real motive power."[41] Inebriated by a surfeit of stimuli and a
veritable orgy of wasting the world's resources, contemporary Western man, without leisure, hostile to repose, staggered along with
his debased sensibility. Instead of seeking to become educated, he
allowed himself to be assaulted by a barrage of printed materials,
half-baked theories, and propagandistic appeals for his allegiance.
Such a figure was Ortega's mass man all over again.

Valéry shared with Ortega the tendency to fluctuate between
extremely dark visions of the future and vigorous calls for the
redefinition by intellectuals of the overarching spiritual unity of
Europe. Both men insisted that although the European spirit was
profoundly disturbed in the early twentieth century, it would not
simply die out, at least as long as it was still alive in men like
themselves. Such was the function of *The Revolt of the Masses* and of
Valéry's cultural criticism, which shared with the work of Mann,
Benda, Mannheim, Jaspers, and others a sense of the existential
shipwreck Ortega had deemed a perennial possibility in all vital
experience of culture.

The stance of such self-styled culture-bearers usually required a
supporting rhetoric to justify their sense of mission. Ortega's key
rubric—"the level of the times"—appeared most prominently as the
title of chapter 3 of *The Revolt of the Masses*, in which he noted:

It is said, for example, that this or that matter is not worthy of the height of a certain time. And, in fact, not the abstract time of chronology, of the whole temporal plain, but the vital time, what each generation calls "our time," has always a certain elevation; is higher today than yesterday, or keeps on the level, or falls below it. The idea of falling contained in the word decadence has its origin in this intuition. Likewise, each individual feels, with more or less clearness, the relation which his own life bears to the height of the time through which he is passing. There are those who feel amidst the manifestations of actual existence like a shipwrecked man who cannot keep his head above water. The *tempo* at which things move at present, the force and energy with which everything is done, cause anguish to the man of archaic mould, and this anguish is the measure of the difference between his pulse-beats and the pulse-beats of the times. On the other hand, the man who lives completely and pleasurably in agreement with actual modes is conscious of the relation between the level of our time and that of various past times.[42]

This notion of a historical curve of cultural and intellectual levels required a definition of modernity, as Ortega immediately observed: "The original sense of 'modern,' 'modernity,' with which recent times have baptized themselves, declares very acutely that sensation of 'level of the times' that I am now analyzing."[43]

The sharp emphasis Ortega gave to the ever-shifting cultural mandates of the present moment derived from his appreciation of the root meaning of "modern," from the Latin adverb *modo*—"just now," "recently." That is, the dilemma of being modern is precisely that of living in the ever-vanishing present, of dancing on the edge of time as it lapses into pastness or burgeons with futurity. Passing time, linear and irreversible, brings to each hour its task and opportunity. To "baptize" oneself as "modern" means to proclaim that, abreast of his historical moment, man either faces the challenge of innovation posed by the new times or fails to rise to the level of that challenge. Failure means archaism, or being outmoded. This understanding of time as progressive and irreversible is based ultimately on the Christian conception of man's historicity and his search for salvation after life in this world. In religious terms, failure to reach toward God in this life casts one away from Him, down into the pit of hell or the moil of purgatory: there is no neutral ground, no moment in which time (and the movement toward final judgment) stops. In the secular terms Ortega employed, one either keeps up with the challenge of one's day (also of one's generation and one's epoch) or suffers the feeling of falling below it. There is no resting place.

To become and to stay modern was the most difficult of tasks. In preferring for himself the appellation of "very twentieth century," Ortega had grasped the dilemma. But he had not really escaped it, for his vision of the level of the times had not a little of the anxiety to keep up, to avoid backwardness, which characterizes the quest for modernity. The quest is anxious because there is no room to *be* in the present, buffeted mercilessly as it is by the weight of the past and the looming of the future. Past and future together virtually annihilate the present, as T. S. Eliot knew when he wrote, "Time past and time future allow but a little consciousness." [44]

A more sympathetic view of the immediacy, the sheer presentness, implied by modernity was given in Baudelaire's aestheticized version of the *Zeitgeist* as it descended from Hegelian thought:

> Modernity is the transitory, the fugitive, the contingent, the half of art, of which the other half is the eternal and the immutable.... As for this transitory, fleeting element whose metamorphoses are so frequent, you have no right either to scorn it or ignore it. By suppressing it, you are bound to fall into the emptiness of an abstract and undefinable beauty, like that of the one woman before the first sin.... In a word, if a particular modernity [in the sense of a particular present moment] is to be worthy to become antiquity, it is necessary to extract from it the mysterious beauty that human life involuntarily gives it.... Woe unto him who seeks in antiquity anything other than pure art, logic, and general method. By plunging too deeply into the past, he loses sight of the present; he renounces the values and privileges provided by circumstances; for almost all our originality comes from the stamp that *time* imprints upon our feelings. [45]

Thus, ironically, one misses the true and the eternal by depreciating the transitory. One does not find the sacred sources of beauty and truth by turning away from the world's concerns, as Julien Benda counseled the *clercs* must do. On the contrary, plunging into time, into what Ortega called one's generational and personal "installation" in history, is the only way to authentic being. The paradox, typical of modern as opposed to ancient Greek thought, is that authenticity resides in the mutable, in the becoming and disappearing of the existent world, rather than in some fixed principle of changeless being. Or, as Eliot puts it, "Only through time time is conquered." [46]

And that conquest does not mean dispensing with time but, much as in the dialectical tension established by Baudelaire, achieving something "timeless" by deep response to the affective imprint of one's own time.

If Ortega followed Baudelaire in embracing the tasks dictated by his cultural and historical moment, he nonetheless entertained something like a coherent, relatively stable vision of modernity. While this vision was not entirely fixed or easily localizable, it did have a core of central attitudes and exemplary works that commanded his respect and called for "translation" into Spanish terms. Much, of course, depended upon the angle and the circumstances from which one bespoke "the modern." There is no definitive list of its attributes, and to call any culture or country "modern" or "premodern" is to pass a sweeping judgment that ignores qualifications and the relativity of the observer's perspective. "Premodern" suggests that one is in a partially evolved state on the way to "the modern," conceived of as final goal. The term "backward" more dramatically suggests the way in which modernity and modernism structure our perception of those parts of the world or of human experience which do not keep step with the self-proclaimed centers of advanced consciousness. It is important to insist that modernity is always self-proclaimed, for one otherwise forgets the essentially arbitrary and relative connotations of a term which originally pointed to what was simply current or in vogue. In *The Revolt of the Masses*, Ortega noted:

> Modern is what exists according to the mode; one understands the new mode, modification or fashion that in a particular present has arisen over against the old, traditional modes that were used in the past. The word "modern" expresses, then, the consciousness of a new life, superior to the former one, and at the same time the imperative to be at the level of the times. For the "modern," failure to be so is equivalent to falling below the historic level.[47]

Ortega's fascination with this idea demands further analysis of the metaphor itself. Discerning the level (or leading edge, center, peak) in "the times" implies claiming a comprehensive grasp on present cultural developments. To some extent, Ortega could validly make that claim: he read widely and perceptively in several European languages, both ancient and modern; he traveled extensively and observed acutely; he was as well educated, in a broad humanistic sense, as any man of his time. But even with this preparation and sensitivity, and with impressive literary talent, this man who liked to see himself as a twentieth-century Goethe also spoke from the perspective of a culture long sunk in rigidified, traditionalist forms of thought and expression. Out of that situation he seized upon his key metaphor as a rhetorical device to dramatize his cultural mission. He took it, of course, from the nineteenth-century German tradition of cultural and philosophical history, in turn nourished by the thought of Johann Gottfried von Herder, Goethe, Hegel, Johann Gottlieb Fichte, and the German pre-romantic and romantic writers. From those sources came one of the richest currents of the historicist movement, with its emphasis on nationalism, historical periodization, and the unique virtues of each form of life created by a given people. Later historians like Leopold von Ranke, François-Pierre-Guillaume Guizot, Jacob Burckhardt, Wilhelm Dilthey, and Karl Lamprecht, refining and giving concrete body to cultural history, bequeathed to the twentieth century the essential notion that particular times and cultures could be understood in unified and comprehensive fashion by the "spirit" (*Geist*) that informed their overall "style."

Much of this conception developed in its early form out of Hegel's vision, in the *Philosophy of History*, of the World Spirit following its own majestic, mysterious course from East to West in the progressive self-realization of its own freedom. It was in immediately post-Hegelian thought that the earlier notions of a general *Geist der Zeiten* or, alternatively, a single *Weltgeist* manifest in different locations at differenft historical moments, shifted toward the idea of a *Zeitgeist*, understood as the characteristic "spirit" of a given time. The young Hegelians carried out a process of secularization, whereby the now radically historicized "Spirit" of Hegel's thought lost its claim to eternity, its quasi-divine status, and became invested with progressivist and futurist import. Or, as Karl Löwith has put it, "the Spirit of the Ages becomes the spirit of the age." He traces its gradual temporalization through Fichte into various writers of the 1830s and 1840s, in whom the phrase took on the quality of "a universal slogan." Thenceforward, with the feeling

> of the radical changes taking place between ages, all events are referred more and more consciously to the spirit of the "epoch," and the feeling of an epoch-making turning point between two ages [roughly, before and after the French Revolution] grows; thus the final age as such becomes the

destiny of the spirit. This is what lends all talk of the spirit of the age that contemporary note which adheres to it even today.[48]

Apart from the German notion of *Zeitgeist*, the same fundamental idea of a discernible spirit characteristic of the culture of an age developed elsewhere in Europe as well. The titles of William Hazlitt's collection of critical essays *The Spirit of the Age* (1825) and Thomas Carlyle's essay "Signs of the Times" (1829) were both indications that English writers too felt that the early nineteenth century could be understood in terms of something like a time-spirit, and that the very concept of an "age" or "the times" was itself important. Although neither of these works includes a concept directly comparable to the German idea of the *Zeitgeist*, John Stuart Mill came closer to it in his "The Spirit of the Age" in 1831. Picking up the stress on contemporaneity and the secular and the futurist overtones of the phrase, he noted the novelty of the expression:

> It is an idea essentially belonging to an age of change. Before men begin to think much and long on the peculiarities of their own times, they must have begun to think that those times are, or are destined to be, distinguished in a very remarkable manner from the times which preceded them.[49]

The resultant hunger for information and orientation among the increasingly numerous and restless masses of men in what Mill termed an "age of transition" led him toward a vision of noblesse oblige for educators; this made them not a little like Ortega's elite, whose mission was to restore to society its necessary hierarchical structure.

In seeing "the level of the times" as that manifestation of cultural preeminence by which the cultural condition of all contemporary peoples was to be judged and reformed, Ortega drew upon the transformation of the Hegelian Spirit into secular terms. Unlike Hegel, who so powerfully envisioned the ruin and stagnation of all but the one blessed world-historical nation (or culture) touched in each age by the Spirit, Ortega appeared to believe that a "backward" nation like Spain could be brought gradually up to the level as defined by German philosophy, French letters, or English civic life. From Hegel's viewpoint, of course, one could argue that Spain had had its world-historical hour and had irrevocably fallen from that one-time-only height. It was thus only natural that it should see itself languishing in the backwaters of history, consigned to aeons of obscurity along with all those parts of the world once—or perhaps never—fired by the Spirit's course.

Such a vision was not unlike that of neo-traditionalist theorists like Ramiro de Maeztu. During the late 1920s and early 1930s, he asserted that Spain's glorious golden age had been succeeded after 1700 by two centuries of revolutionary politics and secular humanism, with the consequent weakening of the Catholic faith that had sustained the nation during its great period of imperial expansion. For Maeztu, José Calvo Sotelo, José María Pemán, Pedro Sáinz Rodríguez, and other intellectuals who gathered around the rightist journal *Acción Española* (founded in December 1931), the true Spirit, however, was the Christian God, who would, they argued, return to restore Spain to its role as the defender of the true faith.

But for Ortega, the *Geist* of *Weltgeist* was lowercase and secular: the spirit of his own time was to be decried by whoever was sharp enough to identify and construe its portent. Here, of course, lay the ambiguity of his claim to clear vision of *la altura de los tiempos*. On the one hand he treated it as self-evidently manifest, awaiting only recognition. On the other, he constructed his own strategic version of it—the one that, perfectly in accord with Mill's observation, emphasized the need for *change*, for shaking Spain out of its historical slumber by sharply distinguishing Ortega's own time from preceding ones. To be up to the level of the times was to understand the present in dialectical relationship to the past and to use history (as he would brilliantly argue in *History as a System*) as a kind of propaedeutic to present action.

Insofar as definition of the level of the times was the particular task of Ortega's generation of Spanish intellectuals, its sociological significance was considerable. The sense (if not the literal use) of the phrase could be applied to various projects of reform and modernization undertaken by a number of Ortega's peers in diverse fields. We have already seeen how the Generation of 1914 distinguished itself from the Generation of 1898 and from earlier nineteenth-century liberal reformers. Acutely aware of the programmatic possibilities of "reading" the *Zeitgeist*, many of the young Spanish scholars and writers who came to maturity in the years just before and during the First World War joined in Ortega's call for improved standards of scientific, artistic, and scholarly achievement. At the same time, this challenge to a nation already very self-conscious about its "cultural lag" served to sharpen the contrast between Spanish mores and those of other parts of the Continent. The self-appointed culture-bearers of the prewar generation thus further developed the already familiar notion that Spain stood outside the movement of modern Western history.

Ortega's idea that he had come not only to escort Spain back into Europe but simultaneously to set aright the philosophical distortions stemming from Cartesian subjectivism and German idealism indicates that he saw himself as no less than the harbinger of a new stage in European culture. Such an immoderate vision more properly characterizes the brilliant, ambitious provincial than the true cosmopolitan, thoroughly conversant with the wider culture to which he belongs. The powerful stimulus of Ortega's self-appointed role made him tenaciously devoted to his mission of articulating the *Zeitgeist*, while he somehow forgot his "peripheral" Spanish position and the consequently questionable quality of his claim to a clear vision of the times. This oversight was not mere foolishness but more the consequence of a certain cultural "posturing" almost inevitable for intellectuals who work in countries removed from the acknowledged centers of cultural invention and authority.

Ortega's program for the Europeanization of Spain was of the type fraught with risks for any gifted intellectual who feels he speaks from outside the pale, for he is thus tempted to a facility and pretentiousness that will do him little credit with posterity or with the more sophisticated public of other countries. He may, especially if he is the kind of "born" writer Ortega was, fail to develop depth and a necessary degree of specialization. Ortega, as we shall see, eventually but grudgingly recognized the absence of a central area of concentration and of philosophical rigor in his own work. His effort to come to terms with his real place in European and Western philosophy—a place that was less than he had imagined but more than his detractors admit—involved him, in later years, in frequent and sometimes petty apologies for his most fragmentary and impressionistic pieces. His frequent criticisms of Heidegger, for example, were the clearest evidence of his anxious desire to "scoop" the philosophical news of the day.[50]

Since Ortega believed the highest function of cultural criticism to be the discernment and fulfillment of that vision of high culture which it befell one's generation to have, he felt that the critic was something of a seer, one who could read the face of contemporary events for the timely soul within them. This notion of his own role inspired many of his most felicitous and cogent essays, in which he developed the specific implications of the call to be modern. It was imperative, for example, to read Kant in order to correct the distortions of neo-Kantianism; it was impossible to be modern without some sense of the enormous advances in theoretical physics and mathematics; and it was crucial to encounter Cézanne or Proust if one were to comprehend the "level" attained by art and literature in the early twentieth century. The choices one made, the exemplars one identified, depended upon what Ortega called the "installation," or situating, of the person and the generation in history. This notion of the generational grounding of one's cultural agenda concretely tied Ortega's notion of "altura"(level, height) to biological rhythms, cultural patterns, and historical processes. The more general and predictable course of biological generations interacted with the far less certain arrangement and rearrangement of the historical scenario in which one was called to act.

Ortega further qualified these ideas by suggesting that there was both a *general* level of the times, which at any given moment defined the world's most advanced development or the highest level of creative energy in any given field, and a *specific* level proper to each generation and individual in national and historical context. Although the two not entirely separate levels (that for the world and that for a given locale) might coincide, as in the case of German philosophy around the turn of the century, the local level normally suffered by comparison with the worldwide one. Thus, for example, Spaniards wishing to introduce European science and philosophy into Spain might achieve the highest fulfillment of *their* national generation's historical role at home without ceasing to lag behind the higher level of the most advanced European cultures. Or, as a second example, Ortega might bring his countrymen philosophically up-to-date without thereby producing any work perceived as truly original by his German, French, or English peers. Ortega's qualifications of what would otherwise be the simplistic notion of a single level required analysis of the various cognitive maps afforded one by one's "moment" in history and by the culture into which one was born:

> [m]an is always born into an epoch. That is, he is called to exercise life at a
> determined level of the evolution of human destinies. Man pertains
> consubstantially to a generation, and every generation installs itself not

just anywhere, but very precisely on the preceding one. This means that it is necessary to live at the *level of the times*, and very especially at the *level of the ideas of the time*.[51]

As I suggested in chapter 1, this historicist perception of man's situation as time-bound and time-driven took on a particular urgency for a number of European thinkers and writers during the close of the century and just before the Great War. The war's impact made the Generation of 1914 both paradigmatic for the whole question of modern generations and exemplary of the growing preoccupation with youth and regeneration.[52] In Ortega's case, the war did not play a very direct role, but its outbreak coincided with and influenced his choice to define his generation's mission over against that of the Generation of 1898. Prone to think in terms of historical watersheds, the greatest and most obvious of which was the war itself, he and his Spanish and European peers became self-conscious and self-defining as perhaps no other generational group before them. As witnesses to rapid modernization of their societies and to the progressivist, future-oriented sense of time that had developed since the French Revolution, many members of the Generation of 1914 affirmed two key ideas, as Robert Wohl points out: "the rooting out of the past for the sake of the future and the discontinuous nature of human existence." This view thrust the young forward in opposition to the old:

> If the future was going to be fundamentally different from and better than the past, then the young represented the new. They were the standard bearers of the future in the present; whereas their fathers, the adults, were the incarnation of the past in the present and thus a pernicious obstacle to progress and change. To struggle against the older generation, therefore, became the duty of all men who identified themselves with the cause of the future.[53]

This vanguardistic generational consciousness led Ortega and other intellectuals from France, Germany, England, and Italy to adapt the idea of generations to the purposes of social and political change. In this context, Ortega's "level of the times" represented simply another claim to privileged awareness by that small, self-selected number who would grasp and declaim the fleeting, shifting essence of modernity. The rubric "Generation of 1914" was, in Wohl's words, "[a]n exercise in self-portrayal that never described more than a minority within the elite of the European educated classes . . . and also proved inadequate when used as a conceptual device by men and women born in the late nineteenth century to explain their history." [54]

Nonetheless, the rubric was a key ideological element that helped to define them as not only the latest but also the most rigorous harbingers of cultural modernity. Generational consciousness also functioned as a means to transcend provincialism. The resultant cosmopolitan outlook depended upon the feeling that the most advanced voices of one's epoch shared one's judgment both of nineteenth-century culture and one's vision of the emerging contemporary culture. Likewise, a sense of generational membership served to counter some of the anxiety connected with the emergence of mass society and the corollary dissolution of old class structures. [55] The same organizing device had political consequences because it offered an ideological framework that cut across old party or class allegiances, grouping men together either because they were born in the same short span of years or because they shared a set of convictions. Finally, the generational idea permitted middle-class European intellectuals who were, as Wohl notes, "torn between their desire to wrest power from the former elites and their fear of a 'rebellion of the masses'" to dream of "a spiritual revolution that would eliminate the exploiters and the exploited and fuse all sectors of society into a unified and conflict-free community." [56]

Such aspirations come to have ambiguous and self-serving purport as they take on moralistic and generally progressivist connotations. To identify, in accord with Ortega's analysis, the highest development of a culture or of a branch of learning is almost inevitably to vest interest in it. One cannot simply delineate a stage of cultural evolution without evaluating it in terms that are morally weighted, generally in one's own favor. Thus the vision of a politics above partisan and class divisions, espoused by Ortega and many of his European peers, gave its supporters a unifying cause that could lay to rest the outworn concerns of their fathers and grandfathers, providing a stay against the collapse of decrepit social and political structures. Their sense of the urgency of this task promoted a feeling of self-importance, of privileged understanding of the springs of history.

In sum, the phrase "level of the times" and its many variants (e.g., "edge of history," "wave of the future," "cultural mainstream") were and are myths developed by critics and intellectuals seeking legitimation for their own cultural politics. They wish to construe history in their own image—as the history of ideas. Such a project inevitably includes a strong element of parochialism insofar as one's own vision is proclaimed as the center of advanced consciousness. That is so even when the proclamation is formulated at the apparent center of innovation or creative energy, for its proponents are generally too certain of the centrality of the cultural values they affirm. They unwittingly commit themselves to a ruthless dialectic of "archaism" and "innovation," neither of which evaluative category adequately describes the deepest sources of creative energy in a given time and place. The real "level"—complexly textured and insusceptible of empirical verification—is neither archaic nor wholly innovative, but more like a subtle point-and-counterpoint between tradition and modernization as they interact in the present.

Ortega's key metaphor, however dubious in import, became a brilliant piece of organizational rhetoric. His highly developed taste, his philosophical training, and his exceptional literary talent saved him from becoming a dilettantish purveyor of novelties; and, in fact, he was not unaware of the dangers inherent in his pursuit of modernity. Realizing that an unbridled appetite for the modern subjected one to the transient fashion of the moment, he wittily declined to ride on that particular merry-go-round by proclaiming himself "not at all modern, but very twentieth-century."[57]

In essence, Ortega's cultural mission posed two problems for his writing. One was the risk of saying that the new as such was good; the other, more apparent in his writings of the 1930s, was the danger of making culture subservient to the demands of "my life," and so of judging art and ideas by their relevance to immediately present priorities. The present-centered, potentially antihistorical bias is not often noted by his critics, with the exception of those Catholics who, in defense of the "eternal verities" of the faith, have often charged Ortega with a rootless relativism they see as implicit in his "perspectivism." In theory, this doctrine—that each man constitutes a point of view on the universe and on the ultimate unity of truth—acknowledged and respected the variegated nature of human experience in what William James called a "pluralistic universe"; nonetheless, Ortega sometimes assessed the culture of his day as if his limited individual outlook were a sovereign voice for the *Zeitgeist*. For example, he asserted in the essay on "dehumanization" that his age declared its imperative through the novelty of a "young" art that demanded primary attention. Yet this idea evaded the issue of quality in order to emphasize the power of novelty, as Renato Poggioli has pointed out in *The Theory of the Avant-Garde*:

> Because it is absolutely indispensable to distinguish the spurious from the genuine avant-gardism which results in art . . . we must ultimately deny the validity of the position taken by Ortega: according to him, new art would remain a primary and absolutely important phenomenon even if it were to prove itself unable to generate a single masterpiece. If that affirmation contains any truth at all, it is the implicit recognition that the contemporary artist, independently of the results of his own efforts . . . must always accept the historical task of his own time, which is to work in the present for the future.[58]

Ortega, of course, needed to believe in his own cultural priorities, but it is well to remember that the leading edge of the cultural vanguard cannot be located with the certainty he seemed to assert. Comparable to the limiting conditions described by the uncertainty principle in modern physics are those experienced by the cultural critic, whose likelihood of exactly pinpointing the creative center diminishes in proportion as he tries to measure its significance. He may of course anchor his analysis in specific places, works, figures, or cultural "moments" (e.g., impressionism in Paris after the middle of the last century), but these all too often detach themselves from specific referents and become associated with some version of the unifying "spirit" of an era. At that point, corrective work must be done—for example, in close textual interpretation, cultural history, and the sociology of knowledge. Otherwise, faced with the Hegelian march of spirit through history, "the critic," as E. H. Gombrich has argued,

> can watch the signs of the times, but he has no right to judge them. Every person can hope to be the mouthpiece, indeed almost the incarnation of the spirit. Hegel called Napoleon "the world spirit on horseback" and Gertrude Stein claimed to be the embodiment of the *Zeitgeist*. But in a sense everything is, at least everything and everybody can become, an instrument of the spirit.[59]

6
POLITICS AND PHILOSOPHY:
1930–1936

During the heady period of transition from Primo de Rivera to the beginning of the Second Republic, Ortega cultivated the Platonic dream of a republic of philosophers. He entered the new decade, at the age of forty-seven, with the fervent hope that he would be called to play a central role in the formation of that new Spain for which he had so long called. If he had not been an unambivalent republican in earlier years, the ground swell of pro-republican sentiment evident on every hand by 1930 helped convince him that no other form of government could bring Spain to the political level of the times. And it seemed to him a natural turn of events that those men and women who had led the struggle for cultural modernizaton should also become the mentors who would guide *la niña bonita* (the pretty girl, as nineteenth-century republican conspirators had referred to their fairest dream) through the trials to come. The gritty thickness of daily politics, however, as we shall see, had another lesson to teach him.

As regards both Ortega's aspiration to political leadership and his philosophical development around the turn of the decade, it is well to remember that his vision of the peak achievements of European high culture and of the condition of Spain depended upon his perspective as a *madrileño*. In the relative "oasis" of a cosmopolitan center set in the middle of a predominantly rural and agrarian culture, he had invested most of his hope in the still-exiguous select circles to whom high culture truly mattered. In truth, relatively few Spaniards could be expected to concern themselves with the programs and ideas Ortega championed; yet, even without the leaven of philosophical learning, Spain during the twenties had undergone social and economic changes that had brought greater prosperity to a growing middle class and opened new horizons of interest for many people.

(While a dramatic increase in the university population under Primo had meant more potential readers for *El Sol* and for the many publications fostered by Ortega through the Revista press and in Espasa-Calpe, the more elite monthly *Revista* never printed above three thousand copies per issue, and even these were never sold out.) Spain's economic boom during the twenties had brought new wealth, technological innovation, and urban development.Towns of over ten thousand grew dramatically (although those under that figure remained almost stagnant), while the population of Madrid swelled by twenty-seven percent (from 750,000 to 952,000) and that of Barcelona by forty-one percent (from 710,355 to 1,005,039) between 1920 and 1930. Both of the large cities, together with smaller ones like Valencia, Zaragoza, and Bilbao, felt the impact of internal migration, as thousands of families and workers abandoned the countryside (especially in the south) in search of new opportunities and sensations.

The cities now offered movie houses, spectator sports, and other recreational facilities for the growing masses, whose presence Ortega uneasily noted in *The Revolt of the Masses*. Shlomo Ben Ami points to the "spectacular proletarization of Madrid" during this period, as working-class neighborhoods swelled and slum districts began to ring the capital. At the same time, the face of the older city center, where five thousand taxis circulated by 1928, was being transformed by large new buildings and grandiose cinemas. The subway system of Madrid, begun in 1919, was completed under Primo; preparations began for the construction of the Barajas airport; and the rapid development of the nation's road system accommodated an increase of four hundred percent in automobile traffic.[1] Spaniards were unquestionably more mobile than ever before, with suburbs and summer cottages springing up beyond the rims of the two largest cities. Private consumption of electricity increased dramatically, as did the number of telephones in Spain; and radio and the movies became staples of daily life for millions.

As Ortega had observed, ordinary men and women were beginning to enjoy a level of life previously reserved for the wealthy few. One result of this process was a democratization of taste that actually worked against his purposes, but another was an increased impatience with the old forms of life to which the ideology of the dictator's nondemocratic political structure appealed. Primo, for example, tried to encourage Spaniards not to abandon the countryside and flood the cities, arguing that people must curb their appetite for worldly sensations. Conservative supporters of the regime's official morality also bemoaned the growth of music halls, modern dancing, salacious novels, and pornography, which threatened to invade even the backward villages. Meanwhile, plagued by unproductive business and trade policies, Primo's government was rapidly losing the support of industrialists, bankers, big landowners, and the growing bourgeoisie. In Ben Ami's summary, "The growth of wealth and urbanization as well as the steady process of de-archaization of the social structure in the 1920's were increasingly becoming incompatible with autocratic norms of government." In the same vein, Gregorio Marañón commented in 1929: "The time is ripe in Spain for the most profound transformations that the country's social and political structure has ever undergone. In fact, these transformations are taking place at this very moment." [2] In sum, a regime that had arrived in he manner of the old-time *golpe de éstado* (coup d'état) from the past century sat atop a powder keg of expectations that favored the growth of republicanism and a generalized impatience with the waning dictatorship.

The feeling in Spain, during Primo's last year, that the immediate future was great with possibilities surely heightened Ortega's own sense of changes that would reach beyond the lecture hall and the classroom. The excitement surrounding his lectures on the "new level" of European philosophy in the recently completed Teatro Infanta Beatriz perhaps seemed to promise that his analyses of "decision" and "destiny," however philosophical, would prompt Spaniards to abandon the tottering government of his old adversary. (Yet he remained surprised by the sudden rush of interest in the abstruse matters he had so graciously and charmingly tried to convey to the packed halls during the spring of 1929, for his posture during much of the preceding decade had been marked by a distinct turn away from journalism and political activity toward a deepening of his philosophical calling.)

Although Ortega's best hopes were, in theory, for Spain as a whole, he tended to see the struggle for the modernization of Spain as being played out in Madrid—in its *tertulias*, classrooms, and publishing houses. Almost never did he refer, for example, to the obvious cultural importance of Barcelona, in many ways Spain's most advanced and

European city, where a Catalan modernist vanguard was vigorously
active. Looking instead to the Europe of Marburg, Heidelberg,
Berlin, and Paris, he had little to say (until the early period of the
Republic) of either Catalonia or of Spain's unenlightened provinces.
Despite his later recognition, in the early thirties, that the centralist
bias of Madrid and Castile was indeed a grievous error that mis-
represented the complex interregional tensions of Spanish history, his
intellectual vocation drew him away from concern with the relations
between center and periphery in his own culture and ever more
steadily toward Spain's future place in the European community of
nations.[3] Thinking of *The Revolt of the Masses*, one might say Ortega
was more concerned with the "re-vertebration" of Europe—the
recreation of a hierarchical social and cultural order that would
respect excellence in all fields—than he was with the internal social
skeleton of his nation, a problem he had already analyzed, rather
unsatisfactorily, in *Invertebrate Spain*. He had in fact continued the
metaphor of "invertebration" in his analysis of modern society in the
later book, which was on display in the windows of Madrid bookstores shortly after Primo fell on January 28, 1930. Rooted as it was in
a Nietzschean division between the ordinary soul and the man capable of self-transcendence, the new book offered a dehistoricized and
structurally oversimplified picture of things which only tangentially
reflected the Spanish crisis. Indeed, its rapid translation into several
languages—it became a minor best-seller in the United States during
the 1930s, for example—suggests that it succeeded in striking a
general vein of cultural pessimism felt by many readers on both sides
of the Atlantic during the years following the economic crash of 1929
and preceding the outbreak of war in Europe.

After securing Primo's resignation, King Alfonso appointed General Dámaso Berenguer head of a provisional government on January
30, in a lame effort to restore the parliamentary system that the king
himself had tacitly agreed to suspend in 1923. This move did no more
than extend the interim structure of Primo's directory. As Ortega and
others observed, there was no way back, for Alfonso's original support
of Primo had scotched the old constitutional order once and for all.
"By his adherence to rebellion against constitutional legality," Ben
Ami writes, "the king had helped to create the myth of his ' responsibility' for the Dictatorship and, consequently, had put himself in an
unconstitutional position."[4] Alfonso's move in 1923 was partly moti-

vated by the fact that the Spanish Cortes (the traditional bicameral legislature) had been about to investigate the disaster of Annual in the Spanish Sahara, where in 1921 the Spanish army suffered a bloody, humiliating loss. The king's support for Primo had been distinctly antiparliamentary because he sought thereby to avoid close scrutiny of the army's and his own Moroccan policy by a parliament that threatened to become more vigorous.

The Berenguer government, which lasted just over a year, had little chance of defending the monarchy and of restoring, as it proposed to do, the Constitution of 1876. Republicanism in manifold forms was everywhere in the air, and many conservatives and moderates who would not otherwise have embraced the idea of a republic did so as a kind of vote against Alfonso's dream of turning back the clock. Seeking to avoid the appeal to a Constituent Cortes, Berenguer dragged his feet, finally summoning the Cortes for March 1931. All the while, confidence in the monarchy—and in the person of Alfonso himself—was quickly waning. In August 1930 a group of pro-republican conspirators met in San Sebastián to plan the overthrow of the government in December, with the projected support of a nationwide strike to be led by the Socialists. The Revolutionary Committee of San Sebastián, later to become the Provisional Government of the Second Republic, had its hand forced by a premature uprising in the army barracks at Jaca, led by a Captain Galán, who was to become, together with his co-conspitrator Captain García Hernández, a martyr for the cause. The San Sebastián group supported the barracks revolt and was imprisoned by the Berenguer government. The projected strike failed as well, but the days of the stopgap government were strictly numbered, as Ortega had made clear only a month earlier in one of his most famous articles, "El error Berenguer" (*El Sol*, November 15, 1930), a declaration that helped the General's government to its inglorious finish on February 14 of the following year.[5] In that article, the brunt of Ortega's attack fell upon the monarchy rather than the man who embodied its error, and upon the cant that put forward this interim government in the facile spirit of a "return to normalcy." Such a statement, he saw, amounted to contempt for all those who knew plainly that the dictatorship had been a shameful farce. Instead of openly admitting that and seriously undertaking to reconstruct the state, "the regime" (meaning, essentially, the king) had passed off on Spaniards this nondescript government whose best achievement was to have stayed free of major troubles for ten months. A break with normality as major as that of Primo's regime could not simply be placed in parentheses as a kind of interregnum; moreover, before Primo the nation had already been living for many years in an abnormal state of affairs that had passed for normal up to its interruption in 1923. Since the monarchy was remiss in its duty to its subjects, "the man in the street" took it upon himself to proclaim "Spaniards, your state is no more! Reconstruct it! *Delenda est monarchia.*" [6]

In January 1931 there was an official announcement of election to the traditional Cortes. The news was met by strong objections from all sides and the growing demand for a Constituent Cortes to establish a new constitution and government. When Berenguer fell in February, the former Conservative minister José Sanchez Guerra tried but failed to form a government. Flailing about for a temporary solution, the king appointed the essentially nonpolitical Admiral Juan Aznar prime minister on February 18, with a cabinet composed largely of old-fashioned monarchists like the Count of Romanones and Juan La Cierva. The imprisoned Revolutionary Committee daily gained prestige, and violent student protests combined with the impromptu organization of a "free university" (supported by Ortega and other professors) in early 1931 to add fuel to the fire. Aznar's brief government was destined to be the last before the municipal elections of April 12 made clear the wide extent of support for a republic, giving Alfonso no choice but to abandon ship. Counseled by Romanones to cede gracefully, the king left Madrid for Cartagena, en route to Marseilles, on April 14. The Provisional Government, released from prison, assumed power. A rapid, bloodless transition had taken place in just two days, and on April 14 the Second Spanish Republic was officially declared under Prime Minister Niceto Alcalá Zamora, an Andalusian *cacique* (local land-holding political boss) who had gone over to the new cause in the spring of 1930.

In the first days of February 1931, with the help of his friends the novelist Ramón Pérez de Ayala and Gregorio Marañón, Ortega founded the Agrupación al Servicio de la República, an organization designed to mobilize intellectual and middle-class professional support for the forthcoming Republic. While the other two founders had for some time made no secret of their pro-republican sympathies, Ortega was slower to cleave to the cause. By this time, however, he had realized that his earlier calls for the "nationalization" of political activity in the general interest of the nation's future could best be heeded under the umbrella of republicanism. While the relative vagueness of this concept bespoke Ortega's distance from the machinery of party politics, the Agrupación represented the first step in his bid to play a major role in Spain's immediate political future. Holding its first meeting in Segovia on February 14, it presented a loose enough platform to attract a good crowd. As Ben Ami has written of its early life:

> The ASR appealed mainly to students and intellectuals, but the fact that it was conceived as a "levy-*en masse* against the Monarchy" rather than as a "party" in the strict sense of the term, enabled many people who already belonged to other parties to join it.... A fortnight after its foundation, the ASR had 15,000 members, a figure which in April had risen to 25,000.[7]

The new organization published a manifesto in *El Sol* on February 10, signed by its three founders and stating the urgent need for a better understanding of "national affairs" at this historic juncture. The last stage of "decomposition" of the old state had been reached, it declared, and a republic responsive to truly national needs and able to bring all Spaniards into the reconstructive effort was imperative. The triple aim of this intellectual pressure-group was, in Ortega's words, first, "to mobilize all Spaniards of an intellectual calling to form a large contingent of forecasters and defenders of the Spanish Republic"; second, to pave the way for the "triumph" of the republic "in constituent elections carried out with maximum guarantees of civic order"; and third, to organize "from the capital to the village and the farm the new public life of Spain in all its aspects."[8] While Ortega had long written in the pages of *El Sol* against the old regime, this was the first clear declaration of his firm adherence to the republic as the necessary next step.[9] He was concerned particularly that the transition to the new government be orderly, thoughtful, and nonpartisan—and of course that it make room for the counsel of men of ideas. More particularly, according to notes Ortega did not publish at the time, the Agrupación favored unionization for workers of both sexes, a constitutionally guaranteed balance of power, increased regional autonomy without federalism, centralized organization of economic development, separation of church and state, and mild socialization of private capital.[10] But though its original manifesto called forth a warm response from an appreciable educated public, its program remained too general, too dependent on the rhetoric of grand beginnings, to have major organizational effects.[11]

Meanwhile, an internal political crisis in the management of *El Sol* was about to bring Ortega's distinguished tenure with that paper to an abrupt end. In the course of 1930, a shift in financial control of the Madrid daily left Nicolás María de Urgoiti, who greatly admired Ortega and who had personally authorized the publication of the key article on Berenguer, no longer in the dominant position he had occupied since 1917. Ortega's call in November 1930 for the destruction of the monarchy had piqued Alfonso XIII, who in turn threatened La Papelera Española (the Spanish Paper Company), the controlling interest in *El Sol*, with a lowered tariff on foreign paper and consequent ruin. Urgoiti had been a director of the company until the end of 1925, when he left to devote full time to *El Sol* and its evening edition, *La Voz*. But he had continued to rely on friends on the board who were also major stockholders in *El Sol* to support his liberal, laic policies as founder of the paper. When, in response to pressure from the king, these men turned their concern to the survival of La Papelera Española, Urgoiti was confronted with an ultimatum: he must either espouse a pro-monarchy position in the two newspapers or give up his role as their effective head.

Thus, much as Ortega's "Bajo el arco en ruinas" had not only caused his own break with *El Imparcial* in 1917 but also upset Urgoiti's plans to take it over (the upset leading then to the establishment of *El Sol* as an alternative), now "El error Berenguer" lay behind Urgoiti's dilemma with the king and the paper company. After a brief and valiant struggle against insuperable odds, Urgoiti lost control, and on March 25, 1931, the last number of the paper under him (and under the directorship of Felix Lorenzo) appeared on the street with the following terse note from Ortega:

> Since the founding of this newspaper in 1917, I have written in it and—in Spain—in it alone. Its pages have carried almost my entire work. Now it is necessary to go forth in search of another intellectual home. Soon that will be found. Goodbye, my readers![12]

In times as mercurial and politically important as those weeks preceding the municipal elections that ushered in the Republic,

Ortega and Urgoiti could hardly remain without a forum for the former's commentary; hence *Crisol*, (Crucible), a triweekly publication, appeared with its first number on April 4, 1931. Thus after a brief shipwreck, Ortega was launched again. This time it was on a frankly republican venture, for it was now abundantly evident that there was no other path upon which to proceed. While Ortega's attack on the monarchy had clearly precipitated the end of his collaboration with *El Sol*, Alfonso's vigorous counterblow through La Papelera Española turned his intellectual opponent more markedly toward republicanism and may even directly have occasioned the formation of the Agrupación al Servicio de la República.[13]

The first numbers of *Crisol* celebrated the peaceful and swift arrival of the Republic in a moderate tone, emphasizing the importance of proceeding without undue haste and of avoiding disruptions of civil order. As the time drew near for elections to the Constituent Cortes on June 28, *Crisol* editorials warned that while the Republic had arrived de facto, its true establishment would require a dynamic faith in the nation's political future: once again Renan's notion of a nation made by daily plebiscite could be divined in this counsel, which obviously came from Ortega himself.[14] He relished the delightful prospect of building a nation, creating a future from the ruins of the past hundred years. Charged with this heady sense of opportunity, Ortega presented himself as a candidate for the Cortes representing the nonpartisan Agrupación of intellectuals, which succeeded in winning sixteen seats in the voting. He was elected as a deputy for the province of León. The great bulk of the seats went to the Socialists and the Republican Left, though Alejandro Lerroux's right-center, middle-class, republican Radicals won approximately one hundred places.[15] All told, moderate bourgeois republicans were seriously outweighed by the radical and socialist left.

From the beginning the prospects were not bright that a voice as inveterately literary as Ortega's and as restrained in its welcome of the Republic would play a decisive role in this historic convention. Indeed, except for his significant contribution to debate on the statute for Catalan autonomy, Ortega's parliamentary rhetoric tended to be more appropriate for the very early days of a transpartisan welcome to the Republic than for the inevitable later polarization of the extreme Left and Right. As he continued to write in *Crisol* and its successor *Luz* and to speak in the Constituent Cortes, the sonorous

and grave call to national unification (with respect for limited regional autonomy) became too obviously his note.

There are three major sources in which one may find the main lines
of Ortega's political ideas as a deputy to the unicameral Constituent
Cortes of 1931–1933: the book of articles published originally in *El Sol*
in 1927–1928 and collected under the title *La redención de las provincias y
la decencia nacional* in March 1931; the collection of articles published
periodically in 1931 and collected, together with a lecture that gave
the volume its title, in *Rectificación de la República* in December 1931;
and, also published in *Rectificación*, the three speeches given in the
Cortes on the Catalan Statute debated in the spring and summer and
passed in September 1932. Seeking in the first book to rectify the
relative lack of concern for the provinces that had characterized his
earlier intellectual campaign of Europeanizaton, Ortega set out to
analyze the relationship established by the Constitution of 1876
between the national center (Madrid) and the peripheral provinces.
He believed that the crucial problem of that document, drafted on
French and English models, lay in the connection ordained between
the Cortes, elected from the various provinces, and the national
government in the capital. Further, the Spanish Cortes followed the
French and English tendency to sanction two great dominant parties
—in Restoration Spain, the Liberals and the Conservatives. These
tended to be moved by ideas, by relatively abstract national programs, which could hardly be simultaneously designed for the nation
as a whole and in response to very concrete local needs in particular
provinces. Thus the ideological orientation of the parties was fitted
more to the proclivities of a literate urban electorate (particularly in
the capital) than to those of the provincial population, which suffered
from the imposition of such a political structure upon the entire body
of Spain.

The solution, Ortega believed, would be to seek a balance between
centralism and some form of local autonomy, in the hope of creating
leaders from the provinces who would help to integrate local interests
with national priorities. As things stood, Madrid sent only eight deputies out of four hundred to the Cortes, and altogether the remaining large cities of Barcelona, Seville, Bilbao, and Valencia sent only
some thirty more. The rest—the vast majority—came from smaller
provincial capitals and rural districts with widely varying needs.
Working with the national government for national interests, most

parliamentarians could hardly comprehend the intricate patchwork of such local priorities, even though about three-quarters of them came precisely from small provincial towns and rural districts. Thus the Cortes, subject to pressure from the interests of bureaucrats, intellectuals, and entrepreneurs from the larger cities (especially Madrid), tended to impose a set of more abstract national priorities on large areas of the country that had very different ones.

This discrepancy could have been overcome either if the predominant classes of the cities effectively predominated throughout the nation as a whole or if the spirit of Madrid in fact radiated out to animate the whole nation. Neither of these was the case, however. Indeed, the Spanish capital, unlike Paris, was more like an island, for, Ortega observed, "six kilometers from Madrid the cultural influence of Madrid stops." Drawing upon cultural sources from abroad, the capital was still "more cultivated than cultivating," hence too weak to exert formative pressure on the culturally distant provinces.[16] Insofar as the parliamentary system of the Restoration years had encouraged attention to national "ideas" over against neglected local "realities" that became progressively the concern of local *caciques*, Spain had had a provincialist politics of the worst sort. As power brokers at home, local bosses forced the central government to cater to their immediate interests, meanwhile supporting electoral abuses that made a farce of representative government. A system of local "oligarchy and caciquism," in Costa's phrase, was the result: the national parliament, said Ortega, tended to "be composed of fifty authentic elected representatives [from the large cities] and three hundred and fifty mandatories of the worst localism."[17] Like Lilliputians, the hundreds of local districts kept the Cortes as bound as Gulliver with their vested interests, and provincial voters ended up electing agents who could procure state favors rather than effective representatives to a national legislative body.

Such had been the situation from 1876 to 1900, during which time, Ortega argued, "the real Spain" had clashed with "the unreal constitution."[18] From 1900 to the time he penned the essays on provincial "redemption," however, things had grown worse, for the constitution had been essentially eliminated as electoral corruption had worsened and the de facto system of local compromises and concessions engineered over the people's heads had corroded the last vestiges of legal procedure. *Caciquismo* had indeed usurped the potential political power of the provinces, leaving Spain shattered into hundreds of petty political fiefdoms. While contributing nothing to the national welfare, these demanded more and more favors from the central government and the Cortes. Local bosses, able to sell votes outright to candidates seeking election to the Cortes, had become the actual representatives of Madrid in the provinces, and since the local constituency benefited in some fashion from bossism, it joined its immediate leaders in "the subversion against Madrid." [19] This whole situation was a significant feature of the "invertebrate Spain" Ortega had analyzed seven years earlier.

Freed from the suspension of political life represented by Primo, Ortega now moved from his pessimistic analysis of recent political history to hail a grand future just out of reach: "It is a matter of... outfitting the Hispanic ship for the high seas. It is necessary for our people to make history once again." [20] He in fact had something like a concrete antidote for the civic decadence he had diagnosed. Faced with the "invertebration" of Spain, in which the historic parties had lost the vigor to work effectively at a national level, Spaniards must escape their centrifugal and "centrophobic" provincialism by replacing the arbitrary provincial boundaries with the larger geographic and historical regions (*comarcas*). These would be Galicia, Asturias, Old Castile, the Basque provinces, and Navarre, Aragon, Catalonia, the Levant, Andalusia, Extremadura, and New Castile. [21] Assigning to each of these its proper sphere of autonomous responsibility would in fact forestall the long historical drift toward separatism and "particularism." The central state should reserve to itself only the indispensable powers (not unlike those accruing to the federal government of the United States). There should be regional assemblies elected by universal suffrage and empowered to form regional governments, while the services and offices of the central government should be concentrated in a single urban center for each region. [22] Thus a comprehensible image of the state—no longer august and distant in Madrid—would be represented for the local peasant or tradesman, who would once more find politics accessible because scaled to his grasp. Like what Ortega wrote on other occasions of the making of a nation or the future of a European community, his plan for regional revitalization rested on a shared dream of the future, for "[t]he true local political unit will be that interior grouping of Spanish collective life which possesses the greatest potential for acting." [23]

On December 6, 1931, in the Cínema de la Ópera in Madrid, almost six months after his election to the Constituent Assembly, Ortega presented a lengthy assessment of the first months of the new government under the title "Rectification of the Republic." Later that month he published the lecture in a little book of the same name, in which he also incorporated articles written since April 1931 and three parliamentary speeches. The titular speech was his first major analysis of a dangerous "detour" from what he had hoped would be the course of the republic: a policy of "national unity" coupled with a moderate tone and the minimum of partisan divisiveness. Several times since the spring of that year Ortega had remarked on the disturbing tendency toward haste in certain legislation (particularly that against the religious orders and the parochial schools in Article 26 of the new constitution) and toward a potential dictatorship of the Left. In the speech of December 6, a scant three days before official ratification of the new constitution, he spoke out in favor of a distinctly democratic republic (as against a "conservative" or "bourgeois" one) and a lay state in which the Church would no longer receive state protection. But he warned that neither democracy nor laicism could be achieved through violent rejection or even persecution of opposing interests. To single out for persecution either the capitalists of Spain or the national religious orders was to begin the process of civic disintegration that Ortega shrewdly foresaw as the Republic's eventual fate. But, he felt, the new order was still young, the damage was not yet great, and his own proposal of "a party of national amplitude" would provide the necessary tonic to heal the body politic.[24] Most important also was a centrally coordinated national economic policy that would limit laissez-faire abuses and integrate the Spanish worker and the entrepreneur into a program of overall economic growth, thus avoiding the need to take away from the latter to give to the former. He concluded by indicating the former minister of the interior of the provisional government, Miguel Maura, as a potential leader of the proposed new party.

Maura was a conservative liberal and a Catholic who had formed part of President Alcalá Zamora's Liberal Republican Right in 1930 and had come into the new government along with his chief. During the episode of the burning of churches and convents which erupted in several Spanish cities in early May 1931, Maura, who advocated calling in the Civil Guard to suppress the violence, had fought for and finally won from the cabinet permission to respond firmly to this first dramatic instance of deep national division over the religious issue. After that episode, Maura lost favor with both the Catholic right (for whom he had acted too slowly) and the Socialist left (for whom he was the oppressor of the people). It was perhaps indicative of the quixotic note in Ortega's proposal to rectify the "tone" and "style" of the Republic that he should choose for a leader a man with diminished charisma and a dim political future.

In the other pieces gathered in *Rectificación de la República*, Ortega spoke of the uniqueness of Spain's bloodless transition to the new regime and of the danger of imported models for revolutionary change. He saluted War Minister Manuel Azaña's successful reorganization of the Spanish army, quarreled with Minister of the Treasury Indalecio Prieto's critique of his rhetorical manner in parliamentary debate, and, in a famous phrase that had first appeared in *Crisol* on September 9, 1931, spoke for all those republicans who feared that increasingly radicalized ideologies of left and right portended trouble: "¡No es esto, no es esto?" (That's not it!).[25] The three major pieces besides the "rectification" lecture were the parliamentary speeches of July 30 and September 4 and 25. In the first of these he defined his minority role, as the voice of the Agrupación, to be that of a nonpartisan watchdog who sought to integrate unnecessarily opposed positions. Now, like Julien Benda in France, Ortega was tending to claim this watchdog role as the proper one of the intelligentsia—they should remain free enough of ordinary political commitments to achieve a theoretical view of priorities. In this case, he was there to declare republican government the only one that came up to the "historic level" the times required.[26] Additionally, he signaled the primacy of "the economic problem" and urged replacement of the old language of "capitalism" and "collectivism" with a more de-ideologized approach to planning for a modern industrial economy.

In the long speech of September 4, Ortega offered his assessment of the projected constitution, laying special stress on the need for "profound local reform" (outlined in the terms of *La Redención de las provincias*) and "the organization of society into a nation of workers."[27] The latter phrase meant that each Spaniard, of whatever class, profession, or political and religious persuasion, was to find his proper place and contribution in the building up of a new state. Intellectuals would be understood as workers, alongside miners, farmers, and mechanics; and aristocrats of the old stamp would have to join the corporative effort required of all. An organized democracy would grant responsibility to all men insofar as each one learned to make his personal contribution. Similarly, regional autonomy would revitalize the provinces by redeeming those that were sunk in mere bossism and strictly local concerns. Finally, though Ortega had made quite clear his support of a lay state, he censured the Assembly for what he considered its naive decision to write specific legislation against the Church into the constitution as Article 26, which suspended the state budget for clerical salaries after two years; forbade the religious orders to teach in parochial schools; required them to register property, income, and investments; reduced their property to what was necessary for the performance of religious duties; and, finally, dissolved all orders that could be a danger to the state or required a special oath of membership (this latter clause aimed at the Jesuits).

This extreme measure had caused the resignation of the two liberal Catholics in the cabinet, Alcalá Zamora and Miguel Maura, and had begun the dissolution of an already fragile spirit of compromise. One did not, Ortega argued, liberate oneself from the past with hatchet blows and the self-indulgence of wrath, for violence only wrought future violence. The constitution should simply designate the Church as a legal corporation subject to the same state controls as any civil body.[28] Such was the balanced secular position he was to reiterate in more personal form three months later in the Cínema de la Ópera:

> Ladies and gentlemen, I am not a Catholic, and since my youth I have taken care to formalize in non-Catholic fashion even the humble details of my private life. But I am not about to have imposed on me the wild figureheads of an archaic anticlericalism![29]

In short, enlightened secularism defined the level of the times: anti-clericalism fell below it into political and philosophical inauthenticity.

In the shorter parliamentary speech of September 25, Ortega returned to his plea for constitutional recognition of regional autonomy as outlined by him almost four years previously. Judging that his fellow deputies were confusing "federalism" and "autonomy," Ortega defined the first as obtaining when several independent states cede a portion of their power to form a new central state (as in the United States), and the second as obtaining when a preexisting state grants limited self-government to its several regions. Federalism was another archaism, which raised the ghosts of the First Republic of 1873–1875. As such, it would constitute "a disturbance of the new Spanish destiny."[30] The Assembly must recognize that the most appropriate response to Catalan, Basque, and Galician separatism would be to assume that a generous measure of local autonomy could be extended without calling in question the fact that sovereignty remained with the central government.

The basic outlook developed in this speech and in the earlier *Redención de las provincias* continued to inform Ortega's participation in debate on the Catalan Statute through the summer of 1932. In May, June, and July of that year he outlined in greater detail his response to this long-vexing question, toward which few Castilian intellectuals had been as sympathetic as he. In the first of these three parliamentary speeches, he took detailed issue with the proposed text of the Catalan Statute and clarified his sharp opposition to separatism in the name of the long history of a "formidable urge to be Spaniards, to form a great nation and melt into it. That is why this compact Spain has been formed from the plurality of dispersed peoples that were in the Peninsula."[31] Separatism seemed to Ortega a retrogressive impulse, which looked toward the days of feudalism and the defense of local privilege. The national unit, while in itself already inadequate for the future of Western mankind, was closer to the political needs of the times than regional particularism. "For this reason, this history of peoples like those of Catalonia and Ireland is an almost incessant complaint; for universal evolution ... consists in a gigantic impulse and movement toward ever greater unifications."[32] Over against the highly vocal Catalan separatists, moreover, stood "all the other Spaniards who feel Catalonia to be an ingredient and an essential portion of Spain."[33] The problem would never, Ortega argued, find a definitive solution, but a priori it was necessary to assert that sovereignty belonged to the national state and emanated from Madrid.

On July 27 Ortega spoke on a proposed amendment to the statute which would settle the question of bilingualism in Catalan universities by creating two parallel systems—one regional, the other national. Ortega's counterproposal was to create a single, bilingual state university system that would still recognize Spanish as the official language of the entire nation, while giving Catalan its due, as on the secondary level. He was concerned, as well, to resist a feature of the amendment whereby the *Generalitat* of Catalonia could propose a single, autonomous, bilingual university that would annul the two university systems without belonging clearly either to the state or to the region.[34]

The Catalan Statute and the Statute of Agrarian Reform, in the second of which Ortega had almost no hand, were both ratified in September 1932. By his own account, he ceased to participate actively in parliamentary affairs shortly after his last speech on Catalan universities.[35] In October he dissolved the Agrupación, and noted in a manifesto:

> The Republic is sufficiently consolidated so that the focusing of opinions can and ought to begin. But the Agrupación, by its very genesis, by its initial spirit and intent, cannot be a force adequate to combat other republican forces. It was born to collaborate unconditionally in the advent of the Republic.[36]

It seems appropriate to take Ortega at his word: the original aim of the group had been to promote the orderly and enlightened transition to a new form of political life, not to establish itself as one more among the already numerous parties. But he also had a growing sense that his effectiveness as a parliamentary speaker was waning and that the political climate of the government and the Assembly was not propitious to the critical distinctions so dear to him and other liberal intellectuals. Weighted on the Republican and Socialist left from the beginning, the Assembly had moved quickly to reduce the number of military officers and reorganize the army, to establish economic and political control over the Church, and to draft legislation pertaining to agrarian reform, organized labor, and regional autonomy. Although Ortega had early applauded Azaña's army reform, one might see in the former's movement away from active political involvement at this point his resentment that a relatively obscure intellectual and litterateur like Azaña had, rather incomprehensibly for Ortega, risen so rapidly to political prominence. In the bold moves of this ungainly man and many of his fellow deputies, Ortega was inclined to see undue haste without proper regard for a national consensus. Perhaps, privately, he felt that the course of Spanish politics was falling into what he considered coarser hands than his own, and threatening to substitute a new oligarchy of the left for the old one under Alfonso XIII.

In mid-October 1931, Azaña, who had been minister of war since April, became prime minister upon Alcalá Zamora's resignation in protest over the passage of Article 26. Emerging as the great Republican leader of the first two years of the new government, Azaña was to remain in that post until September 1933. Growing conflict between the Republican Left and the Socialists, coupled with a powerful increase in rightist strength, forced his resignation two months before the elections of November gave a resounding victory to the conservative Catholic right, the centrist Radicals, and the monarchists, an event that confirmed Ortega's concern over exacerbated polarization and partisanship.[37]

Less privileged in his social origins and educational formation than Ortega, whose politics had seemed to Azaña tinged with an antidemocratic bias and an aloof intellectualism, Azaña had in fact been the butt of ridicule by more prestigious intellectuals and men of letters during the 1920s. Ortega had never fully recognized him as a colleague, despite their common membership in the Generation of 1914 and in such organizations as the Liga de Educación Política Española and the Reformist party of Melquíades Álvarez. Yet Azaña not only arose as the leader of the first *bienio* of the Republic in October 1931 but earlier (June 1930) had been elected president of the prestigious Madrid Ateneo. There, however, he had quickly came under attack by those members who wished to radicalize that institution in 1931 and 1932. Though he had been secretary of the Ateneo from 1913 to 1920 and had twice run (unsuccessfully) as a Reformist candidate for congress (1918 and 1923), he had previously been known primarily as a belletristic author and critic who had written the autobiographical novel *El jardín de los frailes* (1926) and some studies of the nineteenth-century novelist Juan Valera. In 1920 he had also founded and edited (with Cipriano Rivas Chérif) the little magazine *La Pluma* (1920–1923), and had then briefly edited *España* (founded chiefly by Ortega in 1915) between 1923 and 1924, the last year of its publication. When Azaña's political vocation became dramatically evident in 1931, Ortega, Unamuno, and others who had aspired to be the major theoretical voices of the Republic were shocked at the ascendancy of this ungainly petit bourgeois. Those who had seen the *Revista de Occidente* as marking the true level of the times had paid little heed to the introspective and retiring figure whose bulky features were to make him prey to innumerable newspaper caricatures during the 1930s. Though his early writings marked him as having a scholarly temperament with poetic inclinations, Azaña has appeared since the publication of his complete works—notably including the *Memorias políticas y de guerra*—as one of Spain's most gifted modern writers. In the 1920s, Unamuno had described him as a "writer without readers," but the *Memorias* have revealed a vivid and complex literary-political mind whose depth of perception and personal anguish during the 1930s have given him posthumously the readership he could not claim during his lifetime.

Since their common membership in the Liga de Educación Política Española (1913), Azaña had considered his gifted colleague Ortega something of a political lightweight who flirted with various affiliations without deep commitment, and Ortega, for his part, had kept a cool distance. Azaña's striking public career developed just as Ortega was encountering clear difficulties in coping with the hurly-burly of parliamentary politics during the first stage of the Republic. In a sense, their fortunes were reversed at that point: the relatively obscure litterateur became a powerful orator and a practiced political leader, while the distinguished philosopher and essayist found himself progressively on the margin of events in the arena of parliamentary discourse, his voice too elegant and literary to be oratorically effective. In fact, Azaña's biographer Juan Marichal points to oratorical style as a clue to the two men's respective political fortunes:

> [I]t is enough to compare one of Ortega's parliamentary speeches with any of Azaña's to perceive immediately that artistic intent was constantly at work in the Madrid philosopher (with obvious neglect of the political thread of his discourse). One notes the very careful preparation of the sentences, and there is hardly any "improvisation" [38]

Azaña, by contrast, blended improvisation with a profound feeling for Spain, greater empirical content than Ortega, and assimilated threads of the earlier grand oratorical style of Emilio Castelar and Antonio Muara. [39]

Ortega's feeling that the style of his parliamentary speeches was perhaps not well received by some members of the Assembly is illustrated by the defensive tone of his rejoinder to a criticism of his "mannered" style of address by the moderate Socialist and first minister of the treasury, Indalecio Prieto. Shortly after the Assembly first met on July 14, 1931, Prieto responded in what Ortega thought "bad-humored and perverse" fashion to his suggestion that the new government had not sufficiently reassured Spanish capitalists that they were not to be singled out for persecution.[40] Ortega took Prieto's remark to heart and launched an elaborate apology for the right "to show myself as I am." He resented Prieto's implication that he was merely posturing, for

> a man of letters, a thinker, a theorist, and an avid student are not things I pretend to be, but rather—the devil take it!—what I am, what I am to my roots. . . . Imagery and melodic phrasing are incoercible tendencies of my being which I have carried into teaching, learning, café conversation, just as, vice versa, I have taken philosophy to the newspaper. . . . Thus I demand my full right to forge a politics that is poetic, philosophical, cordial, and gay.[41]

Prieto had obviously hit upon a delicate point, one that continued to trouble Ortega periodically throughout the fifteen months of his active participation in the parliamentary debates. As a nonpartisan critic and self-appointed "shepherd" of the Republic, he was bound to take a position that evoked little sympathy from those who were fighting for specific programs and had much more experience in practical politics. Prieto and others felt an understandable hostility at times toward the "schoolmasters" gathered under the Agrupación umbrella.

An additional motive for Ortega's early withdrawal from the public arena was his belief that he had seriously neglected his vocation as a writer and a teacher in order to fulfill his parliamentary duties. Thus he could complain in February 1932 that for "more than a year I have not been able to devote a moment—except in my university course—to my standing professional commitments. Do not forget . . . that I live by my pen and that, like it or not, I have to go back to plowing my daily furrow with it."[42] Although he had neglected his philosophical mission during the first year of the Republic, he had, after a fashion, transferred it to the parliamentary debates, for his tendency to instruct, analyze, and meditate aloud was inveterate and present in even the most deliberate of his speeches and political journalism. As he had said to Prieto, he was what he was to the very roots.

Contemporary historians now see Ortega's influence at its peak during the last weeks of the monarchy, the interregnum of the Berenguer government, and the early months of the Constituent Assembly and the Republic itself. It was in this period that the Agrupación did its most effective work in turning middle-class opinion away from Alfonso XIII's floundering regime toward republicanism. Critics of his political activity have said that Ortega lacked the combative spirit necessary for the daily strategies and skirmishes, and that he had no talent for organizational detail. He was, in fact, not very interested in the practical implementation of politics; it gave too little rein to his intellectual independence and too little stimulation to his artistic temperament. In the many projects he fostered in his lifetime, he was never inclined to follow through with the tedious details. This reluctance reached even into his more purely intellectual work. At the *Revista de Occidente*, for example, the devoted labors of his friend and secretary Fernando Vela were essential for the practical operation of the magazine; and many of Ortega's writings over the years remained in their original form as lectures, notes, or fragments, hastily composed and abandoned in the course of a career that included enough varied projects to fill the lives of ten ordinary men. Politically, Ortega was at his strongest in articulating the great liberal hope in the growth of an orderly democratic republic.

Ortega's Agrupación suffered too, like the parties of the Republican left which counted on middle-class support, from the relatively undeveloped political consciousness of the Spanish bourgeoisie. This lack of a solid constituency with well-formed political opinions made it all the more likely that in a pinch Ortega would resort to lyrical effusions and "grand programs" for lack of a clear political direction. His clearest success in building a constituency for his ideas came during the heyday of his career with *El Sol* in the twenties and, briefly, with *Crisol*. Later in 1932 the latter paper, which remained closely associated with Ortega's general political effort, announced that it would be succeeded by a new daily, named *Luz* in accord with Ortega's notion of the intellectual as "luminary" and torchbearer. The last number of *Crisol* went on the streets on January 6, 1932, and *Luz*, destined to be the last, brief fruit of the cooperative ventures of

Ortega and Urgoiti, appeared on the afternoon of the following day.[43] Financial pressure had caused the collapse of *Crisol*, and both men hoped that *Luz*, as a serious republican daily from the start, would fare better.

But Urgoiti found the new venture difficult to carry; meanwhile, a wealthy Catalan speculator named Luis Miquel was planning to take control of *El Sol*, *La Voz*, and *Luz* in order to create a powerful pro-Azaña press.[44] Ortega, about to be squeezed out of his fourth journalistic forum, was reported to be thinking of returning to his old home at *El Sol*. By August 1932 he had indeed ceased to be a contributor to *Luz*, a withdrawal from public life confirmed by the dissolution of the Agrupación in the fall. By his own account, the lack of response to the "Rectification" lecture of December 1931 had already confirmed his decision to give up political aspirations.[45] In early September 1932 the interests headed by Miquel took control of the three papers destined to become the "Azaña press." Now Ortega's long, distinguished journalistic career was effectively at an end. Since his earliest contributions to *El Imparcial* he had always been able to count on a forum for his reflections and political commentary. Left on the sidelines of political action by the fall of 1932, he could well recur to the words in the prologue to his *Obras* published that same year: "To the sea once again, little ship! What Plato called 'the second voyage' has begun!"[46]

There was a coda, however, to this last movement in his prewar public life. On December 3 and 9, 1933, after more than a year of silence, he published in *El Sol* two articles that may be considered the last will and testament of his political life in Spain.[47] Both articles, "¡Viva la República!" and "En nombre de la nación, claridad," followed on the heels of the election of November 19, in which the forces of the right, particularly José María Gil Robles's Confederación Española de Derechas Autónomas (CEDA) had triumphed; both were pleas in defense of the Republic against its potential destroyers from Left or Right. In asserting, in the article on December 3, that the Left had "thrown up all the foolishness it had in its belly" and that the right would now have to do the same so that the Republic could move on, Ortega tried to be optimistic in the face of partisan enmity toward what he felt must be the political destiny of Spain: a republic for the whole nation.

The shout of "¡Viva la República!" was for some, no doubt, a theatrical gesture from a prematurely disillusioned figure whose personal resentment over his political fortunes had caused his withdrawal; but a more accurate reading of both final pieces would recognize their acute analysis of the dangers facing the regime, now some two and a half years old. Ortega impugned both the leftist government of the past two years under Azaña and the newly elected rightist coalition, which seemed quite capable of turning against the Republic itself. If the Left had committed the barbarities of burning churches and expelling the Jesuits, the Right might equally well have the temerity to thrust the Church back into a privileged position. All Spaniards, he felt, must rally to the destiny called for at this "level" of their history: the Republic was their fate, and *amor fati* would be their wisdom. This was especially a call to the young, as yet uncorrupted:

> Will young Spaniards ... be capable of feeling the enormous possibilities contained in the fact that in the midst of a halting Europe the Spanish people was the first radically to affirm the dominion of morality in politics over against all utilitarianism and machiavellianism? Was not that perhaps the business that, in the last analysis, was reserved for the Spanish people? [48]

The refrain of an appeal to youth in Ortega's political commentary of the period indicates his increasingly pessimistic view of the future of the Republic. It is tantamount to an admission that the future of a united Spain could not be the work of his contemporaries, sullied by partisan commitments and the tedious details of daily political work, but must belong to yet another generation, still capable of dreaming of its hour on the stage. Ortega's own hour had not gone well for him, but he had known at least when to retire from public life, his efficacy at an end.

If his voice was now eclipsed in public by those of parliamentarians like Azaña and Gil Robles, Ortega continued to further his career as a philosopher and university professor, reaching, during the years of the Republic, a kind of magisterial height with philosophical work as profound and clear as any he ever did. While it is not simple to determine the precise effect his engagement and eventual failure in the making of the new government had on his writing in those years, one is immediately impressed by the range and penetration of his thought, which was surely activated and deepened by the experience of the nation's political crisis and by more personal reflections on the result of his own aspirations to leadership. His principal projects after *¿Qué es filosofía?* were *Goethe desde dentro* (published by the Revista de Occidente Press in April 1932), "Unas lecciones de metafísica" (university course of 1932–1933), "Meditación de la técnica" (summer course in 1933 at the University of Santander), "En torno a Galileo" (university course of fall 1933), the first draft of "Ideas y creencias" (begun in December 1934), "Historia como sistema" (written in 1935), and "Misión del bibliotecario" (published in the *Revista de Occidente* in May 1935).

The first of these—the work on Goethe—echoes something of Ortega's doubts about the direction of his own life at the time, suggesting, as one critic remarks,

> how his ideas of vital reason, vocation and destiny might be applied to biography.... In every life there is a destiny for which the individual is born; as part of his circumstance it precedes concepts and ideas regarding it. By means of his will, a man may choose or not to fulfill this vital project.... The drama that is life lies in the individual's struggle with his circumstance to fulfill or avoid his destiny.[49]

Ortega charges Goethe with knowingly having denied his destiny, which was presumably manifest to him, by turning aside from his youthful poetic career to busy himself with the nonpoetic labors of his later years in Weimar. Ortega did not often think of destiny as being so evident. His insistence that Goethe contravened the clear knowledge that he was destined to be for all his days a great poet in fact clashes with Ortega's conviction, pervasive elsewhere in his work (both before 1932 and later in the 1930s), that though the destiny of circumstances is evident enough, the shape our lives will take—the fulfillment of our vocations—is never clear before the fact. It is, rather, as if we drew nearer at times to a conviction that we are fulfilling our vocations, and at other times as if we had the vague foreboding that we are not doing so. He generally argues that our destiny must be intuited and searched out, or again, that it has to be "come into"—discovered, acknowledged, and created all at once —through living one's life. In sum, destiny is both made and found in acts of existential decision.

It may be argued that Ortega, in writings on the concept of destiny other than the essay on Goethe, suggests that such acts derive from a kind of intuitive sense of what we must do to make our destiny manifest. If, in that sense, we never make decisions *ex nihilo*, neither do we ever do so with total certainty. Ortega's idea that Goethe had but denied such certainty is a retrospective reconstruction, resting on the dubious assumption that biographical criticism can, as Dilthey had argued, recreate the life-structure and grasp the circumstances of another man distant in time, reliving his dilemmas and choices "from within," as experienced by the subject himself. Yet a central tenet of Ortega's developing understanding of life-as-project was that no one could in fact transpose himself into another's circumstances. His attempt to do so with Goethe derived, one feels, from Ortega's extraordinarily close identification with the German poet, whose putative vocational dilemma Ortega may have seen as somehow like his own. If Goethe presented the case of a great man unfaithful to his deepest self, then Ortega too must have thought by 1932 that politics had become *his* "Weimar," his long detour from his destiny as a thinker. It seems likely that the contradictions and inconsistencies of the puzzling essay on his great mentor reflect Ortega's ambivalence at that difficult juncture in his own life. Until 1933, he moved by turns toward and away from active involvement in national affairs, as he varied in his concept of the proper role and effective force of ideas in history. In fact, he never resolved this dilemma for himself: it was instead resolved for him by the collapse of the Republic; by the resultant civil war, which drove him into exile; and by the Franco regime, which obstructed his efforts to reestablish himself in Spain in the mid-1940s.

Ortega returned in full force to his philosophical calling in the university courses given in Madrid in 1932 and 1933, and in the summer course in Santander in the latter year. His turn toward the lecture hall was simultaneously a turn away from the Cortes, where he had failed to create an enduring audience for himself. He was engaged once again with the School of Philosophy and Letters, which was to occupy the first building finished in the new University City being constructed on the open fields on the west edge of the capital. On this site in the winter of 1932–1933 he offered the brilliant "Unas lecciones de metafísica" (*Some Lessons in Metaphysics*), which was both the mature fruit of his absorption of Heidegger's *Sein und Zeit* and a statement of his own independent emphasis on matters of concern common to both thinkers. The course consisted of a full exposition of the radical reality of "my life" understood as the unified interplay of

"I" and "my circumstances." This theme had of course been addressed toward the end of the series "¿Qué es filosofía?" but each time Ortega returned to it, its implications for a philosophy of human life grew clearer. It may well be argued that the *Lessons*, delivered in a vivid colloquial language obviously pitched to an admiring live audience, represents the peak of his philosophical work before the civil war.

In the published text, taken directly from the manuscript prepared for the lectures, one feels the dramatic, even theatrical quality of Ortega's classroom teaching style. The pages are dotted with thematic *ritornelli* and leitmotivs that lend order to a naturally expansive theme. Fearing perhaps to transcend the grasp of his student audience, he referred to their immediate circumstances as persons who had to decide at each moment whether to stay in his lecture hall or walk out in boredom. Thus he threw his listeners back on the element of existential choice in each thing they did. To study merely because one called oneself a "student" was a case of tautological inauthenticity. To become authentic and escape socially imposed roles, one had to understand that "culture" required "care," or "concern," what Heidegger—whom Ortega gratefully acknowledged in this context —had called *Sorge*. A metaphysics of human life, he reasoned, returns man to the study of the permanent structure of his existence. It must be founded upon care for one's own life as the only legitimate entry into philosophy. The life into which one is cast, however, already has its own lineaments:

> The circumstance, the environment, the world into which we have fallen on coming to life and in which we are prisoners and perplexed, is in every case composed of a certain repertory of possibilities.... Faced with this keyboard of possible things to do, we are free to prefer one or another; but the keyboard, as a whole, is fateful.... [Nonetheless] this fateful character of our surrounding, of the world in which we live, does not oblige us to do or to be any one single thing. Would that it did! Then man's life would be like the life of the stone...directed by cosmic forces....But in what direction you are going to walk has not been decided.... Within the destiny marked out by your environment, you are free; even more, you are fatefully free because you have no choice, like it or not, but to select your future within the range and margin that your fateful environment offers you.[50]

This sense of a historically given destiny was, in part, the mature philosophical fruit of his youthful idea that the Generation of 1914 was called to transform both Spanish and European culture. From his earliest writings Ortega had proclaimed the repertory of tasks and possibilities laid upon him by the culture of his time and by Spanish politics. The keyboard had indeed been fateful! Pulled between the need to creat an audience for his work and the desire to pursue theory as a "spectator," Ortega might well imagine the dumb bliss of the stone with its simple fate.

Some Lessons in Metaphysics stands today as one of the clearest, most succinct expositions of Ortega's mature ideas, which grew increasingly existentialist throughout the thirties. Within that broad tradition of thought, probably no analysis of the human situation has been more explicit. Influenced by Heidegger's example in *Sein und Zeit*, which still seemed to Ortega to have reaped the systematic fruit of seeds he himself had earlier sown, he had ceased by the early thirties to write essays.[51] A single elaborated *aperçu* now seemed insufficient. Yet the graceful essayist of earlier work would not be entirely suppressed, for both the *Lessons* and "En torno a Galileo" were beautifully written. The former distilled his many thrusts at defining human life into a number of memorably simple statements.

In essence, he noted in the second lecture, "[l]ife is what we do and what happens to us."[52] To this seeming truism, Ortega added that life is in fact "evidential"—always undeniably present to us in a "now," a present moment. We need not reflect in order to know ourselves alive in a surrounding world. Yet this basic reality that we "reckon with" (*contar con*) implies that we cannot simply rest in a blissful self-awareness. Being in the world means to be given over to circumstances, to traffic with things and people and the ever-breaking furture. In response to this condition, we must make the decisions that give form to the vital project each of us is. At the same time, we encounter life as "continual and essential perplexity." Nothing tells us with certainty how to decide. Thrust into life without choosing it, we are obliged to create a role for ourselves with no previous script. As Unamuno had put it, man lives his own novel, writing or "telling" himself as he goes, and no one knows precisely how the story will go. Pirandello made the same point in "Six Characters in Search of an Author" (1921), which portrays a handful of dramatic characters

abandoned by the playwright and struggling to "complete themselves" by concluding the play. In a similar sense, obviously spurred
by Heidegger, Ortega saw life as constant disquiet or "preoccupation." It was "given" only in the sense of our being suddenly
confronted with it at birth. Otherwise, it was best defined as what we
must constantly define for ourselves.

Because each man must create his own story, he has no simple
identity. In good part, the world defines him by meeting, resisting,
and shaping the thrust of his choices. Thus, "[t]o live is for me to exist
outside myself." [53] Unlike inert objects, man can realize himself only
by living toward and with things. Incapable of simple self-sufficiency,
he must in each new moment risk himself. In this way, "[m]an is
essentially a stranger, an emigrant, an exile." [54] Yet he cannot strictly
be alienated from the world, for things, experienced as a series of
"conveniences" and "inconveniences," are ineluctably a part of his
life. Previous to all reflection and irreducible to the intellectual constructs "body" and "soul," one's life is the coexistence of "I" (itself a
kind of construct) with things. As one sees oneself obliged to live in
one's circumstances, at once mutable and obdurate, thought, or
philosophical analysis, becomes hermeneutically imperative. Such
reflection amounts to constructing the world as man knows it, for
"world" is not what is "out there" but rather, as its etymology in
English suggests ("age," or "life of man"), that with which I occupy
myself. Thus, to have a world is to transform sheer circumstantiality
and contingency into a meaningful order. Thinking, though in itself
not primary in our lives, is a form of doing something with things. This
position makes explicit Ortega's refutation, in the last four lectures of
Lessons, of realism and idealism as opposing ways of sundering man
from the world. The first does so by making him an object among
other objects (immersing him, as would a modern behaviorist, in a
world without human perspective), the second by placing the world
in his mind.

At various points just before and after the Second Republic was
born, Ortega remarked the promise and the uncertainty entailed by
his understanding of the reality of human life. Many of these observations gave body to the metaphysical principles articulated in 1932–
1933, and revealed as well the mixture of apprehension and great
expectations with which he contemplated Spain's political crisis. In
February 1930, for example, less than a month after Primo de Rivera

had left for Paris, Ortega wrote to Victoria Ocampo:

> [W]hat is characterisitic of that which we call Life, Yours, Mine, Each Person's ... is that it means existing in an inexorably given world, in this one here and now. Your Life depends upon what happens in the world and on what the world is like. You are no more than one of the two important ingredients in your Life: the other is the World. If you wish to be successful in your Life, you must be successful in your ideas and presumptions about the World. ... But the World, what there is around us, our *circumstance*, has layers like an onion, and the most external or superficial ones are less real, less *authentic* than the internal ones. A life is successful when it is lived *toward, with* and *from* the most authentic and substantial part of what is *existing* and *occurring* in today's world. It's useless trying to be admirable if you don't live the substantial part of your era. To do this, your life must cease to slide over the world (being amused, seeing, hearing, entertaining, being capricious); on the contrary, it must be anchored to it. ... *Today's life is in its last hours and a radically different type is forming rapidly*. But ... that new life cannot be found in the street or in store windows. To find it requires work, effort, dedication, *vocation*—not diversion.[55]

Three years later, in the autumn of 1933, he reflected his feelings about the arrival and departure of his generation's golden hour in the university course "En torno a Galileo." These lectures found a more approriate title in their English translation as *Man and Crisis* (1958), for though Ortega nominally based this analysis of the historical dimension of human life upon Galileo's founding of the age of modern physical science, the lectures centrally presented a mature formulation of his idea that culture must periodically be in crisis if it is to respond to changing historical conditions and new imperatives. Huizinga, whose *Waning of the Middle Ages* Ortega had already introduced to Spanish readers in translation, had clearly shaped his Spanish colleague's dramatic sense of the rise and decline of cultural periods, for Ortega took as a chief instance of cultural crisis the plight of "fifteenth-century man," who "is lost in himself, torn away from one system of convictions and not yet installed in another, without solid grounding on which to stand; swinging loose on his hinges, so to speak, exactly as man is today."[56] Purportedly, modern man's disorientation resulted from the breakdown of the dominant yet humanly inadequate "physico-mathematical" vision of reality which Ortega had already analyzed in *What Is Philosophy?* But the urgent note in both the theme and sytle of these lectures in 1933 surely came from Ortega's experience during the late days of the Constituent Assembly of the Second Republic, when his own active political role was already behind him. Now, the sense he had long before formed that he was living on the edge of a new age about to be born emerged full-blown as a statement of the human condition, for genuine culture, like authentic human life, was always *in statu nascendi*.

Between the lines of these lectures, however, one senses the implicit correlate that life is also *in statu morendi*, for what is born must also die. Fifty-one years of age when he gave the course, Ortega was a leader of the generation "in force" in the world. He could look both ways, toward the grand hopes of youth and the restricted horizon of old age. A sense of his own mortality may be felt in his reminder that essential to our life in time is its passage and our consequent occupation of successive stages of existence. As the generations march through history, so does each of us move inexorably through the years. In this process, we exist simultaneously in the larger historical and generational structure, and in the related microstructure of our particular biographies:

> Life is time ... and not cosmic time which is imaginary and therefore infinite, but limited time, time which comes to an end, time which is the true and irreparable time. Because of this, man has an age. Age is the fact of man's being always in a certain sector of his scanty time-span ... whether he is a child, a youth, a grown man, or an old man.
>
> But this means that every historic present, every "today," involves three distinct times, three different "todays." Or, to put it another way: the present is rich in three great vital dimensions which dwell together in it, whether they will or no, linked with one another, and perforce, because they are different, in essential hostility one to another. For some, "today" is the state of being twenty, for others, forty, and for still another group, sixty; and this ... creates the dynamic drama, the conflict, and the collision which form the background of historic material and of all modern living together.[57]

In 1933, Ortega was the "mature man," who had just played his hand. As the outstanding representative of the liberal intelligentsia of 1914, he was fast becoming marginal to the great events of the day. Yet he could still affirm in the third lecture, "The Idea of a Generation," that to belong to a generation which is broadly uniform is to have a very different vital destiny, a very different life structure, from belonging to one which is narrow, heterogeneous, and dispersed. And there are generations whose destiny is to break through a people's isolation and to lead them to live spiritually with others, thus integrating them into a much broader unity, taking them out of their retrograde history, freeing them from being individual and housebound, so to speak, and introducing them into the gigantic ambit of universal history.[58]

This larger view of his generation's mission compensated, one may suppose, for Ortega's withdrawal from politics in 1932. From that point on, he would stake his efforts entirely on the long-range work of reforming culture through philosophy.

Apart from reflecting his personal situation, "En torno a Galileo" presented in its fullest form Ortega's theory of the generational structure of human life, a theme he had sketched out ten years earlier in *El tema de nuestro tiempo*. This theory and the related concept of "birth" were part of his plan to systematize the study of history. While the spectacle of history presents the obvious importance of generations in succession, in order to move beyond mere linear chronicle historians must understand the principles governing a man's location in time. Chief among these is his having been generated by those who preceded him and his being capable of generating those who will follow him. Novelty, historical movement, and changing cultural imperatives can all be understood in these terms. The proper study of history and of individual biography requires this type of "historical reason," as Dilthey, whom Ortega claimed to have just "discovered" in 1929, had already abundantly pointed out.[59] Thus life is understood, first, from within the drama of man's effort to create a meaningful "world" and second, as a series of changes in that world, each of which is accompanied by "a change in the structure of the vital drama." History then becomes "the study of the forms or structures which human life has taken since we had any information about it."[60]

A key structure is that of human generations. By Ortega's reckoning, biological generations succeed each other roughly every thirty years. But the coexistence at any given point of the youth, the mature man, and the old man—in familial terms, son, father, and grandfather—means that the world is interpreted in different terms by "contemporaries" who are yet not "coevals." Ortega defined coevality in terms of the "zone of dates" covering one's birth and determining at what point in history one passes through the five chronological stages of life. These go by intervals of fifteen years, comprising childhood (birth to fifteen years), youth (fifteen to thirty), initiation (thirty to forty-five), dominance (forty-five to sixty), and old age (sixty to seventy-five). Biographically, the third and fourth are the crucial stages, during which men (and possibly women, though Ortega neglects to mention them) put the stamp of their particular "vital sensitivity" on the world: "Hence I could say that an historic generation lives fifteen years of gestation [from thirty to forty-five years of age] and fifteen years of creation [from forty-five to sixty]." [61] There followed a dubious method for dividing "historic time" into similar intervals in order to correlate generational rhythms with the substance of history. Ortega assumed "that the face of the world changes every fifteen years." [62] A man's age when this happens will determine the role or roles he plays within this pattern. At best, this sketch toward a full-fledged theory of generations remained very approximate, though it at least affirmed the useful idea that an effective generation of coevals will, by confronting together the same historical circumstances, share a set of formative experiences and a resultant worldview.

The rhythm of individual lives and that of the changing "tone" of history, both governed by the fifteen-year unit, take place within the much larger pattern of cultural ages, which presumably mature, decay, and suffer the crisis of dissolution. Certain generations, like those of Galileo and Descartes, and, three hundred years later, that of Ortega, are called upon to usher in the epochal change that coincides with their maturity and gives them their exalted task in history. These are the select paladin-generations that incarnate the human need for periodic cultural renewal. The generations of Galileo (1564–1642) and Descartes (1596–1650) gave us the modern scientific worldview regnant down to the end of the nineteenth century. Now the generation of Ortega and his contemporaries was presumably destined to develop the new view of human life understood not through models provided by science but in terms of life's quintessential temporality and organic continuity. Nicely enough, Ortega envisioned this very same generation as "epochal" for Spanish history; thus he was able to fuse his political with his philosophical destiny.

Closely tied in theme and tone to his lectures on the crises inherent in all human culture, Ortega's course "Meditación de la técnica" (summer 1933) was his contribution to a theme that in one fashion or another attracted most of the major thinkers of his day.[63] Seeing modern technology as a legacy of Cartesian reason, he analyzed *technē* as man's inclination to build a world that at once reflected his commerce with his circumstances and allowed him to understand them as an extension of himself. Rather than leading man in search of "hidden" or "withdrawn" Being (Heidegger), philosophy must illuminate man's changing "answers" to the challenge of living, since man, unlike other animals, is not concerned primarily with being for its own sake, or simple self-preservation; instead, he seeks well-being (*bienestar*). To name the basic necessities of his life (food, clothing, shelter, etc.) is not to say much, for man is the animal who in order to live must live better. He does so through the "second nature" of the cultural worlds he creates. In this context, technique and technology have been part of the human venture since the beginning. It is only one long step from fire and stone axes to central heating and modern pile drivers. In man's quest, through technical means, to save effort or to make its effect more beneficial, he creates what Ortega calls an "invented life." The emergence of technology is preprogrammed, as it were, in the encounter of *homo faber* with the world, which presents itself to him as a repertoire of obstacles and opportunities. (Unlike man, the dog, for example, does not find these at hand, or at least does not reflect on them.) Man's being-in-the-world rests upon the creation and satisfaction of desires through the application of technique. Thus, Ortega clearly saw, there is no sharp line between so-called 'basic" needs and luxuries. The task of the philosopher and the historian is to discern the context in which certain desires make sense, for a given ideal of civilization will determine what technology will be cultivated, and vice versa.

For Ortega, three stages of technical development correspond, broadly speaking, to the history of civilization. First, there is a primitive technology discovered by chance (*la técnica del azar*) as man finds the uses of fire and the earliest tools. At this stage, technology is very close to "natural actions," and thus quickly becomes universal in practice: everybody can soon make fire, bows and arrows, and so on. Yet early man, still unaware of his capacity for invention, stumbles on his novelties, which seem to him almost a part of nature. He is still unconscious of himself as *homo faber*. In the second stage (*la técnica del artesano*)—in ancient Greece, pre-imperial Rome, and the medieval period—the figure of the artisan becomes typical. Simultaneously inventor and worker, he specializes in certain refined techniques; but since his craft is immersed in a long tradition and passed on through workshops of masters and apprentices, he cannot be considered a self-aware inventor. Technology as such is still invisible. At this stage, the tools of a trade are relatively simple extensions of the body. Techniques are not perceived as separate from him who practices them, and the machine, strictly speaking, has not yet appeared. Since man has as yet neither distanced himself from nor radically transformed nature, he could still, if his techniques were to fail him, return to an essentially primitive life. He is not radically dependent upon the artificial products of a truly sophisticated technology. Nonetheless, people now look to the trained artisan for skills and products not shared by the entire community.

In the third stage (*la técnica del técnico*), the inventor may be distinguished from the worker. The technician, designer, or engineer creates what others will implement or produce with the aid of machines. Technology is everywhere visible in its own right. Man understands as never before that he has a capacity quite different from that given to him by nature. The fact becomes evident that civilization is second nature. Rather than discovering certain techniques by chance or assigning them to skilled practitioners of a craft, man now perceives technology as a kind of cornucopia of limitless possibilities. The whole understanding of human life begins to shift from an accent on limitation to a mood of astonished expectation of new technical marvels. Ortega finds this last stage disturbing, even "anti-ethical," for modern technology, upon which man is dependent as never before, creates and satisfies needs so abundantly as to foster the illusion that humans can do and be whatever they wish. A certain fairy-tale quality attaches to life, tempting man to overleap himself. The resultant plethora of opportunities, welcomed with a kind of "intoxicated" fantasy about marvelous futures, creates an outlook quite contrary to Ortega's more sober view of the human condition as a combination of difficulty and possibility. The dream of untrammeled technical growth is in fact akin to the bewildering expansion of knowledge he had remarked two years earlier in *Man and Crisis*:

> [T]he man who knows many things, the cultivated man, runs the risk of losing himself in the jungle of his own knowledge; and he ends up by not

knowing what his own genuine knowledge is.... [T]his is what happens to the modern average man. He has received so many thoughts that he does not know which of them are those he actually thinks, those he believes; and he becomes used to living on pseudo-beliefs ... which falsify his own existence. Hence the restlessness, the deep *otherness*, which so many modern lives carry in their secret selves. Hence the desolation, the emptiness, of so much personal destiny which struggles desperately to fill itself with one conviction or another without ever managing to convince itself.[64]

The "jungle" of knowledge, like that of inventions, fosters the development of the "mass man." The ambiguous blessings of modern civilized life threaten man with the loss of authenticity defined as the capacity to live in harmony with himself. The problem of human "identity," so clearly a part of existentialist thought as it develops from Kierkegaard onward, is thus characteristic of high technological civilizations. Moreover, technology itself, anonymous and ubiquitous, becomes our environment. As such, it is semiautonomous, for not only can we no longer live without it, but we must also respond to the agenda it dictates. Since technology cannot determine the ends of human life (though, indeed, through its sheer pervasiveness it would seem to do so), modern life suffers from an ethical vacuum, a sense of emptiness and lostness. Knowing more than ever about how to do things, Ortega's argument runs, we know less than ever what to do and why we must do it. In standing above and enveloping life, as it were, technology, our creation, has severed us from ourselves.

This perception of the situation was not a new one. Wordsworth and Blake had instinctively foreseen what alarmed Ortega. In the 1840s Emerson remarked that "things are in the saddle and ride mankind." Marx had analyzed the plight of the alienated worker who served the machines fashioned by capital in its needs for self-expansion, and throughout the past century a host of thinkers and artists had deplored the dehumanizing effects of the Industrial Revolution. In many European countries and in the United States as well, the arts and crafts movement of the late nineteenth century (represented most typically by William Morris in England) expressed a deep anxiety over the disappearance of a way of life like that of Ortega's second stage. Speaking out of a long tradition of skepticism regarding modern technology, Ortega's was only one voice among those of many twentieth-century thinkers who cried alarm. Yet his analysis of the situation was more dispassionate than, say, Karl Jaspers's or Heidegger's or those put forward by members of the Frankfurt School, like Theodor Adorno, Max Horkheimer, or Herbert Marcuse.

These and numerous other thinkers, predominantly German-speaking, tended to see a demonic purport in the arrogance of what Spengler called Faustian Man. This emphasis is evident, to take a prototypical instance, in Heidegger's "The Question Concerning Technology" (1953), in which he analyzes technology as the audacious project to "enframe" the whole world in order to submit it to the human will to use. Through technology, he argues, man tames nature, only to lose in the process his sense of wonder and his rootedness in life. Then the world can no longer reveal or "uncover" itself to him on its own terms, for the work of "enframing" renders it a "standing-reserve" for eventual exploitation, threatening to "sweep man away into ordering as the supposed single way of revealing." An unleashed and rampant will to technical perfection will end by fabricating a world in which we can see nothing but the reflection of our own handwork. For Heidegger, the consequences of this domination will be disastrous for our well-being.

What Ortega explored in 1933, in an optimistic if still ambivalent tone, as a fundamental human response to being in the world (i.e., the birth of technology from man's desire not only to live but to live well) became in the later Heidegger, especially after World War II, an ominous threat to humanity. Heidegger's dark vision of a planned and managed world governed by scientific research and devoted to the production of "gadgetry" was probably affected by Germany's defeat and by the spectacle of unleashed atomic power in 1946; but his bias against the scientific-technical cast of a "darkened" modern world, where man, no longer the watchful "shepherd" of Being, was plagued by self-forgetfulness, had already been evident in *Sein und Zeit* a quarter century earlier. In his essentially nostalgic preference for an "agrarian" or pastoral vision of existence, his metaphors drawn from the worlds of the farmer, woodsman, and craftsman, Heidegger, like many other thinkers of the period between the wars, rejected a modern cosmopolitan world characterized by the trivialization of life and the distraction of man from his meet "path."

By contrast, Ortega, temperamentally more sanguine than his German colleague, who composed his later work in a Black Forest cabin, saluted and buoyantly accepted the fact that man was, for better or worse, a quintessentially "technical animal." Though he clearly saw the danger of unbraked technology, he registered the perception more soberly, in a more balanced tone, than either the later Heidegger or the pessimistic Jaspers of *Man in the Modern Age* (1931). At bottom less an "irrationalist" than Heidegger, Ortega could not espouse a turn away from the modern world, of which the (for him) indubitable scientific and cultural advances had given impetus to his programs of modernization for Spain. Nonetheless, there remained in his view of man's inherent need to create and recreate civilizaton an undercurrent of uneasy concern. Precisely because man as technician, man with no "nature" but his history of changing vital projects, could be whatever he wished, he was not really anything fully. This ontological "deficiency," if it can be so called, was confronted by Heidegger in his analysis of *Angst* and being-toward-death, but for Ortega it was more the sign of a radically open and in some sense hopeful future. His ambivalent conclusion to the "Meditation on Technology" remained, in fact, present in his later thought, as one may observe in the brief "El mito del hombre allende la técnica" (The Myth of Man Beyond Techinque), presented at a colloquium in Darmstadt in 1951, with Heidegger, who was implicitly challenged in Ortega's title, as a coparticipant. There too Ortega affirmed man's existential commitment to "technique" as the fruit of the evolved cerebral superiority that had distinguished him from the chimpanzee. The consequent human elaboration of an "inner" world of dream and fantasy destined man to be the restless creator of ever-different if not always better human "worlds." By nature an "unsatisfied" creature, a constitutionally "unhappy" animal, he had created through the "new world of technique" what Ortega termed "a gigantic orthopedic apparatus," for "all technique has this marvelous and ... dramatic tendency and quality of being a grand and fabulous orthopedics."[65]

By 1933, Ortega's conviction was well established that human life must be understood not only through a more direct phenomenological analysis of its constituent features but also through the exercise of *la razón histórica* (historical reason), defined as the systematic comprehension of all man's previous "experiments" in being as expressed in the record of culture and civilization around the world. In an expansive essay of 1924 entitled "Las atlántidas" (a reference to the myth of sunken, suboceanic cultures), Ortega had first identified *la razón histórica* as a superb means of access to the story of mankind's intellectual history. The immediate stimulus came from Ortega's passionate interest in recent archaeological discoveries, most notably of the tomb of Tutankhamen in 1922 by Howard Carter (who lectured at the Residencia de Estudiantes in Madrid in November 1924) and Lord Carnarvon. Seeing *la razón histórica* analogously as the philosopher's tool for uncovering buried forms of life, Ortega made the new concept a historicized variant of his earlier *razón vital* (vital reason). It would become ascendant as his career proceeded, receiving a full exposition in *Man and Crisis* and the slightly later essay "Historia como sistema" (History as a System, 1935), contributed to a festschrift for Ernst Cassirer in 1936.[66] Like Benedetto Croce and R. G. Collingwood on the Continent and Charles A. Beard, Carl Becker, and John Dewey in the United States, he emphasized that history was written from the present to account systematically for one's current situation in its dimension of temporal depth. More, that depth, achieved through a historico-logical connection with all that man had been, was the only one available to modern men, who could no longer invoke a timeless "essence" or "soul" bestowed upon them from above. Man does not have a static being; rather, he "goes on being" in various ways, all of which include what he has already been and done:

> Man is what has happened to him, what he has done.... Man is a substantial emigrant on a pilgrimage of being, and it is accordingly meaningless to set limits to what he is capable of being.... The experiments already made with life narrow man's future. If we do not know what he is going to be, we know what he is not going to be. Man lives in view of the past.
> *Man, in a word, has no nature; what he has is ... history.* Expressed differently: what nature is to things, history, *res gestae,* is to man. Once again we become aware of the possible application of theological concepts to human reality. *Deus, qui hoc est natura quod fecerit ...* says St. Augustine. Man, likewise, finds that he has no nature other than what he has himself done.[67]

The optimistic implication of such radical historicism was that man might be almost anything tomorrow—except a repetition of what he had already been. There was a distinctly heartening national correlate to this idea, for it opened the way to freeing Spaniards of attachment to the ghosts of a stagnant national character. If they had been known, for example, to be prideful, passionate, Catholic, and apolitical, there was no inherent reason why they might not become more modest, rational, secular, and politically conscious tomorrow. However burdened they were accustomed to feel by the decline of their earlier golden age in modern times, their future growth was not fixed. At the same time, in order to realize their potential for change and come abreast of the level of the times as currently defined outside Spain, Spaniards would have to study their own national past, which had been so egregiously neglected by them. Looking to understand the problems of forms of life today, men must turn to yesterday, then to the day before yesterday, and so on, building their way systematically back through "human experiences linked in a single, inexorable chain." The chain always began with the radical reality of "my life," out of which one asks after the past because he carries it within.

As if to turn his reflections about history upon himself, Ortega wrote during the years of the Second Republic two extended prologues to his works which are of considerable autobiographical import. The first, for an edition of his *Obras* published by Espasa-Calpe in Madrid in 1932, doubtless reflected his assessment of his own work in comparison with that of Heidegger.[68] Yet Ortega began by disclaiming any interest in the prologue, attributing it merely to an editor's designs. He averred himself too concerned with the future, with work in progress, to relish past accomplishments: "The time for memoirs, for twisting one's head backwards, will come."[69] Looking behind in 1932, he feared he would see only his tracks in the sand, for Spain—unlike other countries, he felt—forced men to beat along their solitary tracks. Elsewhere one might enjoy the "vital luxury" of attempting "to reconstruct the life of other men."[70] But "[c]an a Spaniard hope that some compatriot will feel interest in the secret that was his life?" French, English, or German men could find in biographical curiosity a way to "nourish" themselves by living vicariously a while. Ortega had tried, he argued, to instill this sense in his countrymen, but they were "shipwrecked" in their monadic selves. Hence there was little to be hoped from this presentation of his works:

There is no great probability that a body of work like mine, which though of limited value, is very complex, very full of secrets, allusions, and elisions, very interwoven with an entire vital trajectory, will find the generous spirit that aspires in truth to understand it. More abstract works, disconnected by their plan and style from the life in which they arose, can be more readily assimilated, for they require less interpretation. But each of the pages gathered here sums up my entire existence in the hour in which it was written, and, juxtaposed, they represent the melody of my personal destiny.[71]

The tone of lament (perhaps even a bit of self-pity) evident in this statement doubtless reflects his growing realization that he was not, after all, destined to play a major political role in the new government, as well as his much more long-standing sense of the effect of his circumstances upon his philosophical vocation: "Perhaps this congenital fervor [for intellectual clarity and deep analysis] rapidly made me see that one of the characteristic features of my Spanish circumstances was the deficiency of the very thing that I, by intimate necessity, had to be."[72]

Out of that opposition between vocation and circumstance, of course, had grown his mission of intellectual service to Spain, but the same conditions had diminished his hope for the impact of his work. Having early seen the inadequacy of university chairs and books as means to cure Spain, Ortega had long before turned to the intellectual marketplace of the daily newspaper. But now, in 1932, he continued, Spain had come up to "the level of history." Probably as a vote of confidence for the Republic and—despite his disclaimer —for the impact of his own philosophical work, Ortega now claimed to hold the "radical conviction that the Spanish spirit is saved." Now if the nation fell back into the doldrums, the fault would not be her own but that of Europe, from which blew "a fierce wind of indifference."[73] Thus it was time for him to address his readers beyond the national frontiers, where the loss of cultural vitality was presumably more threatening than at home. Books were the way to do so and would most likely engage his future efforts. He would turn from domestic journalism to his more systematic task: "To sea once again, little ship!"

In 1934 Ortega returned for two weeks to Germany for the first time since his student years. Together with his son Miguel, he visited Marburg and several other cities, paying a brief call on Edmund Husserl. Shortly after returning from a country radically changed from the one he had known before the First World War, and repelled by "the events in Munich in 1934," he refused his German publisher (Deutsche Verlags-Anstalt) the right to publish a lengthy "Preface for Germans" he had written to introduce some of his works translated by Helene Weyl.[74] This piece, generally unknown by readers of Spanish until after Ortega's death and only recently available in English, is of considerable value in lieu of the autobiography Ortega only hinted at writing and the biography of him which still needs to be written.[75]

While it is a revealing personal statement, however, it is even more a kind of *apologia pro philosophia sua*. Philip Silver has seen it as a crucial document for understanding Ortega's claim that he had gone well beyond Husserl's concern with "pure consciousness" and the transcendental ego, and beyond Heidegger's concept of man as a question to Being, by establishing his own philosophy of human life and its structure.[76] Arguing that he had done so as early as 1914 in the *Meditations*, Ortega drew from that text the final paragraphs of the "Preface" of 1934 by way of justifying his choice of a different career pattern from that of the scholarly German *Gelehrter*, whose orderly surroundings and settled life encouraged his "launching his ship on a sea of divine, eternal concerns, and spending the next twenty years thinking only of the infinite."[77] By contrast, Ortega asserted, he had been compelled to think first of Spain in order to be able to think of other things later: "[T]he Spaniard who tries to escape national concerns wll find himself their daily prisoner ten times over, and eventually will realize that for anyone born between the Bidasoa River and Gibraltar, Spain is the first, the whole, the peremptory problem."[78] This insistent loyalty to his Spanish origins paralleled Ortega's discovery, based upon earlier work by Dilthey, Wilhelm Wundt, Brentano, and Scheler, that the groundedness of embodied human life in its social and historical circumstances provided a pretheoretical, given sense of the world immediately present to man on the level of "facility" and "obstacle." That is, the apologia for attending first to Spain and its claims on his pedagogical talents was the autobiographical dimension of his philosophical realization of the limits of Husserlian phenomenology: if, ontologically, my life (which is not simply "me") consists in the dynamic interaction of "I" and "circumstance," then, existentially, I must find the authentic version of this life by attending to that facet of it which the universe proffers me in the form of my native land.

Ortega's commitment to the problem of Spain had already been clearly set forth in 1914, if not already in his Bilbao lecture on social pedagogy in 1910. Similarly, his differences with Husserl, his search for a fundamental reality that would be in itself already systematic as given (thus preceding all rational constructs, all maneuvers of consciousness), appeared several times in his writing between 1912 and 1914.[79] A careful reading of his earliest philosophical essays in light of the "Preface" of 1934 offers a plausible basis for qualified acceptance of Ortega's retrospective claim, around 1947, that he "abandoned phenomenology at the very moment of tasting it."[80] In other words, though he continued to incorporate much of Husserl's epochal work in *Ideen* into his own later work—absorbing and adapting the crucial concepts of intentionality, of the natural attitude toward the world about one, and of the need to overcome "subjective idealism"— Ortega had found Husserl's concern with pure consciousness and his unquestioned and phenomenologically underived assertion of a "natural attitude" to be epiphenomenal derivatives of "reality itself," understood as "the coexistence of the I and the thing."[81] Ortega would later argue that his devotion to more pressing patriotic and pedagogical tasks had presumably delayed the full development of this early critique of phenomenology, but he would also offer, in his postwar book on Leibniz, a futher explanation:

> The reason for my silence was purely and simply ... timidity. Because ... the doctrine [that he was developing in his own philosophy] includes the greatest enormity which, between 1900 and 1925, could be uttered in philosophy, namely, that *there is no consciousness* as a *primary* form of relationship between the so-called "objects"; what we have is man in relation to things and things to man, that is, human existence.[82]

The issue of timidity, sympathetically construed by Julián Marías as a hidden facet of his master's personality, is dubious, and is probably a partial rationalization by Ortega of the more likely truth that his putative "rejection" of Husserl was not as sudden or dramatic as he later preferred to assert.

In another sense, Ortega's claim to have overcome Husserl's faults might be understood as a peculiarly Spanish response to the idealist tradition as it had come down to Husserl through Kant from Descartes. As such, Ortega's idea could be seen as a more sophisticated version of what Unamuno had said in *The Tragic Sense of Life* (1912) about "el hombre de carne y hueso" ("the man of flesh and bone"), whose anguished sense of existence precedes and underlies all conceptualization. Although Ortega's own sensibility, as Pedro Cerezo Galán argues, was distinctly "jovial" and "festive" in contrast to Unamuno's "tragic" and "pathetic" one, both men had something of what Américo Castro called the characteristically Spanish sense of the undifferentiated "whole man," what Unamuno himself elsewhere termed "nada menos que todo un hombre" (nothing less than a complete man). This existential awareness would, presumably, have rendered them both suspicious of the excesses of European philosophical idealism. Questionable as Castro's own idea may be in any rigorous comparative study of cultures, it may still point up an inclination of the Spanish sensibility, formed at a cultural remove from the main currents of modern European thought. The Spanish Krausists too, after all, had converted their contact with a phase of Kantian philosophy into a program of moral reform that centered on the need to make "new *men*."

If Ortega brought from the Spanish "periphery" of Europe some brand of Spanish humanism which heightened his feeling for the primacy of individualized human life, he nonetheless found his own contemporary culture enfeebled by an unreflective, raw "subjectivism"—a kind of parody of true individualism. And he just as certainly, and more explicitly than Unamuno, came to his radical critique of idealism through immersion in the modern German philosophical canon. If being a Spaniard had anything to do with his doubts about "consciousness," it was indeed as "the cocky little fellow [*chulito*] from Madrid who had been through Kant," as he once called himself in conversation with Julián Marías. By sheer temperament, perhaps, he was prone to criticize Husserl's dubious concept of the phenomenological reduction and his excessive claims to make philosophy a pure "science" of essences; but these ideas also seemed questionable enough to him on strictly philosophical grounds, for at bottom they constituted a kind of continuation of the Cartesian split between the *res cogitans* and the *res extensa*. In that sense, they troubled Ortega as an inaccurate and impoverished idea of the way we actually live in and with the world. As a response to the press of circumstances, the "bracketing" of our everyday sense of things in quest of the "essence" of what is known seemed a gross distortion of the enveloping, always particularized quality of human existence.

This "existentialization" of phenomenology, present *in nuce* in the thought of the young Ortega, became prominent in Heidegger's *Sein und Zeit* and in later work by Gabriel Marcel, Merleau-Ponty, and other twentieth-century philosophers, including of course the mature Ortega. But the essential critique Ortega made of Husserl's early work was already clearly present in another, slightly earlier philosopher who also came to European thought from "outside," as it were, though he had steeped himself in it as deeply as any man of his time. In an essay of 1904, "Does Consciousness Exist?" William James raised the very point that seemed so "enormous" to Ortega when he first intuited it a few years later. But James—already in the full maturity of his career—did not postpone his question as too daring, though he clearly realized its radical purport. In fact, it had already been implicit in his *Principles of Psychology* in 1890. Oddly, Ortega nowhere acknowledges James as a crucial precursor of his own philosophy. Unamuno knew James's work well, though his focus was more on the American thinker's views on religion and immortality—especially in "The Will to Believe" (1897)—than on the "radical empiricism" so clearly relevant to Ortega's case. *The Principles of Psychology*, quickly translated into several European languages, was well known in Germany by the time Ortega became a student there, but if he knew the work, he does not mention it.

The German trip in 1934 produced more than the intellectual autobiography of the "Preface." During February and March 1935, Ortega published a series of five reflections on contemporary Germany in *La Nación* of Buenos Aires.[83] Entitled "Un rasgo de la vida alemana" (A Sketch of German Life), these impressions of a culture he had not known at first hand for twenty-three turbulent years of its history turned out to be as much a meditation on social roles in differing cultures as a probe into contemporary German life. Indeed, Ortega announced to begin with that he had only carried away surface impressions from the hasty visit. But, always ready to give his theme another turn, he reflected that the present surface of German life carried underneath a long history—in this case of Germany's mid-nineteenth-century decision to achieve an outstanding organization of its collective life. Thus, for example, the German functionary or citizen had been taught to subordinate his personality wholly to the role he was called to play. By contrast, the Spaniard, given to a kind of anarchic personalism, subverted the role by subordinating it to his whim. For Ortega, the French were really the only major people of Europe wise enough to strike a balance between person and role. He acknowledged that the tyranny of social and cultural convention is necessary to preserve the past in collective forms and save the mere individual from hopeless subjectivity and oblivion. But the most pressing question for him was whether the inevitable existence in any society of some degree of collectivized organizaton had not become in the modern period the quintessential feature of social life in the West. In that case, Germany as observed in the 1930s would offer an unmistakably prophetic sign of the times, only this time on the level of mass society and mass psychology rather than on that of philosophy, science, and scholarship. But after cautiously reserving his judgment regarding German politics of the early 1930s, Ortega concluded by placing Germany once again in the exemplary role of harbinger of "our common destiny."[84]

In April 1935 Ortega and his wife celebrated their twenty-fifth anniversary; the event was publicly signalized later in the year, when Spain's most distinguished thinker was honored at an official ceremony marking his twenty-fifth year in the chair of metaphysics at the University of Madrid. On the same occasion, enlivened by tributes to his magisterial mission by colleagues and former students, he was awarded the Medalla de Oro de Madrid by the city fathers. But just as Ortega was being praised for the fulfillment of his vocation as teacher and philosopher, a rebuke came from another quarter. In "Words of Homage and Reproach Addressed to Don José Ortega y Gasset" in the Falangist journal *Haz* of December 5, the son of Primo de Rivera and cofounder in 1933 of the Spanish Falange, José Antonio Primo de Rivera, called to account the man he had claimed as his ideological and philosophical mentor. This reference marked Ortega as the charismatic intellectual hero of what has been called "the Generation of 1936."

In José Antonio's words, "A generation which has almost managed to arouse Spanish concern, with Ortega y Gasset as its beacon, has imposed on itself... the mission of making Spain vertebrate once more."[85] Following Ortega's own frequent reflections on the relationship between intellectuals and politics, José Antonio asserted that "politics are not the intellectual's business," for politicians work in the temporal world of fairly immediate consequences, but intellectuals pursue "timeless" truths. This lesson of vocational seriousness had indeed been learned from Ortega's work, and it was now turned against him for having entered politics only to abandon it later in disenchantment. "But," continued José Antonio,

> the leaders of men are not entitled to disenchantment. They cannot capitulate and surrender the battered hopes of all those who followed them. Don José was hard on himself and sentenced himself to a long term of silence; but the generation he left out in the cold did not need his silence but his voice. His prophetic and commanding voice.[86]

Recalling Ortega's famous "No es esto" of September 1931, José Antonio looked forward to that day when the revered leader whose silence he rebuked could respond to "the triumphant march past of this generation" with the full assent of " 'Yes, this is really it.' "[87]

José Antonio, who had come into politics partly to avenge the ridicule and opposition his father had met from the intellectuals and the propertied classes alike, had undoubtedly read his Ortega. It is easy enough to find the trace of the older man's ideas and style in his speeches and manifestos: "The *Patria* is a total unity, in which all individuals and classes are integrated.... The *Patria* is a transcendent synthesis, an indivisible synthesis, with its own goals to fulfill."[88] And "*a nation is unity in universal terms*, the level a people attains when it fulfills its universal destiny in history."[89] Echoing Ortega's idea that national destiny required a collectively held "design" or "project" for the future, José Antonio spoke of "the fatherland" as "the culmination, in this world, of a great collective undertaking."[90] In the fundamental ideological program for the Falange, set forth in the first issue of *F.E.* (Falange Española) in December of 1933, he had inveighed against political parties, which "disregard the oneness of Spain" and were an outmoded remnant of the old parliamentary system that must be scrapped in order for Spaniards to "see all political problems with the utmost clarity." Striking a note akin to Ortega's in his concern for a centrally planned national economy, José Antonio added that "class struggle disregards the unity of the fatherland because it destroys the integrity of the idea of *national production*." The Falangist state would "consider the goals of each component group its own," seek a more even distribution of wealth, and establish work as "the best foundation of civic dignity." Its philosophy would be founded on the principles of "authority, hierarchy and order," and must incorporate each individual into his proper place in the functioning of the nation-state.[91]

In its stress on a militantly Catholic philosophy of man, and on the family, the municipality, and the guild (or trade union) as fundamental components of the new state, the Falange program of course differed significantly from Ortega's political outlook, but the rhetoric of José Antonio and some of his ideas were clearly indebted to Ortega and, less directly, to the Generation of 1898.[92] Ortega himself seems to have paid little heed to the admiration he received, along with Unamuno, Ganivet, and Baroja, from youthful Falangist ideologues. Indeed, the connection between the two Josés seems one of a unilateral, indirect influence upon the younger by the older. José Antonio clearly adapted some of Ortega's political principles to the purposes of national syndicalism. What was emphatically missing in the thought of José Antonio and of his comrades Ramiro Ledesma Ramos and Onésimo Redondo (leaders of the Juntas de Ofensiva Nacional-Sindicalista, which fused with the Falange in February 1934 to form the so-called F.E. de las J.O.N.S.) was the depth of historical perspective, the learning, and the stylistic refinement that characterized even the vaguest of Ortega's political pronouncements. One cannot deny, however, that Ortega's lack of a concrete political program—excepting his proposals for regional autonomy and some of his reflections on bilingualism in Catalonia—brought him a few strange bedfellows.

If some young Spaniards coming to maturity in the last years of the Republic found inspiration for a poetic politics of national destiny in Ortega's writings, others of a distinctly different stamp saw him as the outstanding literary and philosophical mentor from the preceding generation. Ricardo Gullón, one of the young writers whose generational "placement" was affected by the outbreak of civil war in 1936, has summarized the crucial issues in the development of the liberal, pro-Republican youth who would find in Ortega very different fruits from those plucked by José Antonio:

> The struggle against the dictatorship of Primo de Rivera, and later political agitation against the government of General Berenguer; the activities of the FUE; the exile of Unamuno; the resignation of their chairs by Professors Jiménez Asua, de los Ríos, Sánchez Román and Valdecasas; the founding of the Agrupación al Servicio de la República by Marañón,

Ortega and Pérez de Ayala; the proclamation of the Republic in 1931
—all these were the background for the generational activity.[93]

In the School of Philosophy and Letters, Ortega exercised full sway
among a group of colleagues and students who clearly acknowledged
his leadership. As Gullón notes:

> Overall, Ortega's influence seems to me greater than that of Unamuno.
> The Generation of '36 is imbued with Orteguianism: María Zambrano,
> Antonio Rodríguez Huéscar, Julián Marías, Pedro Laín Entralgo and,
> not far removed, José Luis Aranguren and José Ferrater Mora confess
> themselves his disciples. Ortega was the master most heeded. We read
> him in the paper each morning; we read him in eagerly awaited books.
> Perhaps never has any other writer of our language—in or out of Spain
> —been able to count upon so much thoughtful admiration or to have had
> such influence on the young as did Ortega until 1936.[94]

The period after 1933 during which Ortega maintained political
silence cannot, we assume, have been so very bleak for him in other
spheres of his life, where the vitality of his philosophical thought and
the power of his teaching were amply recognized. The cultural life
around him during the decline of the Republic's political fortunes was
varied and vigorous, if not paralleled by political stability.

In December 1935, President Alcalá Zamora, conceiving himself
the moderating force intent upon establishing a center coalition,
refused, after the collapse of the combined CEDA-Radical cabinet, to
reappoint CEDA leaders and provide their head, Gil Robles, with the
power to shape the government to his specifications. The interim
ministry under Portela Valladares led to elections in February 1936,
when a Republican and Socialist coalition gained power as a "Popular Front" government. This alliance, which combined the small
middle-class leftist parties and the moderate Socialists with the rapidly growing Communist party and the more radical "bolshevized"
Socialists, won by only a very small margin; but the constitution,
designed to encourage coalitions and avoid fragmentation, gave the
majority of seats in each district to any list that got over half the
vote.[95] Thus, though the voters had in many cases not significantly
changed their opinion since the end of 1933, the government itself
swung radically to the left and greatly increased the likelihood of
violent division.

Alcalá Zamora, who had failed to gather together any center group, now turned to Azaña as the only prime minister who might govern with the Popular Front coalition. He was called to an almost impossible task: the radical left was gaining greater power daily; street violence between opposing factions was rife; the last vestiges of decorum and restraint were everywhere challenged. In early April 1936, the left-dominated Cortes deposed President Alcalá Zamora, replacing him temporarily with its own president, Martínez Barrio. On May 8, Azaña, who during his new term as prime minister had, in Stanley Payne's words, "found himself the virtual prisoner of the extreme left," was duly elected president of the Republic.[96] Though Azaña tried manfully to rule over a rampaging left, which was moving toward revolutionary aims and hailing Francisco Largo Caballero as the "Spanish Lenin," and an essentially beaten right, bitterly resentful of its subjugation by the Popular Front, he could do little to prevent the hastening collapse of political and social order. He had been committed to the electoral program of the Popular Front, which was carried out during the first few months of 1936. But the pendulum could not be swung back without disastrous damage to the clockwork itself, and on June 17, what had for some time appeared an inevitable military uprising began when General Francisco Franco declared a state of war in Tenerife and then flew to the African mainland to assume command over the Army of Morocco.

As the leaders of the Nationalist revolt moved rapidly to take control in the south and the north of the Peninsula during the next few days, Ortega, fearing an attack on his life in the radically destabilized atmosphere of the capital, moved from his residence in the "Colony" of El Viso (Serrano 161) to the Residencia de Estudiantes, which offered asylum at that point to a number of Spanish intellectuals and children and to a handful of British and American summer students. Until this last group was evacuated, the embassies of those two nations flew their flags over the buildings for a short period as a protective sign against feared incursions from ad hoc groups of the radical left. Ortega and his family moved in on July 20 and 21, but were unable to leave until the end of August. His situation during those weeks was greatly complicated by an intensification of the illness (blockage of the bile duct by gallstones) from which he had begun to suffer in the summer of 1935. For a period of days, he was confined to bed with septicemia and fever. At this moment, youths from an organization of antifascist writers, some of them armed, arrived to demand that he and other illustrious intellectual leaders sign a manifesto in support of the Republic. The text was carried up to his room by his daughter, Soledad, who then relayed to the group below her father's refusal on the grounds of disagreement with a number of points in the statement. This especially precarious situation was then resolved by a number of younger pro-Republican professors who were on the grounds, and later that day Ortega signed, together with Marañón and Menéndez Pidal, a modified statement more in accord with his own ideas. He was quite aware, of course, that his name could readily be manipulated for partisan ends, and had long before made clear his distrust of the political extremism that forecast the doom of the Republic. Apart from this brief final statement made under duress, he continued to observe the silence on political questions he had imposed on himself in 1933.

On August 30, through the intervention of the French embassy, Ortega and his family managed to take a train to Alicante; from there, on the following day, they embarked on a French freighter bound for Marseilles. When the ship that carried him into exile left the harbor, he was not to see Spain again for another nine years. During this time—and, indeed, until the end of his days—he provided no more than the most oblique hint concerning his reflections on the ruin of the nation that had been for so long the ultimate source of his political and philosophical concerns.[97]

7
THE SECOND VOYAGE: 1936–1947

This chapter will trace Ortega's wanderings in exile after his flight to Paris in 1936. These difficult and lonely years added a chapter to his life of the kind that may be found in the biographies of a very great number of Europeans, intellectuals and nonintellectuals alike, during the first half of this century. Having sought refuge first in France, Ortega later left that country for the familiar ground of Argentina, whence nostalgia and the cessation of war in Spain eventually drew him back to the Peninsula, first to the suburbs of Lisbon and then, tentatively, to Madrid in 1945. Preferring to maintain his residence in Portugal, he chose not to reside permanently in his own country ever again; for though he was free to come and go in Spain without obvious harassment, he found the political and cultural atmosphere there unpropitious for the public pedagogy he hoped once again to pursue. By comparison, Portugal offered a comfortable *pied-à-terre* where he could turn to the more intimate business of philosophical writing.

The Spanish Civil War marked the great watershed of Ortega's career; indeed it redefined the lives of millions of his compatriots, brutally breaking many of them. The story of his own years in exile is, of course, only a minute part of the terrible chronicle of those Spaniards who, having escaped death on the battlefield or later imprisonment and execution at the hands of the victors, became melancholy wanderers—refugees, émigrés, expatriates—in many parts of Europe and of North and South America. Yet the war alone was not responsible for Ortega's turn away from politics toward a more strictly philosophical vocation, as we have seen. Already in 1932 he had characterized the shift in his work with the Platonic metaphor of "the second voyage," an image of intellectual renewal. Indeed, from the time of "¿Qué es filosofía?" through "Historia como sistema" (1929–1935), Ortega reached his full intellectual maturity, even as he attempted, with acute disappointment, to fulfill what he considered his political destiny. Clearly, the political and social turmoil that characterized the fall of Primo de Rivera and the transition to the Republic also stimulated the development of Ortega's already deep sense of man's existential condition, honing his understanding of the venture of philosophy as a response both to the challenges of daily life and to moments of crisis. For him, philosophical reflection had never been simply a dialogue with the dominant great texts of the tradition, but was rather a way to construct a *modus vivendi* in the world.

Since the events in Spain that began in 1929 had already given to his philosophical work an unprecedented tone of urgency and authenticity, the "second voyage" he announced in his prologue to his *Obras* in 1932 was actually well under way at that time, and consisted of producing work that would confirm his belief that Spain had indeed reached "the level of the times." And in fact, the books that Ortega, in the prologue, predicted he would write were to come only haltingly (often in the form of unrevised lecture texts or collected shorter pieces), and even his major postwar work on Leibniz and "deductive theory" would appear only posthumously, in 1958. In truth, when the civil war began, most of Ortega's liveliest and most penetrating work already lay behind him. In his writings of the 1920s and 1930s, he had developed his most characteristic and seminal ideas, which he only modified and extended in the postwar period. Although he continued to write and lecture extensively between 1936 and his death in 1955, the later work often failed to come up to his announced expectations. Marías argues that his master was buzzing with new ideas and projects by the time he settled in Estoril, near Lisbon, early in 1942, but a cool consideration of the later career persuades one that, for all the diversity of his postwar concerns, Ortega never really recaptured the élan and the brilliance of his earlier work. The dreamed-of second voyage, that is, was never as clear as he had hoped in that brave announcement of 1932.

After disembarking at Marseille early in August 1936, the Ortegas proceeded to Grenoble and thence to Paris, where in November they took up residence at 43 rue Gros in the sixteenth *arrondissement*. Promptly their apartment became a temporary shelter for numerous family members in flight from the havoc at home. Ortega continued to suffer from gallstones and resulting complications, but the pressure of financial necessities kept him at his desk. His main source of income in this period was journalism, particularly for *La Nación* of Buenos Aires. In the spring of 1938, he was invited by the Dutch historian Huizinga to give a series of lectures at the University of Leiden. After speaking as well in Rotterdam, Delft, Amsterdam, and the Hague, he summered at Saint-Jean-de-Luz, France, near the Spanish border, as close as he could come to his beloved Zumaya, where the family had so often spent summers before the war. Returning to Paris in September, he fell gravely ill, and had gall bladder surgery in October. By February 1939, he had recovered sufficiently to spend a three-month period of convalescence at Portimão in the south of Portugal. The civil war had ended by the time he returned to Vichy and then Paris in the late spring, but Spain, filled with hunger, suspicion, and ruin, was hardly the place for a recuperating patient with unclear political allegiances. In any case, his interests in Madrid were represented by his older son, Miguel, an officer in the Nationalist army, who bought up a majority of the stock in the *Revista de Occidente* and saved the offices from being sequestered by the Franco government. Faced with the uncertainties posed by Nazi aggresssion (France would delcare war on Germany on September 3, 1939), Ortega accepted an invitation from the Amigos del Arte—the group that had invited him to Argentina in 1928—to visit Buenos Aires again, and embarked with his wife and daughter from Cherbourg in August 1939.

Despite the warm friendship of certain Argentine intellectuals like Victoria Ocampo and Eduardo Mallea, and an active lecture schedule in the first months, Ortega did not find the atmosphere as welcome as during his previous trip, particularly at the University of Buenos Aires. During the visit of 1928 he had been introduced there by the philosopher Coriolano Alberini, who had made slighting remarks about Argentine higher education, insulted the Argentine writer José Ingenieros, and generally alienated many in the audience. By association, Ortega had been implicated in their minds with a mordantly derogatory view of their native culture. Later, when his essays "La pampa ... promesas" and "El hombre a la defensiva" had appeared in volume 7 of *El espectador* in 1930, they had felt their idea confirmed that he was a patronizing visitor from the mother country who was unfit to judge them. For his part, Ortega experienced frequent depressions in the Argentine capital, not all of which, to be sure, may be laid to the hostile reception. His health was still not sound, and perhaps more important, he was suffering from the general trauma of exile.

Nor could he have found the political climate in Argentina very reassuring. Although by the late 1930s Buenos Aires was clearly the most sophisticated and Europeanized of all the Latin American capitals, political leadership was entering a period of acute crisis. Former President Irigoyen's Radical Party had been ousted by a military coup in 1930, leaving a conservative oligarchy in effective power. After the administration of Augustín Justo (1932–1938), the Radicals returned to power under President Roberto Ortiz, a wealthy lawyer who sympathized with the Allied cause in Europe. But Ortiz was ailing, and the command soon passed to his also infirm vice president, Ramón Castillo, under whom the government took an ultranationalist, isolationist, and pro-Axis turn. As Castillo reversed Ortiz's efforts to restore the integrity of democratic institutions, Argentina became a center for Axis sympathizers. Then Castillo was in turn overthrown by a military coup in June 1943. Two provisional presidencies under Generals Pedro Ramírez and Edelmiro Farrell gave way eventually to a palace revolt in 1944 by a group of military officers who, shortly after, delivered the power to Colonel Juan Perón. Although Ortega had by then left the country (the family sailed for Portugal early in 1942), the instability of Argentine politics must have been painfully obvious to him while he was there; and that instability, coupled with growing pro-Axis and anti-Semitic sentiment and with the prominence of the military in public life, could only have been ominously reminiscent for him of the recent history of Spain.

After just over a year of residence in Buenos Aires, his own summary of the immediately preceding years clearly reflects his unsettled condition in exile. With a dateline of "Buenos Aires, October, 1940," he wrote:

> For five [sic] years now I have been wandering about the world in labor with the two thick books that condense my work during the last ten years. One is titled *Aurora de la razón histórica* [The Dawn of Historical Reason] and is a huge philosophical book; the other is titled *El hombre y la gente* [Man and People] and is a huge sociological book. But mis-

fortune seems to take pleasure in not letting me polish them up by giving them that last touch that is nothing and everything.... I have lived these five errant years in one country or another and in another continent. I have suffered misery, I have suffered long illnesses in which one deals with death face to face, and I must say that if I have not succumbed in those rough seas it has been because the dream of finishing those books has sustained me when nothing else did. When, as with the annual migration of birds, a little peace and quiet returned to my life again, I found myself far from the libraries without which that finishing touch is absolutely impossible. Thus I find that now less than ever do I know when I will be able to finish them. Never have I felt with such force the old truth of *Habent sua fata libelli*. In view of all this and motivated by the convenience of providing a complement to my present course in the School of Philosophy and Letters of Buenos Aires, I have resolved to publish the first chapter of the above-mentioned books.[1]

During the years in Argentina Ortega's work flowed on two levels, both of which reveal his response to exile. There was, first, the deep philosophical current represented by his increasing preoccupation with a systematic philosophy of human life, and second, a series of lighter sketches of Argentine life, the Creole woman, and Latin American culture. A scant two months after his arrival in Buenos Aires, he published "Ensimismamiento y alteración," the first part of a course entitled "Seis lecciones sobre el hombre y la gente," presented before the Amigos del Arte in the fall of 1939. This course would later become the first chapter of the posthumously published *El hombre y la gente* (*Man and People*). Like many of his postwar writings, this book was to mature very slowly, with multiple announcements of its imminent appearance. Beginning as the six lectures in Buenos Aires, the series grew to twelve by the time it was delivered in Madrid over a decade later, and was finally published by the Revista de Occidente Press in 1957. Ortega's major themes had always required numerous turns before finding their fullest form. Despite the relative solitude he experienced after leaving Spain, this feature of this work did not substantially change as he pursued his hope for a major systematic statement of his ideas in lectures, courses, fragmentary essays, and the expanding pages of his notebooks.

"Ensimismamiento y alteración" (Being in One's Self and Being

Beside One's Self), more than an attempt to clarify Ortega's ideas
about society and "the social," was also an oblique response to the
destruction of the Spanish Republic, the state of international violence, and the radical falsification of culture which seemed to have
led Europe into the barbarism of pure *alteración*—alienation, loss of
self-possession, and depersonalization. In reaction against a thought-
less worship of reason and culture for its own sake, what Ortega
called the "cant" or "bigotry" (*beatería*) of culture, Western man
had presumably gone over to the other pole, descending into the
animality of *alteración*. In that condition, he was constantly "altered"
(or "othered") by circumstances and stimuli that placed him at
their mercy. Ortega suggested that Europe had been corrupted by
an "intellectualism" rooted historically in the classical Greek stress
on theoretical as opposed to "vital" reason. The error of that noble
enterprise, of which Socrates and Aristotle were the fathers, had
been to see man as quintessentially the reasoning, thinking being.
But, Ortega reminded his audience, man in fact had no "nature,"
for he was always unfinished, an ongoing experiment. Moreover,
the human condition echoed the plight of the individual and the
present crisis of Western civilization:

> [A]t times what happens to man is nothing less than *ceasing to be man*.
> And this is true not only abstractly and generically, but it holds of our
> own individuality. Each one of us is always in danger of not being the
> unique and untransferable *self* which he is. The majority of men per-
> petually betray this *self* which is waiting to be; and to tell the whole
> truth... our personal individuality is a personage which is never com-
> pletely realized, a stimulating Utopia, a secret legend, which each of us
> guards in the depths of his heart.... No human acquisition is stable.
> Even what appears to us most completely won and consolidated can dis-
> appear in a few generations. This thing we call "civilization"... all
> these securities are insecure securities which in the twinkling of an eye,
> at the least carelessness, escape from man's hands and vanish like phan-
> toms.... The fate of culture, the destiny of man, depends upon our
> maintaining this dramatic consciousness ever alive in our inmost being,
> and upon our being well aware, as of a murmuring counterpoint in our
> entrails, that we can only be sure of insecurity.[2]

Ortega was thinking both of Spain, where war had ended at the
end of March, and of Europe, where it broke out anew at the be-

ginning of September. It was odd that in such circumstances he should have to insist on radical insecurity as the only thing certain in our lives, but such had been the sway of intellectualism that he felt people were still wont to see culture as progressive and as a permanent collective acquisition of the human spirit. The consequent separation of culture from life rendered intellect ineffective and gave violent force to unharnessed action. Then the will to power reigned without check. In such times, the task of the thinker was to call men back to *ensimismamiento*, encouraging them to take their bearings in the quiet of the "inner space" that mankind had required aeons to develop and explore. Like the fools of the marketplace whom Nietzsche's "madman" called the murderers of God, killers of truth stalked the land again:

> The demagogues, impresarios of *alteración*, who have already caused the death of several civilizations, harass men so that they shall not reflect, see to it that they are kept herded together in crowds so that they cannot reconstruct their individuality in the one place where it can be reconstructed, which is solitude.[3]

As Carl Becker, borrowing from Aristophanes, had written of the climate of opinion at the beginning of the 1930s, "Whirl is king, having deposed Zeus."[4] "Whirl," of course, was another name for *alteración*, for twentieth-century man's flight from the Enlightenment toward a degenerate worship of vitality and power. This rout could hardly be turned directly around by thoughtfulness alone, but it was the thinker's exemplary task to resist the stupidities he saw around him in the interest of reconnecting thought and action, culture and life. Intelligence as such would never rule the practical, political world, but it was indispensable for reestablishing a balance between the two necessary phases of *ensimismamiento* and *alteración*: "There is ... no genuine action if there is no thought, and there is no authentic thought if it is not duly referred to action and made virile by its relation to action."[5] Of the two, Ortega recognized, man's primary destiny was action. Thought, never given to man as a sure possession, must be conquered again and again in the name of projected future action. "We do not live to think, but the other way round: we think in order that we may succeed in surviving."[6] The particular contribution to human survival which Ortega essayed in the Buenos Aires lectures was a clarification of a cluster of concepts—"state, nation, law, freedom, authority, collectivity, justice and the rest—that today put mortals into frenzy." [7]

Ortega's philosophical horizon during the Argentine years was defined not only by "Ensimismamiento y alteración" but also by the lengthy essay "Ideas y creencias" (Ideas and Beliefs)—a work that he had actually drafted in Spain in December 1934 but that was first published, together with various short pieces, in Buenos Aires only late in 1940, in a volume that took the name of the long piece. The former essay ("Ensimismamiento") would eventually become the initial lecture of the lecture series "El hombre y la gente" (presented in Madrid in the winter of 1949–1950); the title essay of *Ideas y creencias* was conceived as the first chapter of Ortega's projected and often-announced *Aurora de la razón histórica* (The Dawn of Historical Reason). In the prologue to *Ideas*, he suggested that *Aurora* was all but finished; but the status of that putative manuscript has in fact remained unclear. Large parts of it apparently found their way into the posthumously published *La idea de principio en Leibniz y la evolución de la teoría deductiva* (Buenos Aires, 1958; translated in 1971 as *The Idea of Principle in Leibniz and the Evolution of Deductive Theory*), a work drafted largely in the spring and summer of 1947. But already in his draft of the essay "Ideas y creencias," written during the darkening days of the short-lived Second Republic, Ortega had seen that the history of shifting ideas was less the philosopher's true business than was the more profound ground of belief in reason itself:

> Here is a splendid example of what should interest history when it truly resolves to be a science, the science of man. Instead of concerning itself solely with the "history"—that is, with cataloguing the succession—of ideas about reason from Descartes to the present, it will strive to define precisely the nature of the faith in reason and its consequences for life that effectively operated in each age. It is obvious that the plot of the play that is life differs if one dwells in the belief that a benevolent and omnipotent God exists rather than in the contrary belief. And also the life of him who believes, as one believed at the end of the seventeenth century in France, in the absolute capacity of reason to discover reality, differs...from that of him who believes, like the positivists of 1860, that reason is essentially relative knowledge.
>
> A study such as this would permit us to see clearly the modification

undergone by our faith in reason during the last twenty years [1914–1934], and it would cast surprising light upon all the strange things happening in our time.[8]

To write the true history of our changing trust in reason and of changing definitions of its essence would perhaps be the philosopher's most valuable contribution to a world in turmoil. This project demonstrated once again Ortega's commitment to the study of history as an existential necessity, for man could not live intelligently and responsibly in the present without knowing the preceding "projects of life" that underlay his current cultural and historical situation.

In essence, mere *ideas* (perhaps an echo of Husserl's famous title of 1913) were seen as transient, shifting notions one "holds" for a while and then replaces with others. They were the counterpart to the distraction man feels in *alteración*; while *creencias* (beliefs) were the unquestioned ground one counted on in order to live, that *point d'appui* comparable to *ensimismamiento*, the radical solitude of dwelling in oneself. Thus one may link Ortega's critique of unreflective intellect to his view of modern man as emptied of his own history. The two bipolar rubrics around which he was organizing the two large books in gestation during his residence in Buenos Aires were definitely related, though not in a simple or patent fashion. Both a repertory of ideas and a set of fundamental beliefs (what social historians today call *mentalités*) are lived by each generation and each individual as an inheritance from the past and as a horizon of present possibilities. But, Ortega believed, the identification of a person with his ideas (or with thoughts that merely "occur" to him) missed the deeper level where his beliefs lay solidly sedimented. (These too were subject to change, but at the much slower rate of what may be called a "paradigm shift.") The crises in twentieth-century history had left men disillusioned with the creation, manipulation, and criticism of ideas.

Though he did not say so directly, Ortega was again criticizing the entire neo-Kantian tradition for its naive faith in cultural constructs to the neglect of the deeper layers of conviction in which we actually "dwell." One of those convictions, central to neo-Kantian thought, was that reason was adequate for the conduct of life. But particularly since 1914, Ortega believed, men had fallen *into* and were rooted *in* doubt as to the place of reason in life. Since skepticism was an inherently philosophical cast of mind, a condition out of which new intellectual horizons could be descried, Ortega suggested that the horizons of the contemporary world were becoming less "intellectualistic": made aware of the difference between *ideas* and *creencias*, men would ideally put less faith in culture and theory, and spend more time thinking about the hidden assumptions they counted on without question.

Many of these same thoughts about the "career" of reason in history and its status in contemporary life surfaced again, just over a year after Ortega's arrival in the Argentine capital, in a series of five lectures on *la razón histórica* (historical reason) he presented at the School of Philosophy and Letters of the University of Buenos Aires in September and October 1940. (These, together with another course of five different but related lectures under the same title, given in Lisbon in 1944, were finally published posthumously as *Sobre la razón histórica* in volume 12 of the *Obras completas* in 1983. All ten lectures may possibly have belonged, in Ortega's mind, to the great work he never finished as such, *Aurora de la razón histórica*.) Dispirited by the relative obscurity of his life in exile, he nonetheless pursued this major theme of all his writing after 1933: *la razón histórica*, now incorporating and replacing the earlier term *la razón vital* (vital reason), expressed his growing understanding of the contingent condition of all thought and philosophizing. Echoing thoughts shortly to be published in Buenos Aires under the two titles of *Ideas y creencias* and "Apuntes sobre el pensamiento" (Notes on Thinking), in the five lectures he distinguished philosophy from science by arguing that the latter was deduced from posited first principles, while the former consisted of a progressive backward movement toward the roots of its principles, which could never be left entirely unquestioned. Science progressed cumulatively, but philosophy circled back critically on itself. In order to understand philosophical ideas, one had to discover the fundamental, generally unspoken beliefs from which they arose. This search implied that the philosopher must execute a kind of anabasis, going down and back to the most primary questions, a project Ortega carried out in depth in the later Leibniz manuscript.

Reviewing the inadequacies of the "substantialist thesis," which placed ultimate reality in the physical world, and of the Cartesian "answer," which found the only indubitable truth in the cognizing mind, Ortega asserted once more the now familiar primacy of human life as the ground of all philosophizing. Moreover, he argued, Cartesian doubt had not succeeded in abolishing the independent reality of the circumstantial world. Since "the fundamental event of our relation with things can only be correctly described as the bare coexistence of *myself* with *things*," then "consciousness, *cogitatio* or thought... is only an invention, a hypothesis, a theory, and nothing more."[9] The ground of Descartes's *cogito, ergo sum* was itself thrown into question by the further assertion that thought cannot be immediately present to itself, cannot, in other words, think itself in an unmediated fashion. In fact, every act of awareness reminds us of the doubtful world that remains "doubtfully there" all about us, for to cast it into radical doubt is not unquestionably to demonstrate its nonexistence: "[W]e could say that when I doubt the world's reality what remains absolutely real is me doubting and the world 'doubtifying' me."[10] Indeed, modern thought since Descartes had dwelt in doubt—in a sea of doubts—as its natural element. Reminding his Argentine audience of the old aphorism *Primum vivere; deinde philosophari*, Ortega summarized his critique of Descartes:

> [A]ny thesis that was ever proposed, or ever could be proposed, as the first thesis of philosophy, already *presupposes* life as the fundamental reality.... [T]he really fundamental thesis asserts both that life... is the primordial reality and that the principles of the theory of reason are not rational but simply the exigencies of our lives.[11]

The fact that these principles are inherently historical and hence subject to change means that reasoning too has its own "biography" over the centuries. We cannot repeat Descartes's form of making philosophical sense any more than he could repeat that of St. Thomas or Aristotle. Unable to rest on received truths—which are really no truths at all—we are bound always to search for an adequate version of reality for our ever-changing situation. The human "I" is turned constantly toward the future. But this also means that man is "indigent" in the sense that he cannot reach a permanent *entente* with his world, for he must meet its mutable conditions in his search to fulfill the figure he has sketched for his life: "Thus the contour of each *I* presses against its circumstances with the specific profile that it has: and the circumstances will respond differently, according to these contours, warpings, and patternings of the *I* that each of us is."[12] Man's being, unlike that of the stone, is the opposite of self-identical substance, hence not a full being at all. Human life, then, is "a labor of realization and not something that is already there, it is a task, something to be accomplished."[13] This condition gives life a constitutive dimension of unhappiness. As a quintessentially aspiring and hopeful being, man is bound to know frustration and disappointment. Yet, to balance the picture, life also offers the zest of adventure. As Ortega remarked, with a famous colleague in mind, "Life as anguish, Mr. Heidegger? Agreed! But, it is also this: an enterprise."[14]

He concluded the lecture series by reaffirming a central concept from such earlier works as *Man and Crisis* and *History as a System*: "Man has no nature; what he has is history; because history is the mode of being of the entity that is constitutionally, fundamentally, *mobility* and *change*. And this is why pure, Eleatic, naturalistic reason will never manage to understand man."[15] That task obviously remained for the unfolding of historical or "narrative" reason, a discipline still in its first stages of development. Ortega was to pursue this grand project throughout the late 1930s and the 1940s, the quest finding a not altogether satisfactory culmination in the book on Leibniz. In his "Apuntes sobre el pensamiento," published in the Argentine philosophical journal *Logos* in 1941, he noted:

> My aim is to follow into its ultimate consequences the observation that the specifically human reality—man's life—is of historical consistency. Such an undertaking requires that all concepts referring to the integral phenomenon of human life be "denatured" and subjected to a process of "historification." Whatever man is he is not once and for all; he has one day *come to be thus* and will one day *cease to be thus*. Permanence in the forms of human life is an optical illusion from which we suffer, thanks to a certain crudeness of concepts. Ideas that hold only when applied abstractly to those forms are used as if they were concrete and capable of genuinely representing reality....
>
> Whoever aspires to understand man—that eternal tramp, a thing essentially *on the road*—must throw overboard all immobile concepts and learn to think in ever-shifting terms.[16]

One sees a phenomenological thrust—perhaps an echo of Husserl's famous *epochē*—in Ortega's desire to "denature" life in order to discover its reality as a historical process. But if this procedure indeed invites comparison with Husserl's technique for suspending the "natural attitude," Ortega explicitly differentiated himself from the older man later in the same essay by noting that Husserl had failed to include in his theory of consciousness the "pre-theoretical and a-theoretical needs and conveniences" out of which the adoption of a philosophical position proceeds:

> Phenomenology, which lays claim to being the supreme expression of reason, has the formal character of an independent activity and not of a function of life; it is knowledge for the sake of knowledge. In the analysis and definition of reason given by Husserl in *Formal and Transcendental Logic*, the themes of humanity, life, and the functional character of reason are not and indeed could not be taken up again.... The phenomenological attitude is diametrically opposed to the attitude that I call living reason.[17]

In Ortega's view, Husserl, still influenced by the outwash of Kantian idealism, had given consciousness an unwarranted absolute status:

> Now, if *consciousness of* is the absolute reality and as such the starting point of philosophy, philosophy would start from a reality in which the subject—I—exists enclosed within itself, within its mental acts and states. But such existence in the form of *being enclosed in oneself* is the opposite of what we call *living*. Living means *reaching out* of oneself, devoted, ontologically, to what is *other*—be it called world or circumstances.
>
> To start from life as the primary and absolute fact is to recognize that *consciousness of* is solely an idea, a more or less justified and plausible one, but no more than an idea which we have discovered or invented in the process of living and for motives arising from this our living. Living reason starts from no idea and hence is not idealism.[18]

In this refinement of his position, Ortega seemed to be reaching for a kind of philosophical biology. The "life" he spoke of was always "my life" in that it could not be understood without reference to an individual person, but it was also "our lives" as thinking animals whose consciousness had emerged over aeons of time from an organic base in nature. Aspects of this central truth, manifest before Ortega in William James's *Principles of Psychology* and *Essays in Radical Empiricism*, have since been followed out by thinkers as diverse as Maurice Merleau-Ponty, Susanne Langer, Hans Jonas, and Ortega's disciple Julián Marías. In general, post-Husserlian thought, particularly in the work of phenomenological psychologists like Helmuth Plessner, Eugene Minkowski, and Erwin W. Straus, has moved in the direction of Ortega's insistence on a reason grounded in life. As a corollary, he believed, it was also necessary to trace the vital trajectory or "biography" of reason as a historically conditioned faculty that had evolved together with man himself. In that sense, reason was the product of both nature and culture, but, above all, it could not be considered the unchanging essence of the human animal.

The "Notes on Thinking" repeated the essential themes of the lectures on *la razón histórica* and of *Ideas y creencias*. Cognition itself, Ortega suggested, was a historically evolved form of man's mental life rooted in the belief (*creencia*) that the human mind could penetrate the being of the world. By contrast,

> modern physics does not search for being. It contents itself with working out an imaginary, subjective pattern which allows us to take our bearings among appearances but which does not claim to be more than an approximation open at any time to corrections suggested by newly observed phenomena.[19]

Twentieth-century physics and mathematical logic, particularly, prompted Ortega to assert the mutability of all forms of understanding. Traditional cognition, which he believed had originated with ancient Greek philosophy,

> now appears not as an absolute reality to which man is committed forever and ever but as a pure historical phenomenon; not as a "natural" and therefore inevitable occupation of man but as one "form of life" invented in the course of history by way of answer to certain experiences and liable to be dropped in view of others.[20]

In addition to such concerns, the "Notes" also reflected Ortega's turn away from politics toward that stress on the thinker's solitude which became a leitmotiv of his writings after the civil war. In the first section of the essay, "Crisis of the Intellectual and Crisis of the Intellect," he quoted his own words from an article of 1923:

> A situation like this [Primo's takeover] requires that the intellectuals should withdraw from the social heights and concentrate upon their

own concerns.... The intellectual minority must be expected to divest their work of all political or humanitarian "pathos," [feeling] and to renounce being taken seriously by the multitude.... And what a relief to the intellect to be rid of the cumbersome tasks it rashly took on! How delightful to go freely about its own subtle pursuits, again to be set upon itself, to live at the fringe of the busy world unharassed by the necessity of producing premature solutions.... Such a withdrawal... leaves the thinker severed from his fellow men, in unmitigated solitude. When this has come to pass and he is thrown upon himself, thinking assumes a new aspect.[21]

Eighteen years later, Ortega had made his bid to live on the "social heights" and had abruptly come to the dark gestation of exile. Consequently, the "withdrawal" of 1941 was not that of 1923. His intellect was no longer as buoyant as it had been in those days of the founding of the *Revista de Occidente*, a time when, he now averred, "intellectuals still enjoyed great social prestige, in certain respects the greatest they have ever possessed in the course of history."[22] But the present moment seemed an ominous reversal: "It is a fact that thinking is out of fashion. In a few years the place in society occupied by 'intellectual life' has changed completely."[23]

If Ortega was philosophically productive during the two and a half years in Argentina (August 1939 to February 1942), he also continued his old habit of writing occasional pieces in more direct response to his environment. The spectacle of civil and world war, the pain of expatriation, and the burden of illness combined to infuse these writings with a sharpened awareness of the philosopher's precarious place in the world. (Nor was he at this time free from financial worry, picking up income where he could. The "Meditation on the Creole Woman," for example, was given in 1939 as three radio talks sponsored by an Argentine brewery. Ortega had often defined nationality by pointing to the curious inauthenticity that befalls the man who leaves his own country. Now that very situation was his: *de te fabula narratur*. Since "I am I and my circumstance," any major shift in circumstances breaks the fusion of the ego and its customary surroundings, leaving the immigrant a spectator on the sidelines, over whom the essentially opaque drama of a foreign country's life easily slides. "The exiled person feels his life, as it were, suspended: *exsul umbra*, the exile is a shadow, the Romans said."[24] And he pictured himself as a shadow in the crowds of the Argentine capital:

What have I to do in the center of Buenos Aires, will you please tell me? I am the opposite of a businessman. I do not participate in intrigues. I don't have an office. My social relations are moderate, sober. I detest encounters in which people who understand nothing of politics speak of it anyway, resolved to save this country and other countries and, to boot, humanity itself.... Neither have I had the chance to know, with very few exceptions, the intellectuals of Buenos Aires. Can you tell me what my business is in the center of the city with its intestinal streets, its mute facades and narrow sidewalks along which one cannot even stroll?[25]

Like all uprooted persons, Ortega was often obliged to live marginally in his adopted land. His choice of Buenos Aires had doubtless stemmed from warm memories of earlier visits, and he also needed to be "installed," as he put it, in a culture that used his mother tongue. But Ortega found his third visit lean by comparison with the other two, and although he was able to continue working, he experienced bouts of acute depression. In October 1941, he wrote to Victoria Ocampo, with whom he had reestablished warm relations:

I can tell you that since February my existence has not *in the least* resembled what it had been until then and that, *without possible comparison*, I am passing through the hardest stage of my life. Many times during these months I have feared I would die, in the most literal and physical sense, an anguished death. Nowadays many men of my condition are dying in the same way throughout the world.... When the bases of our life have been broken or are gravely ailing, it is impossible to tell even one's best friend what is happening because he simply cannot understand. That would be to falsify and betray our suffering. No: one must keep still, bear up and bury oneself in some corner. Each life is intransferrable and, for the same reason, ineffable.... My health has been bad since March, but this would be the least of it, supposing at least that the malaise does not come from the moral torment. A strange convergence of fate has brought my situation to its most acute extreme, but it is clear that this fate springs from the framework of general causes that affect many people. It would not be unusual, then, for you one of these days to enter a period of bitterness and for this or that source of life to begin to fail you. Now, kindly imagine a moment in which not one but *all the sources of life fail you at once*, and then you would have an idea of what is happening to me.[26]

A good deal of Ortega's response to exile in Argentina can be inferred from several brief essays and from the texts of some radio talks given in Buenos Aires. Three main threads are woven through them: his view of his potential Latin American public, his sense of the fragility of communication and understanding, and his precarious condition as an exiled intellectual. Though he was, by all accounts, a man of great charm and one to whom success and admiration had seemed to come easily, by 1939 he was forced to live out a bitter and literal analogue of the voyaging metaphor he so loved in Plato's seventh letter. Now his earlier speculations on the hazards of his calling came home to him trenchantly. Something of the renewed doubts he suffered can be heard in an undated though certainly postwar appendix ("El oficio de pintar") to his essays on Goya, in which he enviously compared the work of painters and intellectuals:

> The thinker manipulates ideas, beings that offer no resistance and let themselves be combined and deformed abundantly. If he does not discipline himself he is lost. His work will become irresponsible, petulant, and null. That is why an intellectual ineluctably needs to have a clearer awareness [than the artist] of what he is doing. The painter, on the other hand, neither tends to nor need be conscious. The incorruptible consistency of the material his hands encounter acts as if it were the consciousness he lacks. That is why the artist lives more in his work than the intellectual, and when his fingers are still, when they abandon the canvas, the brush, the burin, the clay, or the marble, it is as if he were brainless, and he seems foolish.[27]

This portrait of the artist was, no doubt, shaped by the thinker's idealization of an obviously more manual art, but the description of the intellectual's dilemma is sure, founded in long experience. Those "beings that offer no resistance" were none other than the "ideas" of Ortega's *Ideas y creencias*, volatile, labile things that never touch the bottom of our being. He was fond of quoting Heinrich Heine's coachman, who, when asked to define ideas, reputedly replied, "Ideas, ideas?—Oh, they're those things that they put into your head."[28] With the spectral quality of his own thoughts in mind, Ortega voiced his yearning, in three radio talks of 1939, to change his identity, leave the world of thought, and dance with the creole women. His puzzlement over his role as an intellectual without a constituency, in the midst of a huge foreign city, was clear. Yet these pangs of homelessness did not entirely deter him from his vocation. He warned the Argentines, as he had done in 1916, that intellectual growth was as important as politics, too often an excessive concern in Spanish-speaking countries.

Ortega often made didactic observations to and about Latin America, which needed, he felt, to make fundamental distinctions between bogus and genuine culture. In doing so, he courted the Latin American audience with a blend of enticement, charm, and uncertainty, the latter quality evident in the constant qualifications of the radio talks. In this position, Ortega found it necessary to be, as he had said of the Argentines themselves, "on the defensive." In the last of the talks, he bridled against the sophomoric thrusts directed at him by certain local intellectuals:

> I know very little, very little, much less obviously than the young wise men around here, those who have read four German books and permit themselves to make faces at me, I who am at present one of the writers on matters of thought who has sold the most in Germany for years now.[29]

Ortega's sensitivity to Argentine criticism of his self-appointed role as critic in exile in fact suggests that he saw a parallel between the Argentine and the Spanish situations. While Argentines might be faulted for the posturing and bravado they employed to cover the weaknesses in their culture, Spaniards too, especially since the crisis of 1898, had similarly expressed their sense of inferiority toward the rest of Europe. The difference between the two peoples stemmed, in Ortega's view, from the respective ages of the two countries. Perhaps with this distinction in mind, he peppered his Argentine essays with allusions to Europe and spoke with the authority provided by the older culture. He was enthusiastic about his "discovery" of America, but he remained convinced that it must "enter history" by learning from Europe. The idea that formerly colonial countries could have a radically different development from that of the "mother" nations—skipped stages, unforeseeable innovations—seems not to have entered his asessment.

Ortega's portrait of Argentina did, it is true, include a sense of awe and fascination before the vitality of its people and the abundance of its natural resources, but he had difficulty in achieving a thorough understanding of the "new" world on its own terms, often assuming a speculative viewpoint in order to make sense of what he saw. This difficulty may be seen in a much earlier essay entitled

"Hegel y América" (1928), in which Ortega reviewed Hegel's notion that the native peoples of America, standing outside the classical and European heritage, were primitives who did not figure in the progressive self-unfolding of the World Spirit. As such, they belonged to "pre-history," where nothing had yet begun to happen. In turn, Europeans who emigrated to these lands, overwhelmed by a geography without the spiritual density that a long history created, would retrocede in their spiritual evolution and become, at least for a time, much like the primitive tribesmen whom they conquered or displaced. From this postulate Ortega thought to derive "a fundamental law of history that Hegel never formulated separately," to wit, that

> the history or the spiritualization of the universe is a function of population density. Humanity scattered abroad does not secrete spirit. It must become sufficiently compact that individuals press upon each other. Submitted to pressure, humanity begins to ooze spirituality, and the properly historical enterprise begins.[30]

Such a view naturally accepted the Hegelian premise that the Mediterranean world and Europe remained the central theater of the Spirit's progress through history. As for the fate of teeming Buenos Aires and the energetic ingenuity of the "Yankee" civilization to the north that obviously fascinated Ortega, much remained obscure. Without the aid of European wisdom and experience, it would seem, the peoples of America risked submersion in the vast ocean of their ahistorical geography.

In the essay on Hegel and in other articles on Latin America, Ortega juggled ideas and suppositions as if he had entirely forgotten his own warnings in *Ideas y crencias* that ideas are volatile and perishable. What in fact forms most of our responses—especially since, as Ortega held, most men have neither the time to think nor the habit of doing so—is the basic beliefs (*creencias*) out of which we act, speak, and judge. In his attempt to account for American civilizations, Ortega obviously worked from a fund of Spanish and European preconceptions about America. They gave him his position as cultural mentor, but, unfortunately, he reared upon them a flimsy superstructure of ideas lacking historical integrity and revealing finally the rather conventional judgments of America of an intelligent European in the early decades of this century.

Ortega's influence in Latin America extended chiefly to two nations: Argentina, as we have seen, and, to a slightly lesser degree, Mexico. Thanks both to a native Mexican philosophical movement and the arrival, after 1936, of gifted Spanish intellectuals in exile, Ortega's mark has been more enduring there than in Argentina. Among the Latin American countries, Mexico was something of a case apart, for its native Indian population, while large, had blended with the Spanish and European colonizers more than elsewhere. Hence Mexico was a *mestizo* culture and, as such, would have been a less familiar terrain for Ortega than Buenos Aires and the great pampas, a landscape reminiscent of his own Castile. He never visited Mexico, however, and wrote nothing about it; but his work had been introduced there by some circulation of the *Revista de Occidente* after 1923, and was later widely promulgated by the philosopher José Gaos, his chief prewar disciple, a fervent socialist, and rector of the University of Madrid from 1936 to 1938.

Gaos became one of the most influential and productive of the thousands of uprooted Spanish writers, teachers, and professional people who were so cordially received by the government of President Cárdenas after 1939. In fact, the entire modern political history of Mexico disposed it to sympathy with the lost cause of the Spanish Republicans. Like many of the cultural elite of prewar Spain who found asylum there, Gaos rapidly became active as a university teacher, lecturer, and writer. His work eventually formed the most important bridge between the existential and phenomenological traditions of European thought and native philosophical currents in Mexico, still imbued, when he arrived, with the residue of their positivistic past. Under Ortega's tutelage in Madrid, Gaos had absorbed the same philosophical currents that had deeply influenced his mentor, and in his second career in Mexico he devoted himself to translating, during some thirty years of residence there, fundamental works of Heidegger, Hartmann, Husserl, Scheler, Dilthey, Jaspers, and others. Together with earlier translations fom German that had become available in the pages of the *Revista*, Gaos's work allowed Continental philosophy to cross the seas and take vigorous root in a culture where it had previously had little influence. His efforts were supplemented by an active group of Spanish émigré scholars who, for the publishing house of Fondo de Cultura Económica alone, translated over a hundred titles in the fields of European sociology, philosophy, history, and political thought. Eugenio Imaz, Wenceslao Roces, Vicente Herrero, and others joined Gaos in carrying forward in exile the project of cultural modernization begun years earlier by Ortega and his circle in Madrid.

In the early twentieth century, Mexican philosophical studies had developed largely under the influence of two major figures who, partly inspired by Bergson, had turned Mexican thought away from positivism and toward an outlook sympathetic to the incipient influx of existential and phenomenological philosophy. These were Antonio Caso (1883–1946) and José Vasconcelos (1882–1959). One of Caso's students and an early reader of Ortega, Samuel Ramos, explains in his *Historia de la filosofía en Mexico* the beginning of Ortega's Mexican influence well before Gaos's arrival in 1938: "An intellectual generation which began to act publicly between 1925 and 1930 felt dissatisfied with the philosophical romanticism of Caso and Vasconcelos," and simultaneously discovered Ortega's work and increased its respect for Mexican culture in its own right. Writers, mural painters, and architects included indigenous themes and national history in their works:

> Meanwhile philosophy did not appear to fit within this ideal picture of nationalism because she has always pretended to look at things from the standpoint of man in general; hence, opposed to the concrete determinations of space and time, that is to say, to history. Ortega y Gasset came... to solve this problem by showing the historicity of philosophy in his *El tema de nuestro tiempo*. Assembling these ideas with some others he had expounded in *Meditaciones del Quijote*, that Mexican generation [of the 1920s] found the epistemological justification of a national philosophy.[31]

Ortega, of course, was not the first modern thinker to proclaim the historicity of philosophy, but for Latin America—and especially Mexico—he was the harbinger of this liberating doctrine, which received its wider diffusion thanks to Gaos's emigration.[32] Mexican philosophy in recent decades has been shaped by the continuing influence of Caso and Vasconcelos, together with the introduction of contemporary German thinkers via Ortega, Gaos, and other Spanish exiles. Out of this background, more recent Mexican thinkers have arisen: Leopoldo Zea, Edmundo O'Gorman, Justino Fernández and Octavio Paz.

In February 1942, Ortega and his wife left Buenos Aires by sea to take up residence in Estoril, a Portuguese resort area just west of Lisbon. This was a significant step closer to Spanish soil, but since the political situation at home was still unsettled and even hazardous for those who had supported the Republic, he decided for the time being to carry on his work in the relative comfort and politically stable atmosphere of the neighboring country. Through his daughter, Soledad, who returned to Madrid in March 1940, and his sons, Miguel and José, Ortega kept in touch with news from the Spanish capital. Julián Marías too maintained an active correspondence with him from Madrid between 1942 and 1945, and of course afterward. Although Gaos had been the outstanding disciple of the prewar years, Marías was now emerging as a brilliant follower, eager to further Ortega's work, to collaborate with him, and to have his approval. As for the Franco regime, it did not actively discourage Ortega's return, though it remained clear that any writing or teaching he might do in Spain would be subject to the strict censorship that now controlled the nation's cultural and intellectual life. In fact, it would have been a fine feather in the regime's cap if this grand prewar figure could be shown to have made his peace with the victors, but Ortega was not about to have his reputation put to partisan political use again. While, as we shall see, he attempted to establish himself in Spain later in the decade, he never made formal peace with the new regime. Indeed, he rejected a later offer of a chair at the University of Madrid and, in 1953, refused the state retirement pay for his prewar university career due him on his seventieth birthday. By 1948, he had established a residence in Madrid at number 28 Calle Monte Esquinza but he continued to keep his Lisbon quarters and his residency status in Portugal until his death.

Ortega's years near the sea in Estoril were quiet, withdrawn times of fruitful work and searching for new directions. Not unhappy in his new setting, by far preferable to Buenos Aires, he was determined to give his scattered work of the prewar years systematic form in fully developed books. Continuing to remain aloof from political commentary and journalistic assignments, he worked on the manuscripts that would later appear as *Origen y epílogo de la filosofía*, *El hombre y la gente*, and *La idea de principio en Leibniz*. During this time, Marías spent portions of the summers of 1944 and 1945 in Lisbon in intensive conversation with his former teacher, who doubtless saw in the devoted younger man a promise for the continuation of his work in Spain. This intellectual encounter led Ortega to undertake in 1943 an epilogue to Marías's *History of Philosophy*, which had enjoyed immediate success in Spain after its publication in 1941 and was now going into a second edition. In January 1944, Ortega wrote to Marías:

> The "Epilogue" to your work will touch upon etymology and many other weighty topics. I have been engaged on it for months. Everything nowadays, though, is so problematical, there are so many interferences to interrupt one's work, that I do not dare to venture on great promises. But I do want you to know that I am up to my ears in your epilogue.[33]

By June of that year it was clear that this "back matter" had assumed the proportions of an independent work, for Ortega wrote to Marías that it was now to be a 400-page volume published separately under the title *Epílogo a la "Historia de filosofía" de Julián Marías*. In November and December he incorporated the finished portions of it into five lectures on *la razón histórica* that he gave in Lisbon, and informed Marías that the final manuscript would consist of 700 pages. By the summer of 1945 Ortega told Marías he would publish a separate section of the larger work as *El origen de la filosofía*. Like many of his other texts, this one had an obscure and circuitous trajectory in the following years. In 1946 Ortega announced two separate titles in preparation as *Epílogo a la "Historia de filosofía" de Julián Marías* and *El origen de la filosofía*. While the former has never been published as such, a portion of the latter appeared first in German translation in a festschrift for Karl Jaspers (1953).[34] The final Spanish text appeared posthumously when the Mexican house Fondo de Cultura Económica brought out in 1960 a modest 132-page volume entitled *Origen y epílogo de la filosofía*. This text, apparently incorporating portions of both previously announced titles, was later included in volume 9 of Ortega's *Obras completas* and subsequently published in English translation with the simplified title *The Origin of Philosophy* (1967). Its abrupt ending— in the midst of a speculation on the philosophical discovery of

Being—and its length both point to its fragmentary quality as part of a work-in-progress. One may therefore suppose that the projected magnitude of the piece, as conceived in 1944 and 1945, meant that Ortega originally thought of it in close connection with his magnum opus then supposedly in progress, *Aurora de la razón histórica*, much of which presumably became the posthumously published book on Leibniz. The contents of *The Origin of Philosophy* confirm this surmise: the text of ten short chapters attempts to establish the historical ground for the necessity of thinking philosophically, and is thus the first "chapter" of the story of *la razón histórica* understood as the tool man uses to ground his present situation in the dialectical development of past thought, itself a series of vital "solutions" to problems now obscured and in need of recovery. To understand why one pursued philosophy in the twentieth century, for example, one had to recreate (much in the manner of Croce and his follower Collingwood) the urgent conditions of the original pursuit; that in turn was possible only if one studied the past with a genuine need to know how to live in the present. Otherwise, inquiry about philosophy would be reduced to what Croce termed mere "chronicle," the opposite of lived history. This perspective led Ortega to reflect on philosophy's future:

> [Philosophy] came about one fine day in Greece and has indeed come down to us, with no guarantee, however, of its perpetuation. Without attempting now to formalize an opinion on this matter, I wish to suggest the possibility that what we are now beginning to engage in under the traditional aegis of philosophy is not another philosophy but something new and different from all philosophy.[35]

This new activity was a kind of "metaphilosophy" aimed to sum up, rectify, and transcend the long Western tradition Ortega meant to throw radically into question. In accord with his idea that man has no other nature than his history, and that he may do almost anything in the future except repeat one of his previous "experiments in being," Ortega rejected the notion that the need to do philosophy was a consubstantial part of man. As he later remarked in his book on Leibniz:

> Not only is there no *philosophia perennis*, but philosophizing itself does not become perennial. It was born one fine day and will disappear on another.... One can speak of the history of philosophy as describing pro-

gress in philosophizing. This progress can, finally, consist in our discovering some fine day that not only this or that philosophical "way of
thinking" was limited and therefore erroneous, but that, absolutely
speaking,... all philosophizing is a limitation, an insufficiency, an error,
and that it is necessary to inaugurate another means of intellectually
confronting the universe which is neither one of those anterior to philosophy nor philosophy itself. Perhaps we are in the dawn of this other
"fine day." [36]

Despite the apocalyptic overtones of that pronouncement, Ortega
knew that the philosophical past was continually reconstructed in a
kind of conversation with past thinkers, "a perpetual dialogue and
dispute held in a common tongue, namely the philosophical viewpoint itself and the perennial existence of the same difficult problems." [37] At the same time, insofar as post-Hegelian philosophy is on
this side of what many thinkers have seen as a kind of "watershed"
dividing the great traditions of antiquity and the Christian Middle
Ages from the historicist outlook of modern times, this dialogue becomes particularly problematic. Ortega knew that one went
beyond a tradition only by absorbing it, but the radical position he
took regarding the entirety of Western philosophy points up his perception that the "tradition" was in question precisely in its root
sense of "handing down." The alleged modern break with tradition
implied that the latter could be encountered only obliquely, with a
kind of critical, inventive freedom unknown to those who had stood
more solidly within it in earlier times. Clearly, tradition was not
simply "there" to be transmitted from one age or generation to the
next.

In his concern after 1940 with his relation to the Western philosophical past, Ortega explicitly sought systematic order in his
writing. He was after the big theme and the finished book, vowing
to answer by example the critics who had labeled him an impressionistic thinker, perhaps at best a brilliant journalist. But the
later works, for all his hope to establish with them a dramatically
new stage in his career, are too often digressive and occasionally
overblown. The tight, "athletic" quality of the earlier works—
despite their obvious sketchiness—had saved them from the dis-
tension that is evident in *The Idea of Principle in Leibniz*. Generally,
Ortega dealt with Spain—the concern that had goaded much of
his most spirited writing—much less in the works after the civil war

than in those before. As an obvious response to the wars in Spain and the rest of Europe, he turned progressively in later work to the theme of the continuity and future of European culture. His audience also changed: after 1939 he began of necessity to speak to the West at large. This was a diffuse public not easy to assess; hence the focus previously provided by the response of his native public now became rather blurred. Partly as a result of this profound dislocation in his career, the major late writings—two of which were given as lecture courses in Madrid in 1948–1949 ("Una interpretación de la historia universal") and 1949–1950 ("El hombre y la gente")—did not achieve the level of order and conceptual innovation of which he dreamed in brave announcements of the birth of books he had allegedly carried in gestation for years. His announced aim was to leave a systematic statement of the scattered leitmotivs of his earlier work, but all the later pieces, written under essentially nomadic circumstances, show the detrimental effect of an ill-defined public. By contrast, his earlier successes had exemplified Virginia Woolf's maxim, "To know whom to write for is to know how to write."

The malaise of exile can in fact be sensed in the version of his Argentine lectures on historical reason that Ortega repeated for a Portuguese audience in November and December 1944. Significantly changed since their presentation in Buenos Aires four years earlier, the Lisbon talks were studded with defensive sallies and elaborate apologetic asides. Nowhere in his postwar writing does one see more clearly the toll taken on his work by geographical and cultural displacement. The first lecture was a rambling consideration of the intellectual's social role throughout history. Ortega flattered himself by comparing it to that of the Old Testament prophets: "The intellectual must tell others what he discovers in his fruitful solitude; he must broadcast his solitude to mankind from the desert life he has undertaken. The intellectual is above all a *Vox clamantis in deserto*."[38] The second lecture, even more circuitous, took up the question of making philosophy "of the present" by connecting it to its entire historical trajectory; the talk concluded with an attempted comparison between the prophet Amos and the philosopher's vocation. Somewhat self-servingly, Ortega remarked:

> The true mission of the intellectual is neither to praise nor flatter, but to oppose and rectify; make straight in the desert a highway for our God,

as Isaiah said. Such a destiny is harsh, difficult and terrible—inasmuch as it is one of the rarest examples of the most authentic manliness.[39]

In effect, he observed, the intellectual's only real power lies in his ability to oppose the world by "seducing" men into thought.

In the third lecture, Ortega embarked on a defense of his style of philosophizing, derogatorily called "literary" by certain critics in his audience. In a lengthy digression on the inauthenticity of the man who practices his vocation in a stereotypical manner, he refused to "be what others want me to be—a carnival mask, a uniform, a wrapping! ... I like others not to know what to expect from me, to wonder if I am a philosopher or a poet or if, perhaps, I am neither but a rare duck-billed platypus—an apposite theme, that one."[40] Veering about in search of his theme, he discoursed briefly on his itinerant condition, his perambulatory style, the relation between strolling and thinking, the "chuckleheaded" pseudo-intellectuals who derided his work, and the irresponsible speech habits of "Iberian man." In conclusion, he proclaimed grandly that the rule of law had virtually disappeared from the world, a thesis he left undeveloped. Seeming entirely to have lost his ostensible theme of *la razón histórica*, he declared his "insignificance" as an intellectual of the "minor Latin nations," who noticed "with shame and sorrow the superficiality, the theoretical weakness, the complete lack of acuity and depth with which the great intellectuals of the major nations have dealt in recent years with contemporary problems."[41] His performance on this occasion remained unequalled in his entire career for sheer posturing and braggadocio. In almost complete intellectual disarray, he showed the scars of the loneliness and isolation he had borne for nearly a decade since leaving Spain.

Notwithstanding his querulous tone in the third lecture, Ortega sprang back in the fourth to his predilect themes, proclaiming human life as the virgin territory yet unexplored by philosophy:

[W]hen he comes to the end [of the road of life], man discovers that he carries, stuck there on his back, the entire roll of the life he led. In other words, he is weighted down with "life experience," just as the harvest grape in autumn has hoarded, stored up inside, all the summer sun. This delightful subject, the "life experience," has scarcely had any attention; until now it has never been raised to the status of theory.[42]

This projected study implied the work of autobiography, to which Ortega prompted every member of his audience. Like all men, he added, they lived their lives in ignorance of "the hidden basement" of their existences, "where the tender vessels of the drama that is each of your lives quiver in the dark."[43] Although he never wrote his own autobiography—a genre of relative rarity in Spanish literature—Ortega repeatedly invoked the autobiographical impulse in his fascination with the hidden authentic destiny that each man must discover for himself. In this lecture, he envisioned the day when a true science of being—a revolutionary ontology—would be forged from the cumulative testimony of millions of individual lives understood in their uniqueness as well as their structural typicality. Only then could man transcend the philosophical scandal of living his life without really comprehending or taking stock of it.

The final lecture dramatized again the contemporary state of intellectual crisis; and it was not human life alone that required to be understood fully for the first time, as he hyperbolically noted:

> No one knows what to do in politics...but, then, neither does the physicist know what he is doing in physics, nor the mathematician in mathematics, nor the logician in logic...nor the poet in poetry, nor the musician in music, the painter in painting, the capitalist with his capital, nor the worker at his work, nor the father with his family, and since the family too is in crisis the relationship between the sexes is also a problem now.[44]

The intellectual shaking of the foundations Ortega divined most clearly in twentieth-century physics, mathematics, and logic reached, in one way or another, into all areas of life: "[T]he principles and suppositions of Western life have suddenly turned into questions, enigmas."[45] To a largely Portuguese audience in a conservative Catholic culture sustained by the political illiberalism of Premier Salazar's corporative economy, these pronouncements must have sounded exotic indeed. And what was his public to make of his closing remark that the true subject of his course was what went on not only in the physics laboratories and the studies of mathematicians but as well "in the streets and squares, the houses and the social clubs, in bars and taverns,...on the sea, on earth, in the air and beneath the sea, in the abyss, or even beyond the air, in the stratosphere."[46] They were, in any case, left to ponder this invocation of philosophy's bold sweep, for the course was interrupted at that point and never thereafter completed.

Immersed in these melancholy reflections, Ortega yearned in his Portuguese retreat for native soil. The force of that nostalgia may partially account for the vigorous style of a prologue (English translation, *Meditations on Hunting*, 1985) he completed in Estoril in June 1942 for his old friend Count Eduardo Yebes's *Veinte años de caza mayor* (Twenty Years of Hunting Big Game). Not incidentally do some of Ortega's happiest turns in this piece evoke the hunter wandering far afield in the fastnesses of the Sierra de Gredos west of Madrid and south of Ávila: the body of Spain, the feel of the Spanish earth, underlies the whole meditation. This long and beautiful essay, seventy-three pages in the *Obras completas*, harked back in the felicity of its prose and the concentration of its thought to the best of Ortega's prewar work. Ostensibly a diversion from his major philosophical projects, it in fact offered an exquisitely realized statement of his matured view of the drama of human existence. Throughout his career, in fact, he had engaged his central concerns with quick thrusts of thought couched in the rhetorical flourishes and ingratiating style demanded of him by the particular medium he chose and the public he had to address. In this prologue, as often before, Ortega demonstrated that he knew how to concentrate in the ostensible digression or excursus the essence of his wisdom. His salute to Yebes's book was a generous response to a friend's request for a kind of imprimatur, but Ortega made of this odd circumstance—being, as he pointed out, rather "cowardly" and hardly an accomplished hunter—a basis for sustained reflection and a means of regaining touch with Spain.

Puzzling over his old friend's request, Ortega recalled how, "leaping like a buck deer, the theme of hunting had many times cut across his horizon as a writer."[47] Now the moment had come for a true phenomenology of this universal and age-old human activity. Hunting had often been considered, he pointed out, a mere diversion; but done rightly it required skill, courage, and an almost monastic sense of discipline. As such, it revealed a central facet of the structure of human life—our need to decide what we will do with our lives insofar as they are free of the mandates of necessity. In this sense, life becomes "a poetic task": each must write his own story, freely elaborating the plot that will occupy or fill the time granted him. Much of our allotted time is occupied for us by tasks we neither choose nor are free to deny, but happiness consists in deciding how to fill the unresolved portions of our existence. Curiously, Ortega observed, the classic forms of happy leisure, cultivated most frequently by the aristocracy, had been rather limited and could almost be reduced to four: hunting, dancing, the races, and social gatherings (*tertulias*). Of these, hunting in particular transcends the status of simple pleasure. The Count of Yebes, after all, pursued lynx and deer through some of the wildest countryside of twentieth-century Spain, planning his expeditions with masterly care.

Ortega conceived of hunting as essentially an encounter between two animals, the hunter and the hunted. As such, it reflected a zoological hierarchy, a necessary inequality of condition. Yet it also always involved risk and chance, for by definition the spoils of the hunt could never be guaranteed. The rabbit might be lower in the hierarchy of strength than the fox, but the weaker creature had his wiles and his sheltering retreats. When man entered the scene, he had to accept certain limitations on his superior position in the animal kingdom. Some of these were imposed on him (e.g., the inferior status of his instincts as compared with those of the wild animals), but some he imposed on himself (e.g., not poisoning a river to catch all its fish). If he was to know what hunting was, he could neither do it with a camera—as some misguided English humanitarians had proposed, greatly irking Ortega—nor from a speeding car. To hunt was to go out on foot into nature with one's weapons and one's dogs (which compensate us for our weakened instincts); it was to pursue the animal on his own ground, scaling peaks, standing in thickets, wading in deep pools. Herein lay much of the deep appeal of sport hunting, for it represented a return to an activity essential to human life since man's earliest beginnings. It was a fundamental part of the natural order of the world, a reminder of the quintessence of animal existence.

As human reason had matured and civilization had advanced across the globe, Ortega continued, wilderness, and thereby hunting, had necessarily been reduced. While a certain scarcity of game—or at least the perception of scarcity—had always been essential to true hunting, the modern world had imposed a new kind of scarcity by eliminating the ecological base for the chase. With the long evolutionary and historical attenuation of his hunting instincts, modern civilized man had lost much of the wild, primal alertness of his senses; and though they might be stimulated by all manner of sophisticated occupations and entertainments, something crucial was lost to him who could no longer conceive of hunting. Civilized man risked falling into what Ortega called "inertial thinking," the tendency to take for granted one's habitual assumptions about reality.

Cosmopolitan and urbane as he was, Ortega himself had hunted in his youth, and he saw in this pursuit a means to rediscover an ethical stance toward the natural world that would have pleased Thoreau or John Muir, though neither of them was a hunter. We cannot, he argued, treat even the stones of the sierra as mere raw material or, more grotesquely, as a convenient natural billboard upon which some upstart optometrist from Madrid may paint his advertisements.[48] Hunting too, staged in nature and requiring man's return to it, had its ethic. One must not, for example, kill needlessly (i.e., if not at least to eat the meat); yet neither could one abolish the kill and still say he had hunted, for even in hunting as sport, there remained an attenuated tie to the earlier issue of sheer survival. We stalk our prey until it escapes or is killed; yet we do not dispatch it heedlessly, for we must recall that it is a fellow creature that not only supplies us with food but treads the same earth, caught like us in a body vulnerable to myriad ills and dangers. We have built civilizations to protect us from the ravages of the natural state, but we have done so at our peril, for too great a forgetfulness of our animal condition blunts our sense of reality and weakens our natural defenses. In true hunting, we grant some advantages to our quarry in our desire to return to his level—hence hunting has changed very little as a process over the last five thousand years—for our pleasure is rooted in reestablishing contact with deep paleolithic layers of our human past, wherein man's reason was almost entirely instinctual. As we hunt, we momentarily throw off the burdens of progress and civilized life. We take a "holiday," as it were, from our evolved human condition, touching upon its primal roots among our hunter-gatherer ancestors. Moving thus from history into nature, we also enter into the countryside as we can in no other way, for the hunter neither contemplates nor exploits the land around him: he makes his way through it in agile pursuit of a prey whose wiles he must in some degree imitate in order to succeed, even to the point of disguising himself in its skins.

Having laid bare the elements of the chase, Ortega leaped to his larger point—that the hunter is "man alert," in the same sense in which Emerson speaks of "man thinking," man in process of understanding and making his way in the world. The Count of Yebes's final lesson for hunters applied to the philosopher as well: be attentive to what is before you, look and look again. As the hunter cannot engage in leisurely contemplation of the landscape, so the thinker, rooting about in the dense thickets of ideas and of sensory evidence, cannot simply stand back from life to judge it in Olympian detachment. Alert to the soft and often delusive security civilization seems to promise, the hunter-philosopher remembers the underlying danger of existence and the need for decisive interpretation. Here as elsewhere in his work, Ortega was revising the ancient Greek and Christian emphasis on the *vita contemplativa*: assimilating the philosopher to the hunter, he stressed intellectual action and mercurial readiness. Though he took from Plato the notion that the philosopher is a "devotee of looking" ("un amigo de mirar"), and from Aristotle the idea that philosophy begins in wonder, he radically altered the classical stress on transcendent theory, which seeks its highest fulfillment in steadily gazing upon the truth:

> [I]n effect, he alone thinks who, faced with a problem, instead of looking straight ahead toward what habit, tradition, topical ideas, and mental intertia would presume, stays alert, ready to accept that the solution may spring up from the least foreseen point on the great circle of the horizon.[49]

These were familiar themes from Ortega's earlier work, but the spirited and finely modulated prose of the prologue, together with its buoyant tone, make it one of his more felicitous pieces. The inspiration for it perhaps lay in the simple fact of affection and admiration for an old friend, and in the pleasant memories, evoked by the theme, of rambles with a gun through the rugged Spanish countryside of Ortega's youth. Whatever the case, it is a decidedly jovial piece of work and redolent of what Pedro Cerezo Galán has called its author's "voluntad de aventura" (will to adventure).

By the time he completed the prologue, Ortega knew that the

doleful days of exile in France and Argentina were well behind him. Estoril, the Lisbon suburb where he was living, offered tranquility for daily work, which he apparently pursued with gusto. Turning sixty on May 9, 1943, he seemed to have regained some of his youthful energies of earlier days. Both Julián Marías and Ortega's daughter, Soledad, refer to the Lisbon years of the mid-1940s as a productive and not unhappy period in his life. Nonetheless, the pull of Spain was strong, and on August 8, 1945, Ortega returned to Madrid for the first time since the summer of 1936, going on to spend the summer in Zumaya on the Basque coast. What news he had received of Spain during his absence is difficult to assess precisely. His three children continued to reside in Madrid, where the younger son, José, had assumed directorship of the Revista de Occidente publishing house. Although the monthly review itself would not appear again until 1963, the related press became active as soon as the war was over. In 1940 it published two translations by Marías from the German (Scheler's *De lo eterno en el hombre* and Aschoff's *El dinero y el oro*) and in 1941 Marías's own *Historia de la filosofía*. Numerous other Spanish and foreign authors soon appeared under the familiar logo of the Revista owl. More important, Ortega's irregular periods of residence in Madrid during the last decade of his life (1945–1955) were sweetened by the renewal of the Revista *tertulia* (this time with a different membership), which had been so central a part of his life before the war. After 1945, it met morning and evening whenever he was in residence. As Marías has written:

> In free and spontaneous conversation, with no preconceived plan and with deference to Ortega...who from time to time reoriented the talk, we spoke for an hour or an hour and a half before the late mid-day meal of Madrid, and for two hours before supper. If one considers the pressures of life and understands how hard one had to work in order just to live, one can measure what that "loss" of time meant, which some of us considered the best possible, because the most disinterested, way of investing it.[50]

On May 4, 1946, Ortega made his first public appearance in Madrid in ten years at the hallowed Ateneo, traditional home of Spanish liberalism and free thought since the mid–nineteenth century. Since the postwar Ateneo was, like most prominent Spanish institutions at the time, under government control, it seemed odd to some that he had chosen such a setting. And his theme as well was ostensibly unpropitious. Some undoubtedly expected a reference to the last decade of Spanish history, but his topic was the theater and dramatic masks. One could speculate on associations between theater and politics, but in fact the talk seemed devoid of such intentions. Nevertheless, Ortega's lecture was the social and intellectual event of the season. Crowds of admirers and curious newcomers turned out to see the old master, who had delivered the same talk some weeks before in Lisbon. The text carried a special added preface for his Ateneo audience, in which Ortega's mood was openly sentimental:

> A whole generation of youths has neither seen nor heard me, and this encounter with them is so problematic for me that I can only hope that, after seeing and hearing me, they will want to repeat . . . the verses of the old ballad that tells what people sang to the Cid . . . when he, after long years of expatriation in Valencia, . . . entered Castile once more, and which begin: "Old you come, my lord, / Old you come and green again" ["Viejo que venís el Cid, / viejo venís y florido"].[51]

There was an intriguing ambiguity in his affirmation on this occasion that Spain had emerged from war with a "surprising, almost indecent health," but that remark remained an almost coquettish hint—one of many that appear in his postwar work—of his thoughts on the war and its aftermath. It had always been characteristic of Ortega to suggest grave pronouncements for which he avowed neither the time nor the place suitable. In the Ateneo that day he was, of course, on Franco's ground and had obvious reasons to leave things unspoken. His culminating invitation to the youth of Spain to explore with him the nature of politics was similarly tantalizing. Despite war and exile, he appeared to have retained something of his liberal faith of earlier days: "[I]t is necessary that we all put our heads together . . . to confront the enormous, brand-new, unheard-of problems that man has before him today, with agility, with perspicacity, with originality, and gracefully."[52] The periodic roll of the phrases, the abundant adjectives, rang a bit hollow in this setting, and in fact Ortega could do very little to carry out the implicit promise of this overture to postwar Spanish youth in 1946. In this lecture, he began with great panache but soon lost the edge of his intensity. With rhetorical inflation, he called the nature of politics a topic "no thinker until now had confronted in depth, seriously, and straight-on."[53]

Many people were disappointed and puzzled by the talk. The major Madrid papers reported it, glossing over the remark on Spain's "indecent health" to treat Ortega's return as support for the "New Spain." The Falangist organ *Arriba* and the rightist Catholic *Ya* printed derogatory reviews, but other papers asserted that Ortega had come home to his old post as cultural mentor. In fact, the Ateneo talk on theater marked the beginning of Ortega's contention with the postwar Spanish press. Criticism of that lecture and of others he gave in Madrid during the winters of 1948 and 1949 often played on his obviously heterogeneous public. The most carpingly critical papers (*Ya* and *Informaciones*) delighted in caricaturing his audience as a socially pretentious mélange of duchesses, "egg-heads," bullfighters, and wide-eyed students.

Such people did, in fact, attend these sessions, and Ortega, who had often cultivated the women of Madrid's high society, was particularly flattered by feminine admiration. The one or two bullfighters in his postwar audiences were personal friends, particularly Domingo Ortega, no kin but a passionate devotee of his namesake. The students at Ortega's lectures in the late 1940s were clearly his most critical audience. For them he was more an illustrious name than a present force. His work seemed to belong to a time historically more distant than simple chronology suggested. Further, in the reconstructed version of modern Spanish history proffered by the Franco regime's intellectual apologists and supported by many leaders of the Church, Ortega was chief among the perfidious liberal intellectuals who had planned the Republic and so led Spain into disaster. Those of the young not brainwashed with pseudohistory must, in any case, have found little in the postwar Ortega that spoke to their immediate situation, for they lived with a narrowly doctrinaire educational system, a strictly censored press, and a political vacuum, in which debate and criticism were unknown.

The press's inaccurate portrayal of Ortega's widely varied public created an almost grotesque image of the man. It was true that titled nobility and society figures had been part of his entourage for years, partly because of his haut bourgeois class origins and those of his wife, Rosa Spottorno Topete. But facile criticism of his postwar public forgets that Spain's intellectual community had been decimated by war and exile. Many of Ortega's followers and former students were abroad, and those who had remained in Spain were often more concerned with survival than philosophy. While the situation in some of the better urban secondary schools was by no means unilaterally bleak, there was no unrestricted or unbiased study of recent Spanish history, and students could hardly be expected to form a just concept of the role of the liberal intellectuals during the prewar decades. On a higher level, where a young audience inclined to philosophical studies might have been formed after the civil war, the formerly illustrious School of Philosophy and Letters at the University of Madrid was now staffed by utterly mediocre professors who had sworn allegiance to the Franco regime in order to obtain their posts. In short, it is difficult to see from where Ortega might have drawn an adequate and intelligently responsive audience during those lean years. His own disillusionment, for that matter, was reflected in the apolitical cast of most of his postwar writing and, perhaps, in his heightened tendency toward self-indulgent pontification: if he could not change the world, he could at least entertain it! This distinctly unflattering side of the man as he grew older, and as his ideas seemed to some acerbic critics tired and clichéd, is caught in the novelist Luís Martín Santos's portrait of Madrid's favorite philosopher lecturing in his later years:

> [S]olemn, hieratic, self-aware, disposed to lower himself to the necessary level, wrapped in the highest grace, with eighty years of European idealism behind him, gifted with an original metaphysic, gifted with friendships in the great world, possessed of a great head, lover of life, rhetorician, inventor of a new style of metaphor, taster of history, revered in provincial German universities, oracle, journalist, essayist, talker, he-who-had-said-it-all-already-before-Heidegger began to speak, doing so more or less in this fashion: "Ladies (pause), Gentlemen (pause), this (pause) which I have in my hand (pause) is an apple (long pause). You (pause) are seeing it (long pause). But (pause) you see it (pause) from there, where you are (long pause). I (long pause) see the same apple (pause), but from here, from where I am (very long pause). The apple that you see (pause) is different (pause), very different (pause) from the apple that I see (pause). Nevertheless (pause), it is the same apple (murmurs of astonishment)....
>
> What happens (pause) is that you and I (long pause) see it with different perspectives (tableau).[54]

By October 1945, the Ortegas had set up temporary quarters in Madrid, though they continued to spend long stretches of time in Lisbon. After the Ateneo appearance, Ortega and his wife spent the summer in San Sebastián on the northern coast, then returned to Portugal for the winter. There, in a burst of work during spring and early summer of 1947 (Marías estimates that the task occupied eighty days), he wrote almost the entire manuscript of *The Idea of Principle in Leibniz and the Evolution of Deductive Theory*, which appeared, in its final, posthumous form almost a decade later. Portions of it were originally to be published in 1948 as an introduction to the projected first Spanish edition of Leibniz's *Essays* by the Hemeroteca Municipal (Municipal Newspaper Archive) of Madrid. But after Ortega had revised part of the draft and added some pages, other obligations distracted him from that task, which was never completed according to its original plan. The full text as we have it today was found among his papers after his death.[55]

The conditions of its composition (Ortega was working in relative isolation and without a large library at hand) and its obviously unfinished state must be borne in mind, for the book seems at points to reel about from one topic to another. Beginning forthrightly with the matter of principles in Leibniz, it moves into a general definition of the term and then undertakes a prolonged analysis of the difference between physics (as representative of the natural sciences) and philosophy. This leads to a number of chapters on algebra, analytical geometry, logic, and the notion of a "concept." Then, by way of a review of "pre-Cartesian deductive theory," we enter several chapters on Greek thought, with specific reference to the Aristotelian idea of principles as derived from a "sensualist" view of the world. This is interrupted by a "Parenthetical Note on Scholasticisms," defined as any form of uncritically received doctrine; an indictment of the Stoics' worldview follows shortly. Next comes an elaboration of "ideoma" and "draoma," neologisms designed to restate the earlier Orteguian distinction between *ideas* and *creencias*, those ideas one merely "has" and those deeper ones, substrata of convicton, out of which one acts. From there the book moves through familiar territory regarding the role of doubt in the creation of philosophy, its historically contingent career, and its "dramatic" and "jovial" features. Finally, as if to turn back a quarter century to *El tema de nuestro tiempo*, Ortega gives an analysis of "the Cartesian way of thinking." Obviously broken off *in medias res*, the main text is followed by two appendices, "Concerning Optimism in Leibniz" and "Renaissance, Humanism and Counter-Reformation," the latter an interrupted portion of the original draft of the main text.

This forbidding book has received almost no cogent general analysis either by professional philosophers or by specialists on Ortega.[56] One means of entering it is provided by the simple assumption that it gathers up and restates many of its author's predilect themes, particularly those he presumably intended to expound in full in the projected (but never published, and apparently never fully drafted) *Aurora de la razón histórica*. Indeed, Ortega believed that wandering or "migratory" thematic motifs wax and wane within us, and must, if we are lucky enough to catch them in apogee, be enunciated at that moment. In this sense, the root themes of one's life have their own fate, so to say, and recur in varying transformations over long periods of time, much like the memories of childhood courted by the narrator of Proust's *Remembrance of Things Past*. The book on Leibniz is indeed an excellent example of the tenacity of certain of Ortega's earlier themes, set now in a more ambitious historical framework than ever before. Like most of his other writings, it is also a reflection of his relation to his public (or lack of it) and to contemporary history. Precisely in this study of Leibniz, the great theorist of optimism, we must look for Ortega's postwar restatement of what men can hope for as rational beings, since questions of faith and doubt, belief and skepticism, optimism and defeat are woven throughout the text in which Ortega pondered anew the question of philosophy's historical "career" and its possible ending.

As the painter who declares art a bourgeois trinket and the novelist who speculates on the "death" of the novel still continue to seek new forms for their work, the philosopher too, Ortega implied, must expect the form of his pursuits to change over time. Ortega enjoyed pointing out the fundamental absurdity of the very term "philosopher," arguing that originally in early Greek it had been an awkward neologism invented to describe an activity without a clear social function, and that the original situation of this "dislocated" vocation had returned to haunt philosophers throughout history since then. In the study of Leibniz, Ortega aimed to trace the career (what Marías would later call the "biography") of this quasi-utopian calling as a historical series of responses to the human condition, none of which was good for all time. Thus the very early Eleatic assumption of a Being beyond the shifting appearances of the world of becoming, like the later Platonic theory of changeless ideas, simply reflected the Greeks' need for some form of permanence in the midst of flux. Aristotle had developed his own theory of a "Prime Mover" to account for the activity of the world of appearances, and St. Thomas had created from Aristotle a theological version of that same principle. In turn, Descartes, seeking in the *cogito* an invulnerable defense against his fear that an "evil demon" deceived him in the visible world, had committed philosophy to the sovereignty of self-validating cognition. These positions, like others, far from enunciating "eternal" verities, had all been phases of the career of *la razón histórica* or *viviente* ("living" reason).

The fundamental line with which Ortega aligned himself in the tradition was that from Plato through Descartes, Leibniz, and Kant, all exponents of deductive, synthetic reason, which arrives by intuition at those principles that give order to experience. Like the great paradigm shifts and conceptual leaps characteristic, as he had learned, of science at its most creative, so too deductive theory in philosophy must precede and "discover" experience rather than work slavishly from it on the level of sensory evidence. By opposition, the line from Aristotle through the Stoics, Thomas Aquinas, the later Scholastics (including the great Spanish thinker Francisco Suárez), Locke, and (here Ortega takes us by surprise) Heidegger had established a tradition that committed the sin of *petitio principii* by unwarranted inductive reliance on prima facie evidence. In aligning himself with the former group, Ortega meant to affirm philosophical theory as the a priori means of building a conceptually integrated world, an idea that harked back to his youthful definition of philosophy (in *Meditations on Quixote*) as "the general science of love" (Plato's *amor intellectualis*). The particular forms and terms of this theoretical ordering—the key metaphors and tropes of the various philosophers—would of course change from age to age, but the constant in the many avatars of historicized reason must always be its function as a perspective in which man is enabled to make a rational clarification of what would otherwise be the blur of unreflective existence immersed in immediate sense impressions. In the classical world, for Ortega, the "cataleptic imagination" of the

Stoics, a degenerate continuation of the school of Aristotle, was the most egregious instance of a "philosophy of common sense which, take note, is not intelligence but, like everything called 'evidence', is *blind assumption through collective suggestion.*"[57] In the present age, Heidegger presumably repeated the basic error by the unjustified assumption of an ontology that, in Ortega's critique, failed to clarify the various senses of "being" (or "Being") he employed. His error, in Ortega's argument, was to lose in the mists of neologism and etymological play the senses of a term that he intended to clarify by a variation of Aristotle's method of enumeration.

The polemic with Heidegger plays a central role in the later chapters of the book, and is based on Ortega's dubious assumption that his German colleague—falling into a kind of scholasticism—had taken over from Thomistic thought the distinction between "essence" and "existence," thereby "finding" a kind of ready-made and unjustified ontology. In turning to Leibniz, whose work he had long admired as the noblest form of the rationalist phase in post-Cartesian thought, Ortega was ultimately seeking to distinguish his own form of existential analysis from that of other modern philosophers (chiefly Heidegger) who, he believed, lacked the "optimism" he divined in Leibniz's "dynamic conception of being." By the latter he understood the effort to bring the merely possible to self-realization: "Leibniz was the one who first saw clearly that man is not, as is the stone, inside reality in a direct or immediate way. The fact of our being in reality is extremely strange: we are always arriving at it from the outside, from possibilities."[58] In Orteguian terms, we realize the best possible outcome of the manifold possibilities of our existence by moving from a present situation toward a future one according to a chosen project of life. This is not, in Sartre's phrase, to be "condemned to freedom" but rather to embrace it as a condition of openness to life. Such was the essential import of Leibniz's "optimism of being" as Ortega understood it.[59] The "world" constituted by each man's response to life exemplified the good faith of his intention to be as fully as possible what he must be in order to realize his destiny.

In this regard, Ortega believed that existentialist thinkers of a darker cast, like Heidegger and Sartre, had forgotten the role of philosophical doubt as a constructive force. In their irrationalist vision of a world dominated by *Angst,* they failed to remember that skepticism (*askepsis*) was the cleansing gesture of the truly refined thinker. If philosophy is born, in Ortega's view, from the tonic of doubt (which dualizes, divides, from *duo, dudare*, etc.), it can maintain its authenticity only by refusing to accept as given a particular impression of the human situation. Thus Ortega rejected that type of contemporary thought (especially in the now prominent work of Sartre) which pivoted on the need to "engage" or commit oneself. For him, this act of commitment was the very contradiction of a genuinely philosophical attitude, which consisted in the "negative capability" *not* to commit oneself but to remain open to further analysis. The *engagé* thinkers, for whom Kierkegaard had provided the basic model, had mistaken the Danish thinker's religious position for his philosophical one. In religion, the "leap of faith" was quite acceptable, in fact necessary; in philosophy, it was the death of true speculation. (Similarly, when Aristotle and the medieval Scholastics had posited principles based on induction, Ortega felt they had made a disastrous jump to unjustified "first things.")

In his dissent from the fashionable idea of engagement, Ortega showed once more his temperamental disagreement with those whose philosophy turned on anxiety, homelessness, and the threat of despair. He argued that though we think in order to save ourselves from the "shipwreck" (*naufragio*) of our projects, philosophy itself cannot be conceived in a desperate state, back against the wall. In order to retain its "liberating" power, it has to achieve some independence from the struggle out of which it is born. Therefore, its origin, like that of culture in general, is in "joviality," the attitude the Greeks called proper to Jove. If philosophy can be seen as a quasi-divine, sportive venture in which we deploy our spontaneous energy above and beyond attention to survival and the completion of pragmatic tasks, then it is so, in one sense, by virtue of its "natural" status as an inherent feature of human being. Aristotle, arguing that man desires by nature to know, had identified the beginning of philosophy in the experience of "wonder" or "curiosity" before the world. But Heidegger, rejecting the inauthenticity that resulted from the trivialization of this impulse, had asserted that man as *Dasein*—as the only kind of being in the world that can and must do so—had always asked after Being. For Ortega, who also revised Aristotle in this sense, Heidegger's critique was telling, though his position seemed both unreasonably dehistoricized and marred by a generalized "inflation" of the concept of Being. Ortega's own insistence on philosophy as an undertaking that began "one fine day in Greece" and would doubtless someday end did not deny man's natural condition as one of estrangement from the world, but any inquiry into being was for him a metaphysical task to be conducted within the historically contingent framework of philosophy as a series of thought experiments, ultimately temporary solutions to the constituent dilemma of man's "homelessness." If Heidegger saw human existence as the arena in which the question of Being is raised, his view of this drama seemed paradoxically timeless, quite unlike the Diltheyan "biography" of philosophy Ortega attempted in *The Idea of Principle in Leibniz*: "Heidegger clearly recognizes that, in general, man is historical, but he does not do this well in his analysis of any individual theme." [60]

If Ortega's historicist perspective became clear in his writings of the mid-1920s, by the time of *What Is Philosophy?* in 1929 he had begun, under the impact of reading Heidegger, to develop his own progressively independent understanding of the "antinaturalistic" nature of cognition as something that man, far from having it as part of his "nature," had to achieve against the grain, as it were. This idea led him, with help from Dilthey and the later Scheler, toward the radically historicized *Idea of Principle in Leibniz*.[61] By the late chapters of the book, particularly in "El nivel de nuestro radicalismo" (The Level of Our Roots), he could write:

[M]an is *a nativitate* estranged from the world; he is a stranger in it, a foreigner ... notwithstanding that he has not always been occupied in philosophizing, and moreover, has almost never done it. This initial error proliferates in Heidegger and forces him to maintain that man *is* philosophy and this—one more error—because man, in the face of the world's failure as a combination of *chattels and playthings*, of things-that-are-useful, discovers that these do not really belong to him, while at the same time they have a Being of their own and man's Being consists in asking about them and demanding them.... It is not true that man has always been asking himself about Being. On the contrary he did not ask himself about Being until after 480 B.C., and then it was a matter of a certain number of men in a certain number of places. It is no use to stuff philosophy with illusions.... Heidegger's exaggeration of the concept of Being becomes obvious if one notes that his formula "man has always asked himself about Being" or "*is* a question about Being" makes sense only if by Being we understand everything about which man has asked himself; that is to say, if we make of Being the great illusion, the "bonne à tout faire" and the *omnibus* concept.[62]

To be more precise, Ortega charged Heidegger to distinguish between a serious understanding of Being "*in modo recto*" and the more ridiculous one "*in modo obliquo*," for "[t]he difference between the two ways is decisive: because if we understand *being* as formally, terminologically Being, then it is wholly false that 'the comprehension of Being' is inborn in man, and if we understand *being* as anything that man has understood, then Heidegger has not said anything at all."[63] Ortega could now claim his (or "our") "serious" position as a mature form of the antinaturalistic cognitive enterprise different both from the theoretically "playful" Greeks and the ultimately "confused" Heidegger.

The seriousness of which Ortega spoke was, however, a spirited and heroic one, after the manner of Nietzsche, as becomes, clear in the chapter entitled "The Jovial Side of Philosophy." There Ortega distinguishes philosophy from the historically earlier triad of myth, poetry, and religion, all forms of belief "among which there exists a perfect continuity, so that their reciprocal frontiers are indistinguishable."[64] In coming after the mythopoeic view of the world, philosophy was a hermeneutical rather than an explanatory undertaking, a problematic effort to uncover and examine "fundamentals." As such, it must remain free to play with possible interpretations, preserving its "acrobatic" spirit. (Here Ortega felicitously fused his earlier "sportive" with his later more "serious" understanding of the operation of thought in the world.) Yet once philosophy appeared on the historical stage and moved inevitably away from belief toward theory, it became, in its passionate play, the most serious and authentic way of "confronting the enigma of living."[65] In other words, "philosophy is born and reborn when man loses his faith or his system of traditional beliefs, and therefore falls into doubts at the moment when he believes himself to be in possession of a new *way* or method for emerging from this doubt. In faith one is, into doubt one falls, and in philosophy one emerges out of this to the Universe."[66] Having passed through other kinds of understanding before beginning to philosophize some five centuries before Christ, man is duty-bound to pursue philosophy until something better is discovered, always recognizing that no perspective is entirely adequate to the task of "uncovering" truth. In this sense, the history of philosophy becomes a kind of graveyard of attempted solutions to the dilemma of living, though we can understand our own situation only by examining of the once-live projects behind the names and terms of the illustrious dead.

The effort to reconstruct the succession of man's "landings" from the energizing sea of doubts in which he is obliged ever again to swim is not, we must remember, a grim enumeration of failures. In the recreation of former systems, as in the elaboration of our own in the present, we discover that theory as intellectual gaiety becomes antidotal to the melancholy error of the *engagé* thinker and the Heideggerian pessimist. In Ortega's view, the essential failure of the philosophy of *Angst* was its monochromatic quality, its betrayal of the many-sidedness of truth:

> On whichever side one takes existentialism, one sees that the other side, the opposite, is equally true and basic. For example, the World as the *unheimlich*, the "strange" and disquieting. Good; already in Dilthey the World is proclaimed as *resistance*, but one does not stop there. On being resisted, the World reveals itself to me as "other than I" and as being that other. But on rejecting this, I discover that in the World there is also something "good," favorable, useful, pleasant. A shipwrecked man, I yearn for that wonderful feeling which is the "resistance" of solid ground. Because the World is not only a great sea in which I am drowning, but also a beach that I can reach. In short, the World as resistance to me, shows me the World as "assistance." If it were only *unheimlich*, disquieting, unfamiliar, I would already have left it, and the sentiment of "unfamiliarity or disquiet" would not exist unless its opposite—the cozy and restful—were also existing. So the World is equally rough weather and warm hearth.
>
> I do not, then, believe in the "tragic sense of life" as the ultimate form of human existence. Life is not, cannot be a tragedy. It is within life that tragedies are produced and are possible.[67]

In affirming the "playful" theory born of doubt, Ortega, doubtless remembering Johan Huizinga's portrait of *homo ludens*, perhaps overstated the jovial side of things and the "optimism" of Leibniz in order to counterbalance a prevalent, even fashionable mood of much postwar European thought. In any case, the philosopher, he believed, was obliged to deny himself the dull comfort of "residing" in the truth. Such certainty was really tantamount to despair of the endless quest of philosophy. The "engaged" position may be considered the desperate posture of those who feel life's absurdity and rebel against it; but, for Ortega, that was the barbarian's way, incidentally not unlike the crude simplicity of the Aristotelian-Scholastic insistence on direct intuition of reality through sensual-empirical induction. By contrast, he affirmed, one came to principles only through the inspired leaps of theory, taken from a metaphysical springboard. From such theory are deduced the constructs of philosophy, science, and poetry, none of which directly reflects the world or can be induced from empirical evidence alone.

Ortega's critique of existential *Angst* as a kind of wrongly posited first principle was essentially the same one he brought against the entire empiricist-sensualist tradition. The fault in question was the "vulgar" assumption (a form of commonsense belief) that reality is what lies under our noses, and may adequately be grasped through direct observation. This debased philosophy amounted to an acceptance of mere *doxa* (popular opinion), whereas Ortega affirmed that true philosophy was *paradoxa*. As such, "it *began and consists...* precisely in denying to the senses the jurisdiction of truth," for they constitute the realm of the *idola fori* (the idols of the marketplace).[68] The "cataleptic" entrancement of the Stoics with sensory eivdence, for example, was hopelessly at odds with the mind's noble ability to discover principles that, in their deductive sweep, enable man to map new dimensions of reality.

This distinction between common sense and the "aristocratic" thought of the true theorist returned to Ortega's much-worked rubrics of "ideas" and "beliefs," only this time with positive emphasis on idea-as-theory and a downgrading of belief-as-opinion. Whereas the earlier analysis had stressed the indispensable substrate of beliefs upon which we must base our lives, depicting ideas as shifting surface currents of little vital consequence, the two terms underwent a semantic shift in the Leibniz study: belief as it emerged from the empiricist-sensualist tradition would always be impoverished, while ideas (harking back to the Platonic and Neoplatonic tradition) were indispensable for the discovery of reality. Thus Ortega could claim that Augustine was far superior to St. Thomas as a philosopher, casting the latter as merely the "unsurpassable *administrator* of the Greco-Arabic-Gothic philosophic heritage."[69] The root problem for medieval Scholastic thought, in his view, was its nature as received doctrine, assimilated Aristotelianism adapted to the demands of faith in search of rational explanation. What might have become a truly *Christian* philosophy animated by a profound faith became instead, under the aegis of Aristotle, a form of *fides quaerens intellectum*, taking as its official philosopher a "man of science," a "radically naturalistic and profane thinker."[70] Aristotle's methodological course from sense observation to principles (e.g., from observed cases of rational human behavior to the principle that man is a rational animal) necessitated an unwarranted jump. For Scholastic philosophers, it could be explained by one or another deus ex machina, like the Jesuit Francisco Suárez's posited *lumen naturale*, which allowed men to believe they discerned the divine principle implicit in sense data.[71] In Aristotle and Suárez, then, principle was the beginning rather than the end point of theory.

Convinced that each moment of culture, like each human life, must be seen in its unique, unrepeatable circumstances, Ortega evoked the atmosphere of Athenian public life—"an infinite *tertulia*"—where, he added, a gentle climate and places propitious for endless conversation stimulated much of Greek thought. But "[a]ll of that is a unique venture not made for exportation."[72] From the circumstantial uniqueness of Greek thought derived the absurdity of the Scholastic attempt to revive it in the chill cells and cloisters of European monasteries centuries later. Just as no man's life could be lived by another, the Greek "venture" could not really be restaged. Yet the Scholastics had tried to do just that by squeezing a once-vigorous faith into the intellectual iron maiden they built out of Greek philosophy. Thus, so-called Christian "philosophy" was actually an inauthentic fusion of Greek ontology and the supra-rational faith of the Middle Ages. To call this anomalous historical hybrid the "perennial philosophy," as modern neo-Thomists did, seemed to Ortega a *contradictio in adjecto*. For the Aristotelian-Thomistic tradition to be truly perennial, it would have to come to terms with modern secular thought. Outside of a dialectical relationship with other forms of thought, it became little more than an ossified curiosity anachronistically surviving in the present, a fate of which Ortega found abundant evidence in the contemporary Spanish intellectual climate. Medieval theologians, he averred, might better have developed a theology frankly founded on faith qua faith. In this argument, Ortega seems to have made a considerable oversimplification of the actual historical marriage of faith with rationalistic theology, though there was validity in his charge that the confluence of Greek and medieval thought in Scholasticism bequeathed a strange legacy to the later Church.

The French historian of philosophy Alain Guy points out that Ortega had not always been as critical of Scholasticism as he was in this study. For example, in *En torno a Galileo*, he had positively appraised medieval philosophy as, in Guy's words, the "progressive triumph of reason and even of humano-centrism."[73] Ortega asserted there that St. Anselm's insistence on reason as a positive adjunct to faith was crucial for the maturity of rational thought. The integration or cooperation of faith would, ideally, strengthen both. Also in that book he had seen St. Thomas as a great humanist who proclaimed the rights of rationalism and made God accessible to reason. By contrast, the Leibniz critique of Scholasticism defined it rather ahistorically as any form of received ideas. In the final analysis, it was a generic phenomenon of human culture to be found wherever there was a sclerotic hardening of thought into transmissible doctrine. But as Guy wisely objects, Ortega's insistence on the ever-renewed beginning of philosophy in skeptical inquiry emphasizes the existential source of thought at the expense of its history, for not even the first philosophers could begin wholly anew. All had received some kind of inherited repertoire of problems, assumptions, and definitions from the respective cultural situations in which they arose.

The Idea of Principle in Leibniz argued centrally that Plato, Descartes, Leibniz, and Kant were the great exemplars of the way reason works on empirical reality. Finally, there was no "proof" that Aristotle's empirically derived principles were inferior, but Ortega trusted more what he called the Platonic inclination to "flee" the world of sensory evidence in order to catch it, as it were, by surprise, returning to it obliquely from the perspective of myth or archetype. While Aristotle took sensory evidence at face value, Plato preferred the visionary order of forms (ideas). In a similar fashion, Leibniz's metaphysics rested in the realm of "possibles," from which reality presumably comes to be. While Aristotle made mere *idola fori* the point of departure for his descriptive, casuistic work, Plato, by supreme contrast, established theory as the opposite of accepted *creencias*, which were the mere "opinions" of the shadow-world of the cave. To Plato, Ortega reminds us, we owe the truth that philosophy must fly in the very face of what normally "one says" (*se dice*) or "one does" (*se hace*). He pointed out that this distance of theory from the realm of ordinary usage and custom was largely responsible for the classic charge against the philosopher that he cares too little for worldly affairs. However, the fact was that concern for the truth led philosophy (though not necessarily the philosopher as a human being) away from the immediate sensory world in the name of understanding it better:

> When Plato wants to know a thing that is close to him, his first action is to run off in the opposite direction, separate himself from it completely, go beyond the stars, and then, coming back as from a "supercelestial place," he sees what can be said with meaning about the things of this world which are so meaningless. This Platonic *flight in order to approach* seems to me the most inspired invention of a theoretic nature which has been produced on this planet.... Plato's method is basically paradoxical, as every great philosophy perforce must be. Aristotle and his time adopted an opposite method, which coincides with public opinion and common sense.[74]

The insistence that man qua philosopher must separate himself from the world of daily commerce with his fellow man became a tenet of this book—a study written in the partial exile of Lisbon and out of Ortega's determination to devote his remaining years to a kind of work from which, he now believed, the imperative needs of postwar Spain had consistently diverted him. But the aloofness of the late "autumnal" book on deductive theory sounds odd in a man who had spent decades before 1936 building a philosophical culture for his native public:

> It is not the man who philosophizes but philosophy itself which detaches itself from ... others. It does not need them, as does poetry, which is essentially a matter of speaking to another and needs that other, even an anonymous and indeterminate other. Nor is it, like science, in need of collaboration. Philosophy is not a form of speaking to another, but of talking to oneself. It is not a business of sociability but a need for solitude. Philosophy is a form of playing Robinson Crusoe. This is especially so because the philosophic Crusoe does not live on a desert island but on a "deserted island" where previous inhabitants have all died. It is an Island of the Dead, of dead philosophers, the only companions whom philosophy in its solitude needs and will traffic with.[75]

The search for a systematic statement of high theory in the later years involved perhaps an august rationalization of Ortega's realization that, as a survivor of a vanished era, he had no true circumstantial base for his work. It is true that the impulse to turn away from a more public role had surfaced often before and had been progressively noticeable in his thinking since his disillusionment with politics under Primo de Rivera, although the arrival of the Republic had brought him back briefly to his earlier dream of a more worldly role for intellect. But the desire manifest in *The Idea of Principle in Leibniz* to develop a philosophy in communion with the great shades sprang from Ortega's forced separation from the community of his contemporaries, from the "vital project" that had prompted his most seminal work. However "derivative" that work may have been, in the sense that he had absorbed key ideas from others' texts—and what major thinker does not do so?—nonetheless it had been "original" because it sprang from and addressed a world that was authentically his own. Before 1936, Ortega had indeed "saved" his circumstances. Paradoxically, as he tried in the Leibniz study to make his own mark among the other creators of "big books," he appeared as more of a professional philosopher, a member of the guild, than as the unique intellectual voice he had previously been in and for Spain. As Cerezo trenchantly puts it, "Ortega had died as an intellectual in the collective death of Spain."[76] Having begun his career with grand hopes for the power of thought in the world, Ortega at work in Lisbon believed that the function of reason as a guide to action had changed radically. But, revolted and pained by the spectacle of ruin to which his own culture had been reduced, he was in fact admitting, whether he knew it or not, that the golden hour of his life and of his generation had passed forever.

8

THE FINAL YEARS: 1948–1955

While Ortega's dark asides in *The Idea of Principle in Leibniz* on the "village culture" of the Spanish capital provide a hint about his more personal thoughts upon return from exile, they do not begin to suggest the unspoken agonies of millions of Spaniards which lay behind the cultural decadence that offended and disheartened him. Nor could one infer from his efforts to establish himself again in Spain after 1945 the actual condition of the nation's intellectual life under the pall of Francoist ideology and censorship. The extreme poverty and political repression that scarred and crushed the lives of so many Spaniards in those years of halting recovery from the war found its cultural analogue in the miserable condition of secondary and university education, journalism, publishing, libraries, and scholarship. The wealthy few, who had indeed survived the war in a state of "indecent health," might well be untroubled by such things, but Ortega could hardly expect his work to thrive in that atmosphere. If he had worried over the absence of a sufficient middle-class public for his ideas before the war, he discovered that the situation was much worse in the late 1940s. The exciting intellectual atmosphere of Madrid in the 1920s and 1930s was gone; in its place stood a bomb-scarred city faced with enormous problems of daily survival and a ruthlessly repressive regime.

Even as Ortega resolutely pursued the august history of reason since the time of Descartes, Spain had entered the period, in the words of one historian, of the "fascist university," the moment when Spanish higher education "had reached its lowest point in modern history: over-bureaucratized, corrupt, legalistic, unexpanding, rigid, and, worst of all, dogmatic and poor."[1] Since Franco's victory, the universities had become virtually confessional: priests and laymen imposed Aristotle, St. Thomas, and Suárez as the bases for thought and morals; religious education was obligatory; and the Opus Dei, founded as a small Catholic lay organization in 1928, played an increasingly prominent role in the founding of *colegios mayores* and as the dominant force within the government-sponsored Consejo Superior de Investigaciones Científicas (CSIC), established in 1939 to administer a network of foundations, institutes, journals, and scholarly activities. The CSIC promoted an orthodoxy of outlook aimed at reestablishing a Christian unity of the sciences, crowned, as in the Middle Ages, by the queenly discipline of theology. The Opus Dei, privileged by its close ties to this powerful organization and promoting a quasi-monastic ethos of self-forgetful service, attracted many of the brightest young men of the postwar intelligentsia. The rapidly growing lay order thus became an indispensable part of the cultural program of National Catholicism, as the movement to unite state and church was called. Offering physical confirmation of cultural decline, a new, red brick university city was being built in an insipid "official" style on the western outskirts of Madrid, where the prewar campus and buildings had been destroyed during the Nationalist siege. One now entered this precinct through a triumphal arch commemorating Franco's victory of 1939.

The self-seeking and ambitious among postwar Spanish intellectuals, while defaming the culture of the prewar liberals, set about to create a new ideology based on the wholesale condemnation of the modern liberal and Europeanizing tradition. In its place they promoted a selective celebration of "glorious" episodes from the distant past. History was rewritten to perpetuate the myth that Spain had detoured, somewhere in the seventeenth century, from her sacred path as the imperial defender and propagator of the faith. The eighteenth and nineteenth centuries were dismissed as contrary to the real spirit of the nation, reinforcing the idea, prevalent in another form when Ortega began his career, that Spanish history after 1600 was a story of decadence and error. But while the Generation of 1914 had exploited this myth in order to dramatize its program of cultural modernization, it had clearly continued the work of the Krausists, Giner de los Ríos, and the Generation of 1898. Postwar Catholic intellectuals, by contrast, worked to bury that legacy. Instead, they taught, as Raymond Carr and Juan Pablo Fusi remark, that

[t]he task of the historian was to glorify Castile as the "hammer of here-
tics," as the austere architect of a national unity based on religious uni-
formity. This was combined with the new regime's vision of itself as the
heir to the imperial tradition. The result was a proliferation of works on
the Catholic kings, the discovery of America and the soldier-saint
Loyola, founder of the Jesuit order.[2]

In other cultural areas, literary critics and poets turned for inspiration to the work of Garcilaso, Lope de Vega, and Cervantes; painters chose to accentuate pious religiosity and return to the representational mode decried by Ortega in *The Dehumanization of Art*;
and architects busied themselves in imposing on Madrid prominent
examples of the "Escorial style" favored by the government.

The work of such postwar reform was greatly facilitated by the
disappearance, in exile or in death, of thousands of the most gifted
teachers, writers, historians, and artists of the prewar period. What
some have called the "silver age" of Spanish culture had been, both
in Castile and Catalonia, the brightest efflorescence of talent since
the sixteenth century. Beginning with the writers of 1898, it had developed vigorously with Ortega's generation and had produced, in
the Generation of 1927, a group of poets comparable only to the
major figures of the golden age. The major universities in Madrid
and Barcelona had kept pace with this remarkable concentration
and growth of cultural energies. But the close of the civil war found
most of the country's prewar university teachers either dead or in
exile. In fact, as José Maravall has noted, "[b]etween 1939 and
1944, one hundred and fifty-five professors acceptable to the regime
were appointed—56 per cent of all professors in Spanish universities in 1944."[3] Thus mediocre intellectuals and government
toadies were allowed to fill the posts of illustrious predecessors.
Second-rate Catholic critics and thinkers rose to eminence, finding
in the new regime the shelter they had lacked under the Republic.
A vapid traditionalistic theology poured from unfortunately inspired pens, and the Spanish clergy—as distinguished from some
outstanding lay Catholics—became the most reactionary of any
in Europe. All the while, the regime strengthened its ties with the
Vatican, making an agreement as early as 1941 to govern the
appointment of Spanish clergy, and establishing in 1943 the Ley de
Ordenación de la Universidad Española, which specified that
"[t]he university shall adapt its teaching to Catholic dogma and

morality and to the norms of canonic law in force."[4] This strategy to build a strong, united, and Catholic nation sought to recapture the spirit of imperial Spain, militant vanguard of the Counter-Reformation. The modern "crusade" culminated in the postwar years with the Madrid-Rome Concordat of 1953, establishing Roman Catholicism as the state religion and giving Franco the power to nominate the bishops of the Spanish church.

Well before the Concordat—in fact even before the civil war had concluded—a legal structure had been established to guarantee state control of education. In November 1937, Franco had stated, "No Catholic university will be needed because all our universities will be Catholic and a religious higher education will be provided by them." The Ley de Ordenación spelled out the postwar conditions of university life, adding to the establishment of Catholic dogma and morals the stipulations that teaching must accord with the program of the Falange, that university rectors must be appointed from among professors who were "militants of Falange," and that "a single and state-controlled student union, the Sindicato Español Universitario (SEU), was to be in charge of the indoctrination of students into the 'spirit' of the Falange." The SEU, a prewar fascist union, was organized after 1939 "on the same pattern as the official state-controlled trade unions... that is, it followed the lines of the *corporazioni* of Fascist Italy." The Ley de Ordenación also declared that "the University is the theological army to fight heresy and the creator of the missionary phalanx that must affirm Catholic unity." As Minister of Education Ibañez Martín had noted in introducing the law to the Spanish parliament:

> What is indeed important from a political point of view... is to eradicate from teaching and from scientific creation ideological neutrality and to banish laicism, to train a new youth imbued with that Augustinian principle that science does not bring one any closer to the Supreme being.[5]

During the postwar period, religious instruction formed a fundamental part of all education from the primary school on up. But since the university had so often before the war been the source of inflammatory protest, particularly under Primo de Rivera, higher education provided the most glaring example of the regime's intention to suppress intellectual freedom. The historian and journalist

Max Gallo writes:

> Orthodoxy prevailed everywhere; by plundering untranslated foreign
> works, Spanish scholars built up reputations that were unassailable.
> ...Students, at their examinations, had to produce their teachers'
> lessons word for word. Praise of Francoism, or of the thirteenth century,
> considered as the golden age of Western civilization, had to be accepted
> without argument. Tracts were even distributed in certain universities
> demanding the restoration of death by fire, as under the Inquisition. In
> crucial subjects such as history and philosophy, the systematic distortion
> of facts was the rule, and whole sectors of these diciplines disappeared or
> were condemned in the name of Spanish Catholicism and its traditions.
> The period was one of intellectual asphyxia. Yet the student body did
> not react....Their topics of conversation were football, films and
> women. The better pupils learnt what they were taught; their gift was
> for repetition rather than for invention or criticism. Those in opposition
> were a tiny minority.[6]

Yet despite these conditions and the dreams of many ecclesiastics
that Spain would again become the pope's arm in the world, there
was growing debate among Catholic intellectuals as the postwar
period advanced. The most enlightened of them tended to be either
former students of Ortega's or sympathetic readers of his work. He
himself had generally maintained a discreet silence toward the
Spanish Catholic intellectual tradition and the role of the Church
in national life, although his pointed critique of Scholasticism and
neo-Scholasticism in the book on Leibniz can certainly be read, in
part, as a response to the dominant tenor of postwar Catholic
thought in Spain.

The critical vanguard of intellectual (and, eventually, organized
political) resistance was largely constituted by old Falangists still
engaged by the ideals of the movement and increasingly critical of
the evolution of the Francoist state, which was working to edge the
Falange to the sidelines. Men like Dionisio Ridruejo (Franco's director general of propaganda from 1938 to 1940), Antonio Tovar,
and Pedro Laín Entralgo were conscious that their original hopes
for social reform were not to be met by a state rapidly moving
toward the restitution of old privileges and, in due time, toward a
capitalistic economy. For them, Ortega was a congenial figure
whose writings, quite apart from the issue of political differences,
provided the obvious model of excellence in modern Spanish prose.

Some years later, in 1953, Ridruejo would write in the liberalizing weekly *Revista* (not the prewar *Revista de Occidente*, which would not begin publication again until 1963) a tribute to Ortega's seventieth birthday: "Is there in Spain a single man dedicated with the least seriousness to the tasks of the spirit who does not have to recognize himself, in some degree, a disciple of Ortega, who does not ... have a debt to pay to Ortega."[7] Like Ridruejo, whose own political development remains perhaps more interesting than that of any other figure of the postwar years, many sincere national syndicalists in the Falangist ranks attempted to incorporate certain ideas from the great liberal philosopher into an ideological program that would offer an appealing alternative to National Catholicism and to the atheistic Marxism that later animated the radical left in its opposition to the regime. As it became clearer that Franco had no intention of accepting Falangist proposals for reforms such as the creation of labor syndicates and the nationalization of banks, the more sensitive minds in the Falange became openly critical of the prevailing atmosphere of cultural mediocrity, official corruption, and bureaucratic mindlessness.

The appearance in 1941 of the magazine *Escorial* (edited by Ridruejo and Laín) was a clear sign of the enlightened Falangists' desire for a unified Spain healed of its war scars and nourished once again by its best traditions. Here too the influence of Ortega's earlier work was indirectly evident. Laín, who was a devoted reader of the philosopher's essays, wrote prose that often seemed a slightly pedantic, more pedestrian imitation of the master's own. But, more important, *Escorial*'s concern with a national unification aimed at overcoming the deep rifts created by the war clearly echoed Ortega's own prewar call for the "nationalization" of politics above and beyond partisan interests. In the atmosphere of 1941, it was a brave venture. Most of the *Escorial* essayists helped the magazine to survive by discreetly avoiding overt criticism of the regime; indeed they even shared, on the surface, its professed commitment to the revitalization of Christian culture in Spain. However, while Laín remained a devout Catholic, it could not be said that the politically liberalizing Falangists as a group were primarily concerned with Catholic values, except insofar as they could be construed as support for a social and political program that inclined some of the bolder reformers toward democratic socialism. This relative ideological openness allowed them to see Ortega's essentially a-Catholic writings as a model of intellectual excellence and moral integrity.

In general, postwar Spanish intellectual responses to Ortega's work were divided between the sympathetic liberals and the sharply antagonistic conservatives and reactionaries. Several of his most astute followers among liberal Catholics (Laín, Julián Marías, and José Luis Aranguren, for example) were and have continued to be men not averse to criticism of the institutional role of the Church and the clerisy in the postwar Spain. They have stood for an intellectually rigorous reading of Ortega, tending to argue that the hostile label of "secular relativist" badly misconstrues a man whose work they perceive as a complement to the most essential ethical teachings of Catholic Christianity.[8] Of course, this view often—particularly in the case of Marías—glossed over the master's lack of interest in religious questions; but in the restrictive atmosphere of the postwar Catholic state, such disciples and interpreters of his work have been both his fairest Spanish critics and his staunchest defenders.

Opposed to the liberal Catholic continuators of Ortega's work who emerged in the 1940s stood a large number of traditional Catholics who saw in him an undesirable, even a perfidious, influence in Spanish culture. Several of them joined an attack on him after his death in an attempt to reduce his growing reputation as one of the nation's greatest modern writers. Numerous others throughout the 1940s and early 1950s vilified him, Unamuno, and other leaders of prewar liberal opinion. Debate between the traditionalists and the more liberal critics was, in microcosm, a kind of intellectual civil war. The clash may be read as a revealing chapter in modern Spanish intellectual life, a sign of its politicized and bitterly polemical tone after 1939.[9] Reading the old-guard Catholics, one finds an intense and defensive dislike of Ortega, whose work they attempt to link with the Krausist legacy. Some of those who struck at this tradition even lent credence to reports of a conspiracy of international Masonry behind all Spain's ills in the last century and a half.[10] Also, certain Catholic intellectuals argued that Ortega, his followers, and the *Revista de Occidente* writers generally, constituted a kind of cultural "establishment" that had sought to impose on the nation its own hierarchy of intellectual and moral judgments. Conservative Catholics were not alone in this critique; however, what distinguished theirs from other assessments was an astonishing lack of intellectual integrity.

Although the cultural atmosphere of Madrid in the 1940s seemed, on the whole, quite unpromising for Ortega's hopes of reestablishing himself there, he planned, shortly after his initial return in 1945, to found a journal called *Estudios de Humanidades* and devoted to a reexamination of those studies that could be grouped under the venerable Ciceronian rubric "humanities." The idea was to break through the abstract "crust" of the term in order to discover its original nucleus: "human-ities," human things, *de rebus humanis*. The project much resembled what Ortega had sketched out almost two decades earlier in his lecture "Mission of the University," when he had called for a fundamental reorganization of higher learning. With extensive help from Julián Marías, he hoped to bring out the first number by June 1947. However, long delays by potential contributors to the issue caused the eventual abandonment of the project altogether. Quickly taking a new tack, he and Marías established the Instituto de Humanidades under the legal shelter of the already existing Aula Nueva de Preparación Universitaria, a private tutoring center for pre-university students established in 1940 by Marías, his wife-to-be Dolores Franco, Soledad Ortega, José Ortega Spottorno, and others. Uncertain of the reception the Instituto would receive if presented under Ortega's name as an independent venture, he and Marías managed to launch it as a nominal extension of the Aula.

Envisioning the new undertaking as a center for research, seminars, and lectures for a public restricted both by relatively erudite subject matter and substantial matriculation fees, Ortega announced in his statement of purpose:

> We do not address ourselves to the public, nor do we seek it out. The purpose is to form a completely private collaborative group that does not pretend to exercise the least influence on national life nor to practice proselytism.... The major part of the themes that will occupy us automatically exclude, by their very character, large audiences. We are inviting a certain number of people to work in a corner apart.[11]

At the same time, reflecting on the changing social role of the intellectual, Ortega criticized those whose pride in individual possession of knowledge made them arrogant:

The vanity of knowledge, and, even more generally, intellectual vanity, is today a formally anachronistic attitude. Man's present situation makes it impossible as a normal passion. The reasons are many, but ... it is important to point out three. First: the interests of the masses, no matter to what social class they belong, predominate almost exclusively in ... all countries. There is, thus, no public attention left to contemplate the intellectuals, to evaluate them according to a hierarchy of merit, and to applaud their activities. Second, the very intellectual function of knowing has ceased to be, as it was until recently, a *performance*, an exercise of skill and virtuosity before which people retained the role of spectators charged with witnessing the acrobatics, admiring and applauding its performers.... The third reason is the most intimate: ... It was not plausible that, human life having come to a situation as critical as the present one, solely the sciences and the intellectual function should enjoy a tranquil and satisfying frame of mind.[12]

In a time when European cultural traditions had been either destroyed or shaken to their roots for the second time in three decades, Ortega argued that the old style, from which he wished to dissociate himself, really belonged to the generation preceding his own:

> The last generation in which this [showmanship] happened fully was that of Unamuno and Bernard Shaw.... So it is that in their magnificent gesticulation, constantly referred to a public of spectators, they seem like grand "musical eccentrics" of thought, knowledge, and letters. Note that this diagnosis does not involve any censorship. They fulfilled their destiny being that way, as we would fail in ours by trying to repeat that "number."[13]

Despite the high matriculation fees—there was no other means of support—650 students registered for Ortega's first Instituto course, given in the capacious quarters of the fashionable Madrid club Círculo de la Unión Mercantil in the fall and winter of 1948–1949. Announced as "Sobre una nueva interpretación de la historia universal. (Exposición y examen de la obra de A. Toynbee, *A Study of History*)" (On a New Interpretation of Universal History. [Exposition and Examination of the work of, etc.]), the lectures were ostensibly a critique of Arnold Toynbee's great work-in-progress (1934–1954); but in fact Ortega used them to develop his own still-fragmentary philosophy of history as a critique of and in contrast to the English historian's pattern of "universal" history.

Toynbee's uncompleted magnum opus was much in vogue in those years, but, like many other contemporary European writers, he was still little known in Spain. The audience was widely mixed, running the gamut from ladies and gentlemen of high society to university students eager to hear this by-now-legendary figure of Spanish letters. Ortega was quite aware of the oddly variegated public, to whom he addressed many cajoling asides throughout the series. Indeed, he might well have applied to this occasion a definition of public lectures which he had formulated many years earlier:

> Every lecture ... is an animal, an individual organ that has its possible biography of a life that usually lasts an hour. What the orator says is only one of the organs of that fleeting being, perhaps only the skeleton.... [A lecture consists of] the coughs, the collective stirring, the tension of curiosity in a dangerous curve drawn by the orator's monologue, or the fatigue that suddenly comes over the public. And a door that squeaks, and a flicker in the light bulbs, so dramatic, which passes like a shadowy threat. And then that terrible abyss that unexpectedly opens before the speaker when he finds himself without the word on which to stand and waves his arms in mortal fright ... or the magnificent, heavy, meaty, pliable paragraph that swells marvelously in the air like a great balloon, and, suddenly—ding! ding!—the six, the seven strikes of the clock which lance it, perforating it and making it lose its gas. Or else the sheaf of lost notes and the consequent dive of the orator into the high tide of his papers; after swimming to the bottom, he breaks the surface with the elusive pearl between his teeth.[14]

Characteristic of Ortega's acute sense of the drama of the spoken word, this passage also points up his constant temptation to posturing before a diverse and largely uninformed public. Despite his protest that culture must not be a show put on by the elect few for the benighted multitude, Ortega often recurred to his deep sense of theatricality in order to capture his public.

Ortega's strategy in the lectures was to use the English historian's theses to build his own countercritique of a philosophy of history. From the start, his attitude toward Toynbee was ambivalent. On the one hand, he was obliged to recognize the man's greatness and to admire him as a representative of English culture; on the other, he suggested that Toynbee's pretensions to the novel profession of "internationalist" might distort his historical perspective by causing him to overlook the way his judgments were rooted in his British circumstances. Later in the series, this critique led Ortega to reflections on the English concern with world empire as the paradoxical result of a markedly provincial and ethnocentric sense of culture. In the long run, he felt, Toynbee erred by presuming to make the whole world an arena for his donnish, Oxfordian ruminations. At stake here, of course, were Ortega's own most intimate questions about the place of modern Spain in the world, for Spaniards had once laid claim to an empire as universal as that which the English were in the process of losing. Further, the modish calling of "internationalist" was largely the result of increased media of travel and communication; and Ortega noted, using Toynbee for a measuring stick, that this new "closeness" of previously disparate and distant parts of the world might delude intellectuals into claiming a greater understanding of things than was in fact possible.

Any historian who pretended to sketch general patterns for the rise and decline of world civilizations must work with special care, distrusting his system more than Ortega felt Toynbee had done. Over a decade before the Toynbee lectures, in 1937, Ortega had written from exile in Paris to his friend Ernst Robert Curtius in Germany, enunciating the reasons for extreme care in construing a nation's history as it were "from within," a statement that may also suggest why Ortega refused to speak out publicly for either side in the civil war then raging in Spain:

> What is secret, that is, what is destined to silence, is of two kinds. There are things ineffable because they are too elemental or simple: they tolerate neither analysis nor, therefore, verbal expression. They are the "infra-tacit." But there are secrets whose ineffability proceeds inversely from all that it would be necessary to say in order to speak of them. Strictly speaking, everything historical is of this sort. For that reason, there has not been until now an effective historical *logos*, or there has been only the merest stammering of it. Whoever lives the life of a people as a native possesses its reality in an unexpressed manner, and will know for himself the secrets of which this people consists, and that these are secrets not in any mystical sense, but because they are history and history is infinite. Every historical phenomenon, even the most modest— for example, the pronunciation of a word—is the foreshortening of a profound past. This would constitute the "supra-tacit" secret.[15]

Hence the "internationalist" historian's profession was dubious: first, he might be deceived by the apparent accessibility of foreign cultures to modern research; second, and especially true for

English-speaking scholars, Ortega believed, he might well mistake a mass of empirical material for an integral perspective on the life of another people. These points have their validity as a critique of Toynbee's enormous project, but they are also equally revealing of Ortega's own subtle, unstated defense of Spain as a country so readily misunderstood from without and so little a part of the modern devotion to "scientific" analysis. As he stressed the "secrecy" of a people's history, he was speaking out of his own intimate circumstances of the mixture of timidity and assertiveness implied in being a Spaniard in a time when Spain appeared to play a minor role in the world.

In the first of the lectures on Toynbee, late in 1948, Ortega alluded to the "Epilogue for Englishmen" he had added to *The Revolt of the Masses* in April 1938 for an edition published in the midst of the Spanish Civil War, when it was becoming abundantly clear that neither England nor the United States would offer support for the Republic. At that time, without actually espousing such a step, Ortega had come as close as he ever did to breaking the political silence he had imposed on himself after 1933. Praising England lavishly in the epilogue for the quality of its "national character," he wrote:

> The nervousness of recent months has made almost all nations live mounted on their own frontiers, that is, affording an exaggerated spectacle of their most congenital defects. If we add to this that one of the principal themes of dispute has been Spain, it will be clear how much I have suffered from whatever in England, France, and North America represents lack, torpor, vice, and defect. What has most surprised me is the decided will in the public opinion of those countries not to be well informed about things; and what I have most missed with respect to Spain has been some gesture of a generous spirit, which is, in my judgment, the most estimable thing in the world. In the Anglo-Saxon—not in his governments, but rather in those countries—intrigue, frivolity, hard-headedness, archaic prejudice, and new hypocrisy have been allowed to run free without bounds. The greatest stupidities have been seriously attended to as long as they were indigenous, and, on the other hand, there has been the root decision not to wish to listen to any Spanish voice capable of clarifying things, or to hear it only after distorting it.[16]

Ortega clearly saw at that time that foreign understanding of the war's complex domestic origins was very limited, and that other nations and observers were likely to project upon Spain their own priorities. Unlike the atypical postwar book *The Spanish Labyrinth* (1943), by Gerald Brenan, most foreign views of the Spanish tragedy were colored by habits of thought pertinent to the observer's own culture, or, in the case of so many foreign writers and poets who rallied to the crisis in Spain, by romantic projections upon a land that had long fed the fantasies of travelers and cultural adventurers. In that sense, the Spanish Civil War functioned as a kind of vast Rorschach blot, eliciting as many interpretations as there were dreams and programs that embraced it. This tendency could, of course, be explained by the investment of foreign political interests in the outcome of the war; but in a longer perspective, for outsiders Spain had often been over the centuries more an object of fantasy than of serious study. Its literature, for example, was not seriously studied (even by Spaniards themselves) until German scholars of the early nineteenth century became interested, among other things, in the theater of the golden age; and nineteenth-century travelers like Dumas, Gautier, George Borrow, and Richard Ford had all reveled in the country's romantic "difference" from the rest of Europe.

A continuation of this spirit in the work of many foreign writers during the 1920s and 1930s actually complicated the task of beginning to understand Spanish history "from within," as Ortega was wont to say. Something of the sense of Spain as the object of others' needs is caught in W. H. Auden's "Spain 1937," in which the various nations of the world, witnessing the defeat of the Republic, invoke the long-past power of the great nation that founded an empire. But contemporary Spain, where "We are left alone with our day, and the time is short and / History to the defeated / May say alas but cannot help or pardon," can only reply:

> "O no, I am not the Mover,
> Not today, not to you. To you I'm the
>
> "Yes-man, the bar-companion, the easily-duped:
> I am whatever you do; I am your vow to be
>   Good, your humorous story;
> I am your business voice; I am your marriage.
>
> "What's your proposal? To build the Just City? I will.
> I agree. Or is it the suicide pact, the romantic

> Death? Very well, I accept, for
> I am your choice, your decision: yes, I am Spain."
>
> Many have heard it on remote peninsulas,
> On sleepy plains, in the aberrant fishermen's islands,
> In the corrupt heart of the city;
> Have heard and migrated like gulls or the seeds of a flower.
>
> They clung like burrs to the long expresses that lurch
> Through the unjust lands, through the night, through the alpine tunnel;
> They floated over the oceans;
> They walked the passes: they came to present their lives.
>
> On that arid square, that fragment nipped off from hot
> Africa, soldered so crudely to inventive Europe,
> On that tableland scored by rivers,
> Our fever's menacing shapes are precise and alive.[17]

Unlike Ortega, Auden portrays the voice of Spain as endlessly compliant, without resources to shape the history that is befalling her. There is, of course, a marked difference between the poet's utterance and the philosopher's, not the least of which is that Ortega wrote the epilogue of 1938 from "within the whirlwind," while Auden in his picture of "that fragment nipped off from hot / Africa" ironically perpetuated the tradition of exoticizing Spain. Yet his words are still, in some sense, to the point, for Ortega's anger was directed ultimately against the presumption and blindness of those outsiders who ultimately judged themselves in their uncomprehending judgments of Spain. Moreover, the epilogue makes clear, the English, "so frugal with serious historical mistakes," had just committed the very grave one of adopting a naive pacifist stance toward German aggression in Europe. The reference, written in April 1938, is undoubtedly to Neville Chamberlain's policy of appeasement toward the Italian conquest of Ethiopia, which he agreed to recognize on April 16 of that year in an attempt to keep England out of the Spanish Civil War. Characteristically, Ortega did not make the reference specific, contenting himself simply with the closing observation, "Of all the causes that have generated the present misfortunes of the world, perhaps the clearest is the disarmament of England."[18]

Appended to the introduction to the English edition of *Revolt* was Ortega's earlier essay "En cuanto al pacifismo" (Concerning Pacifism), originally published in the English review *The Nineteenth Century* in June 1937 and now dated "Paris, December 1937." Noting that the "construction" of peace is as much an active task as the making of war, Ortega chided England in this essay for a naive approach to the goal of European unity, which was not to be won by a withdrawal from the proper and necessary assertion of strength. Lest we repeat the folly of the League of Nations, he warned, we must design a concept of international law supple enough to meet the challenges of our time. A policy of sheer appeasement was not sufficient, he argued, doubtless thinking again of the Conservative cabinet in London. More pointedly, he also mentioned the recent Labor party vote against union with the English Communists for a proposed "Popular Front." The irony here, Ortega observed, is that the very same Labor party had been willing to support the Popular Front government in Spain after 1936. This flagrant double standard pointed to the kind of ill-conceived internationalism against which *The Revolt of the Masses*, he liked to think later, had ultimately been aimed. No lasting European peace could be built without an awareness by leadership elites of the specific historical destiny of each cooperating nation in its own terms. Even Albert Einstein was rebuked in these pages of 1937 for a recent statement on the Spanish Civil War, in which he had displayed "a radical ignorance about what has happened in Spain now, over the centuries, and always. The spirit that moved him to this insolent intervention is the same that for some time now has been causing the intellectual's universal loss of prestige."[19] Ortega closed the essay on pacifism with a call to overcome the "abstruse internationalism" then in vogue. In fact, only by passing through a phase of exacerbated nationalism, he believed, could Europe hope to achieve a functioning community of nations. As much as predicting the European war that was little over a year away, he foresaw a continent split between "a new liberalism" and a "totalitarian" camp. The coming clash between these positons would supposedly temper and purify the liberal vision and ensure its eventual triumph: "This will save Europe. Once again it will become plain that every form of life has need of its antagonist."[20]

It is quite plausible to adduce these earlier criticisms of English policy as an explanation of the acerbic undercurrent in the postwar lectures on Toynbee in Madrid during the winter of 1948–1949.

How, after all, could that Oxford don who proclaimed himself a master of international affairs square his claims to a catholicity of understanding with the example of his nation's ignorance of Spain's dilemma, not to mention England's narrowly self-interested position during the collapse of the Republic? In this perspective, Toynbee seemed to Ortega a sentimental devotee of a secular, vaguely internationalist "religion" of humanity. At the same time, he insisted that Toynbee was representative of the pragmatic and empirical cast of the English mind. However plausible some of his interpretations might seem, Toynbee had not, Ortega concluded, thought through the theoretical bases of the *Study of History*.

Apart from Ortega's reflections on Spain and England and the long rumination on Roman history which formed a good part of the lectutres, he also hinted at unvoiced feelings about his own position as a "survivor" of the prewar period now living in what he elsewhere called "a phantasmagoric Spain." For example, his deeper response to the disaster at home may be read between the lines of his prolonged consideration of legitimacy and illegitimacy in the Roman Republic and Empire. At one moment in the eighth lecture he implied a link between ancient Rome and modern Spain, speaking of "the analysis we are making today of life constituted in illegitimacy, of which the two gigantic examples are the declining period of the Roman Republic and the times in which we ourselves are living."[21] At other moments he was careful to deny any close link betwen his far-ranging theme and the immediate facts of Spanish life under General Franco. In speaking of the biblical prophets as men who cried out against their people, he concluded: "Let us leave this matter...and may nobody start to trivialize it with momentary political interpretations when it is a matter of the perennial and desperate mission of the intellectual in this world, a mission already almost three times millenarian."[22]

In the twelfth and last lecture, speaking of the deterioration of the law as a body of fundamental rights (*el Derecho*), he seemed to draw painfully close to contemporary Spain, yet again he denied that he was speaking politically, positing the existence of a depth beyond politics in the collective life of peoples:

All the great countries have contributed to the destruction of all law, and nowadays nobody has rights because there is no Right [*derecho*].

... Certain circumstances of pure chance have permitted an appearance or thin layer of law to subsist in the civic life of some countries, and availing themselves of it they attack for political reasons those in which even that appearance has been lost. But I have nothing to do with politics, nor is anything that I am saying political, but rather enormously deeper and graver than all politics....

I do not now speak especially—not even principally—about Spain. I made clear in my first lesson that after fifteen years of almost total silence, I was renewing my public activity, though strictly of an intellectual sort, as an activity from Spain. From here, then, my anguished cry goes forth on the winds to all the powerful of the earth that they may become fully aware of the enormity they have committed, that they are committing, in destroying Right in the human sphere.[23]

It is difficult to imagine that the specter of Franco did not lie behind Ortega's pained meditation on the eclipse of right and law in the world. Also, high-minded and sweeping as this meditation on universal history sounded, there seems little doubt that his earlier concern with English "neutrality" in the late 1930s combined with his dislike of Toynbee's "legislative" internationalism to prompt this lengthy polemic *in absentia* with the English historian.

Although attendance was impressive at these lectures, clearly the most vital project of the Instituto de Humanidades, several newspapers responded with hostility. *Informaciones* announced that "marquises, bullfighters and 'other intellectuals'" constituted the public, averring that "Don José's great miracle has been to make philosophy in vogue and get marquises to speak of a new interpretation of history at tea-time, and bullfighters to read Dilthey."[24] The stereotype of the ridiculous public had become a staple of *ad hominem* attacks on Ortega, who occasionally came to his own defense in the venomous social atmosphere of postwar Madrid. His picture of the city's cultural life, for example, was not charitable:

Madrid has lost the bit of alertness to ideas that was awakened in her: she has quite become again the eternal Manchegan village that she always was at bottom.... Madrid has been delivered—as one delivers a good sheep to the beast of prey—to the provincial "intellectuals" and the amateurs.[25]

Unwittingly corroborating his dismal picture of the capital, some papers carped at the social spectacle of the lectures, noting the rush for seats by women in mink coats and feather boas. One critic noted sardonically that certainly no one was bored, for Ortega had entertained royally: he cracked jokes, gave "a beautiful definition of love," and reminisced about the Madrid of his childhood.[26] When Ortega referred at one point to the savagery under the surface in civilized men, and characterized the intellectual isolation of Spain as its "tibetanization," several papers reacted with snappy humor: Are we in the Himalayas or in Madrid? The daily *Pueblo* ran a series under the heading "Do You Feel Savage?" asking well-known singers and actresses to respond. The dominant tone of press coverage was, finally, trivializing and mean-spirited. As such, it confirmed the fact that Ortega was essentially persona non grata in official circles, as had already been made clear in the mandated restriction to twenty lines of any announcements the Instituto placed in the Spanish papers.[27] Resistance of that sort, combined with a precarious financial situation that prompted Ortega to appeal for American foundation monies, would in another year bring about his decision to end the Instituto's activities. For all the social stir and ephemeral excitement caused by the lectures on universal history, their reception met the problems one might well have expected under the prevailing conditions; and their positive effect was further reduced by their digressive, often frankly disorganized structure. The old bugaboo of "system" which had troubled Ortega at least since his encounter with Heidegger's *Sein und Zeit* raised its ugly head again as he attempted to develop his own philosophy of history and culture over against that of Toynbee.

Burdened by unpromising prospects in Madrid, Ortega accepted with evident pleasure an invitation to make his first visit to the United States in July 1949. The Chicago business executive Walter P. Paepcke had asked him to be a featured speaker at the Goethe Festival in Aspen, Colorado, where a major celebration was being organized to commemorate the bicentennial of the German poet's birth. Together with Albert Schweitzer, Giuseppe Borghese, Stephen Spender, Ernst Robert Curtius, Thornton Wilder, and Robert M. Hutchins, whose idea the event had originally been, Ortega lent eminence to this unusual exhibition of international culture in the Colorado Rockies. Goethe, of compelling interest to him from early in his career, was to be hailed as the model of enlightened European humanism, vital to the cultural reunification of the postwar West. This was a model Ortega aspired to follow in his own career as one of the Continent's preeminent men of letters and an outspoken proponent of European unity. Perceived by Paepcke as a kind of twentieth-century Goethe, Ortega was a natural choice for the occasion.

He delivered two addresses on separate days during the two-week festival. In the first, he invoked Goethe's understanding of the sacred duty of the individual to fulfill his unique personhood. This mandate, he reasoned, represented one of the richest fruits of European culture, which had been built from a striving toward self-fulfillment by multitudes of men and women. Now that Europe was in crisis, Ortega continued, it needed the inspiration of this legacy in order to rally from its pessimism, which had been irresponsibly exacerbated, he added, by those existentialist thinkers who, like Heidegger and Sartre, stressed *Angst* and the threat of nonbeing. Goethe, who could offer modern people an alternative vision, had himself been a kind of precursor-existentialist, but of a more affirmative turn. Not content to rely upon a received cultural heritage, the great poet had asserted that culture was made for man rather than vice versa. In this sense, the Goethe Ortega invoked in Aspen was a more heroic figure than the one he had sketched out in "Goethe from Within" in 1932. The Goethe for the new times knew well the uncertainty of life—the constant possibility of "shipwreck" —and the imperative existential project that is each human destiny. This figure, who had refused the illusions of cultural security in order to face the unfolding future, was, Ortega believed, the proper guide for a Europe (and a world) seeking to reorient itself after the apparent collapse of its spiritual foundations:

> Here you have the grand Goethean task upon which, in my judgment, Europe is entering—the construction of a civilization that starts out expressly and formally from human negativities, from inexorable limitations, and bases itself on them in order to exist fully. The European peoples have by now dealt out the whole deck of illusions. Now it is a question of the final illusion—that of living without illusions, of feeling delight in contemplating the naked reality of things, of adjusting our ideas to its contours and, like good sailors, tightening our sails into the wind.[28]

In the first lecture Goethe emerged neither as the classic figure of world literature nor as the curious "failure" of "Goethe from

Within" but as the navigator-hero who dared the open seas of the future.[29] In the second, a few days later, Ortega returned to his concern with the uncertainty of the human prospect, noting that is was more accurate to say that man "is" future rather than that he "has" a future. Goethe too had understood this, he remarked, though his complex dual nature had led him to assert, in a kind of pantheistic optimism, that man developed organically like a plant. This *Naturphilosophie*—derived by Goethe from the Stoics, a cursory reading of Spinoza, and his own botanical studies—was in fact sharply at odds with the poet's more intimate awareness of the role of chance, character, and destiny in human life. The genuine Goethe, ambivalent in his conception of life, destined to live out the "innumerable and profound dualities" of his epoch, did not affirm without ambivalence the "stoical-humanistic-rationalistic pantheism of the eighteenth century and the beginning of the nineteenth"; yet he took shelter from his uncertainties in that doctrine and in the retreat offered him by Weimar.[30] Here Ortega returned to the critical judgment of "Goethe from Within," tantalizing his audience with the prospect of a truer and fuller "Goethe without Weimar." He added, seeming to reverse his judgment of the first lecture:

> The age of Goethe is perhaps that in the entire history of humanity in which the future seemed least insecure, at least as regards the human community. The idea of... Progress had just been invented, according to which humanity would inevitably arrive at happiness through an infinite but certain process. On the other hand, perhaps never as during the current time has the human future revealed with such terrible violence the uncertain threat that it constitutes by its very nature.[31]

The reaction of the audience and the newspapers to Ortega's two presentations was warmly enthusiastic, though Thornton Wilder, who translated the second lecture for the listeners, remarked, "I really do not know what to think of it," for it seemed the work of "a great and fertile mind being strangely willful and naughty—shooting out suggestive half-truths without organization or basic coherence."[32]

In accepting the invitation to Aspen, Ortega initiated a continuing relationship with Walter Paepcke, producer of the grand colloquium. President of The Container Corporation of America in Chicago and an enlightened patron of the arts, Paepcke was a notale figure in a series of remarkable postwar collaborations between men of ideas and leaders of the business community. This "romance of commerce and culture," as James Sloan Allen has dubbed it, owed its existence to the confluence of several currents in the years just before and after World War II. The arrival in Chicago of two leading figures of the German Bauhaus—László Moholy-Nagy in 1937 and Ludwig Mies van der Rohe in 1938— made that city, already the birthplace of modern architecture in the work of Louis Sullivan and others, an American center for the extension of the modernist architecture and design so brilliantly realized in Germany in the 1920s. Mies established himself at the Armour Institute (later the Illinois Institute of Technology), while Moholy-Nagy founded his own New Bauhaus, later renamed the School of Design. Paepcke, who had already introduced modernist design as a feature of Container Corporation advertising, came to Moholy-Nagy's support until the latter's death from leukemia in 1946. Shortly after this, Paepcke became an enthusiastic convert of the campaign for education through the Great Books developed some years earlier at Columbia University by John Erskine and brought to Chicago by Mortimer Adler and Robert Hutchins. This remarkable popularization of high culture was to be a cornerstone of what Allen calls "the Chicago *Bildungsideal.*"

In the powerful city, which more than any other seemed to embody the driving energy of American industry, numerous leaders of the business and educational communities, led primarily by Paepcke and Hutchins, dreamed of uniting material and intellectual culture on a grand scale. The University of Chicago, with its tradition of involvement in the life of the city, was the natural nucleus for this project; and Hutchins, its controversial leader, was to be the great salesman of ideas. He, Adler, and Paepcke all imagined that the propagation of the Great Books reading plan throughout the country would be the best possible antidote to postwar materialism in a nation newly arrived at a position of world leadership for which it seemed ill prepared. The friendship between Hutchins the entrepreneurial intellectual and Paepcke the idealistic captain of industry eventually led to plans for a cultural center in the little mountain town of Aspen, envisioned by Paepcke as the perfect retreat in which to meditate on the heritage and future of Western civilization. The Goethe Festival of 1949 was the culminating event in a long series of steps he took to make Aspen a backcountry acropolis with a high cultural atmosphere. Not content with the idea of a tony resort, Paepcke "wanted to make Aspen something of a *Kulturstaat,* a civilized state organized around culture and thriving on it." [33] But the promotion of the Festival required enormous material outlay. As Allen observes:

> Mass marketing, mass communications, and public relations, the engines of the consumer culture, made the Goethe Festival the historic public event it was, putting Aspen on the map, making a folk hero of Albert Schweitzer, and, as Hutchins bragged in the aftermath, becoming "one of the most significant programs for adult education" ever undertaken. [34]

This projected American Weimar in the mountains, created by large outlays of money and adroit advertising techniques, appealed to Ortega's flamboyant imagination, particularly after having found the going so difficult in Spain. Prompted by his striking success at the festival in July, he wrote Paepcke in October to suggest the founding of an Aspen Institute for Humanistic Studies that would be modeled on his own Instituto de Humanidades in Madrid. Focusing on advanced studies and adult education, the projected center in Aspen would, he hoped, avoid the problems confronted by overextended and overspecialized modern universities, though it would retain the university ideal of interpreting the general structure of the culture as articulated in Ortega's prewar "Mission of the University." This conception accorded remarkably well with the spirit of Hutchins's and Adler's Chicago endeavors, for its "synthetic teaching would be made on the basis of a *library with very few but masterly chosen volumes.*" From these, students would learn "to *really* absorb an important book." [35] Idealistically, Ortega imagined that the classic European notions of "Spartanism" and "elegance," embodied in the new institute, would serve as a counterweight to American materialism. He fancied that students in Aspen could renew the monastic ideal by engaging in useful physical labor while they studied the classics. Such a program would be an implicit challenge to the increasing prominence of the mass man Ortega perceived in the United States. While the winter season in Colorado would, he foresaw, impose character-building rigors on the participants, summer would ensure the edifying presence of "gens du monde," who would be drawn to play and learn in the mountains. Students at the Institute could learn simply by observing the elegant manners and taste of this cultured minority. The elect few and those who watched them live would together form a new American elite destined to elevate the entire tone of the nation's cultural life.[36] His snobbish side all too obvious in the letter to Paepcke, Ortega dreamed of a bastion in the New World established against the incursions of mass society, the recreation, in the improbable setting of the former Colorado mining town, of a high culture gone forever from Europe. The mote in his eye—and in Paepcke's as well—was evident, as Allen makes clear:

> Like Ortega, Paepcke conceived of elegance in Aspen as the unity of Spartan austerity and cultural refinement. But since both Paepcke and Ortega had themselves acquired elegance more through economic and cultural privilege than through Spartan difficulty... it is nicely ironic that they should have felt the need to impose, by severe means, the elegance they enjoyed on their social opposites: the unprivileged, undisciplined, unrefined Mass Man.[37]

The Aspen Institute for Humanistic Studies was founded on December 30, 1949. Although in good part Ortega's brainchild, it was soon to undergo a dramatic turn away from his original conception at the prompting of Henry Luce, who envisaged it as the setting where business leaders, together with their peers in government, education, and the arts, could raise the intellectual level of American business culture. While this idea was not a salient part of Ortega's picture, it did accord nicely with Paepcke's original dream for Aspen. (The Institute in fact followed Luce's plan of development and is still thriving today.)

Meanwhile, Ortega was busy pursuing his burgeoning career as a kind of world-class intellectual-at-large. After a visit in New York on his way home from Aspen, he returned briefly to Spain, only to leave in late August 1949 for the German Goethe Festival in Hamburg, where he shared the stage with Schweitzer and Thomas Mann. This was the first of a series of appearances he made in Germany late that summer and during the fall. With the exception of a very brief visit to Germany in 1934, the date of his "Preface for Germans," he had been absent from the country for almost forty years, since his last studies there in 1911. Long past was the flowering of German philosophy, letters, and science which had originally drawn him and had continued to fascinate him during the Weimar Republic. But at least in postwar Germany, as in the United States, he enjoyed an enthusiastic, receptive public. Older members of his audience in Hamburg and elsewhere remembered well the earlier translations of his very popular essays, particularly *Estudios sobre el amor*. More certain of the German public's admiration than of any he might face at home, Ortega nonetheless kept his by-now-accustomed silence on political issues, turning instead to the theme of Europe's spiritual reconstruction. Surprisingly to many, he made no reference to the rise of Hitler, the Holocaust, and the wholesale destruction of Germany's earlier cultural life.

It is conceivable that Ortega's silence about the German defeat came out of a sense that it was inelegant to criticize the defeated or those who are in trouble in their own house. As a citizen of a nation that had, as he elsewhere remarks, "won everything and lost everything," Ortega, we have seen, was excruciatingly sensitive to foreign criticism of Spain; and his care after World War II not to review the German record probably reflected his old conviction (hardly honored in Argentina) that an outsider could not really understand the internal affairs of another nation. More important, however, is the possibility that the silence of this deeply political man stemmed from his shock at the destruction of the world in which he had been formed. Despite his idea that orders of culture must rise and fall, or pass like the seasons, he doubtless found it difficult to accept the collapse of that very cultural height that had compelled his youthful admiration. He knew in theory that all cultural forms were transitory; yet, in his dedication to the liberal, enlightened ideal of historicized reason at work revitalizing the Western cultural tradition, Ortega was at odds with himself. Like many others of his generation all over Europe, he was more attached to a historically limited version of culture than he knew. And for all his alarm at the prospect of mass society, his picture of the world did not perhaps wholly encompass the massive anticultural and antihumanist forces eventually unleashed in the very Europe whose threatened cultural hegemony in the world he could still at least invoke in *The Revolt of the Masses*. Of course, the outbreak of war in Spain unquestionably drove home the lesson of catastrophic collapse, but from the distance of Argentina and later of Portugal Ortega had only very indirectly felt the repercussions of the Spanish war and the subsequent larger one in Europe as a whole. In any case, the theme of political structures and hierarchies, implicit in his thinking since the early *Invertebrate*

Spain (1921), appeared after 1945 in his hope for a unified federation of European states to be held together by a sense of shared destiny and by the common legacy of classical culture.

However, despite Ortega's optimistic assertion that Germany and Europe as a whole would recover from its crisis—a prophecy that has proved abundantly true—we may wonder whether, in regard to the German disaster, he was able to accept the apparent contradiction of his earlier tendency to think that high culture was a clear mark of human progress. As a young man just back from study in Germany, as we noted in chapter 2, Ortega had recognized flaws in German culture and had written that they must someday be transcended, presumably in the interest of a larger European community. But that issue had become relatively dormant in his ensuing devotion to transmitting to Spain the best fruits of German thought; and the whole prickly matter of Germany's political evolution in the twentieth century seemed really to have sunk from sight in his writings. In addition, his essentially Spenglerian theory of cultural cycles, as presented, for example, in *Man and Crisis*, would seem to have been challenged by the course of recent history, for the collapse of mid-century Germany was no autumnal "waning" of an old and decadent culture, but a shocking eruption of brutality in the midst of a young nation of great cultural energies.

If his response to it all was buoyant and hopeful, there was surely an untold side to the story. In the cataclysms that shattered the liberal vision of a civilized Europe, Ortega was confronted with the devasting failure of culture and reason and even with their most cunning perversion. The wars in Spain and on the rest of the Continent challenged the sufficiency of his *razón histórica*, whether he believed so or not. Ortega had often proclaimed that each generation made its own destiny and could not expect the past to provide it with much valuable counsel in that respect, but his dilemma as one who outlived the world that gave him his cultural foundations is best suggested in the French poet René Char's grave maxim, coined in the middle of World War II, "Notre heritage n'est précédé d'aucun testament" ("No testament precedes our inheritance").[38] Ortega himself had observed the same of his own age in *The Revolt of the Masses*: "[F]or the first time we meet with a period which makes *tabula rasa* of all classicism, which recognizes in nothing that is past any possible model or standard."[39] Earlier he had sounded the same note, though apparently more affirmatively, in *The Dehumanization of Art*:

> This grave dissociation of past and present is the generic fact of our time and the cause of the suspicion, more or less vague, which gives rise to the confusion characteristic of our present-day existence. We feel that we actual men have suddenly been left alone on the earth; that the dead did not die in appearance only but effectively; that they can no longer help us. Any remains of the traditional spirit have evaporated. Models, norms, standards are no use to us. We have to solve our problems without any active collaboration of the past, in full actuality, be they problems of art, science or politics. The European stands alone, without any living ghosts by his side; like Peter Schlehmil he has lost his shadow. This is what always happens when midday comes.[40]

Deprived of the counsel of tradition, modern man (and particularly Spanish man, who very slowly and reluctantly gave up his position as the defender of Catholic Christianity in the post-Reformation world) stands, in this vision of 1925, secular and alone, yet guided by the blazing noonday light that limns "our present life that feels itself as ampler than all previous lives."[41] But this pre–civil war evocation of the modern stance, this almost futurist celebration of "the times," was not to remain the tone of the chastened and deepened Ortega of the bad years to come.

In September 1949, Ortega presented, to a huge crowd of students at the Free University of Berlin, a lecture titled "De Europa meditatio quaedam," in which he spoke of the birth pangs being suffered by postwar Europe as it entered a new, still-unclear mode of existence.[42] He acknowledged that it was a time of doubtful recovery, but claimed to find in it a sign of regeneration:

> Certainly everything in Europe has become questionable. But I need immediately to add something so that you will not twist my diagnosis of the situation through which Europe is passing.... The fact that our civilization has become problematic for us, that all its principles are *without exception* questionable, is not necessarily sad or lamentable or the danger of death agony, but perhaps signifies on the contrary that a new form of civilization is germinating in us; that therefore under the apparent catastrophes... a new form of human existence is being born.[43]

These sentiments seem strangely incongruous uttered in a blockaded Berlin still under the control of a four-power government at the start of what would later be known as the Cold War era. Much as in the earlier essay on English pacifism, "En cuanto al pacifismo," Ortega seemed now determined to descry the spectacle of a new Europe arising like the phoenix from its ashes. Obviously referring to Oswald Spengler's prophecy in *The Decline of the West* of a downward curve in the historical fortunes of Europe, he proclaimed himself in Berlin a *matinalista* (advocate of the dawn) rather than a *vespertinista* (advocate of the evening), invoking once again the old Nietzschean metaphor of a breaking dawn. The allusion clearly meant that there was no *Untergang* (decline) in prospect, only the sloughing off of an old skin. In this lecture Ortega attempted to establish the antiquity of both the idea and the political reality of Europe as a cultural-linguistic unity traceable to the tenth and eleventh centuries. In his view, it was then that Europe as a project of common *convivencia* (living together) had been forged. Historically, the evolving meaning of Europe had been defined in terms of the gradual emergence of the various national states, the oldest of which was Spain, whose origin dated back to the fifteenth-century union of the kingdoms of Castile and Aragon. In his concern to justify historically Europe's reconstruction, Ortega renewed his prewar convictions—clear though implicit in *The Revolt of the Masses*—that nationalism was the "greatest danger" of political life in mass society, and that the dramatically weakened European cultural hegemony could hardly be replaced by anything better. It was Europe at the top again or chaos—and not only Europe, but, specifically, select European citizens who would form a transnational elite able to articulate the fundamentals of a renewed culture as he had sketched it out in *Mission of the University* (1930) and "Misión del bibliotecario" (Mission of the Librarian, 1935).

Ortega was convinced that in the long run the depth and strength of European culture, particularly as manifest in recent times in England, France, and prewar Germany, would again provide the entire world with an insuperable model of excellence. True, Latin America had awakened his catholic curiosity; the United States had puzzled and fascinated him; and Asia and Africa were ethnologically interesting; but no other part of the globe could, he felt, match the cultural and scientific development of Europe as the inheritor of Greco-Roman antiquity. While Ortega had contributed to the self-critical revision of Europocentric consciousness through the studies in non-European anthropology, ethnology, geography, and history that had appeared in the *Revista de Occidente* or under the auspices of the Revista press, he had done so always from the standpoint of his own European identity, the affirmation of which overcame any lingering sense he might still harbor of being a partial "outsider" from the Spanish steppes. He was still, circumstantially speaking, first of all a *madrileño*, next a Castilian, then a Spaniard, then a European; but it was his insistence on the last category, he believed, that validated the other three, saving them from anachronism, decadence, and provincialism.

In the Berlin address, Ortega praised Germany as a youthful nation only recently unified and self-aware, and possessed, he said, of an admirable resiliency. Speaking in German on the occasion, he seemed a cosomopolitan citizen of the West, obviously at home quoting Goethe, analyzing German character, and, incidentally, challenging Arnold Toynbee for his "primitive" notion of nationhood, to which Ortega opposed his own of European unity. Faced with the gratifying attention of eager crowds of young Berliners, he remarked on the limits on the power of intellectuals in political affairs, pointing out at the same time that the split between politician and thinker was a disastrous feature peculiar to modern politics:

> During thirty years one has claimed not to rely on the intellectuals, but in spite of the hostility against them, there is no way to annul the cosmic fact that the intellectual is the only man who *lets things be*, and thanks to this he is the only one one a little bit aware of what they are.[44]

Historically, he argued, the roots of the division between men of thought and men of action were in the mid–eighteenth century, when intellectuals had aspired to guide public affairs; henceforth, and in return, politicians had taken vengeance on them by usurping their role of defining things.

Though this analysis seems a bit too neatly symmetrical to be wholly true, Ortega had himself gone through the role inversion he spoke of. His was a considered caution in assessing the fate of ideas:

> Intellectuality is everywhere a merely eccentric power, only exceptionally and obliquely a factor in effective history.... For a century and a half, as a consequence of three centuries of humanism, historians have tended to place intellectual and artistic groups too much to the fore, which falsifies the true prespective of historical forces.... The true histori-

cal influence of intellectuals is always distant from them and, strictly speaking, is not from them but from their ideas. But the ideas of intellectuals require much time to be converted into "historical forces," since, for this effect, they must cease to be properly "ideas" and become "commonplaces," in use, "public opinion." This is one of the causes that make history march to a slow, "tardigrade" tempo.[45]

This notion is far from his earlier hope that the very power of his bare voice could turn men to reason and reform. In a lecture to Spanish students in the late 1920s, he had cryptically proclaimed that a single word of his would unite the youth of Spain behind him; but in Berlin Ortega spoke as at least a chastened optimist, disposed now to accept the slow transmission of novel thought into action. The shock of war and exile had obviously left him haunted by concern for political stability and international understanding. Consonant with that preoccupation, he saw his postwar writings (which included biographical studies of Juan Vives, Velázquez, Goya, and Goethe, and various short pieces on the place of technology and the role of the "manager" in modern culture) as contributions to the renewal of Europe and confirmations of the intellectual's high task of clarifying human affairs.

In late September 1949, Ortega was back in Madrid to prepare his second series of lectures for the Instituto de Humanidades. There, during the winter of 1949–1950, he presented, in the most extensive form thus far, his long-evolving philosophical sociology under the title "El hombre y la gente" (later translated as *Man and People*). The twelve lessons were charged with ideas long congenial to him. On their posthumous publication in 1957, the editors pointed to the palimpsest-like quality of this work, which, as so often before, Ortega had left unfinished.[46] The first full version was delivered in the Teatro Barceló, where all 1,300 seats were filled. Still, government censorship limited the newspaper announcements of the Instituto de Humanidades to no more than twenty lines, and replies to newspaper criticism were not permitted. Once again, as in 1948–1949, the government organ *Informaciones* was the most hostile. This second lecture series proved to be the last of the Instituto experiments, which had included a variety of smaller courses and seminars by Julián Marías and other colleagues. Frustrated by wrangles with the press and faced with financial strictures, Ortega abandoned his only postwar institutional base after two years.

For many modern social scientists, the fragmentary form and excessively theoretical tone of the *Man and People* lectures robs them of significance. Scholars concerned with methodological models, concrete applications of theory, or empirical studies reject Ortega's principle that we must begin by *thinking* our way into the fundamental categories of social reality. Yet, as one critic of Ortega has justly noted:

> [t]he determination of the kind of reality 'society' is and the place it occupies in the context and hierarchy of other realities is an eminently metaphysical task. And, in fact, the way which Ortega chooses to pursue in disclosing the essence of the social is the very metaphysics of human life.[47]

But it is just that "metaphysical" premise that makes this work seem to many sociologists a step back toward nineteenth-century social thought (Tarde, Durkheim, Simmel, et al.). It is also true that *Man and People* failed to elicit followers, providing few useful ideas for the young Spanish social scientists who began to appear in the 1950s.

For Ortega, the structure of human life in society required analysis on three levels: the individual, the inter-individual, and the social. In experience, these do not, however, present themselves in that order, for the young child's first awareness of the world (which he will later understand as the discovery of the radical reality of "my life") is made up of "others," who, from his earliest waking moment, appear on his horizon. He confronts inter-individual life —without understanding it as such—before he becomes aware of himself as an individual; and indeed this life with selected "others," who become intimate and familar in the course of time, forms the basis both for the notion of society as generalized others and for one's developing sense of individual selfhood. Gradually, through a progressive capacity for *ensimismamiento* (being in oneself), one discovers authentic personal reality in the incorruptible depths of radical solitude. Both this solitude and inter-individual life with friends, family, colleagues, and so forth stand over against society considered as the realm of impersonal usages, conventions, and *vigencias* (practices, law, customs "in force"). In Ortega's view, inter-individual life seems to provide the most promising area in which the fruits nurtured in solitude may fully ripen, but he does not adequately develop its categories. Instead, he places his primary emphasis upon the plight of the individual exposed to social usage and conventional controls in his life in public. Ortega emphasized the dichotomy between the personal and the social, viewing society as the impersonal power that brakes the creative, expressive capacities of the person.

Despite his attention to the inter-individual realm, Ortega's basic outlook in *Man and People* pits personal authenticity against inauthentic (because radically impersonal) social behavior. This division derives from the classic model of nineteenth-century liberal and romantic thought: the sacred self must be defined in opposition to organized constraint; and the ideal condition for this achievement is maximum freedom for each to be what he is or must become, while economic, social, and political interference is, ideally, kept at a minimum. We may suppose that the best fruits of the individual's radical solitude are realized in the inter-individual "middle ground" between *ensimismamiento* and the presumably depersonalized life enjoined by social decorum. But the weakness of *Man and People*—curious, in view of its author's convivial nature—is its failure to offer a convincing picture of life lived among friends, in the *tertulia*, or with one's family. Since one's more strictly public life is subject to the "de-authentication" imposed by society at large, we might expect the lectures to distinguish between the broadly public and the more intimate social spheres; but they do not. Like one's experience with spouse and children, one's public and political activity seems in this context to be without proper category. Ortega's negative vision of social roles, in which men "lead" lives rather than "living" them, undoubtedly came in part from his reaction to twentieth-century Spanish society: class mobility was rare; the roles of church, state, and army officials were strongly marked; much of the population was locked into the peasant's unchanging rural cycle; rhetorical gestures and tropes characterized both the literary and the spoken language; and public life, as noted earlier, was sharply separated from domestic and amatory affairs.

Following his decision to suspend the activities of the Instituto in Madrid, Ortega naturally turned more frequently toward Germany in the last years of his life. His very successful visit there in the fall of 1949, warmly welcomed by his old friend Curtius, encouraged him to spend large parts of 1951, 1952, and 1953 lecturing in various

German cities. By this time he had set up an apartment in Munich as a *pied-à-terre* for his longer stays. In Darmstadt in 1951 he participated with Heidegger in a colloquium on technology and architecture. Ortega's first encounter with his illustrious peer and "rival" produced, approximately a year later, some revealing reflections on philosophical style:

> [I]n what can a good philosophical style consist? In my judgment, in the thinker's immersing himself in common language, avoiding the terminologies in force, but not simply to use it just as it stands, rather reforming it from its own linguistic roots, as much in vocabulary as, at times, in syntax.[48]

On his strongest side, Heidegger appeared to Ortega to be an extreme case of this general rule, for Heidegger's most fruitful linguistic reform lay in a return to etymological sources, a kind of "diving" for the oldest strata in the language. Of course, the issue of the language in which one works was implicit in Ortega's critique, for Heidegger was writing in the language identified by many (and accepted by Ortega and other contemporary Spanish intellectuals) as almost consubstantial with modern philosophy itself. Heidegger himself was bold enough to pronounce Greek and German the two prime cases of inherently philosophical tongues. By contrast, Ortega was always aware of the problems posed for his work by the fact that Spanish provided almost no preexisting philosophical framework or lexicon out of which to build his own radical revision of Western philosophy. In short, he had no choice but to seek the deepest roots of his own tongue for the appropriate resources. In this quest, his marked preference for colloquial diction sharply distinguished him from those who have emphasized the thinker's reliance upon removal from the realm of common speech. Recognizing Heidegger as perhaps the most eminent representative of that tradition, Ortega was at pains in his later essays to contrast his own work—often a bit enviously—with that of his German colleague:

> Heidegger is profound, whether he speaks on *bauen* ["to build or make"; part of the title of a German conference in which both men participated] or on anything else.... I need to add that not only is he profound but that, furthermore, he wishes to be so, and this no longer seems to me so good. Heidegger... suffers from the mania of profundity. Because philosophy is not only a voyage to the profound. It is a return trip and

is, thus, bringing the profound to the surface and making it clear, patent, common knowledge.[49]

Understandably, Ortega's sincerest approval of Heidegger rested on their common conviction that poetry and philosophy were next of kin:

> Heidegger takes a word ... and draws shavings from it. Little by little from the miniscule belly of the term, humanities come forth, all the human pains and joys and, finally, the entire universe. Heidegger, like every great philosopher, leaves words impregnated, and from them the most marvelous landscapes then emerge in all their flora and fauna.[50]

But as Ortega saw it, the real difference between them, and the source of his own self-esteem in the face of Heidegger's accomplishments, came down to Ortega's distinction between the thinker (or philosopher) and the writer. Heidegger he considered the former, himself the latter. Hence he could with all generosity grant that Heidegger had a "marvelous style"—but it was a *philosophical* style and not a literary one:

> The thinker ... uses the language to express his thoughts as directly as possible. To speak is for him to denominate. He does not linger, then, on words nor remain in them. By contrast the writer as such did not come into the world to think accurately, but rather to speak effectively or, as the Greeks said, *eu legein*, to "speak well."[51]

Speech as the writer understands it is never a mere medium for thought; it is first and foremost compelling and beautiful language, which embodies thought less explicitly but also less laboriously than the words of the philosopher. The writer and the poet need not feel themselves bound in quite the same way to the substance of what they say, for they "mean" or intend differently from the philosopher, who seeks truth *through* language rather than *within* the liberating play of metaphor and image.

Despite his choice to cast his lot with the writer, Ortega expended great effort in the postwar years, most notably in the Leibniz study, to produce a scholarly, systematic treatise that would win him a place in the pantheon of major modern philosophers. In the back of his mind was always the acclaim enjoyed by *Sein und Zeit*; but he was also aware that his exceptional literary gifts seemed somehow to have impeded his success as a philosopher in the strictest sense. As he labored over *The Idea of Principle in Leibniz*, gone was the "stylist of dazzling elegance and colorful profusion" Curtius had seen in the younger writer. If in his last major work he drew closer, on a grand scale, to the rigor of the true thinker, something had been lost in the process, for the qualities of plasticity and playful inventiveness that had made him a kind of poet in his best earlier work were sacrificed to the struggle for completeness and depth. In this way, the development of his prose style over the span of his career recreates for us the very real distinction to be made between poet-philosophers like Kierkegaard, Schopenhauer, Nietzsche, or James and the more ponderous, usually more systematic thinkers like Spinoza, Leibniz, Kant, Hegel, and, in certain works, Heidegger. There are rare figures who seem to have a foot in both camps—Bergson or Santayana, for example—but most incline either toward the flight of the eagle or the steady course of the ox.

Although Ortega ploughed many a furrow with the oxen, his writing before the civil war was as much the finest nonfictional prose in modern Spain as it was philosophy. The change in his style after the war reflects both his aspiration to inclusion in the brotherhood of philosophers and his difficulty in identifying his public and defining his social role. Although by then he enjoyed a large international public, he did not know, as he had rather intimately before 1936, the composition of his audiences and his readership. His social role had become both more multiple and more diffuse. Obliged to be a bit of everything to everybody, he suffered the embarrassment of riches which comes with great renown and the consequent temptation to overextend oneself. The inflated and hieratic tone to be noted at times in the lectures and occasional writings of this period would seem to reflect both a sense of professional dislocation and an evident pleasure in his role as a kind of ambassador-at-large for European culture. Indeed, he might well have been foreseeing his future difficulties as a writer when he wrote in 1927: "The seriousness of a writer must reside in what he says, not in the gesture with which he says it. He who adds a solemn or pedantic manner to the expression of his ideas is not sure of their solidity."[52]

Ortega returned to Spain numerous times during those restless years, but after the *Man and People* series he withdrew from an intellectual climate that resembled that of an armed camp. Nothing escaped a kind of politicization, the obvious result of the denial of political activity to all but the chosen Francoist elite. Classified at home by reactionary Catholic and regime circles as one of the perfidious instigators of the "Godless Republic," a man whose "secular relativism" could only pollute the minds of the young, Ortega became, like Unamuno and many other prewar liberals, an obvious target of ideological backlash. Indeed, the charged issue of religious allegiance would intrude even on his deathbed in October 1955.

While summering in Zumaya that year, he had begun to suffer digestive problems reminiscent of the illness that had dogged him off and on since 1935. His son Miguel, a specialist in such disorders, urged him to return to Madrid in September and submit to exploratory surgery. There, Doctor Plácido Duarte operated and found that a huge cancer of the stomach had spread beyond any hope of correction. In the days just before the end, speculation on the state of his soul ran high as sensationalistic journalists raised the question of his possible return to the faith *in extremis*. In anticipation of his death, the Madrid papers had been notified of strictures to be imposed on all coverage of the story, while certain unscrupulous reporters had already bruited rumors of his last-minute conversion.[53] When he was very close to the end, a friend of the family, Padre Félix García, was brought in at the request of Ortega's wife, but Miguel Ortega has written that he believes his father was already unaware of what was happening around him.[54] On October 18, approximately a month after surgery, Ortega died at 11:20 A.M., at home in number 28 Calle Monte Esquinza. On October 20, Minister of Education Joaquín Ruiz Jiménez convoked, in the name of the University of Madrid, a public mass in Ortega's honor. His sons and daughter declined to attend, sending the minister the following statement:

> Our grievous concern—once the possibility of his recovery was rejected—focused on trying to respect his conscience, which, now clouded, could tell us nothing definite. Nobody can have the least doubt that all his life our father took the most circumspect care, with maximum respect, that all his actions would show his intention to live a-Catholically. Neither do we doubt that even hours before his operation he continued in the same feeling and attitude, according to things he told us at that time. After the operation, God alone knows. We paid

heed to the fervent desire of our mother—absolution *sub conditione.* Whether he took this with a clear awareness—which, up to that moment, and as far as the eyes of the doctors and the family can judge, was strikingly lost—or whether he did so with diminished consciousness is a matter that belongs to the mystery of God.... We wish all this to be clear in case on some occasion it is necessary to remember it, and it has seemed to us most appropriate that it be known to you, to whom we repeat our most sincere gratitude.[55]

In keeping with Ortega's often-expressed wish that he might die "in a *tertulia*"—poetically akin to his statement that he had been born "on a printing press" (an allusion to his father's busy journalistic career)—his children and close disciples, at the suggestion of Fernando Vela, spent the entire night before his last morning reading those passages in his work that touched on death. Shortly before, he had said to Miguel, "I'd like to be buried in the civil cemetery, but it's so ugly."[56] In fact, Ortega was buried in San Isidro, the principal Catholic cemetery of Madrid, but the question of whether he had made his peace with the faith remained ambiguous and assumed extraordinary public importance, thanks in good part to the inflammatory tone of the press. For many Spaniards, he had been *the* great liberal thinker whose life and writings had exemplified independence of mind and a moral alternative to professed Catholicism. His criticism of Catholic tradition had always been philosophical, never personal, for he aimed at intellectual liberty rather than doctrinal conflict.

There was a large procession at Ortega's funeral, and a few days afterward hundreds of Madrid students gathered in the old site of the School of Philosophy and Letters in the Calle San Bernardo to honor the man whose death had brought him to their attention. They carried to his grave a funeral wreath bearing the words "Ortega y Gasset, filósofo liberal de la juventud española" ("liberal philosopher for Spanish youth"), at a time when the word "liberal" was still considered a direct challenge to the regime. Proclaiming themselves "a generation without a master," they read passages from Ortega's work. Their acknowledgment that he had lived among them almost unknown pointed up the conspiracy of silence perpetrated by their elders.

This demonstration and others soon to follow made clear that those who had hoped for reform from within (Christian Democrats under Ruiz Jiménez and the remaining idealistic Falangists) could not offer the young a credible alternative. In fact, the event triggered by Ortega's death was the first major public protest of the opposition in postwar Spain. The relatively restrained official response indicated Franco's concern to show the world a moderate face. Eager to solidify economic ties with other Western nations and to appear more progressive than he was in fact, the Caudillo (chief, head of state) had recently (1953) signed an accord with the United States, granting it air bases on Spanish soil, and by 1955 he was hoping for Spain's inclusion in the United Nations. In fact, barely two months after the funeral, on December 15, 1955, the government that had destroyed the Republic was made a full member of that body. Meanwhile, from the demonstration of October forward, the new generation of students was radicalized in the face of increasingly repressive measures taken against it. It might be said, in this sense, that Ortega managed in death to achieve what he had not been able to do in his postwar life, for the catalyst of his memory thrust forward the cause of liberal protest, reminding those who cared of the great "buried" legacy he and his generation had bequeathed to the present.

With the liberal Catholic Ruiz Jiménez as minister of education and his appointee Laín Entralgo as rector of the University of Madrid, a brief period of cultural liberalization coincided with Ortega's death. But the traces were still held tightly, and after mounting student protests early in 1956, prompted in part by the forced cancellation of a National Congress of Young Writers authorized by Ruiz Jiménez for the previous November, the liberal minister was dismissed. This reactionary turn was prompted by the virulent attacks of the conservative Catholic cultural establishment, which went so far as to accuse him of attempting to "deliver over teaching once again to the Institución Libre de Enseñanza."[57] Thus Ortega's death had provided only a brief catalytic effect in an atmosphere charged with profound unresolved tensions.

On November 18, 1955, an act of official homage was organized at the University of Madrid for the deceased colleague who had refused both to rejoin the faculty and to accept the retirement pension due him after his seventieth birthday. The dean of philosophy and letters (Dr. Sánchez Cantón) and a student spoke briefly, but the spotlight shone on Ortega's old friends and colleagues Emilio

García Gómez and Gregorio Marañón, and on his more distant admirer Laín Entralgo. García Gómez spoke on the "ten lessons" that Ortega's example had left (work, intellectual vigilance, clarity, tolerance, etc.) and praised his departed friend's stoic detachment from material interests: "Ortega never received an official salary other than that of professor of metaphysics.... He could have been whatever he wished, but he wished nothing. He has died with neither attentions, nor bands nor crosses nor academic or ambassadorial titles."[58] His exemplary "disinterestedness," García Gómez concluded, was one of the ten lessons he could offer young Spaniards.

Of all those present, Marañón, the great endocrinologist and man of letters, spoke of Ortega with the most obvious authority, for he had known and admired his former colleague in the Agrupación al Servicio de la República early in their careers, and had shared with him the status of charismatic figure for the Generation of 1914. It was Marañón who perhaps most dramatically exemplified Ortega's sense that their generation had the mission to introduce precision, science, and rigor where the preceding one had offered rhetoric, belles lettres, and a poetry of the national soul. Moreover, Marañón had done so without becoming merely a "scientist," for his popular humanistic essays were the fruit of his ability to synthesize learning in science, history, literature, and the visual arts. More than the others, then, he spoke as a kind of natural peer of the philosopher when he said:

> Ortega was not a specialist, for example, not a philosopher, although he has his eminent place among contemporary philosophers; nor a learned man, as Menéndez Pelayo was not either, although both men read everything under the sun; and much less did he claim to do what nobody can to—undertake even summarily to cover the whole panorama of knowledge, which is nowadays like a fathomless firmament. Wisdom consists in knowing what one knows profoundly and in comprehending profoundly what one does not know.[59]

In his call to his listeners to consider this occasion the appropriate honor that a state renders to those who have in the brilliance of their careers glorified it, Marañón touched upon the political aspect of the gathering, in which a "liberal" philosopher was being honored in the halls of a university still strictly administered by an authoritarian regime. Both Marañón and Laín understood that this homage to their old colleague was bound to have far-reaching symbolic significance, particularly among contemporary students, and they hoped to chart a peaceful middle way by invoking a nonpartisan and nonsectarian atmosphere as the proper one in which to honor one of Spain's greatest modern writers.

The final remarks by Laín, another doctor who had cultivated humanistic studies with distinction, were even more indicative than Marañón's words of the political significance of the occasion. He reminded his listeners that he had been instrumental in attempting to have Ortega return to his alma mater during his lifetime, then observed that since Ortega could not now be honored in the flesh, this salute to the man raised two questions: How could the university offer homage to one who had not wished to return to it? And how could it honor one whose teachings many felt should be forgotten? The answer, of course, was that the university would contradict its deepest meaning should it refuse to recognize the compelling excellence of Ortega's work. It must be dedicated first of all to "high, noble and pure ideas," a commitment that would not, Laín asserted, oppose its exalted "Christian and Spanish" purposes.[60] Thus, the university must guarantee that

> under the supreme and consoling leadership of the truth of Christ... there be an efficacious and friendly coexistence between the thought of Saint Thomas and the thought of Ortega, between the theology of Father Arintero and the poetry of Antonio Machado, between the heritage of Saint Ignatius and esteem for all that is estimable in Unamuno, between the spirit of Menéndez Pelayo and the spirit of Ramón y Cajal.[61]

A professed Catholic like Marañón, Laín hoped for a Christian republic of letters, at least in men's minds. And he naturally sought that side of Ortega which would accord with a pluralistic and ecumenical Christian future for the university and for Spain. Thus he concluded with the following statement from Ortega himself, adjuring his listeners to apply its sense to the life and example of their great compatriot:

> The dead do not die completely when they die. They remain a long while present. A long while an uncertain something of them hovers amongst the living who loved them. If during this time we breathe

deeply and open even the smallest avenues of our feelings, then the dead enter into us, make a dwelling place in us and, thankful as only the dead know how to be, they leave us the heritage of the full quiver of their virtues.[62]

The quiver would indeed be passed on to many in the audience, though they would learn to stock it with different arrows and shoot at different targets. Yet even as they did so, they would confirm the teaching of their best "liberal philosopher" that each generation must bring its own irrevocable and inalienable life-project to the great course of mankind's pilgrimage.

EPILOGUE

Ortega was without doubt the chief intellectual reformer of modern Spain. Obliged, in the midst of rapidly shifting political conditions, to present his work to a public unprepared for philosophy and intellectual novelty, he came to be one of the most eloquent and passionate of twentieth-century existentialist writers. Before 1936 he was sure of his capacities as a writer, teacher, and cultural critic; and his various publics—students, readers of *El Sol*, and educated citizens of Madrid—often confirmed these for him. Such was his situation in spite of the sometimes facile praise he received from a public lacking a standard of comparison by which to judge his work in the larger context of European culture. Perhaps that rootedness in Madrid and his ready access to various media for expressing his ideas made him able to write so well about insecurity and "shipwreck" in human life.

Even so, he had a persistent sense of the intellectual's fragile place in the larger arena of political and public life. His resultant disquiet was heightened by his being a *Spanish* intellectual, having always to turn toward Europe for stimulus. By the time of the Second Republic, and even earlier, during the last years of Primo's dictatorship, Ortega showed that he no longer had a firm notion of the relevance of his work in Spain. Previously he had shielded himself from radical doubt about his calling by his deep sense of Spanish citizenship, his belief in his obvious literary gifts, his family position among the politically liberal haute bourgeoisie, and his charisma as the central figure of select literary and intellectual circles. By the late 1920s, however, he had to acknowledge more fully the truth, caught in Manuel Tuñón de Lara's later assessment, that his Spain lacked the support of "a strong, liberal modern bourgeoisie that could break away from the system of the aristocratic-landholding oligarchy.... Such a middle-class force did not exist, nor was there any other capable of hegemonically 'nationalizing' institutions."[1]

With the failure of the Republic and the ensuing years of exile, Ortega came to know intimately the insecurity he had so movingly proclaimed inseparable from the human condition. He went on from the collapse of his native projects to achieve worldwide fame as a major European thinker. The timeliness of his existentialist view of modern man's condition accounts for much of his renown in the Spanish-speaking world and in translation. But the sheer felicity and vitality of his prose is equally important. A distinct voice is present in almost everything he wrote. Believing that "clarity is the philosopher's courtesy," Ortega never lost touch with the colloquial current in his written work. Some consider it a serious fault that his books are often composed of unrevised lectures or articles, but his lively tone and his "light" approach to big ideas are notable virtues of such works. Perhaps because such qualities are atypical of most philosophical prose, Ortega is not even mentioned in many surveys of modern thought. Both he and Unamuno, Spain's two greatest thinkers in our era, have been much neglected by twentieth-century historians of philosophy.

In Thomas De Quincey's famous distinction between literature of knowledge and literature of power, much of Ortega's work belongs in the latter category. Though the poet in the man was early subordinated to the writer of discursive prose, he retained his exceptional gift for pungent metaphor and sonorous phrasing. He could be light and profound at once, as perhaps all fine literature finally must be. In his best work, he moves one, as De Quincey says powerful writers must, by eliciting deep sympathy with truth. The catholicity of his curiosity plays a good part in this effect. As Curtius remarked on first reading him in 1924:

> From Ionic philosophy of science to Cubist painting there does not seem to be anything in which this critic is not passionately interested.... I do not know of any critic in Europe capable of writing with the same sympathy and the same understanding on Madame de Noailles and Simmel, Marcel Proust and Max Scheler. Ortega can and does. And in language sparklingly pointed, nervously clear, sensitive, and unrhetorical.[2]

More striking even than these qualities is the penetrating aptness of his understanding of life as a drama of existence. A passage like the following, in which he seeks to portray "with some clarity the essence of living," is typical:

> Living is not entering by choice into a place previously chosen accord-
> ing to one's taste, as one picks a particular theater to go to after dinner;
> living is finding oneself suddenly—and not knowing how—projected
> into, fallen into, submerged in a world that cannot be exchanged for
> any other, into the world of today. Our lives begin with the perpetual
> suprise of existing without any previous consent on our part, castaways
> on an unpremeditated globe. We did not give life to ourselves, but we
> met it at the very point where we met ourselves. We can compare our
> plight to that of a sleeper who is carried to the wings of a theater, and
> there, awakened with a push, is thrust down to the footlights and before
> the public.... He finds himself caught accidentally in a difficult situ-
> ation, without knowing how or why; somehow, he must, and with some
> decorum, resolve that sudden appearance before the public which he
> neither sought, prepared for, nor foresaw. Fundamentally, life is always
> unforeseen. Before entering on its stage, we have not been prepared or
> announced; yet that stage is always concrete and definite.[3]

The metaphor in this passage is felicitous and memorable. Starting
from the simple fact that each of us occupies a place in the world,
Ortega draws the tragicomic portrait of our improvised efforts to
create our roles in life. The figure of life as a theater is very old, but
it gains fresh currency in the image of the sleeping spectator's con-
tretemps. In this manner, Ortega artfully points up and deepens
what we already know, enhancing and clarifying our intuitive sense
of life. Comparing the pursuit of philosophy, as he often did, to
dancing, bullfighting, falconry, and the strategy of warfare, he
draws the reader charmingly into thought. The philosopher's tendency to cultivate a rebarbative style in the supposed interest of
greater depth and accuracy was for him a kind of misprision, a grasp
on the "point" rather than the entire process of communication.

It is finally not odd that his diverse work has not generally been
assessed accurately, with anything like a balanced and comprehensive sense of his achievements. The effort to do so has been hindered
by several conditions: his political involvement in a period only relatively recently opened for unrestricted study; the rancorous atmosphere of Spanish intellectual life for a long period after the civil
war; the lack of an authorized biographer with access to all his
correspondence and personal papers; and the fact that some of his
best and most revealing writings have become available only one or

two at a time with the publication (often posthumous) of paperback editions or new volumes of the *Obras completas* over the course of many years. In general, the publishing history of many of his key pieces has been, as I have shown, complicated by the circumstances under which they were composed and—in the case of lecture series—delivered. In several instances, important developments in Ortega's thinking have remained in unedited manuscript form for many years before finally appearing between covers; and even then they have often retained—perhaps occasionally to their benefit— the tone and format of unrevised lectures.

Furthermore, despite great efforts in the later part of his life, Ortega did not, as this study demonstrates, become a truly systematic thinker. The very word "system" become something of a shibboleth for him and has remained so for several members of what may be called the later "Revista de Occidente group"—Marías, Paulino Garagorri, Manuel Granell, and Antonio Rodríguez Huéscar, among others. Their perception of an overall structure in much of Ortega's work is generally overstated. In their desire to defend his reputation, they have also painted a depoliticized and ahistorical image of the man. This excess was partly a reaction to the extreme undervaluation and even vilification of Ortega in neotraditionalist Catholic circles during the 1940s and 1950s.[4]

Critics of this persuasion typically attacked his historicist "relativism," alleging that the strictly perspectival knowledge of reality to which, in Ortega's scheme, each man is limited means that no one has access to a "higher" absolute and total truth. But Father Frederick Copleston, the English Jesuit historian of philosophy, has argued that this critism is not entirely valid. Noting that "[p]erspectivism already presupposes some truths which are universally valid" (e.g., the truth of a "transsubjective reality"), Copleston sketches out the limits of relativism in Ortega, while agreeing with him that "any finite mind must occupy some particular point in history," from which "it does not follow that his interpretation of reality must be a purely imaginary and subjective construction simply because it is partial."[5] In fact, against his critics who feel that he does away with a standard of objective reality, Ortega can be read as asserting the self-evident presence of the world at it thrusts itself upon each man. To give primacy to what each knows in his own perspective is not to say that all else is unreal or "nonobjective." It is simply to assert that one cannot know *any* reality except through the ineluctable medium of his individualized life.

Copleston's criticism of Ortega is that the doctrine of perspectivism amounts almost to a truism and does not help us to resolve those views (or philosophies) of reality which are seriously opposed to each other and cannot therefore simply be treated as complementary. This charge—that Ortega did not say anything particularly new—is not an uncommon one. Some historians of philosophy have seen him primarily as a derivative, popularizing thinker who constructed his idea of *la razón vital*, for example, out of the work of Dilthey, Nietzsche, Simmel, Scheler, and others. Certainly there are in Ortega's work salient examples of such derivations (e.g., the notion of a "level of the times" continues from Hegel through Dilthey and appears prominently in Ortega about the time he first read Dilthey in 1929), but this approach begs the question of whether he succeeded in making something new out of the sources that influenced him.[6]

In fact, in grasping the immense importance of history—for him the definitive and comprehensive study—he significantly advanced the critique of abstract and atemporal reason as (in Aristotle's sense) the defining characteristic of man. Works like *Man and Crisis*, *The Origin of Philosophy*, and *The Idea of Principle in Liebniz* make it abundantly clear that it is fruitless to see the enduring essence of the human in a particular, time-bound version of this faculty. Among all the existentialists of his day (Jaspers, Heidegger, Sartre, Marcel, Berdyaev, Unamuno, et al.), Ortega gave the most dramatic and concrete picture of human life thrust into a situation and forced to define itself as a product of free choice. In response to the often abstract and excessively rationalistic quality of earlier Husserlian phenomenology, he developed a more encompassing and concrete picture of embodied and "circumstantialized" human life than any other thinker (perhaps excepting Merleau-Ponty) in the broad tradition of phenomenology and existentialism during the first half of this century. In this sense, he was far more than either a brilliant popularizer of others' ideas or merely the "vehicle" for introducing phenomenology into Spain.

Although, as we have seen, pro-regime intellectuals and some ecclesiastics tried to discredit Ortega's work for a time after the civil war, attacks on him diminished during the later 1950s in the slightly more relaxed atmosphere of a nation by then anxious to achieve at least the facade of liberalization necessary for it to claim a place in the consortium of industrialized Western nations. For many Spanish high-school and university students of the fifties, reading Ortega was a bold step toward mental independence, and as official hostility toward prewar liberals diminished, he was even allowed to become part of what Juan Goytisolo has called the "literary cocktail party" of acceptable prewar writers.

After the Press Law of 1966 legalized the publication and sale of Marxist and other previously forbidden texts in Spain, it was no longer a fashionable sign of independent thought to read and cite Ortega. More "radical" texts, most of them foreign, became the badges of mental liberation. Today he is not an important author for most of the young in Spain, but older men and women of all per-suasions still invoke his name and his ideas to express their views on Spanish culture. Indeed, the political history and cultural alle-giances of many Spaniards over fifty are often revealed in what they think of Ortega. Ultimately, for millions of literate Spaniards and Latin Americans his is still the outstanding modern model of clear, elegant Castilian prose vibrant with the play of wit and intellect. He has permanently elevated and enriched their conception and use of the language. Well over three and a half million copies of his books in Spanish have been sold to date, and the number sold in translation would make for a very large addition to that figure.[7]

Ortega's influence on Spanish thought and expression in this century has been vast and varied—almost alone his work intro-duced European phenomenology and existentialism into the Spanish-speaking world—and the number of Spanish and Latin American intellectuals upon whom he had a formative impact is a large one. The mark of his thought and his vocabulary is obvious in the work of liberal (sometimes ex-Falangist) Catholic humanists like Pedro Laín Entralgo, Dionisio Ridruejo, Antonio Tovar, José Antonio Maravall, Gonzalo Torrente Ballester, Juan Rof Carballo, and José Luis Aranguren; in direct continuers and commentators like An-tonio Rodríguez Huéscar and Paulino Garagorri; in thinkers who were formed and/or influenced by Ortega, García Morente, and Zubiri in the "School of Madrid," (e.g., José Gaos, Julián Marías, Juan David García Bacca, María Zambrano, and, less directly,

José Ferrater Mora and Eduardo Nicol); and in prominent scholar-critics like Francisco Ayala (an early contributor to the *Revista de Occidente*), Juan López-Morillas, and Manuel Granell. After that, the question of influence—at once obvious, pervasive, and subtle—eludes one. In being so deep and widespread, it has entered indistinguishably into the stream of the language.[8]

In recent years, important scholarly studies in several languages testify to the continuing vitality of Ortega's thought both in Spain and abroad. Several of these are mentioned in the following bibliographical essay. Their general purport has been to establish Ortega's rightful claim to a major place in the story of twentieth-century philosophy. The outstanding current study in Spanish, Pedro Cerezo Galán's *La voluntad de aventura* (1984), explores the evolution of Ortega's thought and sensibility with exceptional sympathy and acuity. Apart from the specialized studies, of course, Ortega continues to be read and quoted by many readers throughout the Western world who, without knowing his work as a whole, find nuggets of wisdom in one or another of his books and essays. For this public he is a philosopher in the broad old-fashioned sense of the word, one who offers memorable counsel on the conditions of human life.

It may not, of course, be through a directly traceable influence that one should expect to find Ortega's long-range effect, for his continuing appeal both at home and abroad owes much to his artistic sensibility and the extraordinary grace and verve of his writing style. This enduring quality of his essays is well caught by the Spanish intellectual historian Juan Marichal, for whom Ortega's relationship to German thought is secondary to the exceptional personal vision that will make his best work classic:

> Ortega's oratory would not...have marked the history of the Spanish language with its singular accent if it had consisted only (like that of Castelar) in the lively rhetorical exposition of certain principles of conduct and certain formulas for political or social action. A program of action is not enough for one to be a great writer. And in spite of Ortega's own frequent affirmation that he was above all a writer with immediate objectives, the creator of a "circumstantial" work..., it is clear that an aesthetic impulse was always at work in him....Ortega the verbal artist modified more than once, for aesthetic "reasons," the thought of Ortega the philosopher....In 1906 the Orteguian character "Rubín de Cen-

doya" declares, apparently for the first time in the pages of the Madrid author: "An infinite longing for permanence arises from our deepest center." Does one not find here one of the keys to Ortega's stylistic singularity, to his eagerness to seize "the marvel of the world"[9]

In the currently open, pluralistic atmosphere of Spanish culture and politics, it is now possible to recognize Ortega as both a great writer and one of the nation's most illustrious exponents of liberal humanism. In the era that has followed upon the death of Franco, the time seems right for further study of the charismatic figures of the prewar decades. Until recently, it was fashionable to portray Ortega as a vanguard voice of the naive and politically ineffective prewar bourgeoisie. Accurate as this perception undeniably is in one sense, it fails to note that the present generation of young Spanish internationalists share with Ortega the vision of a cosmopolitan culture that will overcome the traditional image of Spain as a semimodern, backward, "Latin" nation. The new generation of teachers, critics, and theorists will ultimately see that, whatever his political "failures," Ortega brought Spain a large step closer to cultural parity with the rest of Europe, shattering the older image of the decay so brilliantly caught in Antonio Machado's lines "Castilla miserable, ayer dominadora / Envuelto en sus harapos, desprecia cuanto ignora" ("Miserable Castile, yesterday reigning / Wrapped in its tatters, scorning what it knows not"). This tradition-burdened and stagnant self-image of Spain has been repeatedly challenged since the middle of the nineteenth century. Continuing that critique, Ortega's has been the most brilliant of the twentieth-century voices that have spoken against official, pious, and arrogant Spain for her own good.

ADDENDUM

The centennial of Ortega's birth in 1983 saw numerous homages to the memory of Spain's greatest modern philosopher. In the United States, conferences were held at the Library of Congress in Washington and on the campuses of Yale, Cornell, City University of New York, State University of New York at Albany, Hofstra, McGill, the University of New Mexico, and the University of Texas at Austin. Noteworthy among the publications resulting from these gatherings are the volumes *Ortega, Hoy*, edited by Manuel Durán (1985), and *Ortega y Gasset Centennial / University of New Mexico*, edited by Pelayo H. Fernández et al. (1985). The two-day session at the Library of Congress in October 1982 was cosponsored by the Fundación José Ortega y Gasset of Madrid, under the administration of the philosopher's daughter, Soledad Ortega. The Fundación, a private academic research institute with facilities in Madrid and Toledo, is dedicated to furthering the spirit of Ortega's work through series of courses and lectures on contemporary issues and on the history of Spanish civilization. In its programs for foreign students it also belongs in the tradition established by the Junta para Ampliación de Estudios and the Residencia de Estudiantes early in this century. As such, the Fundación embodies Ortega's desire—and that of Francisco Giner and others before him—to open Spain to cultural and intellectual exchange with the world beyond its borders. Its regular and visiting faculty include many of the nation's most distinguished teachers and researchers, as well as distinguished Hispanists from abroad. Under the capable direction of Soledad Ortega the Fundación also coordinates scholarly work on Ortega's personal papers and correspondence, copies of which are available in this country on microfilm at the Library of Congress. In its diverse activities the Fundación represents a late fruit of Ortega's work, illustrating the way a great man's posthumous effect may be continued by those who cultivate his memory and shape his image for posterity. While such work nobly testifies to the unexhausted riches of Ortega's writings, it remains essential that those who would assess his life and his ideas do so with something of the independence of mind that so obviously characterizes them.

NOTES

All note citations of José Ortega y Gasset's *Obras completas* refer to the editions and volumes listed in the first section of bibliography below. All translations of passages from these volumes and from all other works (by Ortega or other authors) cited in Spanish editions are my own unless otherwise indicated.

INTRODUCTION

1. Richard Ellman, *Golden Codgers: Biographical Speculations* (Oxford: Oxford University Press, 1973), p. 121.

2. My view on these matters has been shaped by Rudolph Binion's recent *After Christianity: Christian Survivals in a Post-Christian Culture* (Durango, Colo.: Logbridge-Rhodes, 1986).

3. Virginia, Woolf, *The Captain's Death Bed and Other Essays* (New York: Harcourt Brace, 1950), p. 96.

4. José Ortega y Gasset, *Man and Crisis*, trans. Mildred Adams (New York: W. W. Norton, 1958), p. 87.

5. In his allegiance to Spain's central province, Ortega espoused what one may call a "Castilocentric" version of Spanish history. Such a view is not a completely just reflection of the actual preeminence of Castile in Peninsular culture. One may plausibly argue, in fact, that twentieth-century intellectuals based in Madrid have often unjustly ignored or depreciated both the indigenous culture of Catalonia and the contributions of Catalans to the larger national culture. In turn, Catalonian cultural life has been isolated by virtue of regionalist and separatist tendencies and, in recent history, by the aggressively centralist cultural politics of the Franco regime. Something similar may be said as regards the Basque region.

6. Marion Levy, *Modernization: Latecomers and Survivors* (New York: Basic Books, 1972), p. 9.

7. Edward Shils, *The Intellectuals and the Powers* (Chicago: University of Chicago Press, 1972), pp. 363–364. In this volume and in its companion, *Center and Periphery: Essays in Macrosociology* (Chicago: University of Chicago Press, 1975), the sociological implications of this theme are richly developed. There is, of course, an enormous literature on urban and metropolitan life, the growth of cities, and the cultural significance of cosmopolitanism. Much of the best early work on these matters came out of the

"Chicago School" of sociology, which was itself inspired by the concepts of Simmel, Tarde, Durkheim, Weber, and other European social theorists.

8. Interview with Julián Marías, Madrid, January 10, 1973.

9. Ortega's indebtedness to and critique of these two strands of German philosophy has been treated extensively in the following studies: Ciriaco Morón Arroyo, *El sistema de Ortega y Gasset* (Madrid: Ediciones Alcalá, 1968); Philip W. Silver, *Ortega as Phenomenologist: The Genesis of "Meditations on Quixote"* (New York: Columbia University Press, 1978); Nelson Orringer, *Ortega y sus fuentes germánicas* (Madrid: Editorial Gredos, 1979), *Nuevas fuentes germánicas de ¿Qué es filosofía?* de Ortega (Madrid: Consejo Superior de Investigaciones Científicas, 1984), and "Ortega, psicólogo y la superación de sus maestros," Azafea, no. 1 (1985): 185–236; and Pedro Cerezo Galán, *La voluntad de aventura: Aproximamiento crítico al pensamiento de Ortega y Gasset* (Barcelona: Editorial Ariel, 1984).

10. Francisco Romero, *Filosofía de ayer y de hoy* (Madrid: Aguilar, 1960), pp. 188–189.

11. Ibid., p. 189.

12. José Ortega y Gasset, *What Is Philosophy?*, trans. Mildred Adams (New York: W. W. Norton, 1960), p. 75.

13. José Ortega y Gasset, quoted in Julián Marías, *Ortega y Gasset: Circumstance and Vocation*, trans. Frances López-Morillas (Norman: University of Oklahoma Press, 1970), p. 297.

14. H. Stuart Hughes has used the term "sea change" to describe the far-reaching changes wrought in the careers of distinguished émigré intellectuals and scholars who came to England and the United States as refugees from the Nazi movement and the general upheaval in European life during the 1930s and 1940s. (See Hughes's *The Sea Change: The Migration of Social Thought, 1930–1965,* [New York: McGraw-Hill, 1975].) Unfortunately, like so many other intellectual historians in the U.S., Hughes gives no attention to the diaspora of the late 1930s in Spain, which drastically altered the course of Spanish cultural development by depriving the country of so many of its most gifted critics, writers, historians, scientists, etc. Hughes's limited perspective repeats the pattern of neglect of Spanish affairs found in even the most eminent historians of modern European affairs. Although many of them have written extensively on the fall of the Second Republic and the political consequences of the Spanish Civil War, all too few have dealt with the cultural and intellectual conditions obtaining in Spain during the early decades of this century and resulting from the Nationalist victory in 1939. Such questions are now being explored by a new generation of foreign Hispanists and by the younger Spanish historians. An impressive internal attempt at remedying our ignorance of the specifically Spanish "sea

change," which created a far-flung culture in exile, is the six-volume *El exilio español de 1939* (Madrid: Taurus Ediciones, 1976–1978). Directed by José Luis-Abellán, the work includes many distinguished scholars among the contributors, but it nonetheless often becomes a narrowly empirical biographical record involving hundreds of exiled writers and men of learning. The study lacks, by and large, the skillful integration of biographical detail and currents in intellectual history at which Hughes is so adept.

1. FATHERS AND SONS

1. Robert Wohl, *The Generation of 1914* (Cambridge, Mass.: Harvard University Press, 1979), p. 130.

2. Karl Weintraub, *The Value of the Individual: Self and Circumstance in Autobiography* (Chicago: University of Chicago Press, 1978), p. xii.

3. Frederick B. Artz, *Reaction and Revolution, 1814–1832* (New York: Harper and Row, 1934), p. 183.

4. Bruce Mazlish, *James and John Stuart Mill: Father and Son in the Nineteenth Century* (New York: Basic Books, 1975), p. 18.

5. This formulation is Mazlish's.

6. See Mazlish, *James and John Stuart Mill*, pp. 32–36.

7. Salvador de Madariaga, *Spain: A Modern History* (New York: Praeger, 1958), p. 94.

8. Donald L. Shaw, *The Generation of 1898 in Spain* (London: Ernest Benn, 1975), pp. 211–212.

9. Ibid., p. 213.

10. Wohl, *Generation of 1914*, p. 123.

11. George Tyler Northup, *An Introduction to Spanish Literature*, 3d rev. ed. (Chicago: University of Chicago Press, 1960), p. 395.

12. Julián Marías, *Ortega I: Circunstancia y vocación* (Madrid: Revista de Occidente, 1960).

13. Juan López-Morillas, *The Krausist Movement and Ideological Change in Spain, 1854–1874*, trans. Frances López-Morillas (Cambridge: Cambridge University Press, 1981), p. 4.

14. Juan López-Morillas, *El krausismo español* (Mexico City: Fondo de Cultura Económica, 1956), p. 12. This seminal study has been a major source for some of my preceding observations on Spanish Krausism.

15. José Castillejo, *Wars of Ideas in Spain* (London: John Murray, 1937), p. 113.

16. For a convenient summary of Giner's pedagogical career and its later fruits, see the prologue by Juan López-Morillas, ed., *Francisco Giner de los*

Ríos: Ensayos (Madrid: Alianza Editorial, 1969) and Castillejo, *Wars of Ideas*, passim.

17. Raymond Carr, *Spain: 1808–1939* (Oxford: Oxford University Press, 1966), p. 472.

18. In *Generation of 1914*, Wohl chronicles the development of "generational consciousness" in France, Germany, England, Spain, and Italy. The chapter on Spain deals primarily with Ortega's partially successful efforts to create a full-fledged theory of generations, a task in which he has been followed by his disciple Julián Marías, who has provided a convenient critical survey of earlier generational theories but has not added fundamentally to his teacher's seminal insights. (See Marías's *El método histórico de las generaciones* [Madrid: Revista de Occidente, 1949]; English translation *Generations: A Historical Method*, trans. Harold C. Raley [University: University of Alabama Press, 1970].)

19. See Pedro Salinas, "El concepto de generación literaria aplicado a la del 98," in his *Literatura española siglo XX* (Madrid: Alianza Editorial, 1970), p. 26.

20. See the title essay in Ricardo Gullón, *La invención del 98 y otros ensayos* (Madrid: Editorial Gredos, 1969).

21. Fritz Stern, *The Politics of Cultural Despair* (Berkeley and Los Angeles: University of California Press, 1963), p. xxii.

22. On this apsect of Ganivet's thought, see Shaw, *Generation of 1898*, pp. 24–25.

23. Stern, *Cultural Despair*, p. 10.

24. Ibid., p. 12.

25. Ibid., p. 21.

26. Ángel Ganivet, quoted in Frederick B. Pike, *Hispanismo, 1898–1936* (Notre Dame, Ind.: University of Notre Dame Press, 1971), pp. 49–50.

27. Shaw, *Generation of 1898*, passim.

28. Carr, *Spain: 1808–1939*, p. 301.

29. Hans Jeschke, *La generación de 98 en España*, trans. Yolando Pino Saavedra (Santiago de Chile: Universidad de Chile, 1946), p. 49.

30. Ibid., p. 50.

31. Ibid., p. 55.

32. José Ortega y Gasset, *Meditations on Quixote*, trans. Evelyn Rugg and Diego Marín (New York: W. W. Norton, 1961), p. 72.

33. Ortega, *Obras* 9:480–481.

34. Ortega, *Meditations*, p. 107.

35. This overall view of the Generation is indebted to Shaw's reading of its work in *Generation of 1898*.

36. Thomas E. Willey, *Back to Kant: The Revival of Kantianism in German*

Social and Historical Thought, 1860–1914. (Detroit, Mich.: Wayne State University Press, 1978), p. 172.

37. Ernst Cassirer, *The Myth of the State* (New Haven, Conn.: Yale University Press, 1946), p. 296.

38. Ibid., p. 297.

39. Shaw, *Generation of 1898*, p. 203.

40. This selection of influential sources follows that of Jeschke, *La generación*, pp. 76–89.

41. Pedro Laín Entralgo, *La generación del noventa y ocho*, 4th ed. (Madrid: Espasa-Calpe, 1959), chap. 1.

42. Jeschke, *La generación*, p. 89.

43. None of the Spanish theorists of generations (literary or otherwise) has made serious use of Mannheim's "Das Problem der Generationen." The English version, "The Problem of Generations," is in his *Essays on the Sociology of Knowledge*, ed. Paul Kecskemeti (New York: Oxford University Press, 1952), pp. 276–320. Drawing critically upon earlier work by Dilthey, Pinder, and Heidegger, Mannheim established the term "generation-units," each of which has a social and historical "location" and participates in a "common destiny." The last point is crucial, for it marks the way in which a commonly "located" group of people encounters a set of historical circumstances which allows them to experience a genuine generational complex (*Generationszusammenhang*). In short, neither simple contemporaneity nor coevality nor social status nor physical proximity is by itself sufficient: an effective generation-unit must receive some catalytic charge from its encounter with the times, from its discovery of a shared destiny or fate. Then its members become bound together by a pattern of circumstances which may be rather exactly defined. Interestingly enough, Ortega should have been able to infer as much from his own views on the interaction of person and world and on man's inveterately historical condition, but ultimately his sense of destiny was less sociological than individually existential, laying stress on man's search for his authentic self. Although Ortega participated in a highly self-conscious "generation-unit" in Spain and instinctively understood much about the formation of such groups, he did not articulate in his work the social framework to be found in Mannheim. As a result, Ortega's sketchy theory of generations foundered in its overreliance upon a simple arithmetical scheme and upon the notion of a biological rhythm with which generations succeed one another.

44. Wohl, *Generation of 1914*, p. 78.

45. Ibid., p. 210.

46. Ortega, *Obras* 1: 106–107.

47. Joseph Levenson, quoted in Frederick E. Wakeman, Jr., foreword to

Joseph Levenson, *Revolution and Cosmopolitanism: The Western Stages and the Chinese Stages* (Berkeley, Los Angeles, London: University of California Press, 1971), p. xi.

2. THE YOUNG MEDITATOR

1. Ortega, *Obras* 1:41.
2. Ibid., p. 45.
3. Ibid., p. 47.
4. Ibid., p. 122.
5. Ibid., p. 119.
6. Ortega's letter to Maeztu, July 1908, quoted by E. Inman Fox, "Sobre el liberalismo socialista (cartas inéditas de Maeztu a Ortega, 1908–1915," in *Homenaje a Juan López-Morillas: de Cadalso a Aleixandre*, ed. José Amor y Vázquez and A. David Kossoff (Madrid: Editorial Castalia, 1982), p. 225. The entire article treats of the exchange between Ortega and Maeztu during the years cited.
7. Ibid.
8. Ortega, *Obras* 1:129–132.
9. Ibid., p. 443.
10. Marías, *Ortega* I, pp. 199–200.
11. Ortega, *Obras* 1:207–208.
12. Ibid., p. 209.
13. Ortega was deeply committed to what he judged to be the superior vaue of those authors whose works he caused to appear in Spanish translation, often before they were known in other languages outside their own. Indeed, he exercised the role of intellectual gatekeeper by defining (for the small, intellectually ambitious public who cared) that image of the height of the times most congenial to his own taste and convictions. Thus Spain had, in his view, to go to school to study Dilthey, Brentano, Simmel, Scheler, Husserl, Sombart, Spranger, Huizinga, Jung, and Bertrand Russell, to list major authors whose writings appeared in translation in the *Revista de Occidente* and its associated publishing house. Strikingly absent from this list of major thinkers were Marx and Freud. Evelyne López-Campillo, in *La Revista de Occidente y la formación de minorías: 1923–1936* (Madrid: Taurus Ediciones, 1972), mentions four notable "absences" among those thinkers whose work was central to the *Revista* enterprise: Marx, Croce, Bergson, and Heidegger. The latter's major work, *Sein und Zeit*, did not appear until 1927 and certainly did not offer itself for ready translation in the format of the monthly review; but it may also have posed too great a challenge to Ortega's sense of his own originality to receive his editorial support. Croce's work seems to have been of little interest to Ortega. Bergson initially impressed

him, but he later rejected the French philosopher as a muddled thinker, perhaps finding Bergson's vitalism too much like an irrational, quasi-mystical version of his own *razón vital*. One may suppose that Marx's revolutionary vision of history was inimical to Ortega's hope for gradual evolutionary change defined and guided by a liberal intellectual elite. Freud, whom López-Campillo does not mention in this context, propounded a view of psychic life which Ortega found distasteful in its stress on subconscious motivation and libidinal drive. Although Ortega wrote an early exploratory article on Freud in 1911 and provided a prologue in 1922 to a Spanish edition of his works, it is clear that the father of psychoanalysis was not, for him, a welcome presence on the horizon of contemporary culture. In general, Ortega's distance from the work of these latter two seminal figures reveals something of his vision of the modern world.

14. José Ortega y Gasset, *Phenomenology and Art*, trans. Philip W. Silver (New York: W. W. Norton, 1975), p. 24.

15. Ibid., p. 29.

16. Ortega, *Obras* 1:425–426.

17. Ibid., pp. 211–212.

18. Ibid., p. 209.

19. María de Maeztu, quoted in María Dolores Gómez Molleda, *Los reformadores de la España contemporánea* (Madrid: Consejo Superior de Investigaciones Científicas, 1966), p. 492.

20. Ortega, *Obras* 10:86.

21. Ibid. 1:517.

22. Ibid., p. 516.

23. Ibid., pp. 503–521.

24. Ibid., p. 475.

25. José Ortega y Gasset, quoted in Marías, *Ortega I*, p. 352.

26. A summary view of these issues may be found in Donald M. Lowie's *History of Bourgeois Perception* (Chicago: University of Chicago Press, 1982), chap. 6. "Multi-perspectivity" is Lowie's term. Another survey of changing patterns of perception and experience in this same period is Stephen Kern's *The Culture Time and Space, 1880–1914* (Cambridge, Mass.: Harvard University Press, 1983).

27. Virginia Woolf, quoted in Eudora Welty, *The Eye of the Story* (New York: Random House, Vintage Books, 1979), p. 192.

28. Ortega, *Obras* 2:117.

29. José Ortega y Gasset, quoted in Robert McClintock, *Man and His Circumstances: Ortega as Educator* (New York: Columbia University Teachers College Press, 1971), p. 153.

30. Ortega, *Obras* 2:44–45.

31. Ibid., pp. 252–253.

32. Ernst Robert Curtius, *Essays on European Literature*, trans. Michael Kowal (Princeton, N.J.: Princeton University Press, 1973), pp. 306–307.

33. Marías, *Ortega y Gasset*, pp. 322–323.

34. Ortega, *Obras* 1:272.

35. Ibid., p. 300.

36. The list of signers is given in McClintock, *Man and His Circumstances*, p. 88, and in Marías, *Ortega I*, pp. 530–532.

37. Ortega, *Obras* 1:272.

38. Ibid., p. 275.

39. Ibid., p. 286.

40. Ibid., p. 289.

41. Ibid., pp. 291–293.

42. This connection is remarked by José-Carlos Mainer in his valuable introduction to a work he also edited, *Falange y literature: Antología* (Barcelona: Editorial Labor, 1971), pp. 16–20. Specifically, he writes: "All the historians of the period agree... that the major ideological debts of the Falange refer to Ortega. It owed to the Madrid thinker the idea of the nation 'like a national dogma, like a suggestive project of common life' and a whole regenerationist rhetoric, begun on March 23, 1914, in the Teatro de la Comedia with the 'Old and new Politics' speech, that would be reconstructed in the same place twenty years later in the founding speech of the Falange by J. A. Primo de Rivera" (p. 18).

43. Ortega, *Obras* 1:268.

44. Ibid., p. 243.

45. Jaime Vicens Vives, *Approaches to the History of Spain*, trans. Joan Connelly Ullman (Berkeley, Los Angeles, London: University of California Press, 1970), p. xxiii.

46. The full list is provided in Margarita Saenz de la Calzada, *La Residencia de Estudiantes, 1910–1936* (Madrid: Consejo Superior de Investigaciones Científicas, 1986), pp. 153–154.

47. Ortega, *Meditations*, pp. 105–106.

48. Ortega, *Obras* 1:360–361.

49. Silver, *Ortega as Phenomenologist*.

50. José Ortega y Gasset, quoted in Silver, *Ortega as Phenomenologist*, pp. 9–10. The translation is Silver's.

51. Ortega, *Meditations*, p. 97.

52. Ortega, *Obras* 1:172.

53. Ibid., pp. 55–56.

54. Raymond Carr has noted the historical background of deforestation and the failure of reforestation projects in Spain: "The destruction of forests is the historic crime of agricultural Spain. In the past, sheep and the

privileges of the *Mesta* may have been to blame: but the ravages continued into modern times, long after the great days of sheep.... Apart from the demands of the fleet, the building industry and the kitchen, it was the constant extension of the plough that destroyed forest cover. The hatred of the peasant for trees is one of the most reliably attested and curious features of country life outside the north of Spain: trees harboured sparrows, weakened the corn, and 'wasted' land" (*Spain, 1808–1939*, pp. 424–425). Over against this judgment, a representative lyric passage from Ortega shows dramatically the post-romantic, mythopoeic sensibility of an urban intellectual celebrating the countryside: "A tree is perhaps the loveliest thing that exists: it has strength in the trunk, capricious indecision in the branches, tenderness in the tiny, stirring leaves. And beyond all this an indescribable serenity, a vague, mute, palpitant life that comes and goes hesitantly among the foliage. It seems to me right that the first Egyptians believed the souls of the dead went to live in the branches of trees, and the Argentine Indians placed their offerings to the divine Walechn under a tree" (from "The Pedagogy of Landscape," Ortega, *Obras* 1:55).

55. Ortega, *Meditations*, p. 45.

56. Ortega, *Obras* 1:318–319.

57. Ibid., p. 319.

58. Ibid., p. 46.

59. Ortega, *Meditations*, pp. 91–92.

60. Ibid., p. 95.

61. Ibid., p. 98.

62. Ibid., p. 101.

63. Ortega, *Obras* 1:164–168, 443–468.

64. In fact, Ortega's first book was never finished. The first meditation was concerned primarily with poetry, literary genres, and the nature of the novel. The original prospectus for the book included two further sections of meditations on Cervantes, a meditation on Azorín, one on Pío Baroja, one on "the aesthetics of *Myo Cid*," an essay on "limitation," a section on Goethe and Lope de Vega, a meditation on dancers, one on "the end of things" (*las postrimerías*), one on "the thinker of Illescas" (Julián Sanz del Río), and a final one on "Paquiro, or the bullfights."

65. In 1983 they were incorporated into vol. 12 of the *Obras completas*. The English translation by Jorge García-Gómez was published as *Psychological Investigations* (New York: W. W. Norton, 1987).

66. Jorge García-Gómez, in the introduction to Ortega's *Psychological Investigations*, p. 15.

67. Ortega, *Psychological Investigations*, p. 63.

68. Ibid., p. 164.

69. Ibid., p. 170.
70. Ibid., p. 185.

3. A MATURING VOCATION

1. Carr, *Spain, 1808–1939*, p. 509.
2. Ortega, *Obras* 11:268.
3. For a detailed and copious history of Ortega's journalistic career and of the newspapers with which he was associated, see Gonzalo Redondo, *Las empresas políticas de José Ortega y Gasset*, 2 vols. (Madrid: Ediciones Rialp, 1970).
4. Ortega, *Obras* 10:352–682.
5. Ibid., pp. 386ff.
6. For a list of titles, see Redondo, *Las empresas políticas* 1:309.
7. Ibid., pp. 309–340 passim.
8. José-Carlos Mainer, *Literatura y pequeña-burguesía en España: Notas 1890–1950* (Madrid: Editorial Cuadernos Para El Diálogo, 1972), p. 126.
9. Ibid., pp. 141ff.
10. Madariaga, *Spain*, p. 312.
11. Mainer, *Literatura*, p. 149.
12. Ortega, *Obras* 10:250ff.
13. Ibid. 6:223–225.
14. Manuel Rodriguez Navas, quoted in Pike, *Hispanismo*, p. 14. My remarks on *hispanismo* and *hispanidad* are generally informed by Pike's excellent summary history of the two terms.
15. Ortega, *Obras* 8:384.
16. José Ortega y Gasset, quoted in Pike, *Hispanismo*, p. 314. This statement is moderate, however, when compared with the visionary chauvinism of a conservative Catholic apologist for *hispanidad* like José María Pemán (later a major cultural ideologue under Franco): "Spaniards went to the New World and found an inferior race; but they then applied themselves to the task of whitening the faces of that race and of opening up their limited craniums so as to introduce into them the luminous and civilizing thought of the blessed Castilian race."
17. *El Hogar* (Buenos Aires), December 1, 1916.
18. The following biographical sketch draws from Doris Meyer, *Victoria Ocampo: Against the Wind and the Tide* (New York: George Braziller, 1979).
19. Orringer, *Ortega y sus fuentes germánicas*, pp. 207–233.
20. Ortega, *Obras* 3:329.
21. Ibid., p. 332.
22. Ibid., p. 335.
23. Ibid., p. 336.

24. Meyer, *Victoria Ocampo*, p. 58.

25. Victoria Ocampo, quoted in Meyer, *Victoria Ocampo*, p. 58.

26. Meyer, *Victoria Ocampo*, p. 59.

27. Ortega, *Obras* 2: prefacing pages, unnumbered.

28. Material included in this first volume had been planned for Meditation III of ten projected meditations in the original prospectus for Ortega's *Meditations on Quixote*, and bore the title, "Pío Baroja: Anatomía de un alma dispersa." An essay of the same title was finally published in Ortega, *Obras* 9:477–501.

29. Ortega, *Obras* 9:482–483.

30. Ibid., p. 494.

31. Ibid. 1:322.

32. Ibid. 2:111.

33. This piece too had been part of the original plan for the *Meditations* of 1914, namely, Meditation II, "Azorín: Primores de lo vulgar."

34. Ortega, *Obras* 2:160.

35. Ibid., p. 162.

36. Ibid., pp. 164, 169.

37. Ibid., pp. 170–172.

38. Ibid., p. 174.

39. Ibid., p. 176.

40. Ibid., p. 181.

41. Ibid., p. 185.

42. Ibid. 3:45.

43. José Ortega y Gasset, *Invertebrate Spain*, trans. Mildred Adams (New York: Howard Fertig, 1974), p. 28.

44. Ibid., p. 35.

45. Ibid., p. 77.

46. Ibid., pp. 81, 87.

47. Curtius, *Essays on European Literature*, p. 291.

48. Ibid., p. 299.

49. Ortega, *Obras* 3:151.

50. Ibid., p. 165

51. Ibid., p. 186.

52. Ibid., p. 185.

53. Ibid., p. 179.

54. In *La voluntad de aventura*, Cerezo discusses the connection between the earlier essay, published in *El espectador III* in 1921, and the immediately following *El tema de nuestro tiempo*. Cerezo's understanding of both texts has been helpful at this juncture of my study. For his rejection of the earlier criticism of "biologism" in Ortega, see *La voluntad de aventura*, p. 50n.

55. Ortega, quoted in Cerezo, *La voluntad de aventura*, pp. 202–203.

56. John A. Lester, Jr., *Journey Through Despair, 1880–1914: Transformations in British Literary Culture* (Princeton, N.J.: Princeton University Press, 1968), p. 87.

57. Erich Heller, *The Disinherited Mind* (Cleveland, Ohio: World Publishing, Meridian Books, 1959), pp. 264 and 278.

4. PRAECEPTOR HISPANIAE

1. José Ortega y Gasset, prefacing pages of *Revista de Occidente*, vol. 1 (July 1923).

2. López-Campillo, *La Revista de Occidente*, p. 55.

3. Manuel Tuñón de Lara, *Medio siglo de cultura española (1885–1936)*, 3d ed. (Madrid: Editoral Tecnos, 1973), p. 228.

4. López-Campillo, *La Revista de Occidente*, pp. 91–101.

5. For the essay and the foreword, see Ortega, *Obras* 1:216–238 and 6:301–303, respectively.

6. López-Campillo, *La Revista de Occidente*, p. 93.

7. Ibid., p. 103.

8. Ibid., pp. 83–84, 88.

9. Ibid., pp. 112–113.

10. Ibid., p. 114.

11. Ibid., pp. 133–134.

12. Ibid., pp. 116–117.

13. Ortega, *Obras* 4:489.

14. Ibid., pp. 490–491.

15. Ibid., p. 496.

16. Ibid., p. 499.

17. López-Campillo, *La Revista de Occidente*, pp. 141–142.

18. Ibid., p. 152.

19. Ibid., p. 68.

20. By 1938 the Revista press was able to publish a single title, followed by another in 1939 and four in 1940. When hostilities ceased, it came under the directorship of Ortega's son José Ortega Spottorno. The magazine itself suspended publication during the civil war, and despite Ortega's efforts to reinstitute it in the mid-1940s, it did not appear again until 1963, eight years after his death.

21. Carr, *Spain: 1808–1939*, p. 567.

22. Madariaga, *Spain* p. 344.

23. Luis Cernuda, *Estudios sobre poesía española contemporánea*, 3d ed. (Madrid: Ediciones Guadarrama, 1972), p. 144.

24. Ortega, *Obras* 11:93–94.

25. Noteworthy among Ortega's titles of this period are *España invertebrada* (1921), *El tema de nuestro tiempo* (1923), vols. 3–7 of *El espectador*

(1921, 1925, 1926, 1927, and 1929), *La deshumanización del arte* (1925), *La rebelión de las masas* (1930), the lecture series of 1929 which became *¿Qué es filosofía?*, *Misión de la universidad* (1930), various political writings collected under the titles *La redención de las provincias y la decencia nacional* and *Rectificación de la República* (both 1931), *Goethe desde dentro* (1932), the lecture series "En torno a Galileo" (1933), and "Historia como sistema" (1935).

26. José Ortega y Gasset, *The Dehumanization of Art and Other Essays on Art, Culture and Literature*, trans. Helene Weyl et al. (Princeton, N.J.: Princeton University Press, 1968), p. 7.

27. Ibid.

28. Ortega, *Obras* 3:355.

29. See Renato Poggioli, *The Theory of the Avant-Garde*, trans. Gerald Fitzgerald (Cambridge, Mass.: Harvard University Press, Belknap Press, 1968), especially chaps. 3 and 4.

30. I am indebted for this notion to Lionel Trilling's etymological note in *Sincerity and Authenticity* (Cambridge, Mass.: Harvard University Press, 1972) concerning a very old denotation of the Greek verb *authenteo*, which, besides meaning "to have full power over," also apparently meant "to commit a murder" (p. 131).

31. Ortega, *Dehumanization*, p. 44.

32. Simmel, for example, who clearly influenced Ortega's thought, maintained that in raising life from what he called "the animal level to that of the spirit" and in mediating between these levels, culture encountered "an internal contradiction" by virtue of the inevitable clash between permanent institutionalized structures and still-unshaped life energies (perhaps comparable to Freud's "libido"). Through cultural activity, such energy was sublimated or, as Simmel put it, "spiritualized" in the creation of forms. But as these became self-enclosed and self-perpetuating, they harnessed and often repressed the energy that had originally spawned them. Presumably, human life needed these forms in order not to fall back into the animal realm, but also, as Simmel observes, "[l]eft to itself ... life streams on without interruption; its restless rhythm opposes the fixed duration of any particular form.... This constant change in the context of culture, even of whole cultural styles, is the sign of the infinite fruitfulness of life." But, just as Freud posited the warfare of Eros and Thanatos, Simmel saw a tragic contradiction "between life's eternal flux and the objective validity and authenticity of the forms through which it proceeds." The overall process moved "constantly between death and resurrection—between resurrection and death." This dynamic picture of the genesis of culture and of its vulnerability to demands that sprang from without (or "below") its purview caused Simmel to see it as inherently conflictual. Without wholly sharing the emphasis on man's "animal" nature, Ortega took over a good deal of his philosophy of culture

from that outlook, present in a number of theorists around the turn of the century. (Quoted passages from *Georg Simmel on Individuality and Social Forms*, ed. and intro. Donald N. Levine [Chicago: University of Chicago Press, 1971], pp. 375–376.)

33. Ortega, *Dehumanization*, pp. 45–46.

34. Cited in Raymond Williams, *Keywords: A Vocabulary of Culture and Society* (New York: Oxford University Press, 1976), pp. 49–50.

35. Ortega, *Dehumanization*, pp. 51–52.

36. Ibid., p. 48.

37. Ibid., p. 78.

38. Ibid., p. 93.

39. Ibid., p. 94.

40. Luis Araquistain, quoted by Ignacio Soldevila-Durante, "Ortega y la narrativa vanguardista," in *Ortega y Gasset Centennial | University of New Mexico*, ed. Pelayo H. Fernández et al. (Madrid: José Porrúa Turanzas, 1985), pp. 201–202. The entire article helps to clarify Ortega's role as a mentor for the "vanguardist" generation of 1923 (Aub, Chabás, Salinas, Jarnés, Espina, Ayala). Salinas is sometimes grouped with the poetic generation of 1927.

41. Ortega, *Dehumanization*, p. 103.

42. Ibid., p. 54.

43. Éléna de le la Souchère, *An Explanation of Spain*, trans. Eleanor Ross Levieux (New York: Random House Vintage Books, 1964), p. 114.

44. Ibid., p. 112.

45. Ibid., p. 113.

46. V. S. Pritchett, *Midnight Oil* (New York: Random House Vintage Books, 1973), pp. 146–147.

47. For the figures on this point, see Stanley G. Payne, *The Spanish Revolution* (New York: W. W. Norton, 1970), pp. 59–61.

48. Ortega, *Obras* 3:127.

49. Guillermo de Torre, *Las metamorfoses de Protéo* (Buenos Aires: Editorial Losada, 1956), p. 46.

50. Saenz de la Calzada, *La Residencia de Estudiantes*, p. 28.

51. Ibid., p. 100. For another historical sketch of the Residencia, see William L. Fichter, "A Great Spanish Educational Institution: The Residencia de Estudiantes (1910–1936)," in *Homenaje a Juan López-Morillas*, ed. Amor y Vázquez and Kossoff, pp. 209–220.

52. Miguel Ortega, *Ortega y Gasset, mi padre* (Barcelona: Editorial Planeta, 1983), p. 189.

53. This last point was suggested to me by Prof. Juan J. Linz in conversation.

54. Ortega, *Obras* 3:623.

55. Ibid., p. 626.

56. Ibid. 11:142.

57. Ibid. 3:495.

58. Ibid., pp. 499–500.

59. During the twenties, Ortega's evening *tertulia* ran regularly from 8:30 to 10:00 P.M. and included, among others, Blas Cabrera, José Tudela, Manuel García Morente, Xavier Zubiri, Antonio Espina, Emilio García Gómez, Benjamín Jarnés, Valentín Andrés Álvarez, Gustavo Pittaluga and his son Gustavo, Ramón and Gaspar Gómez de la Serna, Alfonso García Valdecasas, and Corpus Barga (Andrés García de la Barga). This list is given by Miguel Ortega, also a regular participant, in *Ortega y Gasset, mi padre,* p. 92.

60. Ramón Gómez de la Serna, *Automoribundia* (Buenos Aires: Editorial Sudamericana, 1948), p. 47.

61. Carr, *Spain: 1808–1939,* p. 60.

62. These activities are cited in an unpublished manuscript by Soledad Ortega, "Datos biográficos de José Ortega y Gasset," which was provided to me by the author in Madrid. See also Miguel Ortega, *Ortega y Gasset, mi padre,* p. 98.

63. Ortega, *Obras* 8:359.

64. For his use of the term "pre-historic," see Ortega, *Obras* 2:563–576 passim ("Hegel y America").

65. Ibid., p. 348.

66. Ibid.

67. Ibid., p. 351.

68. Ibid., p. 374n.

69. Ibid.

70. Ibid. 2:636.

71. Ibid., p. 637.

72. Ibid., p. 639.

73. Meyer, *Victoria Ocampo,* p. 106.

5. THE LEVEL OF THE TIMES

1. Shlomo Ben Ami, *The Origins of the Second Republic in Spain* (Oxford: Oxford University Press, 1978), p. 36.

2. Ibid., p. 38.

3. Ibid., pp. 40–41.

4. Ortega, *Obras* 7:275–276.

5. Mildred Adams, translator's preface to Ortega, *What Is Philosophy?,* p. 9.

6. Paulino Garagorri et al., editors' preface to Ortega, *Obras* 7:276.

7. Such is the list as given by Orringer in *Nuevas fuentes germánicas*. The work of tracing German sources for Ortega's ideas was begun by Morón Arroyo in *El sistema de Ortega y Gasset*; see for this question pp. 123–133.

8. Nelson Orringer, "Ortega's Dialogue with Heidegger in *What Is Philosophy?*," in *Ortega y Gasset Centennial*, ed. Fernández et al., p. 52.

9. Ibid., p. 54.

10. Ortega, *What Is Philosophy?*, p. 241.

11. The relevant text is given in Marías, *Ortega I*, p. 352.

12. Ortega, *What Is Philosophy?*, p. 218.

13. Cerezo, *La volunted de aventura*, p. 337.

14. Ibid., pp. 337–338.

15. The dedication of the "Mission" essay was excised when the piece was incorporated into vol. 4 of Ortega's postwar *Obras completas* in 1946. The omission pointed to a prudent choice by the editors to present a depoliticized version of his work, for in the controlled atmosphere of the years just following the Spanish Civil War, Ortega was still very much persona non grata with the Franco regime. (The additional omission from that edition of Ortega's prewar political journalism was another act of apparently necessary image-building.) For the dedication to the FUE, see José Ortega y Gasset, *Mission of the University*, trans. Howard Lee Nostrand (New York: W. W. Norton, 1966).

16. Ortega, *Obras* 4:314.

17. Ibid., p. 350.

18. Ibid., p. 338.

19. Ibid., p. 330.

20. For the dates of the original articles in *El Sol*, see Redondo, *Las empresas políticas* 2:168–170.

21. José Ortega y Gasset, *The Revolt of the Masses*, 25th anniversary ed., trans. anon. (New York: W. W. Norton, 1957), p. 96.

22. Ortega's claim to the coinage of the term is asserted by Salvador Giner in his *Mass Society* (New York: Academic Press, 1976), p. 44.

23. Robert Nisbet, *Sociology as an Art Form* (New York: Oxford University Press, 1976), p. 44.

24. Williams, *Keywords*, pp. 159–160.

25. Daniel Bell, *Commentary*, July 1956, p. 77.

26. Ortega, *Revolt*, p. 24.

27. Ibid., pp. 35–36.

28. Ibid., p. 36.

29. Ibid., p. 38.

30. Ibid., p. 44.

31. Ibid., p. 136.

32. Ibid., p. 138.

33. Ibid., p. 141.

34. This now-famous phrase appears in Ortega's article "El error Berenguer" (*El Sol*, November 15, 1930), in *Obras* 11:279.

35. Ortega, *Revolt*, p. 147.

36. Ibid., p. 181.

37. Ibid., p. 182.

38. Paul Valéry, *History and Politics*, vol. 10 of *The Collected Works of Paul Valéry* (Bollingen Series XLV), trans. Denise Folliot and Jackson Matthews (Princeton, N.J.: Princeton University Press, 1962), pp. 131, 135.

39. Ibid., p. 136.

40. Ibid., p. 138.

41. Ibid., p. 139.

42. Ortega, *Revolt*, pp. 28–29. This standard translation employs both the terms "height" and "level" for Ortega's *altura*. I prefer the English term "level."

43. Ibid., p. 32.

44. T. S. Eliot, *Four Quartets* (New York: Harcourt Brace Jovanovich, Harvest Books, 1971), p. 16.

45. Baudelaire, quoted in Matei Calinescu, *Faces of Modernity* (Bloomington: Indiana University Press, 1977), p. 48.

46. Eliot, *Four Quartets*, p. 16.

47. Ortega, *Revolt*, p. 32.

48. Karl Löwith, *From Hegel to Nietzsche: The Revolution in Nineteenth-Century Thought* (New York: Doubleday Anchor Books, 1967), p. 203. A further account of the semantic career of *Zeitgeist* may be found in Maurice Mandelbaum, *History, Man and Reason: A Study in Nineteenth-Century Thought* (Baltimore, Md.: Johns Hopkins University Press, 1971), p. 429 and chap. 10 passim. Mandelbaum notes that the "first entry given in Grimm's *Worterbuch* for the term '*Zeitgeist*' dates from 1789; it is there pointed out that the term was also frequently used by Herder and Goethe." He notes further: "Although Hegel did not use the term itself in his *Phenomenology of Mind* (1807), the concept of a *Zeitgeist* was assuredly implicit at many points in that work, and particularly in Hegel's characterization of the spirit of his own time" (*History, Man and Reason*, p. 429). The rapid spread of the concept in German and in other European languages during the nineteenth century is attributed by Mandelbaum to its solid underpinning by such related terms of the late eighteenth and early nineteenth centuries as *Nationalgeist, Geist des Volkes, Nationalcharakter*, etc. These, or some version of them, may be found in such writers as Karl Friedrich von Moser, Fichte, Herder, and, earlier, Winckelmann and Lessing. Even Montesquieu's *L'esprit des lois* may be cited as an early instance of viewing the legal culture of a people as expressive of a folk or national spirit. As the idea spread and found varied expression in

European thought of the last century, it became impossible to trace its genealogy with any real precision. It is by no means clear, for example, that references by such English essayists as John Stuart Mill, Hazlitt, and Carlyle to a "spirit of the age" or "signs of the times" are directly related to the emergence of similar terms in German thought, though Carlyle, if anyone, would have been aware of their use by Hegel and others in Germany.

49. John Stuart Mill, *Essays on Politics and Culture*, ed. Gertrude Himmelfarb (New York: Doubleday Anchor Books, 1963), p. 1.

50. See especially Ortega, *Obras* 9:625–644 passim.

51. Ortega, *Obras* 4:321–322.

52. This theme is richly developed in Wohl's *Generation of 1914*.

53. Ibid., p. 204.

54. Ibid., pp. 236–237.

55. Ibid., p. 207.

56. Ibid., p. 209.

57. Ortega, *Obras* 2:22–24.

58. Poggioli, *Theory of the Avant-Garde*, p. 164.

59. E. H. Gombrich, *In Search of Cultural History* (Oxford: Oxford University Press, 1969), p. 7.

6. POLITICS AND PHILOSOPHY

1. The precise figures and some other material for this sketch of social and economic change are drawn from Shlomo Ben Ami, *Fascism from Above: The Dictatorship of Primo de Rivera in Spain, 1923–1930* (Oxford: Oxford University Press, 1983), pp. 310–318.

2. Marañón, quoted ibid., p. 317.

3. Ortega's thought on the question of regional relations within Spain varied. In *La redención de las provincias* (1931), he proposed a scheme for partial regional autonomy which would include local assemblies and regional governments, though these were distinctly not to be a federation of independent political entities. As for linguistic independence, both Ortega and Unamuno sharply opposed the official recognition of Basque and Catalan as primary languages in the schools. Their deep affective investment in the Castilian tongue seems to have been at stake in this quarrel.

4. Ben Ami, *Origins of the Second Republic*, p. 9.

5. Ortega, *Obras* 11:274ff.

6. Ibid., p. 279.

7. Ben Ami, *Origins of the Second Republic*, p. 44.

8. Ortega, *Obras* 11:127.

9. Redondo, *Las empresas políticas* 2:210.

10. Ortega, *Obras* 11:137–143.

11. Redondo, *Las empresas políticas* 2:212.

12. Ortega, *Obras* 11:172. With Ortega and Felix Lorenzo went several of the most distinguished writers who had contributed to *El Sol*: Azorín, Antonio Espina, Ramón Pérez de Ayala, Fernando de los Ríos, Ramón Gómez de la Serna, Lorenzo Luzuriaga, Benjamín Jarnés, Américo Castro, Salvador de Madariaga, Fernando Vela, and the brilliant cartoonist Luis Bagaría.

13. Redondo, *Las empresas políticas* 2:251; and on all the preceding, 2:219–252.

14. Ibid., pp. 306–307.

15. Gabriel Jackson, *The Spanish Republic and the Civil War, 1931–1939* (Princeton, N.J.: Princeton University Press, 1965), pp. 41–42.

16. Ortega, *Obras* 11:215.

17. Ibid., p. 221.

18. Ibid.

19. Ibid., p. 226.

20. Ibid., p. 229.

21. Ibid., p. 257.

22. Ibid., pp. 258–259.

23. Ibid., p. 255.

24. Ibid., p. 412.

25. Ibid., p. 387.

26. Ibid., p. 350.

27. Ibid., p. 371.

28. Ibid., pp. 382–383.

29. Ibid., p. 409.

30. Ibid., p. 396.

31. Ibid., p. 459.

32. Ibid., p. 460.

33. Ibid., p. 462.

34. Ibid., pp. 508–509.

35. Ibid., p. 519.

36. Ibid., p. 518.

37. In his *Spanish Revolution*, Payne notes that the Republican parties during the last days of the dictatorship and the first days of the Republic "tended toward extreme fragmentation" (p. 103). He also provides an analysis of their organization between 1929 and 1934.

38. Juan Marichal, *La vocación de Manuel Azaña* (Madrid: Editorial Cuadernos Para El Diálogo, 1968), p. 189.

39. Ibid., pp. 188–189.

40. Ortega, *Obras* 11:358–360.

41. Ibid., pp. 361–362.

42. Ibid., p. 432.

43. Redondo, *Las empresas políticas* 2:411–413.

44. Ibid., p. 499.

45. Ortega, *Obras* 11:520.

46. Ibid. 6:354.

47. Redondo, *Las empresas políticas* 2:550–568.

48. Ortega, *Obras* 11:531.

49. Victor Ouimette, *José Ortega y Gasset* (Boston: G. K. Hall, 1982), pp. 118–119.

50. José Ortega y Gasset, *Some Lessons in Metaphysics*, trans. Mildred Adams (New York: W. W. Norton, 1969), pp. 92–93.

51. Morón Arroyo, *El sistema de Ortega y Gasset*, p. 50, and Ouimette, *Ortega*, p. 103.

52. Ortega, *Some Lessons in Metaphysics*, p. 36.

53. Ibid., p. 59.

54. Ibid., p. 66.

55. Ortega, quoted in Meyer, *Victoria Ocampo*, p. 62.

56. Ortega, *Man and Crisis*, p. 186.

57. Ibid., pp. 42–43.

58. Ibid., p. 44.

59. In "Wilhelm Dilthey and the Idea of Life," published in the *Revista de Occidente* in November and December 1933 and January 1934, Ortega noted: "I did not know the philosophical work of Dilthey until these past four years, and I have not known it sufficiently until a few months ago. Thus I affirm that this ignorance has made me lose approximately ten years of my life." Only sometime in 1933, then, did Ortega feel that he had really absorbed this seminal work of late nineteenth-century *Lebensanalyse*.

60. Ortega, *Man and Crisis*, p. 38.

61. Ibid., p. 60.

62. Ibid., p. 65.

63. Ortega, *Obras* 5:317–375.

64. Ortega, *Man and Crisis*, pp. 110–111.

65. Ortega, *Obras* 9:617–624.

66. Ibid. 6:13–50. The essay appeared originally in English in *Philosophy and History: Essays Presented to Ernst Cassirer*, ed. R. Klibansky and H. J. Paton (Oxford: Oxford University Press, 1936.)

67. José Ortega y Gasset, *History as a System*, trans. Helene Weyl (New York: W. W. Norton, 1961; original English title: *Toward a Philosophy of History*), pp. 216–217. The title essay in this collection was translated by William C. Atkinson.

68. See Silver, *Ortega as Phenomenologist*, p. 4.

69. Ortega, *Obras* 6:342.

70. Ibid., p. 343.

71. Ibid., p. 347.

72. Ibid., p. 351.

73. Ibid., p. 353.

74. Ortega, "Nota preliminar," *Obras* 8, unnumbered page.

75. The first Spanish edition of the "Prólogo para alemanes" was published by Editorial Taurus, Madrid, in 1948. The first English translation appears as "Preface for Germans" in José Ortega y Gasset, *Phenomenology and Art*, ed. and trans. Philip W. Silver (New York: W. W. Norton, 1975). The Spanish text has since been incorporated in vol. 8 of the *Obras completas*.

76. Silver, *Ortega as Phenomenologist*, chaps. 3 and 4.

77. Ortega, *Phenomenology and Art*, pp. 73–74.

78. Ibid., p. 74.

79. Silver, *Ortega as Phenomenologist*, chap. 4.

80. José Ortega y Gasset, *The Idea of Principle in Leibniz and the Evolution of Deductive Theory*, trans. Mildred Adams (New York: W. W. Norton, 1971), p. 280.

81. Ibid., p. 281n.

82. Ibid., p. 281.

83. Ortega, *Obras* 5:184–206.

84. Ibid., p. 204.

85. *José Antonio Primo de Rivera: Selected Writings*, ed. Hugh Thomas (New York: Harper and Row, 1975), p. 220.

86. Ibid., p. 219.

87. Ibid., p. 220.

88. Stanley G. Payne, *Falange: A History of Spanish Fascism* (Stanford, Calif.: Stanford University Press, 1961), p. 39.

89. *José Antonio Prime de Rivera*, p. 74.

90. Ibid., p. 76.

91. Ibid., pp. 58–67.

92. See particularly Payne, *Falange*, chap. 5, and Mainer, *Falange y literatura*, pp. 18–20.

93. Gullón, *La invención del 98*, p. 169.

94. Ibid., pp. 173–174.

95. Jackson, *Spanish Republic*, and Stanley G. Payne, *A History of Spain and Portugal*, 2 vols. (Madison: University of Wisconsin Press, 1973), 2:639–643.

96. Payne, *History of Spain* 2:643.

97. Biographical details concerning Ortega's departure from Spain are taken from Soledad Ortega's introduction to her edited *José Ortega y Gasset:*

Imágenes de una vida, 1883–1955 (Madrid: Ministerio de Educación y Ciencia / Fundación Jose Ortega y Gasset, 1983), pp. 47–48.

7. THE SECOND VOYAGE

1. Ortega, *Obras* 5:379.

2. José Ortega y Gasset, *Man and People*, trans. Willard B. Trask (New York: W. W. Norton, 1957), pp. 25–26. The lecture as initially given in Buenos Aires differs somewhat from the form in which it was incorporated in "El hombre y la gente," a series of twelve lessons delivered in the Instituto de Humanidades in Madrid in 1949–1950. The passage quoted here, however, is the same in both the earlier and the later versions. The original Argentine version is found in Ortega, *Obras* 5:305–306.

3. Ortega, *Man and People*, p. 33.

4. Carl Becker, *The Heavenly City of the Eighteenth-Century Philosophers* (New Haven, Conn.: Yale University Press, 1932), p. 15.

5. Ortega, *Man and People*, p. 29.

6. Ibid., p. 23.

7. Ibid., p. 37.

8. Ortega, *Obras* 5:391.

9. José Ortega y Gasset, *Historical Reason*, trans. Philip W. Silver (New York: W. W. Norton, 1984), pp. 51–52.

10. Ibid., p. 60.

11. Ibid., p. 67.

12. Ibid., pp. 91–92.

13. Ibid., pp. 95–96.

14. Ibid., p. 97.

15. Ibid., p. 118.

16. José Ortega y Gasset, *Concord and Liberty*, trans. Helene Weyl (New York: W. W. Norton, 1946), pp. 74–75.

17. Ibid., pp. 80–81.

18. Ibid., pp. 81–82.

19. Ibid., p. 68.

20. Ibid., p. 72.

21. Ibid., pp. 51–52.

22. Ibid., p. 52.

23. Ibid., p. 53.

24. Ortega, *Obras* 2:378.

25. Ibid. 8:408.

26. José Ortega y Gasset, *Epistolario*; ed. and intro. Paulino Garagorri (Madrid: Revista de Occidente, 1974), pp. 168–169.

27. Ortega, *Obras* 7:570–571.

28. Ibid. 6:31.

29. Ibid. 8:404.

30. Ibid. 2:563ff.

31. Samuel Ramos, quoted in Patrick Romanell, *The Making of the Mexican Mind* (Lincoln: University of Nebraska Press, 1952), pp. 141–142.

32. José Gaos was not the only distinguished Spanish intellectual to be drawn to Mexico after the Republican defeat. Others included Eduardo Nicol, Juan Roura-Parella, Luis Recaséns Siches, José Medina Echeverría, Joaquín Xirau, and Juan David Garcia Bacca. Recaséns, a philosopher of law, and Xirau were particularly influenced by Ortega in their student years.

33. José Ortega y Gasset, *The Origin of Philosophy*, trans. Toby Talbot (New York: W. W. Norton, 1967), p. 7.

34. Ibid., pp. 7–8.

35. Ibid., p. 8.

36. Ortega, *The Idea of Principle in Leibniz*, pp. 274–275.

37. Ortega, *The Origin of Philosophy*, p. 29.

38. Ortega, *Historical Reason*, p. 129.

39. Ibid., p. 154.

40. Ibid., pp. 160–161.

41. Ibid., p. 181.

42. Ibid., p. 188.

43. Ibid., p. 190.

44. Ibid., p. 208.

45. Ibid., pp. 199–200.

46. Ibid., p. 209.

47. Ortega, *Obras* 6:419.

48. Ibid., p. 463.

49. Ibid., pp. 490–491.

50. Julián Marías, *Ortega** las trayectorias* (Madrid: Editorial Alianza, 1983), p. 165. In a note on the same page, Marías lists the membership of that *tertulia*, including regular and sporadic participants: Ortega's sons, José and Miguel; his brother Manuel and his cousin José Gasset; also Fernando Vela, José Ruiz Castillo, Pepe Tudela, Antonio Botín Polanco, Antonio Rodríguez Huéscar, Luis Díez del Corral, José Antonio Maravall, Tomas R. Bachiller, Alfonso García Valdecasas, Emilio García Gómez, José Vergara; and on occasion, Pedro Laín Entralgo, Xavier Zubiri, and Dámaso Alonso. Paulino Garagorri became an assiduous participant after 1955, and unexpected visits were paid from time to time by Edgar Neville, Julio Camba,

Antonio Díaz Cañabate, Domingo Ortega, Fernando Chueca, Julio Caro Baroja, José Germain, and José Miguel Sacristán.

51. Ortega, *Obras* 7:443.

52. Ibid., pp. 444–445.

53. Ibid., p. 445.

54. Luis Martín Santos, *Tiempo de silencio* (Barcelona: Seix Barral, 1965), p. 133.

55. Ortega, *The Idea of Principle in Leibniz*, pp. 7–8.

56. A laudable exception, which is, however, perhaps too exclusively concentrated on the matter of Ortega's sources, or *fuentes*, is Nelson Orringer's "La crítica a Artistóteles de Ortega, y sus fuentes," in *Ortega, Hoy: Estudio, ensayos y bibliografía sobre la vida y la obra de José Ortega y Gasset*, ed. Manuel Durán (Xalapa, Mexico: Universidad Veracruzana, 1985), pp. 175–223.

57. Ortega, *The Idea of Principle in Leibniz*, p. 248.

58. Ibid., p. 348.

59. Ibid., p. 361.

60. Ibid., p. 287 n. 8.

61. I am indebted for this perception of a particular juncture in Ortega's philosophical development to Orringer's *Nuevas fuentes germánicas*, especially pp. 43–54.

62. Ortega, *The Idea of Principle in Leibniz*, pp. 277–278.

63. Ibid., p. 283.

64. Ibid., p. 325.

65. Ibid., p. 330.

66. Ibid., p. 295.

67. Ibid., pp. 312–313; translation slightly altered by me.

68. Ibid., pp. 243–244; translation corrected by me.

69. Ibid., p. 159.

70. José Ortega y Gasset, *La idea de principio en Leibniz y la evoluoión de la teoría deductiva* (Buenos Aires: Emecé Editores, Biblioteca de la Revista de Occidente, Obras inéditas de José Ortega y Gasset, 1958), p. 177–178. This was the original Spanish-language edition of the work, which was later incorporated into vol. 8 of the *Obras completas*, 2d ed. (Madrid: Revista de Occidente, 1965).

71. Ortega, *La idea de principio en Leibniz*, pp. 197–198.

72. Ibid., pp. 242–243.

73. Alain Guy, *Ortega y Gasset: Crítico de Aristóteles* (Madrid: Espasa-Calpe, 1968), p. 181.

74. Ortega, *The Idea of Principle in Leibniz*, p. 130.

75. Ibid., pp. 34–35n.

76. Cerezo, *La volunted de aventura*, p. 430.

8. THE FINAL YEARS

1. Salvador Giner, "Power, Freedom and Social Change in the Spanish University, 1939–1975," in *Spain in Crisis: The Evolution and Decline of the Franco Regime*, ed. Paul Preston (London: Harvester, 1976), p. 187.

2. Raymond Carr and Juan Pablo Fusi, *Spain: Dictatorship to Democracy*, 2d ed. (London: Allen and Unwin, 1981), p. 109.

3. José Maravall, *Dictatorship and Political Dissent: Workers and Students in Franco's Spain* (New York: St. Martin's, 1978), p. 99.

4. Quoted in Max Gallo, *Spain Under Franco*, trans. Jean Steward (New York: Dutton, 1974), p. 132.

5. Maravall, *Dictatorship and Political Dissent*, pp. 98–100.

6. Gallo, *Spain Under Franco*, p. 134.

7. Dionisio Ridruejo, "En los setenta anos de don José Ortega y Gasset," in his *Casi unas memorias*, with a prologue by Salvador de Madariaga (Barcelona: Editorial Planeta, 1976), p. 319.

8. For an example of this approach to Ortega, see José Luis Aranguren, *La ética de Ortega*, 2d ed. (Madrid: Taurus Ediciones, 1959).

9. Three exemplary conservative figures from the 1950s are Miguel Oromí, Father Santiago Ramírez, and Vicente Marrero. A representative debate between the conservative and liberal positions can be seen in the polemically heated series of assertions and responses beginning with Father Ramírez's *La filosofía de Ortega y Gasset* (Barcelona: Herder, 1958). This is answered in Pedro Laín Entralgo, "Los católicos y Ortega," *Cuadernos Hispanoamericanos*, no. 101 (May 1958), pp. 283ff. Ramírez, in turn, continued the polemic in a second book, *¿Un orteguismo católico?* (Salamanca, Spain: San Esteban, 1958). Julián Marías, Aranguren, and Laín Entralgo all replied to this publication, Marías in *El lugar del peligro: Una cuestión disputada en torno a Ortega* (Madrid: Cuadernos Taurus, 1958), to which Ramírez rejoined in his third book in two years, *La zona de seguridad* (Salamanca: San Esteban, 1959). As early as 1950, Marías had already done battle against Catholic critics of Ortega who combined a spirit of neo-Scholastic revivalism with a startling lack of judgment and integrity. In his *Ortega y tres antípodas: Un ejemplo de intriga intelectual* (Buenos Aires: Revista de Occidente argentina, 1950), Marías examined a rash of books published in the 1940s by three Jesuit priests. These were: Joaquín Iriarte, *Ortega y Gasset: Su persona y su doctrina* (Madrid: Razon y Fe, 1942) and *La ruta mental de Ortega* (Madrid: Razon y Fe, 1949); José Sánchez Villaseñor, *José Ortega y Gasset: Pensamiento y trayectoria* (Mexico City: Editorial Jus, 1943; English translation *Ortega y Gasset, Existentialist*, trans. Joseph Small, S. J. [Chicago: Henry Regnery, 1949]), and *La crisis del historicismo y otros ensayos* (Mexico City: Editorial Jus,

1945); and Juan Roig Gironella, *Filosofía y Vida. Cuatro ensayos sobre actitudes. Nietzsche, Ortega y Gasset, Unamuno y Croce* (Barcelona: Barna, 1946).

10. An example of this view is Cesáreo Rodríguez y García-Loredo, *El "esfuerzo medular" del krausismo frente a la obra gigante de Menéndez Pelayo* (Oviedo, Spain: n.p. 1961).

11. Ortega, *Obras* 7:20–21.

12. Ibid. 9:444–445.

13. Ibid., p. 445n.

14. Ibid. 2:451–452.

15. Ortega, *Epistolario*, p. 105.

16. Ortega, *Obras* 4:283.

17. *The Collected Poetry of W. H. Auden* (New York: Random House, 1945), pp. 183–185.

18. Ortega, *Obras* 4:285.

19. Ibid., p. 307.

20. Ibid., p. 310.

21. Ortega, *Obras* 9:151.

22. Ibid., p. 146.

23. Ibid., pp. 224–225.

24. *Informaciones*, December 13, 1948.

25. Ortega, *Obras* 8:304.

26. *Informaciones*, December 14, 1948.

27. This and other details of the founding and fortunes of the Instituto may be found in Marías, *Ortega** las trayectorias*, pp. 393–412.

28. Ortega, *Obras* 9:568.

29. Ibid., pp. 557–568, gives the text of his remarks at Aspen as amplified for later use in Hamburg. The lectures were substantially the same.

30. Ibid., pp. 560–562.

31. Ibid., pp. 592–593.

32. Thornton Wilder, quoted in James Sloan Allen, *The Romance of Commerce and Culture* (Chicago: University of Chicago Press, 1983), p. 198.

33. Allen, *Romance*, p. 145.

34. Ibid., p. 172.

35. Ortega, letter to Paepcke, quoted ibid., p. 208.

36. Allen, *Romance*, p. 210.

37. Ibid., p. 212.

38. René Char, *Feuillets d'Hypnos*, no. 62 (n.p. 1943–1944).

39. Ortega, *Revolt*, p. 36.

40. Ibid.; Ortega is here quoting himself from an appendix to the Spanish version of *La deshumanización del arte*. For the text in Spanish, see Ortega, *Obras* 3:428.

41. Ortega, *Revolt*, p. 36.

42. Ortega, *Obras* 9:247ff.
43. Ibid., pp. 250–251.
44. Ibid., p. 267.
45. Ibid., pp. 275–276.
46. As the lectures finally appeared in their 1957 Spanish edition (translated into English the same year), they correspond only very roughly to the twelve topics announced by the Instituto de Humanidades in 1949. Moreover, Ortega had originally projected eight additional topics, which were not treated at all. As was often the case, he was probably composing and revising the series in his mind at least until the first lecture that winter. The genesis of this attempt at a philosophical sociology went back to a lecture in Valladolid in 1934, in which he had presented his notion of social usage under the very title "El hombre y la gente." Then in 1939 he published in Buenos Aires "Ensimismamiento y alteracíon," which eventually became chap. 1 of the 1957 edition of *El hombre y la gente*. During that same period in Argentina, he presented a short version of the larger work-in-progress in *cursillos* at the University of Buenos Aires. The presentation in Madrid was the next step, followed by others in Germany and Switzerland in the early 1950s. The editors' note to the "final" version as incorporated in the *Obras completas* remarks that "[t]he text does not cover the whole projected contents...death surprised the author when he was working over the last chapters" (*Obras* 7:72), thus suggesting that this palimpsest-like work haunted Ortega until the end. The lists of the originally projected topics to be covered are given in *Obras* 7:270–272.
47. Juan López-Morillas, as cited and translated in Harold C. Raley, *José Ortega y Gasset: Philosopher of European Unity* (University: University of Alabama Press, 1971), p. 36.
48. Ortega, *Obras* 9:636.
49. Ibid., pp. 631–632.
50. Ibid., p. 631.
51. Ibid., p. 634.
52. Ortega, quoted in Ricardo Senabre Sempere, *Lengua y estilo de Ortega y Gasset*, vol. 18, no. 3, of *Acta Salmanticencia, Filosofía y letras* (Salamanca, Spain: Universidad de Salamanca, 1964), p. 119.
53. The text of the notice to newspapers, submitted by the Vice-Secretary for Popular Education and distributed on October 15, 1955, is quoted as follows in Francisco López Frías, *Ética y política: En torno al pensamiento político de J. Ortega y Gasset* (Barcelona: Promociones Publicaciones Universitarias, 1985), p. xxiii: "In view of the possible contingency of the death of Don José Ortega y Gasset, and supposing that it in fact occurs, that newspaper will publish it with a maximum title of two columns and the inclusion, if desired, of a single encomiastic article, not neglecting his polit-

ical and religious errors and, in any case, always eliminating the name 'maestro.'"

54. Miguel Ortega, *Ortega y Gasset, mi padre*, p. 201.

55. Soledad Ortega, *Imágenes de una vida*, pp. 58–59.

56. Ibid., p. 58.

57. Joaquín Ruiz Jiménez, quoted in Sergio Vilar, *La oposición a la dictadura: Protagonistas de la España democrática* (Barcelona: Ediciones Aymá, 1976), p. 405. The quotation is from an interview with Ruiz Jiménez.

58. Emilio García Gómez, "Diez lecciones de Ortega," in *Acto en memoria del catedrático Don José Ortega y Gasset* (Madrid: Universidad de Madrid, Facultad de Filosofía y Letras, 1955), p. 38.

59. Gregorio Marañón, in *Acto en memoria*, p. 61.

60. Pedro Laín Entralgo, "La razón de un homenaje," in *Acto en memoria*, p. 73.

61. Ibid., p. 74.

62. Ortega, quoted by Laín Entralgo, in *Acto en memoria*, p. 77.

EPILOGUE

1. Tuñón de Lara, *Medio siglo de cultura española*, p. 230.

2. Curtius, *Essays on European Literature*, pp. 282–283.

3. Ortega, *Some Lessons in Metaphysics*, pp. 40–41.

4. Among the works of antagonistic lay critics, two representative ones of some substance and intelligence are Vicente Marrero, *Ortega, filósofo "mondain"* (Madrid: Rialp, 1961), and Gonzalo Fernández de la Mora, *Ortega y el 98* (Madrid: Rialp, 1961). Prominent critiques by priests, in addition to those already cited by Iriarte and Sánchez Villaseñor, are Arturo Gaete's *El sistema maduro de Ortega* (Buenos Aires: General Fabril, 1962) and Hernán Larraín Acuña's *La génesis del pensamiento de Ortega* (Buenos Aires: General Fabril 1962). More sympathetic and balanced studies from a Catholic viewpoint—excepting here the obvious mention of Marías's work—are J. H. Walgrave, O. P., *La filosofía de Ortega y Gasset*, trans. Luis G. Daal (Madrid: Revista de Occidente, 1965), and Ciriaco Morón Arroyo, *El sistema de Ortega y Gasset* (see bibliograhical essay, below).

5. Frederick Copleston, *Philosophers and Philosophies* (New York: Harper and Row, 1976), pp. 178 and 181.

6. This much-vexed question, together with that of Ortega's systematicity, seems finally one of emphasis. A painstaking reading of the entire body of Ortega's work can, it seems, extract something like a "system" in the sense of repeated leitmotivs, patterns of usage and conceptualization, semantic histories of key terms, etc. Such a reading has been done patiently and skillfully by Morón Arroyo, whose work, along with Philip Silver's on

Ortega as a phenomenologist, has done much to highlight Ortega's claims to serious philosophical status. Morón aruges persuasively that Ortega did indeed make something new and valuable of the many German sources on which he abundantly drew. The same argument, as the bibliographical essay below makes clear, has been advanced in the work of Nelson Orringer and in Pedro Cerezo's recent *La voluntad de aventura* (1984), in many ways the most brilliant and just study of Ortega's work yet to appear in Spanish.

7. As of the early 1970s (later figures have not been made available), approximately 610,000 copies of Ortega's books had been sold in German and around 50,000 in French translation. (Figures cited in a letter to the author from José Ortega Spottorno, Madrid, January 30, 1973.) During the first thirty years of his career, Ortega reached readers mainly in Spain and, to a lesser extent, in Argentina, but by the 1940s he was increasingly translated in a dozen or more languages. Continuously popular in Germany from the 1930s on, his work gradually gained an appreciable public in England, France, Holland, and the United States, to name prominent examples. In Germany, the last hundred years have seen a marked cultivation of Hispanic studies. German scholars of the nineteenth and twentieth centuries helped to disseminate Spanish culture in Europe and even to reintroduce some aspects of it (for example, golden age drama) to Spaniards themselves. However, Ortega's broadly popular appeal in Germany, particularly with *The Revolt of the Masses* and *Studies on Love*, cannot be accounted for within a strictly academic context. Perhaps it rested on his ability to offer the German public a more accessible and frankly "literary" version of some of the most seminal ideas of modern philosophy and cultural criticism than they could find in their own somewhat more forbidding thinkers. For versions of his works in German, Ortega had the good fortune to find an excellent translator in Helene Weyl, the wife of the physicist Hermann Weyl. (She is also one of Ortega's translators into English.) With her renditions of his essays, many German readers hardly knew they were reading a foreign author. Since his works sold steadily in German translation both before and after World War II, it was natural that when he could no longer find an adequate public in Spain after 1945, he should turn back to the adopted country and language of his student years, for the German public seemed ready to offer him the enthusiastic response he so avidly sought as he attempted to reestablish his career after the experience of wandering in exile. Ortega's success in American translations has been steady since *The Revolt of the Masses* first appeared here in 1932. Of course, it has come the closest of any of his titles in English translation to being a best-seller, having sold to date well in excess of 100,000 copies. (This figure was provided by Ortega's American publisher, W. W. Norton, in May 1987.) In the Anglo-American world, Ortega's appeal has always been to the general public, for his work

has generally not been studied and respected by professional philosophers in England and the United States. Its apparent lack of rigor and method and its essayistic tendency do not belong to the universe of discourse that obtains in English-speaking philosophical circles. Even so, in American paperback editions, Ortega's numerous titles still sell steadily and continue to be used in college humanities courses and surveys of modern thought. His continuing importance in this country is indicated by the translated titles of approximately the last two decades: *Mission of the University* (1966), *The Origin of Philosophy* (1967), *Some Lessons in Metaphysics* (1969), *The Idea of Principle in Leibniz* (1971), *An Interpretation of Universal History* (1973), *Phenomenology and Art* (1975), *Historical Reason* (1984), *Meditations on Hunting* (1985), and the recently published *Psychological Investigations* (1987).

8. For Ortega's role in creating a Spanish "rhetoric of humanism," see Thomas Mermall's study *The Rhetoric of Humanism: Spanish Culture after Ortega y Gasset* (New York: Bilingual Press, 1976). Mermall is interested in the development of the essay in Spain after the civil war. His major figures are Pedro Laín Entralgo, Juan Rof Carballo, Enrique Tierno Galván, and José Luis Aranguren.

9. Juan Marichal, *La voluntad del estilo: Teoría e historia del ensayismo español* (Madrid: Revista de Occidente, 1971), p. 215.

BIBLIOGRAPHICAL ESSAY

We may best simplify this brief review of major secondary work on Ortega by first addressing titles originally published in Spanish and then those originally published in English.

Ortega's writings and his career have been much discussed in Spain for decades now, but until recently the voluminous secondary literature in Spanish was generally divided between, on the one hand, uncritical exposition of his ideas and adulation of his person and, on the other, ideologized, often *ad hominem* vilification. Since then, there have been some able Spanish expositions of various aspects of his work, considerably advancing our grasp on his diverse career as a man of letters, a political journalist, and a philosopher. Similarly, there has been more sophisticated attention—in Spanish intellectual history if not in Ortega studies proper—to the larger European and Spanish contexts of his work. (But no study, it should be added, has concentrated as fully as the present one on his role as a modernizing intellectual devoted to bringing Spain abreast of the European "level," although everyone acknowledges that he indeed hoped to do just that.)

To date only Julián Marías's lengthy study of the young Ortega has begun to deal directly with the related question of Ortega's debt to the Spanish reformist tradition that preceded him and with his position in the generational groups of modern Spanish intellectuals. This study—*Ortega I: Circunstancia y vocación* (1960; English translation *Ortega y Gasset: Circumstance and Vocation*, 1970)—begins the effort toward a sympathetic, comprehensive treatment of the man's career. When the study was published, Marías announced his intention to complete the picture with two subsequent volumes. Having later revised this plan, he recently published what is obviously the concluding volume, *Ortega** las trayectorias* (1983). While the latter is a more personal work with greater biographical detail than *Ortega I*, both volumes are limited by Marías's unstinting devotion to his friend and former teacher, whose every word seems to call for reverent exegesis. In the later volume particularly, Marías seems rhetorical and verbose, often quoting his own earlier writings at tedious length. The reader may indeed learn a good deal about Ortega from these two books, but he will do so strictly from within that curious extension of a great man's aura which disciples sometimes manage to effect.

Other sympathetic Spanish expositors of Ortega's work, most of them not as worshipful as Marías, include his prewar student José Gaos and a number of somewhat younger writers—often men close to the *Revista de Occidente*—like Paulino Garagorri (who has for many years edited new volumes of the steadily expanding *Obras completas*), José Luis Aranguren, Enrique Lafuente Ferrari, Juan López-Morillas, Antonio Rodríguez Huéscar, Manuel Granell, Juan Marichal, and José Luis Abellán. As Spanish-language efforts toward what might be called the "recovery" of the import of Ortega's career, the following titles deserve mention. A few years after Marías's first volume, J. H. Walgrave's *La filosofía de Ortega y Gasset* (translation from Dutch, 1965) provided a balanced and dispassionate introduction to Ortega's thought. In the following year, Antonio Rodríguez Huéscar published an exhaustive study of a central aspect of Ortega's work entitled *Perspectiva y verdad: El problema de la verdad en Ortega* (1966). As the title suggests, the author's principal concern is with the charge that Ortega's "perspectivism" relativizes whatever truth his work may be said to attain. Working through the entire body of the writings between 1902 and 1950, Rodríguez Huéscar convincingly reconciles the apparent conflict between the two key terms of the title.

In 1968, Ciriaco Morón Arroyo published *El sistema de Ortega y Gasset*, an attempt to go beyond Marías's generally uncritical book and, as the title indicates, to settle the wearisome debate over the presence or absence of "system" in Ortega's works. Morón's scrupulous examination of the primary texts produced thirteen categorical chapters and a "coda" covering the conceptual range of the man's thought. He has a great deal to say on Ortega's debt to such German mentors and contemporaries as Cohen, Scheler, Simmel, Spengler, Hartmann, and Heidegger, material that richly illumines his final judgment that Ortega's originality lies in what he made of assimilated ideas and currents of thought from German philosphy. Morón argues that Ortega's strength was his gift for creatively reconceiving the sources from which he drew and elaborating them with consummate literary skill. While the general argument for a "systematic" Ortega is not altogether convincing—the stages of his intellectual development are too neatly drawn, tending to compartmentalize what was a more organic and sometimes messy process—Morón refutes for good the foolish notion that Ortega was little more than an impressionistic journalist. In the regard, his ambitious book accomplished something unachieved by any previous study. Nonetheless, Morón's stress on Ortega's relation to the history of ideas tends to minimize the social and historical context of his intellectual biography. In addition, there is a passing attempt in chapter 13 to reconcile Ortega's thought with contemporary neo-Thomism. This intrusion of an evidently extraneous doctrine—for Morón's attempt is forced and quite unconvincing—mars a book that otherwise offers the reader a thoroughgoing analysis of all the major themes.

An admirably specialized study of a prominent facet of Ortega's work (particularly evident in the postwar writings) is Enrique Lafuente Ferrari's *Ortega y las artes visuales* (1970). Lafuente provides first an overview of the theme of visual art in the work as a whole, then a close scrutiny of Ortega's essays on Velázquez, and finally a strongly biased, somewhat schematic defense of *The Dehumanization of Art* as a prophetic work. The first two sections of this book remain its best. On a very different tack, Gonzalo Redondo's two-volume *Las empresas políticas de José Ortega y Gasset* (1970) gives an informative chronicle of Ortega's political development from 1917 to 1934, which is closely coordinated with key events of the time and richly detailed in its central analysis of his ties to the newspapers *El Imparcial, El Sol, Crisol*, and *Luz*. Redondo's main flaw is a tendency toward abundant elaboration at the expense of a clear narrative or conceptual order. His work was followed by Javier Lalcona's *El idealismo político de Ortega y Gasset* (1974), a critique of the vagueness and ambiguity characteristic of what Lalcona sees as Ortega's historically outmoded and impressionistic approach to the major political issues of twentieth-century Spain.

Five years later, Nelson Orringer, a young American scholar, opened a new chapter in Ortega studies with the publication of *Ortega y sus fuentes germánicas* (1979). Orringer draws precise and very suggestive lines between many of Ortega's key concepts over the course of his career and certain texts by German philosophers and psychologists whose work he demonstrably knew and often possessed in his personal library. Orringer fills out and extends many of the links between Ortega's intellectual development and his lifelong study of modern German thought suggested by Morón Arroyo in 1968. By close comparison of parallel texts in German and Spanish, Orringer is able to show Ortega's great gift for the absorption and recreation of the profound legacy of modern German thought with which the then-young Spanish philosopher became acquainted during his trips to Germany in the early years of this century. It becomes abundantly clear, in this perspective, that Ortega continued to draw upon this fund of inspiration throughout the rest of his life. A careful reader of the *Obras completas* might suppose as much, but the documentation for this supposition, widely shared among students of his work, had heretofore been missing. Form the very early essay "Adán en el Paraíso" on through his reflections on phenomenology, aesthetic theory, psychology of the feelings, theory of mass society, the work of Goethe, and the paintings of Velázquez, Ortega's thought appears to have drawn impetus and focus from a host of German theorists and scholars. Yet, as Orringer makes quite clear in his conclusion, this indebtedness to a tradition he could hardly have done without—for a young Spanish intellectual of his day could not nourish his thought on any comparable native cultural tradition—does not make Ortega merely a pale imitation of key German thinkers, as so many have erroneously and even rancorously charged. On the contrary, his superb gift for transforming suggestions from others into a genuinely original and full-fledged philosophical corpus of his own seems even clearer after one has traced the detailed history of his passionate immersion in German thought. Ortega, Orringer concludes, was original not in thinking what others had not previously thought but rather in "giving origin" in the root sense to a work that bore his own inimitable stamp. In his hands, in fact, the frequent ponderousness of German thought became spirited and nimble, while its tendency toward speculative excess often found more felicitous and accessible expression.

In the last few years, three further studies of genuine interest have appeared in Spain. Antonio Elorza's *La razón la sombra: Una lectura política de Ortega y Gasset* (1984) is a cogent Marxist critique of the movement of Ortega's political thought from a rather naive early socialist phase to its presumably more conservative and consistently elitist form by the time of the Republic and afterward. Elorza's analysis provides a good complement to Lalcona's earlier work and is a more ordered, conceptually sophisticated treatment than Redondo's, apart from the fact that Elorza's political standpoint is entirely different. The second title is Pedro Cerezo Galán's *La voluntad de aventura: Aproximamiento crítico al pensamiento de Ortega y Gasset* (1984). This remarkably suggestive study is in many ways the finest overall appraisal of Ortega's thought yet to appear in Spanish. Eschewing consideration of the political phases of the career, it repeatedly illumines the interplay between the man's temperament and his ideas. Like Morón and Orringer before him, Cerezo debunks Marías's uncritical veneration of Ortega, justly faulting it for its almost complete absence of attention to a developmental account of Ortega's thought. For Marías, we can now clearly see, Ortega seems to spring full-blown in 1914 as a thinker who has miraculously overcome any previous ties to his neo-Kantian teachers and to Husserl, whose influence on him in Cerezo's account is pervasive and enduring. While Marías insists to this day upon seeing Ortega as *the* outstanding thinker of the century—who not only brought Spain philosophically up-to-date but soared beyond all comparable figures, including Heidegger— Cerezo astutely acknowledges the man's constant dialogue with his German sources (a fact one could hardly ignore after Orringer) and also delineates his very real differences both from them and from his great contemporary Unamuno. More justly and adequately than anyone else, Cerezo treats the subtle relationship to Heidegger's work, enormously influential in Ortega's "high period" between 1929 and 1936, and develops a vocabulary for measuring Ortega's brilliant revision of the earlier influence of Cohen, Natorp, and Husserl. The central concept of "the will to adventure," finally, illumines Ortega's "heroic morality"—at once earnest and "playful"—as exemplified in his "enthusiastic feeling for the infinite vitality of the world" and his venturesome resolution that philosophy must make men "poets of existence." This splendid study, which abundantly deserves an English translation, is indispensable for any reader who wishes to penetrate the subtle weave of Ortega's work. As Cerezo shows, it may finally lack system, but it clearly has an organically developed perspective that must be understood through its affective tone and rhetoric, as well as its conceptual lexicon.

The most recent Spanish study is Francisco López Frías's *Ética y política: En torno al pensamiento político de J. Ortega y Gasset* (1985). Referring to the nineteenth-century Spanish political background, the ethical implications of Ortega's socialist phase, and his attitude toward the First World War, López Frías treats the career up to the beginning of the Republic. The heart of the book is an analysis of the concepts of "mass" and "minority," particularly as they are employed in *The Revolt of the Masses*. In addition, there is a prolonged, highly repetitive consideration of the social determination of personal individuality. Presenting itself as an exercise in political philosophy, this study is flawed by a certain tendency toward rhetorical inflation, wherein theory seems at points to move undesirably away from the close reading in historical context that is otherwise characteristic of the book.

Turning to English-language studies, perhaps the first noteworthy picture of Ortega's thought as a whole was José Ferrater Mora's *Ortega y Gasset: An Outline of his Philosophy* (1957; revised edition, 1963). It is still a good place for the neophyte to begin, though its remarkable compactness and penchant for too-orderly division of the career into distinct phases will leave him ready to look elsewhere. Written as one of a series of short studies of modern masters, Ferrater's "outline" makes no effort to give more than the rudiments of historical and biographical background. It is the work of one philosopher assessing another, and as such remains sagacious and penetrating.

Six further titles in English, by order of publication dates, should be mentioned. The cultural historian Karl J. Weintraub devotes a concise and informative chapter of *Visions of Culture* (1966) to Ortega as a philosopher of culture in the company of Voltaire, Guizot, Burckhardt, Lamprecht, and Huizinga. This is an illuminating way to focus on his work and one not generally taken by other critics. Weintraub lays particular stress on Ortega's view of the sociocultural role of generations, his distinction between "ideas" and "beliefs," and his notion that culture is a set of "solutions" men periodically dismantle and renew in order to cope with existential problems. The same author has since developed Ortega's central idea of the self as defined in its circumstances in *The Value of the Individual* (1978), a cross-cultural study of Western autobiography.

Harold C. Raley's *Ortega y Gasset: Philosopher of European Unity* (1971) is a judicious and illuminating review of the relation between Ortega's overall thought and his writings on the concept of Europe and the place of Spain in the larger whole of European history and culture. Raley provides a valuable unifying thread along which to order the diversity of Ortega's many writings on the subject, but only the last chapter ("Ortega and Spain") attempts a strict correlation of the theme of Europe with the thinker's career. A further limitation of this otherwise commendable work is its unvaryingly affirmative attitude toward Ortega, who deserves a more psychologically and socio-logically complex reading than he finds with this admiring student of his work.

Robert McClintock has written a mammoth study entitled *Man and His Circumstances: Ortega as Educator* (1971), seeking to develop an entire philoso-phy of pedagogy out of an expansive analysis of Ortega's notion of "social pedagogy." This work is strong and weak by turns. It is well informed and assiduously footnoted, but Ortega is often lost from sight in the flights of inflated rhetoric toward a comprehensive philosophy of education. And the author, in his full-throated enthusiasm, cultivates too little critical sense: when he declares that "Ortega met life with chest out, without stopping to bemoan lost opportunities and without bothering to correct misimpression," he is both factually misinformed and prone to project his own ideal vision onto the reality of the man.[1] Nevertheless, one can learn something from this work of an undeniably central aim of Ortega's entire career—his determi-nation to bring philosophy and high culture to the larger Spanish public.

Oliver W. Holmes's *Human Reality and the Social World: Ortega's Philosophy of History* (1975) is a compact though somewhat abstract treatment of the historicist, phenomenological, and existential backgrounds of Ortega's thinking on the historicity of human life. As regards existential elements in his thought, this study represents a great improvement over an earlier attempt in English, Janet Winecoff Díaz's *The Major Themes of Existentialism in the Work of José Ortega y Gasset* (1968). Holmes sketchs out the web of philosophical influences that played upon Ortega's attempt to delineate the human life-structure as set in historical time, social space, and generational sequence. (Marías's first volume, written from "within" Ortega's early thought, still offers a key perspective on these questions which is not entirely encompassed by Holmes's more compact work.) Finally, Holmes seems to overstate the case when he says that his study is an example of "intellectual history" which aims "to inquire into the interrelationships of Ortega's social and intellectual experiences with the formation of his ideas."[2] There is a brief, accurate biographical introduction, but it adds nothing to what is generally known of Ortega's life. If one considers Ortega's "intellectual experiences" to consist in the creative assimilation of the three interrelated lines of historicism, phenomenology, and existentialism, then Holmes has indeed fulfilled his promise; but the reference to "social" experience seems vague, and there is little strict connection established between particular aspects of Ortega's thought and those thinkers (Dilthey, Husserl, Scheler, et al.) who helped shape it. Moreover, Holmes fails to set Ortega's grand themes fully in the context of his career as a Spanish writer turned as much toward his pedagogical mission at home as toward the world of German thought.

Philip W. Silver has published a much-needed and carefully delimited study of a central facet of Ortega's thought which had previously been neglected or simply passed off nonchalantly. His *Ortega as Phenomenologist: The Genesis of "Meditations on Quixote"* (1978) is a companion volume to his translation of selected early essays by Ortega, published in English as *Phenomenology and Art* (1975). The former work studies in close detail Ortega's early philosophical development and his critical reaction to the Marburg neo-Kantians and to Husserl's work in the years immediately preceding *Meditations on Quixote* (1914), a book that Silver takes to be a declaration of philosophical independence from the German mentors and colleagues. In fact, by Silver's argument, Ortega had already worked out his essential critique of Husserl's concepts of consciousness, intentionality, and the transcendental ego before the youthful *Meditations*, wherein he supposedly revealed his discovery of human life as the radical reality, which is given with a "built-in" systematic structure that need not be discovered through bracketing and phenomenological intuition. The author claims three merits for his study: that it reveals a "crucial stage" in the formation of Ortega's notion of vital or historical reason; that it sets his thought "in its proper European context, the movement known as existential phenomenology"; and that it explains the centrality of the *Meditations* by showing that it contains "Ortega's principal philosophical discovery."[3] Silver's painstaking work presents a fresh perspective on Ortega as a formal philosopher belonging to a major tradition of modern European thought, though it needs to be read together with Orringer and Cerezo, who disagree with it on various points. Even so, any future discussion of Ortega's thought will have to incorporate or meet Silver's argument that Ortega is perhaps the first existential phenomenologist.

The most recent English-language study of Ortega, Victor Ouimette's *José Ortega y Gasset* (1982), is a survey of Ortega's career designed to fulfill the general purposes of the series to which it belongs (Twayne's World Authors). Ouimette emphasizes, in broadly historical fashion, the development of the main lines of the philosopher's thought as they may be seen in the major works, with concise reference to the social and political background of Spain in the first half of this century. Despite a certain lack of feeling for the existential drama of Ortega's intellectual quest, this book provides a clear and solid introduction to his thought for the American and English public.

A final reference must be made to the very useful *José Ortega y Gasset: A Bibliography of Secondary Sources* (1986), compiled by Antón Donoso and Harold Raley. A considerable step beyond Udo Rukser's *Bibliografía de Ortega* (1971), which was usefully organized by countries of publication for both primary and secondary materials, this new work on secondary materials alone includes over four thousand alphabetically listed entries and an introduction, a subject index, and two appendices on "late confirmations" and materials "in process." In addition to written materials, it also lists a number of radio transcripts, slides, recordings, and "unpublished materials open to the public." Needless to add, it is a boon to all current and future research on Ortega.

BIBLIOGRAPHICAL ESSAY

1. McClintock, *Man and His Circumstances*, p. 2.
2. Oliver W. Holmes, *Human Reality and the Social World: Ortega's Philosophy of History* (Amherst: University of Massachusetts Press, 1975), p. ix.
3. Silver, *Ortega as Phenomenologist*, p. ix.

BIBLIOGRAPHY

PRIMARY SOURCES

Ortega's Works in Spanish

Epistolario. Edited and introduced by Paulino Garagorri. Madrid: Revista de Occidente, 1974.

La idea de principio en Leibniz y la evolución de la teoría deductiva. Buenos Aires: Emecé Editores, Biblioteca de la Revista de Ocidente, Obras inéditas de José Ortega y Gasset, 1958.

Obras completas. 4th ed. Vols. 1–6. Madrid: Revista de Occidente, 1957.

Obras completas. 3d ed. Vol. 7. Madrid: Revista de Occidente, 1969.

Obras completas. 2d ed. Vols. 8–9. Madrid: Revista de Occidente, 1965.

Obras completas. 1st ed. Vols. 10–11. Madrid: Revista de Occidente, 1969.

Obras completas. 1st ed. Vol. 12. Madrid: Alianza Editorial, Revista de Occidente, 1983.

Unas lecciones de metafísica. 3d ed. Madrid: Alianza Editorial, 1970.

Selected Works by Ortega in English Translation

Concord and Liberty. Translated by Helene Weyl. New York: W. W. Norton, 1946.

The Dehumanization of Art and Other Essays on Art, Culture and Literature. Translated by Helene Weyl et al. Princeton, N.J.: Princeton University Press, 1968.

Historical Reason. Translated by Philip W. Silver. New York: W. W. Norton, 1984.

History as a System. Translated by Helene Weyl and William C. Atkinson. New York: W. W. Norton, 1941.

The Idea of Principle in Leibniz and the Evolution of Deductive Theory. Translated by Mildred Adams. New York: W. W. Norton, 1971.

An Interpretation of Universal History. Translated by Mildred Adams. New York: W. W. Norton, 1973.

Invertebrate Spain. Translated by Mildred Adams. New York: Howard Fertig, 1974.

Man and Crisis. Translated by Mildred Adams. New York: W. W. Norton, 1958.

Man and People. Translated by Willard B. Trask. New York: W. W. Norton, 1957.

Meditations on Hunting. Translated by Howard B. Wescott. New York: Scribner's, 1985.

Meditations on Quixote. Translated by Evelyn Rugg and Diego Marín. Introduction by Julián Marías. New York: W. W. Norton, 1961.

Mission of the University. Translated by Howard Lee Nostrand. New York: W. W. Norton, 1966.

The Modern Theme. Translated by James Cleugh. New York: W. W. Norton, 1933.

On Love: Aspects of a Single Theme. Translated by Toby Talbot. Cleveland: World Publishing, 1957.

The Origin of Philosophy. Translated by Toby Talbot. New York: W. W. Norton, 1967.

Phenomenology and Art. Translated and with an introduction by Philip W. Silver. New York: W. W. Norton, 1975.

Psychological Investigations. Translated by Jorge García-Gómez. New York: W. W. Norton, 1987.

The Revolt of the Masses. 25th anniversary ed. Translator anonymous. New York: W. W. Norton, 1957.

Some Lessons in Metaphysics. Translated by Mildred Adams. New York: W. W. Norton, 1969.

What Is Philosophy?. Translated by Mildred Adams. New York: W. W. Norton, 1960.

SELECTED SECONDARY SOURCES

Abellán, José Luís, ed. *El exilio español de 1939*. 6 vols. Madrid: Taurus Ediciones, 1976–1978.

Allen, James Sloan. *The Romance of Commerce and Culture*. Chicago: University of Chicago Press, 1983.

Amor y Vázquez, José, and Kossoff, A. David eds. *Homenaje a Juan López-Morillas: De Cadalso a Aleixandre*. Madrid: Editorial Castalia, 1982.

Aranguren, José Luis. *La ética de Ortega*. 2d ed. Madrid: Taurus Ediciones, 1959.

Baroja, Julio Caro. *Los Baroja*. Madrid: Taurus Ediciones, 1972.

Becarud, Jean, and López-Campillo, Evelyne. *Los intelectuales españoles durante la II república*. Madrid: Siglo XXI de España Editores, 1978.

Becker, Carl. *The Heavenly City of the Eighteenth-Century Philosophers*. New Haven, Conn.: Yale University Press, 1932.

Ben Ami, Shlomo. *Fascism from Above: The Dictatorship of Primo de Rivera in Spain, 1923–1930*. Oxford: Oxford University Press, 1983.

———. *The Origins of the Second Republic in Spain*. Oxford: Oxford University Press, 1978.

Berlin, Isaiah. *Russian Thinkers*. Edited by Henry Hardy and Aileen Kelly, with an introduction by Aileen Kelly. New York: Viking, 1978.

Binion, Rudolph. *After Christianity: Christian Survivals in a Post-Christian Culture*. Durango, Colo.: Logbridge-Rhodes, 1986.

Black, C. E. *The Dynamics of Modernization: A Study in Comparative History*. New York: Harper and Row, 1966.

Bolloten, Burnett. *The Spanish Revolution*. Chapel Hill: University of North Carolina Press, 1979.

Borel, Jean Paul. *Introducción a Ortega y Gasset*. Translated by Laureano Pérez Latorre. Madrid: Ediciones Guadarrama, 1969.

Boyd, Carolyn P. *Praetorian Politics in Liberal Spain*. Chapel Hill: University of North Carolina Press, 1979.

Brenan, Gerald. *The Spanish Labyrinth*. Reprint. Cambridge: Cambridge University Press, 1967.

Buckley, Ramon, and Crispin, John. *Los vanguardistas espanoles: 1925–1935*. Madrid: Alianza Editorial, 1973.

Chcho Víu, Vicente, *La Institución Libre de Enseñanza*, vol. 1: *Orígenes y etapa universitaria (1860–1881)*. Madrid: Ediciones Rialp, 1962.

Calinescu, Matei. *Faces of Modernity*. Bloomington: Indiana University Press, 1977.

Carr, Raymond. *Spain: 1808–1939*. London: Oxford University Press, 1966.

————. *The Spanish Tragedy: The Civil War in Perspective*. London: Weidenfeld and Nicolson, 1977.

————, ed. *The Republic and the Civil War in Spain*. London: Macmillan, 1971.

Carr, Raymond, and Fusi, Juan Pablo. *Spain: Dictatorship to Democracy*. 2d ed. London: Allen and Unwin, 1979.

Cassirer, Ernst. *The Myth of the State*. New Haven, Conn.: Yale University Press, 1946.

Castillejo, José. *Wars of Ideas in Spain*. London: John Murray, 1937.

Castro, Américo. *Aspectos del vivir hispánico*. Madrid: Alianza Editorial, 1970.

————. *The Spaniards: An Introduction to Their History*. Berkeley and Los Angeles: University of California Press, 1954.

————. *The Structure of Spanish History*. Translated by Edmund L. King. Princeton, N. J.: Princeton University Press, 1954.

Cepeda Calzada, Pablo. *Las ideas políticas de Ortega y Gasset*. Valladolid, Spain: Universidad de Valladolid, 1968.

Cerezo Galán, Pedro. *La voluntad de aventura: Aproximamiento crítico al pensamiento de Ortega y Gasset*. Barcelona: Editorial Ariel, 1984.

Cernuda, Luis. *Estudios sobre poesía española contemporánea*. 3d ed. Madrid: Ediciones Guadarrama, 1972.

Clarke, H. Butler. *Modern Spain, 1818–1898*. Reprint. New York: AMS Press, 1969.

Copleston, Frederick. *Philosophers and Philosophies.* New York: Harper and Row, 1976.

Costa, Joaquín. *Oligarquía y caciquismo.* 2d ed. Edited and with a prologue by Rafael Pérez de la Dehesa. Madrid: Alianza Editorial, 1969.

Crispin, John. *Oxford y Cambridge en Madrid: La Residencia de Estudiantes (1910–1936) y su entorno cultural.* Santander, Spain: Publicaciones La Isla de los Ratones, 1981.

Curtius, Ernst Robert. *Essays on European Literature.* Translated by Michael Kowal. Princeton, N.J.: Princeton University Press, 1973.

Díaz, Elias. *La filosofía social del krausismo español.* Madrid: Editorial Cuadernos Para El Diálogo, 1973.

―――, ed. *Unamuno: Pensamiento político.* Madrid: Editorial Tecnos, 1965.

Díaz, Janet Winecoff. *The Major Themes of Existentialism in the Work of José Ortega y Gasset.* Chapel Hill: University of North Carolina Press, 1968.

Donoso, Antón, and Raley, Harold C. *José Ortega y Gasset: A Bibliography of Secondary Sources.* Bowling Green, Ohio: Bowling Green State University / Philosophy Documentation Center, 1986.

Durán, Manuel, ed. *Ortega, Hoy: Estudio, ensayos y biblografía sobre la vida y la obra de José Ortega y Gasset.* Xalapa, Mexico: Universidad Veracruzana, 1985.

Edie, James M. *Edmund Husserl's Phenomenology: A Critical Commentary.* Bloomington: Indiana University Press, 1987.

Eliot, T. S. *Four Quartets.* New York: Harcourt Brace Jovanovich, Harvest Books, 1971.

Ellman, Richard. *Golden Codgers: Biographical Speculations.* Oxford: Oxford University Press, 1973.

Elorza, Antonio. *La razón y la sombra: Una lectura política de Ortega y Gasset.* Barcelona: Editorial Anagrama, 1984.

Ermarth, Michael. *Wilhelm Dilthey: The Critique of Historical Reason.* Chicago: University of Chicago Press, 1978.

Fernández, Pelayo H., et al., eds. *Ortega y Gasset Centennial / University of New Mexico.* Madrid: José Porrúa Turanzas, 1985.

Fernández Almagro, Melchor. *Historia política de la España contemporánea.* 3 vols. Madrid: Editorial Alianza, 1968.

Fernández de la Mora, Gonzalo. *Ortega y el 98.* Madrid: Rialp, 1961.

Ferrater Mora, José. *Ortega y Gasset: An Outline of His Philosophy.* New rev. ed. New Haven, Conn.: Yale University Press, 1963.

Fox, E. Inman. *La crisis intelectual del 98.* Madrid: Editorial Cuadernos Para El Diálogo, 1976.

Gaete, Arturo. *El sistema maduro de Ortega.* Buenos Aires: Compañia General Fabril, 1962.

Gallo, Max. *Spain Under Franco.* Translated by Jean Steward. New York: Dutton, 1974.

Gaos, José. *Sobre Ortega y Gasset.* Mexico City: Imprenta Universitaria, 1957.

Garagorri, Paulino. *Unamuno y Ortega.* Barcelona: Salvat Editores, and Madrid: Alianza Editorial, 1972.

Gil Cremades, Juan José. *El reformismo español: Krausismo, escuela histórica, neotomismo.* Barcelona: Ediciones Ariel, 1969.

Giner, Salvador. *Mass Society.* New York: Academic Press, 1976.

———. "Power, Freedom and Social Change in the Spanish University, 1939–75." In *Spain in Crisis: The Evolution and Decline of the Franco Regime,* edited by Paul Preston, pp. 183–211. London: Harvester, 1976.

Gombrich, E. H. *In Search of Cultural History.* Oxford: Oxford University Press, 1969.

Gómez de la Serna, Ramón. *Automoribundia.* Buenos Aires: Editorial Sudamericana, 1948.

Gómez Molleda, María Dolores. *Los reformadores de la España comtemporánea.* Madrid: Consejo Superior de Investigaciones Científicas, 1966.

———. *Unamuno, "agitador de espíritus," y Giner (correspondencia inédita).* Madrid: Narcea Ediciones, 1977.

Gullón, Ricardo. *La invención del 98 y otros ensayos.* Madrid: Editorial Gredos, 1969.

Guy, Alain. *Ortega y Gasset: Crítico de Aristóteles.* Madrid: Espasa-Calpe, 1968.

Heller, Erich. *The Disinherited Mind.* Cleveland, Ohio: World Publishing, Meridian Books, 1959.

Herr, Richard. *The Eighteenth Century Revolution in Spain.* Princeton, N.J.: Princeton University Press, 1958.

———. *An Historical Essay on Modern Spain.* Berkeley, Los Angeles, London: University of California Press, 1974.

Holmes, Oliver W. *Human Reality and the Social World: Ortega's Philosophy of History.* Amherst: University of Massachusetts Press, 1975.

Hughes, H. Stuart. *Consciousness and Society: The Reorientation of European Social Thought, 1890–1930.* New York: Knopf, 1958.

———. *The Sea Change: The Migration of Social Thought, 1930–1965.* New York: McGraw-Hill, 1975.

Iriarte, Joaquín. *Ortega y Gasset: Su persona y su doctrina.* Madrid: Razon y Fe, 1942.

———. *La ruta mental de Ortega.* Madrid: Razon y Fe, 1949.

Jackson, Gabriel. *The Spanish Republic and the Civil War: 1931–1939.* Princeton, N.J.: Princeton University Press, 1965.

Jeschke, Hans. *La generación de 98 en España.* Translated by Yolando Pino Saavedra. Santiago de Chile: Universidad de Chile, 1946.

Jiménez Fraud, Alberto. *Historia de la universidad española*. Madrid: Alianza Editorial, 1971.

———. *La Residencia de Estudiantes*. Introduction by Luis G. de Valdeavellano. Barcelona: Ediciones Ariel, 1972.

Jiménez-Landi, Antonio. *La Institución Libre de Enseñanza y su ambiente*. Madrid: Taurus Ediciones, 1973.

Kern, Robert W. *Liberals, Reformers and Caciques in Restoration Spain, 1875–1909*. Albuquerque: University of New Mexico Press, 1974.

Kern, Stephen. *The Culture of Time and Space, 1880–1918*. Cambridge, Mass.: Harvard University Press, 1983.

Lafuente Ferrari, Enrique. *Ortega y las artes visuales*. Madrid: Revista de Occidente, 1970.

Laín Entralgo, Pedro. *La generación del noventa y ocho*. 4th ed. Madrid: Espasa-Calpe, 1959.

———. *Menéndez Pelayo*. 2d ed. Buenos Aires: Espasa-Calpe Argentina, 1952.

Lalcona, Javier F. *El idealismo político de Ortega y Gasset*. Madrid: Editorial Cuadernos Para El Diálogo, 1974.

Landeira, Ricardo. *Ramiro de Maeztu*. Boston: G. K. Hall, 1978.

Larraín Acuña, Hernán. *La génesis del pensamiento de Ortega*. Buenos Aires: General Fabril, 1961.

la Souchère, Éléna de. *An Explanation of Spain*. Translated by Eleanor Ross Levieux. New York: Random House Vintage Books, 1964.

Lester, John A., Jr. *Journey Through Despair, 1880–1914: Transformations in British Literary Culture*. Princeton, N.J.: Princeton University Press, 1968.

Levenson, Joseph. *Confucian China and Its Modern Fate*. Berkeley and Los Angeles: University of California Press, 1958.

———. *Revolution and Cosmopolitanism: The Western Stages and the Chinese Stages*. Foreword by Frederick E. Wakeman, Jr. Berkeley, and Los Angeles, London: University of California Press, 1971.

Levine, Donald N., ed. *Georg Simmel on Individuality and Social Forms*. Chicago: University of Chicago Press, 1971.

Levy, Marion. *Modernization: Latecomers and Survivors*. New York: Basic Books, 1972.

Lida, Clara E., and Zavala, Iris M., eds. *La revolución de 1868: Historia, pensamiento, literatura*. New York: Las Américas, 1970.

Linz, Juan J. "From Great Hopes to Civil War: The Breakdown of Democracy in Spain." In *The Breakdown of Democratic Regimes: Europe*, edited by Juan J. Linz and Alfred Stepan, pp. 142–215. Baltimore, Md.: Johns Hopkins University Press, 1978.

———. "The Party System of Spain: Past and Future." In *Party Systems and Alignments: Cross-National Perspectives*, edited by Seymour M. Lipset and Stein Rokkan, pp. 197–282. New York: The Free Press, 1967.

————. "Tradition and Modernity in Spain." Unpublished paper, 1968.

Lipp, Solomon. *Francisco Giner de los Ríos: A Spanish Socrates.* Waterloo, Ontario, Canada: Wilfrid Laurier University Press, 1985.

Livermore, Harold. *A History of Spain.* New York: Minerva Press, 1968.

López-Campillo, Evelyne. *La "Revista de Occidente" y la formación de minorías: 1923–36.* Madrid: Taurus Ediciones, 1972.

López Frías, Francisco. *Ética y política: En torno al pensamiento político de J. Ortega y Gasset.* Barcelona: Promociones Publicaciones Universitarias, 1985.

López-Morillas, Juan. *Hacia el 98: Literatura, sociedad, ideología.* Barcelona: Ediciones Ariel, 1972.

————. *El krausismo español.* Mexico City: Fondo de Cultura Económica, 1956.

————. *The Krausist Movement and Ideological Change in Spain, 1854–1874.* Translated by Frances López-Morillas. Cambridge: Cambridge University Press, 1981.

————, ed. *Francisco Giner de los Ríos: Ensayos.* Madrid: Editorial Alianza, 1969.

Lowie, Donald M. *History of Bourgeois Perception.* Chicago: University of Chicago Press, 1982.

Löwith, Karl. *From Hegel to Nietzsche: The Revolution in Nineteenth-Century Thought.* New York: Doubleday Anchor Books, 1967.

Madariaga, Salvador de. *Spain: A Modern History.* New York: Praeger, 1958.

Maeztu, Ramiro de. *Los intelectuales y un epílogo para estudiantes.* Madrid: Ediciones Rialp, 1966.

Mainer, José-Carlos. *Literatura y pequeña burguesía: Notas 1890–1950.* Madrid: Editorial Cuadernos Para El Diálogo, 1972.

————. *Modernismo y 98.* Barcelona: Editorial Crítica, 1980.

————, ed. *Falange y literatura: Antología.* Barcelona: Editorial Labor, 1971.

Mandelbaum, Maurice. *History, Man and Reason: A Study in Nineteenth-Century Thought.* Baltimore, Md.: Johns Hopkins University Press, 1971.

Mannheim, Karl. *Essays on the Sociology of Knowledge.* Edited by Paul Kecskemeti. New York: Oxford University Press, 1952.

————. *Ideology and Utopia.* Translated by Louis Wirth and Edward Shils. New York: Harcourt, Brace and World, Harvest Books, n.d.

Maravall, José. *Dictatorship and Political Dissent: Workers and Students in Franco's Spain.* New York: St. Martin's, 1978.

Marías, Julián. *Acerca de Ortega.* Madrid: Revista de Occidente, 1971.

————. *El método histórico de las generaciones.* Madrid: Revista de Occidente, 1949. English translation, *Generations: A Historical Method.* Translated by Harold C. Raley. University: University of Alabama Press, 1970.

————. *Ortega I: Circunstancia y vocación.* Madrid: Revista de Occidente, 1960.

———. *Ortega y Gasset: Circumstance and Vocation.* Translated by Frances López-Morillas. Norman: University of Oklahoma Press, 1970.

———. *Ortega**las trayectorias.* Madrid: Editorial Alianza, 1983.

Marichal, Juan. *La vocación de Manuel Azaña.* Madrid: Editorial Cuadernos Para El Diálogo, 1968.

———. *La voluntad del estilo: Teoría e historia del ensayismo español.* Madrid: Revista de Occidente, 1971.

Marichal, Juan, and Paz, Octavio. *Las cosas en su sitio.* Quito, Ecuador: Alejandro Finisterre, 1971.

Marrero, Vicente. *Maeztu.* Madrid: Ediciones Rialp, 1955.

———. *Ortega, filósofo "mondain".* Madrid: Ediciones Rialp, 1961.

Martín Buezas, Fernando. *El krausismo español desde dentro: Sanz del Río, autobiografía de intimidad.* Prologue by José Luís Abellán. Madrid: Editorial Tecnos, 1978.

Martín Santos, Luís. *Tiempo de silencio.* Barcelona: Seix Barral, 1965.

Mazlish, Bruce. *James and John Stuart Mill: Father and Son in the Nineteenth Century.* New York: Basic Books, 1975.

McClintock, Robert. *Man and His Circumstances: Ortega as Educator.* New York: Columbia University Teachers College Press, 1971.

McNair, John M. *Education for a Changing Spain.* Manchester, England: Manchester University Press, 1984.

Menéndez Pidal, Ramón. *The Spaniards in Their History.* Translated by Walter Starkie. New York: W. W. Norton, 1950.

Mermall, Thomas. *The Rhetoric of Humanism: Spanish Culture after Ortega y Gasset.* New York: Bilingual Press, 1976.

Meyer, Doris. *Victoria Ocampo: Against the Wind and the Tide.* New York: George Braziller, 1979.

Mill, John Stuart. *Essays on Politics and Culture.* Edited by Gertrude Himmelfarb. New York: Doubleday Anchor Books, 1963.

Morón Arroyo, Ciriaco. *El sistema de Ortega y Gasset.* Madrid: Ediciones Alcalá, 1968.

Northup, George Tyler. *An Introduction to Spanish Literature.* 3d rev. ed. Chicago: University of Chicago Press, 1960.

Orringer, Nelson R. *Nuevas fuentes germánicas de ¿Qué es filosofía? de Ortega.* Madrid: Consejo Superior de Investigaciones Científicas, 1984.

———. "Ortega, psicólogo y la superacíon de sus maestros," *Azafea,* no. 1 (1985): 185–236.

———. *Ortega y sus fuentes germánicas.* Madrid: Editorial Gredos, 1979.

Ortega, Miguel. *Ortega y Gasset, mi padre.* Barcelona: Editorial Planeta, 1983.

Ortega, Soledad, ed. *José Ortega y Gasset: Imágenes de una vida, 1883–1955.*

Madrid: Ministerio de Educación y Ciencia / Fundación José Ortega y Gasset, 1983.

Ouimette, Victor. *José Ortega y Gasset*. Boston: G. K. Hall, 1982.

Payne, Stanley G. *Falange: A History of Spanish Fascism*. Stanford, Calif.: Stanford University Press, 1961.

————. *A History of Spain and Portugal*. 2 vols. Madison: University of Wisconsin Press, 1973.

————. *Politics and the Military in Modern Spain*. Stanford, Calif.: Stanford University Press, 1967.

————. *The Spanish Revolution*. New York: W. W. Norton, 1970.

Pérez de la Dehesa, Rafael. *El pensamiento de Costa y su influencia en el 98*. Madrid: Sociedad de Estudios y Publicaciones, 1966.

Pike, Frederick B. *Hispanismo: 1898–1936*. Notre Dame, Ind.: University of Notre Dame Press, 1971.

Poggioli, Renato. *The Theory of the Avant-Garde*. Cambridge, Mass.: Harvard University Press, Belknap Press, 1968.

Prado, Angeles. *La literatura del casticismo*. Madrid: Editorial Moneda y Credito, 1973.

Preston, Paul. *The Spanish Civil War, 1936–1939*. New York: Grove, 1986.

Primo de Rivera, José Antonio. *José Antonio Primo de Rivera: Selected Writings*. Edited by Thomas Hughes. New York: Harper and Row, 1975.

Pritchett, V. S. *Midnight Oil*. New York: Random House Vintage Books, 1973.

Raley, Harold C. *Ortega y Gasset: Philosopher of European Unity*. University: University of Alabama Press, 1971.

Rama, Carlos M. *Ideología, regiones y clases sociales en la España contemporánea*. Madrid: Ediciones Júcar, 1977.

Ramírez, Santiago. *La filosofía de Ortega y Gasset*. Barcelona: Herder, 1958.

————. *¿Un orteguismo católico?* Salamanca, Spain: San Esteban, 1958.

Ramsden, Herbert. *The 1898 Movement in Spain*. Manchester, England: University of Manchester Press, 1974.

Redondo, Gonzalo. *Las empresas políticas de José Ortega y Gasset*. 2 vols. Madrid: Ediciones Rialp, 1970.

Renan, Joseph Ernest. *La reforme intellectuelle et morale*. Edited by P. E. Charvet. New York: Greenwood Press, 1968.

Rial, James H. *Revolution from Above: The Primo de Rivera Dictatorship in Spain, 1923–1930*. Fairfax, Va.: George Mason University Press, 1986.

Ridruejo, Dionisio. *Casi unas memorias*. With a prologue by Salvador de Madariaga. Barcelona: Editorial Planeta, 1976.

————. *Escrito en España*. 2d ed. Buenos Aires: Editorial Losada, 1964.

Ringer, Fritz K. *The Decline of the German Mandarins: The German Academic*

Community, 1890–1933. Cambridge, Mass: Harvard University Press, 1969.

Robinson, Richard A. H. *The Origins of Franco's Spain: The Right, the Republic and Revolution, 1931–1936*. Devon, England: David and Charles, 1970; Pittsburgh, Pa.: University of Pittsburgh Press, n.d.

Rodríguez Huéscar, Antonio. *Perspectiva y verdad: El problema de la verdad en Ortega*. Estudios Orteguianos, no. 1. Madrid: Revista de Occidente, 1966.

Rodríguez y García-Loredo, Cesáreo. *El "esfuerzo medular" del krausismo frente a la obra gigante de Menéndez Pelayo*. Oviedo, Spain: n.p. 1961.

Romanell, Patrick. *The Making of the Mexican Mind*. Lincoln: University of Nebraska Press, 1952.

Romero, Francisco. *Filosofía de ayer y de hoy*. Madrid: Aguilar, 1960.

Rubia Barcia, José, ed. *Américo Castro and the Meaning of Spanish Civilization*. Berkeley, Los Angeles, London: University of California Press, 1976.

Rukser, Udo. *Bibliografía de Ortega*. Estudios Orteguianos, no. 3. Madrid: Revista de Occidente, 1971.

Saenz de la Calzada, Margarita. *La Residencia de Estudiantes, 1910–1936*. Madrid: Consejo Superior de Investigaciones Científicas, 1986.

Salinas, Pedro. *Literatura española siglo XX*. Madrid: Alianza Editorial, 1970.

Sánchez, José M. *Reform and Reaction: The Politico-Religious Background of the Spanish Civil War*. Chapel Hill: University of North Carolina Press, 1964.

Sánchez Ron, José M., and Glick, Thomas F. *La España posible de la Segunda República: La oferta a Einstein de una cátedra extraordinaria en la Universidad Central (Madrid, 1933)*. Madrid: Editorial de la Universidad Complutense, 1983.

Sánchez Villaseñor, José. *Ortega y Gasset, Existentialist*. Translated by Joseph Small, S.J. Chicago: Henry Regnery, 1949.

Senabre Sempere, Ricardo. *Lengua y estilo de Ortega y Gasset*. Vol. 185, no. 3 of *Acta Salmanticensia, Filosofía y letras*. Salamanca, Spain: Universidad de Salamanca, 1964.

Shaw, Donald L. *The Generation of 1898 in Spain*. London: Ernest Benn, 1975.

Shils, Edward. *Center and Periphery: Essays in Macrosociology*. Chicago: University of Chicago Press, 1975.

———. *The Intellectuals and the Powers*. Chicago: University of Chicago Press, 1972.

Silver, Philip W. *Ortega as Phenomenologist: The Genesis of "Meditations on Quixote"*. New York: Columbia University Press, 1978.

Sobejano, Gonzalo. *Nietzsche en España*. Madrid: Editorial Gredos, 1967.

Stern, Fritz. *The Politics of Cultural Despair*. Berkeley and Los Angeles: University of California Press, 1963.

Stromberg, Roland N. *Redemption by War*. Lawrence: The Regents Press of Kansas, 1982.

Thomas, Hugh. *The Spanish Civil War*. New York: Harper and Row, 1961.

Torre, Guillermo de. *Del 98 al barroco*. Madrid: Editorial Gredos, 1969.

———. *Las metamorfoses de Protéo*. Buenos Aires: Editorial Losada, 1956.

Torrente Ballester, Gonzalo. *Panorama de la literatura española contemporánea*. Madrid: Ediciones Guadarrama, 1965.

Trend, J. B. *The Civilization of Spain*. Oxford: Oxford University Press, 1944.

———. *The Origins of Modern Spain*. Cambridge: Cambridge University Press, 1934.

Trilling, Lionel. *Sincerity and Authenticity*. Cambridge, Mass.: Harvard University Press, 1972.

Tuchman, Barbara W. *The Proud Tower: A Portrait of the World Before the War: 1890–1914*. New York: Macmillan, 1966.

Tuñón de Lara, Manuel. *Costa y Unamuno en la crisis de fin de siglo*. Madrid: Editorial Cuadernos Para El Diálogo, 1974.

———. *Historia y realidad del poder*. Madrid: Editorial Cuadernos Para El Diálogo, 1973.

———. *Medio siglo de cultura española (1885–1936)*. 3d ed. Madrid: Editorial Tecnos, 1971.

Turin, Yvonne. *L'Education et l'ecole en Espagne de 1874 a 1902: Liberalisme et tradition*. Paris: Presses Universitaires de France, 1959.

Tusell Gómez, Javier. *La España de siglo XX*. Madrid: Dopesa, 1975.

Valbuena Prat, Angel. *Historia de la literatura española*. 3 vols. Barcelona: Editorial Gustavo Gili, 1957.

Valéry, Paul. *History and Politics*. Vol. 10 of *The Collected Works of Paul Valéry*, Bollingen Series XLV. Translated by Denise Folliot and Jackson Matthews, with a preface by François Valéry and an introduction by Salvador de Madariaga. Princeton, N.J.: Princeton University Press, 1962.

Vicens Vives, Jaime. *Approaches to the History of Spain*. Translated by Joan Connelly Ullman. Berkeley, Los Angeles, London: University of California Press, 1970.

———, ed. *Historia de España y América*. 5 vols. Barcelona: Editorial Vicens Vives, 1961.

Vilar, Pierre. *Spain: A Brief History*. 2d ed. Oxford: Pergamon Press, 1977.

Vilar, Sergio. *Historia del antifranquismo, 1939–1975*. Barcelona: Plaza y Janes, 1984.

———. *La oposición a la dictadura: Protagonistas de la España democrática*. Barcelona: Ediciones Aymá, 1976.

Walgrave, J. H. *La filosofía de Ortega y Gasset*. Translated by Luis G. Daal. Madrid: Revista de Occidente, 1965.

Weintraub, Karl. *The Value of the Individual: Self and Circumstance in Autobiography*. Chicago: University of Chicago Press, 1978.

———. *Visions of Culture*. Chicago: University of Chicago Press, 1966.

Willey, Thomas E. *Back to Kant: The Revival of Kantianism in German Social and Historical Thought, 1860–1914*. Detroit, Mich.: Wayne State University Press, 1978.

Williams, Raymond. *Keywords: A Vocabulary of Culture and Society*. New York: Oxford University Press, 1976.

Wohl, Robert. *The Generation of 1914*. Cambridge, Mass.: Harvard University Press, 1979.

GENERAL INDEX

BIBLIOGRAPHICAL INDEX

WORKS BY OTHER AUTHORS:

(The title is generally listed as it is used in the text)

Designer:	U.C. Press Staff
Compositor:	Asco Trade Typesetting Ltd.
Text:	11/13 Baskerville
Display:	Baskerville
Printer:	Maple-Vail
Binder:	Maple-Vail